THE BOOK

OF

JACK LONDON

VOLUME I

"A KIND OF NAPOLEON OF THE PEN"
Anna Strunsky

JACK LONDON STATE HISTORIC PARK
Charmian Kittredge London

THE BOOK OF JACK LONDON

BY

CHARMIAN LONDON

ILLUSTRATED WITH
PHOTOGRAPHS

VOLUME I

1921

ILLUSTRATED WORKS OF JACK AND CHARMIAN LONDON
PUBLISHED BY

SEAWOLF
PRESS

PUBLISHED BY SEAWOLF PRESS

Printed in the U.S.A.

FIRST EDITION INFORMATION
The first edition was published by The Century Company in 1921. The release consisted of two volumes.

SeaWolf Press
P.O. Box 961
Orinda, CA 94563
Email: support@seawolfpress.com
Web: http://www.SeaWolfPress.com

About *The Book of Jack London*

Several years after Jack London's death, his wife Charmian released a 2-volume biography of his life. Volume I starts with the origins of his parents, John and Flora, and covers Jack's childhood and early life growing up in the San Francisco Bay Area. It also covers his oyster pirating, Klondike trips, and time spent riding the railroads. The book is full of his letters to Cloudesley Johns, Anna Strunsky, and others. The first volume ends with his voyage to Asia to cover the Japanese-Russian War.

About Charmian Kittredge London

Charmian Kittredge London was raised and educated by her Aunt in Oakland, California. Charmian became a symbol of the New Woman at the turn of the century. She met Jack in 1900, and finally married him in 1905 after his divorce from his first wife, Bess. Charmian and Jack built a sailboat, the Snark, and set out for an around the-world-trip in 1907 which ended prematurely the next year. She became Jack's "mate woman" and loved to accompany him on his adventures. Charmian published four books and died in 1955 at the age of 83.

Books by Jack London

COLLECT ALL THESE SPECIAL SEAWOLF PRESS EDITIONS

Son of the Wolf (1900)
The God of His Fathers (1901)
Children of the Frost (1902)
The Cruise of the Dazzler (1902)
A Daughter of the Snows (1902)
Kempton-Wace Letters (1903)
The Call of the Wild (1903)
The People of the Abyss (1903)
The Faith of Men (1904)
The Sea-Wolf (1904)
War of the Classes (1905)
The Game (1905)
Tales of the Fish Patrol (1905)
Moon-Face (1906)
White Fang (1906)
Scorn of Women (1906)
Before Adam (1907)
Love of Life (1907)
The Road (1907)
The Iron Heel (1908)
Martin Eden (1909)
Lost Face (1910)
Revolution (1910)
Burning Daylight (1910)
Theft (1910)
When God Laughs (1911)
Adventure (1911)
The Cruise of the Snark (1911)
South Sea Tales (1911)
The House of Pride (1912)
A Son of the Sun (1912)
Smoke Bellew (1912)
The Night Born (1913)
The Abysmal Brute (1913)
John Barleycorn (1913)
The Valley of the Moon (1913)
The Strength of the Strong (1914)
The Mutiny of the Elsinore (1914)
The Scarlet Plague (1915)
The Star Rover (1915)
Little Lady of the Big House (1916)
The Acorn Planter (1916)
The Turtles of Tasman (1916)
The Human Drift (1917)
Jerry of the Islands (1917)
Michael, Brother of Jerry (1917)
The Red One (1918)
On the Makaloa Mat (1919)
Hearts of Three (1920)
Dutch Courage (1922)

Books by Charmian London

The Log of the Snark(1915)
Our Hawaii (1917)
The Book of Jack London(1921)
(2 volumes)

TO

ELIZA LONDON SHEPARD

PREFACE

Here in his own workroom, at his own work-table, which, like himself, is deep-grained, beautiful, unshamming even to its rugged knots and imperfections, I write of the Jack London whom I knew.

"That one of us should go before the other is *unthinkable*," he often said. Or, "It is beyond my imagining that I should be without you. . . . By rights we should go out together in some bright hazard, gallant shipwreck in a shouting, white gale, or shoulder to shoulder in some forgotten out-land where the red gods have called us." And again, "If I should go first, Mate Woman, it would be for you to write of me—if you dare be honest," always he challenged.

"But you could hardly do it," he would consider. "I fear you'd not want to write of my shortcomings, which you know only too well, and your work would be valueless without them.—Also, neither you nor I, unless it should be when I am very old, and when others are gone past wounding, can write without restraint of the very circumstances and characters that helped to make or mar me. And, anyway, my dear," was his familiar conclusion, "I'm going to live a hundred years, because I want to; and I'm going to beat you to it some day and write my own book of myself, and call it 'Jack Liverpool'—and it's going to make everybody sit up!"

In some such fashion we would speculate, summer afternoons, perhaps riding over the Beauty Ranch, or lying on the slant deck of a ship in the Trades, or tooling our alert four-in-hand across a mountain range.

I warn, therefore, that this book is written only for those sincere and open-minded folk who want to know the real and living facts that I can tell. So unusual a man should be honored with an unusual biography, and mine is bound to be frank beyond the ordinary, since I must approach it with frankness or do a spurious piece of work. I do not minimize the criticism to which I subject myself, but my philosophy is of a sort that transcends fear on this score. For Jack London was my man of men, and because I have answered these many years to his call of "my woman", I am unafraid. I am privileged to speak my mind about him, what of his own desire; and I can but feel that I knew him somewhat, if only because he said so. I am forever enslaved to him for his love, for his teaching, for his infinitely manifested charity and sweetness," and this enslavement is guerdon of my existence, in that it has taught me freedom, and led to where, within my capacity, I might view and explore the wide spaces of life and thinking.

But only name him,—and forthwith a thousand vivid, trenchant thoughts clamor for delivery. Even more sharply than during his life I now realize how he was eternally whelmed by surging ideas, whenever his embracing mind laid hold of a theme. Often and often I have seen him near despair at the impossibility of capturing and holding, for presentment to his listener, the myriad related thoughts that crowded hard under a single impelling one.

The material at my hand is manifold and priceless. Much of it I shall forego, lest I wound where he hesitated to wound. But, within limitations dictated by like consideration for those he spared, I must in simple justice to him bring to bear all possible illumination. That is my passionate committal of myself and what of himself he lavished upon me.

One book of mine, "Our Hawaii," has been termed by some readers as "too personal," whatever that may signify. But in my sense of the word, "personal" is precisely what that narrative set out to be. And now, suppose that I, of all biographers, assume a conservative, too-proud-to-explain pose concerning this intimate man-soul, who of his admirers misled, or at best puzzled by popular misreport, and desiring more light upon his gripping personality, is to acquire what only I have to offer? Would a woman court happiness with such as Jack London, she needs must learn to regard life broadly. Her reward, if she be wise enough to claim reward, is obvious. What I absorbed of Jack London was by means of throwing wide a willing intelligence toward his nature and mental attitude. And since he went out in the midday of his brave years, I have sensed him in still subtler ways.

I summon the dear ghosts of all he has meant to me, in the largess of his sharing, and always he shared;, all heritage from him of unclouded vision, purpose, straightness of speech; whatever I have meant to him; all these I beg to help me in my loving and difficult task. For at the outset I am appalled by what is ahead of me. Almost it looks a vain endeavor, one I would far better abandon, and confine my revelation to the commonplace, if commonplace can be found in such a life, lest I invite failure by reaching too wide and deep.

None but a fool dwells upon the small irks of a journey that has been undertaken all the way and back, for love and service and adventure. It is the long, long run that matters. The big basic considerations, the rudimental integrities, these are the saving things that buoy up life and persuade from us at the end that we "liked it all." And so, in reviewing what was in our long run a rainbow trail round the curve of the world, though I shall try to write from the height of my head, making honest this document, as he would have it, without sainting his humanness, I know I shall find myself most often directed from the depth of my heart toward a bountiful estimate of his abounding lovableness, charm, and variety.

I should be glad if I could believe that he, friend, lover, husband, for a dozen rich years, were now consciously standing over me guiding my pen—his pen, with which I begin his portrait; glad for my own sake, at the same time decrying the selfishness to stay him one moment from that Field of Ardath that ever, to him, in his fairest hours, meant dreamless rest. But since I cannot even in his loss find hope and faith in what he did not believe for himself, for me, for any one, I can yet know that what of his gift there resides in my being from those long, comprehending years together drives brain and hand to lay what I may of him "cards up on the table," as he fearlessly played his own game of living.

Shortly after his death my already awakened mettle to write of him was spurred by the remark of an American author to a common friend, "Jack London was a far greater man than some of his intimates may let us know." I, at least, shall not merit this curious implication. Jack London gave so greatly to all who could see and hear and feel. Those who gained worse than nothing from the privilege of association with him, neighbor, sharer, young patriarch whose burdens were so nobly borne, I can only designate as the deaf, the dumb, the blind.

This, then, is my goal: to strive to expound him through the evaluations he placed upon himself which untiringly he strove to make clear to me. And to my everlasting joy and benefit, my lamps were always lit that I might less and less blindly gaze into the unfailing wonder which I found him. The vision I cherish rises undimmed, definite, appealing to be revealed as he would declare himself.

Once more, as in other prefaces, I crave indulgence for that I must appear somewhat profusely in my own pages. Verily, in order to make a book about Jack London, I should have to make a book about myself—which indeed would be all about Jack London.

Here I give to the world my Jack London—a virile creature compounded of curiosity and fearlessness, the very texture of fine sensibility, the loving heart and discerning intuitions of a woman, an ardent brain, and a divine belief in himself. And since he was first and foremost his own man, I render, as nearly as may be in the premises, also his own Jack London. If I prove candid to a degree, let it be remembered that he would be first to have it so.

Charmian London

Jack London Ranch,
Glen Ellen, Sonoma County,
California

CONTENTS

CONTENTS

LIST OF ILLUSTRATIONS

LIST OF ILLUSTRATIONS

THE BOOK

OF

JACK LONDON

THE BOOK OF JACK LONDON

PROLOGUE

AND A MEETING

I WISH you'd meet this remarkable boy of mine, this Jack London," my aunt remarked one morning in the spring of 1900, with a laugh in her earnest blue eyes. "I should like to have your opinion of him. The fact is, I have only talked with him once, myself, but already I feel as if he belonged to me."

"Very well," I replied rather absently, pinning on my straw sailor before a diminutive silver-trinketed dressing-table that was my especial pride. For my mind was bent on other matters than this vague young writer whose stories in the *Overland Monthly* I had heard the family discussing with fervor for months past. "Very well," I repeated, "when shall it be?"

"He's coming here to-morrow afternoon," she considered, "though too early for you. But in a few days I'm to meet him at the museum in the Ferry Building, to pose him for a picture in Alaskan furs, to illustrate my article. How would this do?—I'll take you to lunch!"

"Why should *you* take *him* to lunch!" I cried, stung to protest.

"My dear child—I know he hasn't an extra cent to spend. No, I will entertain the pair of you, at half past twelve."

"I don't know what you will think of him," she called after me, in a doubtful tone, as I hurried off for Dwight Way station, which was near our home in Berkeley. "He is not a bit like your college and society friends!"

But their afternoon's interview lasted until six o'clock. My latch-key was already clicking in the lock as Auntie turned the knob for the egress of a rather odd caller, clad in shabby bicycle trousers and dark gray woolen shirt. A nondescript tie, soft bicycle shoes, and a worn cap in one hand, completed his outfit, while the other held fast a copy of Boyd's Composition, borrowed from his hostess. There was a hasty introduction in the dim hall rainbowed by the sunset through a stained glass window. Then the apparently abashed young fellow ran lightly down the steps, pulling the dingy cap over a mop of brown curls, and rode away on his wheel.

"So *that's* your wonderful Jack London," I chaffed. "You will admit he is not a very elegant afternoon caller!"

"Granted," Auntie concurred; but added swiftly, "I do not think he missed your hardly concealed critical look, my dear. Nothing escapes that boy. And you must remember," she admonished gently, "with genius, clothing doesn't matter. Besides, I doubt if he can afford better."

"Well," I retorted, a trifle guiltily, "he is not the only genius amongst your friends, but certainly none of them ever came to our house looking like this one."

Seeing me really contrite, she told me laughingly how Hannah had come to her with puzzled brow, after answering the door bell:

"'I do not think this can be the gentleman Mrs. Eames expects. He is only a boy, in rough clothes, and walks like a sailor.'" Whereupon Hannah had flushingly received a rebuke similar to mine.

On the day set for the lunch, I exchanged noon hours with my pretty assistant. For, in a big San Francisco shipping and commission firm, my shorthand and typewriting earned bed and board, party gowns, the services of Hannah, the immaculate Swedish maid, not to mention fodder and stabling for my beautiful saddle mare. For we were not in opulent circumstances. My aunt and foster mother, Ninetta Eames, wrote for the magazines, while her husband acted as business manager of the beloved old *Overland Monthly*, whose funds were notoriously meager—no one better than Jack London knew how meager. As for myself, I had taken a hand in my own maintenance from my fourteenth year, when I had mastered Uncle Roscoe Eames's Light Line Shorthand and assisted him with his classes, on to the year at Mills College, where I worked my way as secretary to its President, Mrs. Susan L. Mills.

Promptly at twelve-thirty I reached the entrance of the restaurant my aunt had named—Young's, I think it was, on Montgomery, not far from Market Street. If I am a shade misty, it must be borne in mind that this was almost six years before the time when the Great Fire, following upon the Great Earthquake, destroyed landmarks in this section of incomparable old San Francisco.

Already they were on the spot, my small, blue-eyed, dark-haired aunt, and beside her the boyish figure of medium height in a sack-coated gray suit, patently ready-made and almost pathetically new. He wore a small black tie, low-cut shoes, and a neat visored gray cap that did not hide a wavy brown forelock. And this was the first and last time we ever saw Jack London arrayed in waistcoat and starched collar.

My clearest vision of this moment when I first looked fairly upon the man who was destined to play such momentous part in my life, is of the cheerful-gray aspect of him; for, under the meeting low line of his brows, the wide-set, very large, direct eyes were as gray as the soft gray cloth, but more blue for the tan of his blond skin.

Another unclouded mental impression that persists across the years, is of the modest quiet of his manner, and, still more distinctly, the beauty of his mouth, full-lipped, not small, with deep, upturned ends that my aunt happily described as "pictured corners"—a designation too lovely for analysis. And there was about this feature a chastity, an untried virginity of expression, that seemed greatly at odds with recalled rumors of the romantic if rather dubious career of this sailor-shouldered, light-stepping man of twenty-four, as gamin, redoubtable member of dread hoodlum gangs in Oakland, bay pirate, vagrant, adventurer in Alaskan gold fields—not to emphasize a smear of actual jail-birding, if truth prevailed. That he was moreover an exceedingly active member of the Socialist Labor Party was no shock to my propriety, albeit his Socialism was of a ruggeder, more militant sort than that with which I was familiar in my own home.

Ever my initial picture of that baffling mouth must hold its own with the great gray eyes, in their almost appealing candor a similar unbelievable childlikeness. "Looking for something he has never known," was the fancy that drifted through my brain, as my own eyes fell from his to the small hand he extended—half-timorously it seemed to me, as I noted an absence of grip.

"Jack London is the gentlest man I have ever known, "I once heard an old woman say. And that is what also comes down to me from this early contact with a personality that made its thoroughgoing masculinity only slightly felt through an alight repose of demeanor, an expectant passivity, which very little advertised vibrant nerves and quick underlying dominance. That is it—sitting across the table in the buzzing, bustling café, I seemed to sense that he was expecting something, something we two women had for him of *our* personalities, *our* ideas, *our* good will. In those long-lashed eyes that had mirrored much of life's most unbeautiful presentments, there was a waiting, a continual asking, and their own response was swift and sweet toward any gift of frank idea or fellowship. He displayed interest in the fact that I was self-supporting; and once, when my Aunt had addressed me, he raised that full gray look to mine and slowly pronounced, as if listening to the sound of his own pleased voice:

"*Charmian . . . Charmian* . . . What a beautiful name!" I have little recollection of the conversation that lasted out the meal, nor of what Jack London ordered. It is safe to say that, barring his half-fed tramp days, or some outlandish delicacy temporarily in favor, few privileged to contact with him remember him for his appetite. The morning's visit to the museum came up, along with his delight in once more seeing the familiar Klondike habiliments. Then, while my Aunt drew him out concerning himself, Rudyard Kipling's name was mentioned, and Jack's whole face lighted as he exclaimed: "Oh, have you read 'The Brushwood Boy'?—There is no end to Kipling, simply no end." Gone was that half-deferential diffidence; remained only his kindling enthusiasm for the work of his British idol, treasured possession of which without delay he would share with responsive companions.

It had proved inevitable, upon the appearance of young London's "Odyssey of the North" in the *Atlantic Monthly* for January just past, that this new writer's revolutionary method of presenting the primal, raw, frigid life of the savage North should call forth comparison with Kipling. I felt at a disadvantage in that I had missed reading this tale and the other eight that had been running in the *Overland*, beginning with "To the Man on Trail" in the January 1899 issue, and ending with "The Wisdom of the Trail" in December. The entire nine I learned were by now in the hands of Houghton, Mifflin & Company for book publication, under the title of "The Son of the Wolf"—the Arctic Indian's name for the conquering white man. Simultaneously with the *Atlantic Monthly*, he had broken into two other eastern publications, with an article, "The Economics of the Klondike," in *The Review of Reviews*, and a story, "Pluck and Pertinacity," in *The Youth's Companion.*

"Charmian," Mrs. Eames was suddenly struck with the idea, "why can't you review 'The Son of the Wolf'—perhaps in the same number of the *Overland* with my article on Mr. London?"

For as has been seen, at this period we were closely associated with the old magazine of the Golden West, that had cradled the first born of Bret Harte's genius; even I, urged on by my family, had dabbled sporadically and unambitiously at certain unimportant book reviewings. Besides, had not my maiden position, after leaving Mills College, been as assistant sub-scissors in the *Overland* sanctum? But far more than with literary leanings was I occupied, outside my office hours, with University of California "hops," and "proms," and "senior balls," to say nothing of week-end yachting on San Francisco Bay, horse-back rides, and youth's joy of living generally.

Jack beamed upon me from under his marked, mobile brows that just touched over the square bridge of a precisely not-too-short nose:

"Is it a go, Miss Kittredge?—I'll hold you to that! And I'll send you my duplicate proof-sheets soon, so you won't have to wait for the book."

When we parted he asked, meanwhile rolling and lighting a cigarette with quick, definite motions of his tapering fingers:

"Mrs. Eames, may I bring a friend to see you? His name is *Herman* Whitaker, 'Jim' we call him, and he can give you lots of points about me that I can't think of, for your article."

An early night was determined upon, and the engagement was fulfilled, shortly followed by a second. While my aunt's interviews with Mr. Whitaker were in progress, it devolved upon me to entertain their subject.

Of these occasions, nothing consecutive lives in memory, and only two incidents stand out: one, that I complied with my aunt's request to play on the piano for Mr. London, she having discovered his intense fondness for music; the other, that I introduced him to my "den" where, among other cherished objects, were my books, reproductions of my favorite marbles and paintings, and an absurdly elaborate little tea-table. I had the feeling that he was brightly aware of the feminine individuality of the room; and he showed interest in my various girlish activities, whether in music, or drawing, riding, even dancing. Years afterward that rosy little apartment, Venus Crouched and all, figured as Dede Mason's, in "Burning Daylight."

"I never danced a step in my life," he regretted bashfully. "Never seemed to have time to learn those soft, lovely ways of young people. But I like to see dancing."

For the music and the books he was almost equally hungry. Fled beyond recall is the memory of what I played, except that he asked if I had the de Koven "Recessional"—Kipling's verses; and he told me he sometimes bicycled to San José to visit friends, and there he had heard the song. It happened that I was able to gratify him, since I possessed quite a repertory of vocal music; for although no singer, I played accompaniments unprofessionally in the Bay region concerts.

Together we several times hummed through the stately invocation, and Jack was all alight with emotion, his great eyes shining, while he begged for it over and over. He had no apparent singing voice, although to a pleasanter, more expressive speaking tone I had never listened, especially when he descanted upon Kipling.

But more vividly than any other picture of him at that time, he rises standing by my side at the tall bookcase in my "den." His glowing eyes ranged rapidly over the volumes, and he seemed in a fine fervor, murmuring titles and authors or touching the backs with his small hands. Soon we were talking very fast, discussing works we had both read, and he urged me not to neglect Thomas Hardy's "Jude the Obscure." "Tess of the D'Urbervilles" had not come his way. This I lent him, together with Maurice Hewlett's "The Forest Lovers" and "Flood Tide," by Sallie P. McLean Green.

And once, turning toward him, I met a pair of fathomless sea-blue eyes, and experienced a sudden and unexpected impact of his mental and physical vitality; felt at-one with him for a high instant, knew his spiritual dignity, recognized him for the warm, human creature that he was. The moment passed quickly, and he was assuring me, unasked, that he had "a conscience about books," and would take the best care of mine. Through the irony of chance, some one spilled a bottle of ink over the cover of "Flood Tide," to Jack London's undying indignation and remorse. To this day I treasure the stained thing.

Often in later years, he and I wondered, had we been further thrown together, if we should have come to care the whole way for each other. And we usually agreed that the hour was not then. "You came in my great need," he would muse. "That early my great need had not developed, or else I did not recognize it."

The second of these calls occurred, I think, in the week of March 26. I aim to be thus explicit, because of headlong happenings in the succeeding week. Of what led to our making an appointment I am not sure; most likely he was sketching his college career for me, which, owing to responsibilities and lack of money, had been limited to half his Freshman year. Be this as it may, there was to me some unfamiliar purlieu of the staid university town that he thought would be of interest. With mutual amusement over the gaiety that would be added to the academic precincts by spectacle of man a-wheel and woman a-horse, we decided upon Saturday afternoon, April the seventh.

Meanwhile, one Saturday there had arrived the promised proof-sheets of "The Son of the Wolf," and when I returned home early for my long ride, on the tiny dresser I found waiting the long, printed slips. While unpinning my hat I started to read. I neither rose nor finished removing the sailor, until my streaming eyes had lifted from the last word of the last tale.

For before the first few sheets had been turned down, I had become thrall to the wonder and wisdom and artistry of "The White Silence," profoundly aware of the awareness of this young protagonist of nature's primordial forces, his apperception of the world in which he lived, and of the heart of man and beast, aye, and of woman—all human and fallible, but shot through with the fineness and courage of the spirit of nobility. This story, one of his first, contains some of the most masterly of the passages which set him amongst the young lords of language. In Mason's parting words are shown Jack's love of his own race, and for children. Indeed, he let us in upon nearly all of himself in that story. In most of the stories I noticed that he never seemed to be far from the consideration of death. His artistry lingered caressingly about the final destiny of man and animal.

Throughout the long afternoon, thrilled alike with the splendid repose and the crackling action of the work, shaken with its power, there blended with spiritual emotion the conviction that I had no business with the reviewing or criticizing of such brain-stuff as Jack London's. Forasmuch as I was intellectually indolent, I even felt no incitement to bestir myself. I would not touch the thing, I declared first to the four walls of the den, later to my aunt, who stood petrified before this breakdown of my accustomed certitude.

In after years, many were the times Jack London half seriously if laughingly charged that my unalterable decision was due, in the last analysis, to occurrences of the ensuing week. But I plead, now as always, complete innocence. Aside from my being more or less absorbed in another and very different person, the man Jack London dwelt in my consciousness little more tenaciously than an unusual book or play.

On Wednesday evening, April fourth, I found a type-written note awaiting me at home. This must have been tossed into the waste basket, for I have not seen it since. But it was worded something like this—he never lost many hours weeding out formal titles:

"Dear Charmian:

"It will be impossible for me to keep that engagement next Saturday. My letter to your aunt by this mail will explain. Sometime in the future, maybe.

"Sincerely yours,
"Jack London."

As I finished reading, Auntie came in, real distress in her face, for she had grown truly fond of her lovable friend, an affection which he reciprocated. In her hand was a similarly typed missive, covering a page and a half. "Listen to this," she said in a dead voice, and read to me the unexpected contents, which were Jack's vindication for the suddenness of his proceeding. I copy:

"1130 East 15th St.,
"Oakland, Calif.,
"April 3, 1900.

My dear Mrs. Eames:

"Must confess you have the advantage of me. I have not yet seen my book, nor can I possibly imagine what it looks like. Nor can you possibly imagine why I am going to beg off from going out to your place next Saturday. You know I do things quickly. Sunday morning, last, I had not the slightest intention of doing what I am going to do. I came down and looked over the house I was to move into—that fathered the thought. I made up my mind. Sunday evening I opened transactions for a wife; by Monday evening had the affair well under way; and next Saturday morning I shall marry—a Bessie Maddern, cousin to Minnie Maddern Fiske. Also, on said Saturday, as soon as the thing is over with we jump out on our wheels for a three days' trip, and then back and to work.

"'The rash boy,' I hear you say. Divers deep considerations have led me to do this thing; but I shall override just one objection—that of being tied. I am already tied. Though single, I have had to support a household just the same. Should I wish to go to China the household would have to be provided for whether I had a wife or not.

"As it is, I shall be steadied, and can be able to devote more time to my work. One only has one life, you know, after all, and why not live it? Besides, my heart is large, and I shall be a cleaner, wholesomer man because of a restraint being laid upon me in place of being free to drift wheresoever I listed. I am sure you will understand.

"I thank you for your kind word concerning the appearance of 'The Son of the Wolf.' I shall let you know when I am coming out, and now, being located, want you and yours to come and see me and mine. Will settle that when I get back. Wedding is to be private.

"Send announcement later.

"Very sincerely yours,
"Jack London."

"Heavens and earth!" wailed my aunt. "Think what the boy is doing! A *sensible*, considered marriage for a love-man like that! 'Only one life . . . and why not live it?'—The boy must be crazy to dream that marrying in cold blood is living life!"

"No, not crazy, but perhaps super-sane—or thinks he is, "I commented, and went down to dinner, probably marveling how "God's own mad lover" may sometimes direct his madness into quite practical channels.

One bitter cold morning in New York City, in the winter of 1918, I was called over the telephone by Jack's longtime friend, Cloudesley Johns:

"Oh, Charmian—I 've been looking over those 1899 and 1900 letters of Jack's I promised for your use, and find this, dated March 10, 1900. Listen:

"'Have just finished reading "Forest Lovers" by Maurice Hewlett. Bead it by all means. . . . Have made the acquaintance of Charmian Kittredge, a charming girl who writes book reviews, and who possesses a pretty little library wherein I have found all these late books which the public libraries are afraid to have circulated.'"

Thus, Jack London, who always decried puns on my given name, was himself not guiltless in this reference to our passing acquaintance of 1900.

Except for one occasion, when he brought his wife, the pair on bicycles, to call upon us, Jack London dropped out of my sphere of interest, save insofar as I desultorily followed his work. My aunt's article duly appeared in the 1900 May *Overland*, while their friendship grew apace, until he came to address her in letters as Mother Mine. Later in the year I sold a piece of Berkeley land in which she had long since wisely overborne me to invest my savings, and a portion of the sum realized I spent on a fifteen months' vacation in the eastern states and Europe. One icy morning, away up in Mt. Desert Island, opening an Oakland, California, paper, I stumbled upon this item:

"LONDON—In this city, January 15, 1901, to the wife of Jack London, a daughter."

A comment read:

> "Jack London, the brilliant young author and essayist, is receiving congratulations upon the advent of a daughter. Mr. London is satisfied that he has a real live subject for the study of psychology and other phenomena in which he is so much interested."

In this wise the young adventurer, who has been dubbed "the most picturesque figure in American literature," pursued the law-abiding domesticity he had calculated so nicely as his duty to himself, his work, and society; while I, like Masefield's "Young April on a blood-horse with a roving eye," rode merrily upon my own dutiful, dancing, musical way that seemed all-sufficient to my needs, unheedful of the future.

CHAPTER I

THE STUFF OF STARS

ALL in all, it is a happy fate that places in one's keeping the rudimental material, blood-drift and magical spirit-stuff, that went into the syntheses of this resultant entity whom men knew as Jack London; who in his time was loved or hated as they reacted to his spacious nature with its varying levels of humannesses, its winging heights, its drowning depths.

In sifting and assembling the details bearing upon Jack London's origin, the keen enjoyment of serving his readers joins with a keener zest in singing his pride of race; in sounding the pean, manifest throughout his work, of his very own Anglo-Saxon breed, upon which he gambled his faith. And the pleasure increases as additional verification is uncovered bearing upon his direct British ancestry.

From the heart of the city of London there sprang two large families that bore the city's name, one of which branches was from Semitic seed, as witness Meyer London, erstwhile Socialist congressman at Washington, D. C., and many another in America; while in England one of my correspondents is a Jewess whom I address as "Mrs. Jack London."

The Gentile group, it seems, owned the land of which Chatham Square is now part. One of the early Londons had a sister Elizabeth, who married a Wellington, and lived at Chatham. When Jack London's sister Eliza was a child, she heard her father say, referring to politics in his part of Pennsylvania: "If the Wellingtons and McLoughlins stood together, they'd carry the elections!" In Jack's direct ancestry, the first person in my available record is Sir William London, who foreswore allegiance to Great Britain and betook himself to America. Here, under General George Washington, he fought valiantly for his ideals, thereby sacrificing no mean estates in the tight little island; for these were promptly confiscated by the jealous Crown, and thereafter figured in the mill of Chancery. I can remember Jack London saying: "One of my childhood recollections is of mysterious sessions held by my mother and father, from which I gathered that he had been approached across the water by the London heirs to lend a hand in fighting for his great-grandfather's seized properties."

But a letter from one Mary London Wilson, seventy years old, writing from Lackawanna County, Pennsylvania, in 1904, gives the following: That nearly thirty years before, an advertisement had been run in the papers, calling for information of London heirs in America. For Lord Eussell London had died in England, the last of his line, leaving a half million for the American heirs if they could be located. From this letter one learns that none of the Londons knew of this advertisement for nearly two years; when a Charley London, with a lawyer, voyaged overseas, only to find that the estate had gone from Chancery to the Crown.

Sir William London's son William named his son Manley. Manley London married Sarah Hess, and became the sire of eight: Mary, Sarah, Rebecca, George, Martha, Eliza, Joseph, and John London, with whom the direct life-story of Jack London begins. And these Londons, one and all, from the redoubtable knight down to and including his great-grandson John, took part in each and every warlike uprising for American liberty. It would not be out of place here to add that the last of the paternal line, nephews of Jack London, namely, Irving Shepard and John Miller, did their part on sea and land in this twentieth century-greatest of all struggles.

John London, great-grandson of Sir William, first saw the light in Springfield County, Pennsylvania, on January 11, 1828. He grew up on a farm, receiving the education attainable in small rural schools nearly a century ago, while he learned the hard, empirical way of agriculture at that early date.

He comes next into view at the age of nineteen, as boss of a section gang in the construction of a great railroad system through Pennsylvania. One day, John reported at the big farm residence of an official of the road, one Hugh Cavett, The latter being absent, his daughter Anna Jane took the message. Eyes and hands struck fire, and in two weeks the pair were married; for John London was a bonnie lad, six feet in his homespun socks, square-shouldered, well-limbed, fine-skinned, with comely hands and feet, and a wealth of soft, wavy brown

MOTHER OF JACK LONDON
FLORA WELLMAN

JACK LONDON'S FATHER
JOHN LONDON

hair—one of Jack London's own physical characteristics. "Finest head of hair I ever barbered!" old Barber Smith of San Francisco declared of John's luxuriant mane thirty years later. And, like Jack's, John's wide-set, gray-blue, dancing eyes and sweeping ways were not to be resisted by mortal woman. What mattered it to him, when kind called to kind, that Anna Jane's father was his employer and a rich man! He was the owner of profitable farmlands, not only in Westmorel, but in Township Patton, Alleghany County; a stockholder in the Wheeling Bridge property in Virginia, and an investor in various other lucrative schemes that were bringing fortunes to foreseeing men of Hugh Cavett's type. Besides, over and above the love that drew the man and maid so quickly together, was not the comely girl John's very ideal of a capable country-house mistress?

After the wedding John London came to live for a time in the big house, where he began the founding of his own line—a generous contribution of eleven olive branches, some sprouting twin-buds, to the family tree. He was absent frequently, sent out, I gather, by his father-in-law on business connected with the railroad. If the other man was at all put out by the forthright methods of the young couple in matters matrimonial, evidently he made the best of the situation and advanced the unexpected son-in-law in line with his abilities. Moreover, the sedately arriving yearly babies, beginning with Tom and Mary, could not have failed to erase any last vestige of their grandfather's pique.

John London's life-long gallantry is illustrated by a little incident that took place upon his homecoming from one of these trips. Finding his bride over-strained by the housewifely labor of entertaining for weeks a full complement of relatives, he expressed his solicitude by dismissing the whole tribe, stating his reasons. He then turned to and helped Anna Jane clear up after them. In quite another setting, half a century later, Jack London said to me:

"When we are married, much as I love an open house, if I cannot afford servants, we'll live in tents so there can't be any entertaining! No domestic drudgery for wife of mine. It's your life and my life, first. Our need of each other lies in different ways than circumscribed domesticity."

Very congenial seem to have been John and Anna Jane. "No one ever saw Jane angry or disagreeable," reads the yellowed fragment of a letter, "nor John London cross or harsh. He was always protecting some one." A roving spirit characterized the London strain, and Anna Jane appears to have been in no wise backward in aiding and abetting its development in her spouse. From the fact that she is not mentioned in Hugh Cavett's will, and by other data, one is led to conclude that he had settled her portion upon her before she and John presently went adventuring up through Wisconsin, with an eye for an abiding-place, thence drifting down to Illinois, where John's mother, a remarkable woman, managed her own stockfarm. Five sons she gave to the Civil War, meanwhile she continued to develop her holdings.

When John London enlisted in the War of the Rebellion, it was from a Missouri farm, and he left behind Anna Jane with seven children. At the close of the war, with one lung out of action as the result of a combined siege of pneumonia and smallpox, he lived with his family in the town of Moscow, Muscatine County, Iowa, in a two-story white house on the town square. Here Eliza was born. On the opposite side of the square stood the flour-mill, and John, among other building work, superintended the construction of a bridge across Cedar River, the stream that furnished power to the mill. Eliza remembers well the close proximity of the watercourse. Priscilla was washing and getting dinner, and asked her wee sister to run and see if papa was coming. Eliza toddled to the bench on which she was wont to climb to the window, and pulled over upon herself the steaming tub of clothing big sister had set there. She never forgot how quickly papa, returning from his bridge-building, answered the summons to aid his scalded baby. Later, they migrated to a quarter section of government land outside of Moscow. When his wife was discovered with consumption, John arranged affairs so that he could devote himself to her, and it fell in with their mutual dreams to play at gipsying. For two years they moved over the prairies in a "schooner," and during this time John came into pleasant contact with the Pawnees, by whom he swore stoutly to his dying day. "Play fair with an Indian," he held, "and you can trust him with anything, anywhere. It's wrong treatment that's made sly devils of 'em."

With the redskins this born outdoors man hunted and trapped raccoons and other prairie game; and, in bee-hunting, proved of keener sight than the aborigines in following to its honey store the flight of a homing worker. Later, when the Indians were camping near the farm, John branded his stock, and, unlike some of his neighbors, never lost a single head to any marauder. Play the game squarely, was his philosophy, and you stand to win.

That Anna Jane did not entirely subscribe to this wholesale confidence in the original American crops out in an amusing anecdote, often told by her husband. He, despite the railing of his familiars, had blithely loaned to an old brave fifty cents and a musket, but forgot to mention the little transaction to his wife. It happened that she was alone when the chief came to redeem his obligations, and being very ill, she was badly frightened when his gaunt frame filled the doorway. In round terms she ordered him away; but the Indian, when she refused to touch the fifty cents, strode furiously in a grandly threw the coins into the middle of the floor, and stood the well-cleaned gun carefully in its corner. Stalking as furiously forth, he met his benefactor coming home, to whom he clipped out that the white-face squaw was no good—too foolish even to take money or guns offered her.

Early in the seventies, John London found himself bereft of his mate, and with an exceptionally large family to consider. One of the sons, Charles, had been injured playing our national game, a ball catching him in the chest. His father conceived a plan whereby he might leave the remaining youngest folk—three of the eleven had died—temporarily with the older sisters and willing neighbors, while he struck out farther West in the hope of benefiting the ailing boy. All was satisfactorily worked out, when John weakened to the wailing of Eliza and Ida, hardly more than babies. At the last moment a rearrangement was effected that included the pair, as well as two friends, Mr. and Mrs. Chase. They, in return for their expenses to California, were to assume the care of Charles and his two little sisters.

John never again saw Iowa. Charles grew rapidly worse, and died eleven days after he looked upon his first ocean. The widower disposed of the farm, and with the proceeds established himself in a contracting business in San Francisco. Meantime he placed Eliza and Ida in the Protestant Orphan Asylum on Haight Street, paying for their living and tuition. Eliza London has always averred that the period spent in the quaint, moss-grown stone home was the happiest of her life, and with the tenaciousness of a devoted nature, she had soon fastened her shy affection upon one of the teachers. Next she came to nourish a fond hope that her beloved papa would share her own adoration for teacher, and bring to his girls a new mother. But she was doomed to secret sorrow and tears, for papa, although never blind to a pretty face and womanly traits, was even then under the influence of wholly a different person.

Many a smart beau of that winsome light-opera star of the long ago, Kate Castleton, will smile with awakened memories to learn that a sweet friendship existed between the lovable young singer and the big, quiet, long-bearded man from the Middle West who had such a way with him. But it was not she—and another ardent desire of the wee Eliza, who still wore a ring her idol had sent her, went glimmering with the first. For the lady of her father's second choice in life was not beautiful. And Eliza, who did not consider lovely her own small, expressive face with its deep-blue, black-lashed London eyes, worshiped beauty, and little considered other possible attractiveness in herself or those about her.

Now the widower, ever alert to new impressions from the world's limitless abundance, never convinced but there was something better for him just over the mutely summoning horizon, and with the death of two dear ones still quick in his consciousness, had strayed from his more or less strict Methodist outlook and observances and had become enamored of the doctrines of a spiritualistic cult. Amongst the devout sisters of this group of seekers after truth he met Flora Wellman, a tiny, fair woman in her early thirties, hailing from Massillon, Ohio. Once more in the London fashion, John wasted no moment in binding to him his desire.

The next visiting day at the orphanage, on which he had planned to escort the betrothed to meet his daughters, found him ill; and when the unsuspecting Eliza and Ida were bidden to the stiff reception-room, imagine their astonishment to see an unknown woman, hardly above their own height, rise and announce that she was to be their new mother.

In Jack London's inheritance through his mother, again the blood of Great Britain predominates, for Flora Wellman's ancestry leads back to England and Wales, and includes strains of French and Dutch. The family traces its American residence to pre-Revolution days. Flora's father, Marshall Daniel Wellman, was born in Augusta, Oneida County, New York, in 1800, son of Betsy Baker and Joel Wellman, both of British stock. Joel was a cooper, plying his trade in the

Syracuse District Salt Wells. When Betsy died, he married a second wife who in turn left him a widower. Whereupon, while Marshall and a brother were yet boys, Joel journeyed to the headwaters of the Allegheny River, where the three built and launched a wondrous houseboat, called a *bateau*, and made the voyage to Pittsburgh. Thence the *bateau* floated them on down to old Beavertown, where Joel had heard there was a demand for pork- and whisky-barrels. In his palmy days, Marshall Wellman loved to boast that he had earned a reputation of turning out the best tight oaken barrels ever seen in the region of Beavertown.

A year afterward they moved farther West, this time to Wooster, Ohio. There, from the ashes of timber burned in clearing this new country, Joel and his sons manufactured "pot ash," which they had learned was one of the few products that sold for cash in Pittsburgh. When he was an old man, Marshall remembered well the mountain of stacked ash we piled up south of the town, Wooster, near the Robinson place." Once a sister came all the way from New York to see their land of promise; but she became homesick and Marshall escorted her, the couple on horses, back to New York. While still under twenty-one, he took a contract for building a section of the Allegheny Canal in Pennsylvania; and subsequently Marshall Wellman rose to be the wealthiest citizen of Massillon, Ohio, as wealth was accounted in those days.

Flora Wellman, born August 17, 1843, was the youngest child of Marshall Wellman's family of five, the others being Mary Marcia, Hiram B., Susan, and Louisa. Her mother, Eleanor Garrett Jones, born in 1810 at Brookfield, Trumbull County, Ohio, had married Marshall in 1852. Her father, a devout circuit-rider of Welsh extraction, called "Priest" Jones, well beloved and valued adviser to the countryside, had been a pioneer settler and upbuilder of Ohio when that state was thought of as the whole West. He passed away an honored member of Wooster's society, full of good works, and incidentally leaving a comfortable fortune to his heirs.

The mother died shortly following Flora's birth, and Wellman remarried when she was four years of age. His bride was Julia Frederica Hurxthal, the Hurxthals being another of the pioneer Massillon families that had amassed riches.

The little girl was nurtured in an atmosphere of luxury and culture, her clothes and her hats and her boots, her books, and her teachers, all especially ordered and delivered from New York City; and she has told me that she possessed distinct talents in music and elocution. That no due family observance might be neglected, Marshall Wellman even summoned a portrait painter from New York, who immortalized all the members of the household on his canvases.

"Few mothers of great men have been happy women," some one has written, and Flora Wellman seems to have been no exception. Capacity for happiness may have been a part of her heritage, but fate was extraordinarily cruel. Somewhere around her thirteenth year, I have it from her, she fell victim to a fever that physically stunted her, and probably accounted for her short sparse hair and for certain melancholic tendencies. "I cannot remember the day when my mother was not old," Jack London more than once declared, while relatives, and friends of long standing, have asserted in her advanced years, "She has always been very much as you see her now." It would seem that the fever almost entirely robbed the unfortunate young soul of youth and gladness. Her eyes were ever fixed upon decline and dissolution, or peering into the hereafter of her spiritualistic faith.

CHAPTER II

BIRTH

JACK LONDON was born in San Francisco, California, on January 12, 1876. At two o'clock of the afternoon came her woman's hour, that is the most lonely of all hours known to the human, and Flora London's voice was joined by the cry of her first and only child. He weighed nine pounds, which was one-tenth of his mother's weight. She called him John Griffith,—the middle name being in memory of Griffith Everhard, a favorite nephew. Flora and John London, having no formal church affiliations, the infant was never christened, and answered to "Johnnie" until the day when deliberately he selected, and made splendidly his own, the terse British name that has girdled the world wherever books and adventure, and abundant life are known.

The house in which he first expanded his fine young chest and made himself audible, was at Third and Bryant streets, occupied by the Slocums, friends of Flora, the master of the home being a prosperous member of a well-known printing establishment. Contrary to the more or less general belief that Jack London was born in a shanty on a sand-lot, the dwelling was a large and not inelegant one. For this had been a fashionable neighborhood in the changing fortunes of the gay western metropolis, and had not yet lapsed into the subsequent "south of Market" social disfavor.

Unluckily, Flora was unable long to nourish her lusty babe, and he speedily grew thin and blue. John London looked about and discovered among the men working for him one whose wife had lost her latest born and who was willing to become wet-nurse to the white child. Mrs. Prentiss was a full-blooded negress, and proud of it. Many a time Jack London has told how she was bartered on the block for a high price, while her mother was sold down the river. Now she became "Mammy Jenny" to an appreciative foster-son whose faithful and affectionate care years afterward she was until his death; since then, I have as naturally assumed the trust, over and above the provisions of his last will and testament.

It was a veritable cherub that the black woman undertook to mother in her essential capacity, white as snow, exquisitely modeled, with dimpled hands and feet surprisingly small for his firm, plump torso. He soon became pink-cheeked, with eyes of violet, his seraphic face haloed in white-gold ringlets too fragile-fine to seem real to the worshiping African, the devotion of whose deprived heart was instant and abiding toward the "teenty, helpless angel." In the Cloudesley Johns correspondence I find this from Jack: "Hair was black when I was born, then came out during an infantile sickness and returned positively white—so white that my negress nurse called me 'cotton ball.'"

When the baby was returned to his family they had moved to a cottage on Bernal Heights. And now upon the maternal Eliza devolved most of the rearing of her half-brother, indoors and out, in the energetic year spent in the cottage. The perambulator containing the baby boy, wheeled by a no less azure-eyed girl-child, became a familiar object of an afternoon on the hilly streets.

John London, man of the open field, with clinging conservative principles in money matters, was no match for the swift Western commercial spirit. But he recognized his inability in time to avert disaster, closed his contracting office, and accepted a position with the J. M. Flaven Company's famous IXL Emporium. In his canvassing about the spreading city, built upon its many hills, he was further enlightened of this Farthest West expansive atmosphere. His bubbling sense of humor unavoidably entered into many a conflict with a fading Methodist viewpoint—as one day, on a steep cobbled declivity of Telegraph Hill, when he paused to rest his benevolent, well-shaped hand upon the towseled pate of the handsomest of a group of urchins playing in the street. "What's your name, sonny?" he asked kindly. In later years, one of the best yarns of this indefatigable story-teller wound up with the shock he had sustained from this pure, sweet little child: "'What t'e hell business is it of yourn what's my name?—an' I ain't your sonny, neither!'"

The next on the list of baby Johnnie's unremembered homes was a new six-room flat opposite the old Plaza on Folsom Street, owned by a family of Cohens who dwelt in the lower apartments. John London had steadily bettered his income, and was now employed by the

Singer Sewing Machine Company, as general agent and collector. To this day one might find a few of the decayed mansions of the section's past grandeur. In one of these, even then long since converted into a boarding house, I once went to take piano lessons. My teacher dwelt in the inexhaustible fragrance of old cedar paneling, and once surreptitiously led me down a maze of marble staircases into the nether regions of the imposing pile. There my ravished eyes roved about dismantled dining halls of maple and gilt, and a fabulous, echoing ballroom walled in mirrors like Versailles; and the ceiling, I verily believe, was a copy of Rubens' plump charmers and cherubs in Queen Wilhelmina's House in the Wood, near the Hague.

But Flora, never content for long in any spot, found a home she liked better, this time at the blind end of Natoma Street. Here it seemed as if they had come upon the nearest that San Francisco ever conceded to their desire. For the two-storied roomy house was set in a sort of court shaped by the abrupt, vine-fenced termination of the thoroughfare. It was a blossomy oasis in the engulfing metropolitan life of the ambitious city, through tacit agreement kept neat by the dwellers therein, who carefully tended their window pots and flowering strips of garden soil.

Not to restlessness, however, but to an epidemic of diphtheria was due the subsequent exodus of the Londons from San Francisco. The baby fell a victim, followed by his shadow, Eliza, agonizing doubly on his account. The terrified mother turned to and heroically nursed the pair of them—as when a girl she had with deathly fear courageously brought through smallpox her sister Mary's son, Harry Everhard. To this day Eliza holds that a certain mortuary suggestion from her stepmother whipped her to consciousness and a winning fight for life. Both she and Johnnie were lying in what the doctor pronounced a condition bordering upon dissolution. The exhausted but thrifty Flora asked him if it would be feasible to bury them in the same coffin, when the aroused girl opened horrified eyes and feebly, but unmistakably, protested.

The physician, having proved a poor judge of their resistance, dropped back upon the time-honored recommendations of a sojourn in the country. But business had to be business to the paternal provider, and with his agricultural intentions dear as ever to his heart, this change was regarded from the viewpoint of an enduring rural residence. The first lap toward this end was merely to the large San Francisco suburb of Oakland, to the east across the bay, that wide expanse of capricious waters that set in Jack London's eyes the far away look of the Argonaut. Thus Oakland, in the County of Alameda, for him came to be the center to which he always referred as his home town, from which he fared forth to the adventures in which he recaptured the spirit of romance for a growingly blasé civilization.

CHAPTER III

BOYHOOD

(Oakland, Alameda, San Mateo)

MY father was the best man I have ever known, "Jack London was wont to say, "too intrinsically good to get ahead in the soulless scramble for a living that a man must cope with if he would survive in our anarchical capitalist system."

John London once more plunged into business for himself, working toward his pastoral goal. His savings were applied to the leasing and cultivating of a tract of land adjoining the race track at Emeryville, suburb of Oakland near the eastern bay shore, and hard by Shell Mound Park, described in "Martin Eden." With the produce, a green-goods store was opened at Seventh and Campbell Streets. This junction was known as The Point by Oaklanders of that day. Here the local and main line trains left terra firma and proceeded out upon a fearsome, teredo-incrusted trestle far into the bay to where the largest ferry steamers in the world conveyed passengers to and from San Francisco. I recall an occasion, in girlhood, when I paddled in the tiny gray-green surf at The Point, and then went indoors for a salt tubbing in water pumped from the bay and heated.

Into this fresh venture John put his savings and his faith, and, despite a rigorous honesty that ranged the most luscious of his justly famed tomatoes at the lowest tiers of the boxes—the "culls" went to less fortunate neighbors—he might have prospered had he let well enough alone. But to his bosom he took a shifty partner, one Stowell, in whose slippery hands he placed the thriving little shop while he traveled in outlying districts. These absences were for the purpose of taking orders and introducing his fruit and vegetables, which were the best Oakland ever enjoyed; and also for buying, at the Stone and the Meek orchards between San Leandro and Haywards, to fill the demand of his own enlarging trade.

One weekend, arriving back unsuspecting from a trip, he discovered that he had been figuratively thrown out, sold out, cleaned out, by his partner. Stowell must have been a clever crook and known his man well, for John was quite unequal to the tangle in which he found himself when he appealed to the law. Fight he did, and manfully; only a pitiful few dollars remained to him at the end of a legal battle.

But with the recurrent youthful optimism that was his chiefest personal charm, he shook those broad spare shoulders free of the sordid morass, threw back his curly poll, and turned toward the race track garden, from which he began supplying the firm of Porter Brothers, commission merchants, who sold his fast augmenting product.

Four successive homes the family occupied during this phase in their fortunes—one at Twelfth and Wood Streets, another on Seventh near Center and Peralta, And then they essayed to cheer the premises known as the Haunted House, the rumor being that a man had hanged himself from a beam therein. Nothing daunted, Mrs. London pitched in and established a kindergarten, in business relations with a Mrs. Kegler. Flora's knowledge of music assisted capitally in this connection, and she taught a few outside pupils as well. Although Eliza and Jack both received piano instructions from her in childhood, they have always united in declaring that they never saw her play. Her method seemed based upon the mechanics of the process, with no attempt to induce the harmonies by personal example.

Jack's own memories reached to this house, mainly because it was the stage of his debut in trousers—albeit hidden by a jumper. But his infantile pride for once soared above shrinking self-consciousness, and rebelled at the ignominy of this concealment. He was wont, in the most public places, to lift said jumper, that all men might bear witness to the uniform of his sturdy sex. An adorable little man he must have been. Eliza found there was hardly any possession her schoolgirl friends would not part with or lend in exchange for the privilege of taking care of him, or having him sit with them at their desks. He went to the highest bidder, of course; and his sister munched many an otherwise unattainable apple or bun, or pleasured in a borrowed ring or bracelet.

Matters began to mend, and from a subsequent home on Twelfth Street near Castro, they moved upon fifteen acres of the Davenport property in Alameda, where now looms the Clark Pottery Company's factory. So full of strange happenings are our lives, it was in this selfsame Pottery the red Spanish tiling was fashioned to crown Jack London's "Wolf House" on Sonoma Mountain—futile dream-house, three years' building, that in a single midnight puffed out in flame and smoke!

John's success led him to spread operations to other convenient locations, one of which was the later site of the Smith Borax Works. Still other fruitful acres branched out from both sides of the old "Narrow Gauge" transbay railway on the Alameda flats. Through commission merchants his produce, ever maintaining its standard of superexcellence, now found ready market in San Francisco. Long after his death, Eliza's ear one day was caught by a familiar note, caroled by a street hawker. She asked if the words he was singing, "J. L. Corn," meant anything to him. Needless to say, to his bucolic intelligence, they signified nothing more nor less than mere corn. And it pleased Eliza to inform the man that her father had been, so to speak, the father of his wares.

Like a bad dream, the little Jack always remembered his first intoxication, which took place, at the tender age of five, just after he came to Alameda. It was his task to toddle at noonday with a tin lard-pail of beer out into the fields where John London mopped his brow amidst his springing green creations. One day, the frothy contents overrunning and biting into the scratches on his chubby legs, the small man was seized with a desire to taste the stuff that so refreshed his elders. It was not the first time that out of a vast latent curiosity he had fallen for the temptation to test forbidden choice morsels intended for older folk, which up to now he had found good. Also, the pail was too full, and his calves smarted. Into the crackly foam he buried his hot little face to the eyes, hoping the taste would improve when he reached the yellow liquid. It did not improve; but driven by that persistence that all through his career forced him to complete what he had begun, the doughty youngling drained what was to his tiny paunch a mighty draught. Sorely that same thirsty organ must have been crowded, for alarm spread in him to see how the beer had receded. With a stick, remembering how stale brew was made to effervesce, he stirred what was left, and was rewarded by a crop of white bubbles that would deceive the onlooker. John London, sweating prodigiously and eager to

JACK LONDON AT ABOUT 9 YEARS—WITH HIS DOG ROLLO

complete his furrow, unnoticing poured the liquor down his dry throat and started up the team, his small son trotting alongside.

The next the inebriated baby knew, he was coming to in the shade of a tree, in his fuzzy brain a crushing terror of flashing steel blades and great shining hooves of plunging horses. Then his eyes, dark with fear, looked up into a reassuring bearded face that bent over him, its solicitude and relief struggling with a mirth it could not quite control. Poor little wayfarer in the fields of chance—he had reeled and fallen between a plowshare and the hind feet of the beasts, and only the plowman's instant halting of the outfit had preserved the baby from being cloven and turned under with the soil.

Another vividly remembered if lesser childish tragedy on Alameda ground was connected with his building instincts, and it came about in this way: Myself a contemporary child in Oakland, transplanted from the indolent Spanish air of Southern California, I remember my aunt and uncle and the neighbors on Thirty-fifth Street discussing the wonder-operetta *Satanella* which they had attended in the Tivoli Opera House, forbidden pleasure to one so young as I. A magical performance it was, if my excited imagining was correct, of inexplicable appearings and vanishings of sulphurous deities, with all the glamour of intermixed Fairyland and Heaven arrayed against black-and-red but enchanting Sin. Whilst I was drinking in my elders' reminiscent snatches of libretto and score, Johnnie London actually, with his own rounded orbs, beheld the absorbing spectacle. Incited thereby, after a night of fire-illumined nightmare, he undertook to build a little hell of his own under the apple tree by the side of the house. He was assisted wonderingly by his chum, Theodore Crittenden, who, as co-creator, was to be constituted only second in importance to his superior's own Satanic Majesty. But swifter hell than had been anticipated broke loose when the Vice-Devil's assiduous spade accidentally split open the prospective Majesty's chubby nose, and Johnnie's lurid dream collapsed in gore and tears on sister Eliza's clean pinafore.

When Jack London turned sadly from the disappointing soil of human society at large, to solve some of its economic problems in the undisappointing if wearied land that he so patiently reclaimed, he sorrowed from year to year, while his terraced hillsides increased their yield, that John London could not be there to behold and rejoice:

"My one greatest regret, always, is that my father could not live to share my prosperity," he would say. "Think of the lasting joy if the two dear old soldiers, your father and mine, could have lived here on the Ranch and watched my blades of grass come up out of the rejuvenated soil—two blades or more where but one grew when I came upon it!" Alas—the years are many since that pair of stalwart, child-hearted real Americans, born in the same year, laid themselves down untimely.

The three London young folk, Eliza, Ida, and Johnnie, attended the West End School, Alameda, on Pacific Avenue below Webster Street. Eliza was just being graduated from grammar grades when Johnnie entered his first schoolroom to study. Here the bashful but trusting little chap recited his first "piece" when he was about six, and with no more liking for public speaking than was his in adult life:

"Christmas is coming, it soon will be here,
The very best time in all of the year.
I am counting each day on my fingers and thumbs
The weeks that must pass before Santa Claus comes.
No hard words to spell, no writing, no sums;
There's nothing but playtime when Santa Claus comes."

To employ his own words, he had "no recollection of being taught to read or write," and "could do both at the age of five." Eliza remembers him as forever with a book in his hands; and, it not being a bookish household, he must have read and reread from the days when she had "read the pictures" to him out of a printed linen Mother Goose. In this manner she had beguiled him to slumber on lonely evenings in San Francisco, when Mr. and Mrs. London were out, probably with their spiritualist friends. In the ten years that the girl constantly companioned her half-brother, she found him intensely alive to impressions, quick to grasp meanings but half explained, and early to make use of his available vocabulary. Of large words he heard few; but out of his simple store he sought and applied the precise best ones adapted to express his thought.

But his glorious endowment of normality was pervaded by a sensitiveness that comported with the delicate skin, the aristocratic hands and feet and small-boned frame that never, in adolescence, bore up unharmed under the demands of contradictory sturdy muscles of shoulder and trunk and limb. This timidity, or shyness, that masked a hunger for sympathy and understanding from moment to moment, was more often expressed by the laying of a dimpled fist into Eliza's ever-receptive clasp. Deep feelings were not habitually demonstrated in the household. "I do not remember ever receiving a caress from my mother when I was young," Jack has said; "but I was at long intervals cheered by my father's comprehending hand laid upon my head, and his kind, 'There, there, sonny!' when things went wrong." Thus Eliza and the boy, both of intensely loving nature, were impelled together in a lasting relation of confidence.

One grateful spot in Alameda memories was the spio and span cottage of Mammy Jenny Prentiss near Willow Street Station. Her bright-eyed foster-baby often ran away to the crooning embrace of the colored woman whose greatest pride was her own untarnished blood, and who always was tastefully and pridefully dressed. There her spoiled white child was sure of welcome and wondrous pastry, dispensed with adoration and a lavish hand, and there "Will and Annie were like cousins." Flora Wellman's own stiff pride of race had already made its mark on Johnnie's subjective operations; but that it had not become a recognized form is shown by his ignorance of the fact that his half-white playmates were other than like himself. One day, Will Prentiss, aged six, was at the house, getting some of the "culls" of fruit and vegetables with which John London so generously favored his friends. Little Johnnie in an uproarious tomato-fight plastered a ripe red one upon the perfect nose Will had inherited from his mother, and cried out with innocent cruelty, to Will's weeping shame: "Oh, gee! *Willy*! I've made your nose as flat as a nigger's!"

As the savings accumulated, Flora's ambition for the Just Beyond urged her husband toward his unforgotten mecca, and they presently returned to the other side of the Bay. This time they leased a seventy-five acre farm, likely the Tobin Ranch, on the "Peninsula" south of San Francisco, in San Mateo County, and near what now shows on the map as Moss Beach. In level sandy loam not far from the ocean, John concentrated upon the perfecting of the finest potatoes in the San Francisco market—his principal triumph on that farm.

Where the money went, over and above necessities, after the expenses of moving had been squared, was a lifelong puzzle to Jack and Eliza. Jack designated himself as a "meat-eater." While there was always enough to eat in the house, flesh-food may at times have been scarce, or delayed in delivery, and he craved it perhaps out of proportion to his need, as children will. Note the following quotation from a letter, written in a fit of blank despondency, to the sweetheart of his early twenties. In view of a possible future with him, she had urged him to forsake writing and cease not from hunting a steady salary.

"Why, as you have laid down my duty in your letter, if I had followed it what would I have been to-day? I would be a laborer, and by that I mean I would be fitted for nothing else than labor. Do you know my childhood? When I was seven years old at the country school of San Pedro, this happened. Meat, I was that hungry for it I once opened a girl's basket and stole a piece of meat—a little piece the size of my two fingers. I ate it but I never repeated it. In those days, like Esau, I would have literally sold my birthright for a mess of pottage, a piece of meat. Great God! when those youngsters threw chunks of meat on the ground because of surfeit, I could have dragged it from the dirt and eaten it; but I did not. Just imagine the development of my mind, my soul, under such material conditions. This meat incident is an epitome of my whole life."

Now, from the foregoing and some other quotations, the reader is likely to gather that Jack was at times given to hyperbole when, driven and discouraged, he reviewed his thorny path. I may be forgiven, considering many years of intimate observation, if I comment upon a tendency he evinced toward self-concentration when overdone by thinking, or work, or trouble. This is a delicate matter upon which to disagree, since he is not here to argue the point. But as I see it, his excessive sensibilities, despite formidable endurance, caused him to suffer more acutely, mentally and physically, than the average run of human beings. Since his increasing ambitions to do and be, goaded him ever to superactivity, his case was hopeless, in that he must undergo weariness of heart and brain. He could not rest, therefore he did not rest. Hence, I occasionally found him prone to exaggerate, not the thing itself, but the enormity of the thing treated. Take that matter of going hungry in childhood. Once, looking up from a volume she was reading, I overheard his mother say to Eliza:

"Here Jack has written that he didn't have enough to eat. And I've heard him say the only time he ever took anything that didn't belong to him, was some meat out of another boy's lunch basket at school. Do *you* remember any time when we did not set a good table? *I* can't. He didn't go hungry in *our* house! He surely must mean when he was off goose-chasing on the creek, or out all night on the streets, or something of that sort. Why, you know, his father always had vegetables, and if meat was ever scarce, there were plenty of chickens."

And Eliza was equally put to it to recall slim fare.

From Jack London's recollection of this phase in his peripatetic life, he drew the rather bleak and depressing coast line, too often muffled in dreary fogs, the scarcity of English-speaking society, his mother's vaunt that she and hers were "old American stock" and not "dagoes" nor immigrant Irish—and the red brand on his gray substance of a second bout with alcohol. It would seem that from his earliest conscious observation of a beckoning world, turn where he would, alcohol appeared as playing a mysterious part in the pleasures of the god-like, enviably unshackled grownup, and in the romance, pleasant and otherwise, but still the romance, of manly, reckless, invincible youth. His father, in no wise a "drinking-man," found smacking satisfaction in a quart-pail of mild beer; nor was his mother averse to the cooling cup. Even the incompetent who reigned supreme in the little box of a schoolhouse enjoyed ill-hidden libations behind his desk, and afterward a one-sided thrill in "licking" the pupils who were too small to retaliate, as the larger sometimes did.

At the long desk with his class, Johnnie had not sat without meditating, no matter to how little purpose, over the very evident pleasurable action upon the grown-ups of beverages other than water. For so precocious a child in book-learning, he was peculiarly and adorably a hero-worshiper of those in authority, whose opinions he accepted as inspired. Until partial disillusionment in late boyhood, this open-souled trustfulness was always a-battle with an intellectual development out of keeping with his age.

And now, the guileless little man came to grips with hitherto unknown breeds of humans upon a temperamental day of mingled Italian and Irish joviality, largely induced by heavy red grape of California, there was literally thrust upon him his second stunning brush with an ambushed enemy he had no wisdom nor preparation for withstanding.

The Week of the Holy Ghost was nigh, and an invitation to unlimited hospitality for seven days and nights to the countryside dwellers of whatsoever nationality or religion, was sent out by an Italian ranchman, "old man Margo." Now, the Signor Margo had married an English-woman who had given him a fair-haired, blue-eyed son,

Dominic, whom it was the father's fond ambition to waste no time in marrying to the right American girl. The trim looks and competent ways of Eliza London, in her earliest teens, had attracted many an approving glance from the old man, and an exceptionally pressing bid was made for the company of her family at his house. The elders declined, but allowed the children to go.

So it came about that on Sunday the three young Londons trudged six miles to the Margo ranch, where a typical Irish-Italian merry-making was in full blast. By this time the small brother's searching mind had begun to lead him out of his timorousness, and the tanned little fists were more often by his sides or occupied otherwise than in feeling for his elder sister's protecting hand. Life was commencing to wave her royal-colored emblems before his awakening eyes, and more and more was he lost in contemplation of her pageantry, to a growing oblivion of the old self-consciousness. But he was an infant at heart, unknowing of evil, and the occurrences of this Sabbath day were burned inerasably on the malleable stuff of his reactive brain.

From the Margo kitchen the strange clamor of a culminating situation, begun with the free drinking of the previous night, only whetted the half-fearful inquisitiveness of our trio, which drew them irresistibly into the reeking dim room. Small Johnnie's big eyes must have nearly burst their expansive spheres at this sudden introduction into a scene where the gamut of human passions was either sounded or indicated. To woman's hysteria he was no stranger—his adult aversion to such uncontrol amounted almost to a hysteria in itself; but the girls' screams, frightened or loudly skittish, at the rough or drink-addled performances of the men with them or with one another, curdled his tender blood and nerves. He sat in a daze. His sense of proportion was all awry. Never, even under tantrums, had he beheld humans acting so illogically—flying tooth and nail at one another's throats one minute, the next clumping to ungainly embraces of forgiveness and reeling good fellowship; while yet others, too sodden to fight, mouthed their tongue-tangled approval or criticism of the changing humors of stronger-headed brethren.

The seven-year-old child, soon fascinated beyond vestige of alarm, sensed the increasing tide of lawlessness as the men poured an incessant stream of liquid down their straightened necks. He saw the now worried girls melt out of the doorways, as the clumsy brawling doubled and trebled among the rough aliens of hot and unruly bloods, until some impetus sent the whole mad company lurching down the sandy road to another ranch.

And the diminutive Jack London here put into practice the first evidence of that tactful sixth sense of fitness that early rendered him, the indomitable, fine one, into the very genius of Mixers. In a few years this intuitive faculty was to earn him the proudest title ever bestowed upon him by the sycophant earth—Prince of the Oyster Pirates. For now a wee Irish lassie, only other child of his age in the maudlin crowd, walked by his side. Like many another gay blade, he never was able to recall the name of his sweet maiden; but the favor in her blue, blue eyes commanded a chivalrous instinct to emulate her older sister's swain, walking just ahead, in all but his gait. Around her plump waist went his dutiful, sympathetic if timid arm, and they bumped along in blissful discomfort for the half of an uneven sandy mile—after which, guided by her consenting eyes, they clasped hands instead.

Turn about, the Irish ranch hilariously welcomed the partially sobered pilgrims, who "tanked up" afresh, till afresh swelled and roared the fun. A hospitable Italian offered Johnnie wine. He declined with thanks, and later a second proffer. And here renewed apprehension quickened his heart-beats, for there loomed suddenly the oft-voiced prejudice of his blonde mother toward all black-eyed men and women, as being actuated by deceitful motives, if nothing more deadly. As for Latins, "dagoes" as they were known to her confiding offspring, their ways were associated in his mind with keen-flashing knives called daggers.

When Italian Pete, with humorous diablerie unguessed by the alarmed boy, clouded his black brows over the lightning of blacker, snapping eyes, in fiery disapproval of this insult to red, red wine, Johnnie's nerves already made him feel the thrusted two-edged metal turning between his ribs. In that semi-autobiography "John Barleycorn," thirty years later he wrote: "I have faced real death since in my life, but never have I known the fear of death as I knew it then." Nevertheless he steeled himself and put his dimpled hands about the heavy glass, which he lifted and drained to the nauseating bitter dregs—and dregs they were, for this was the cheap "red paint" made from the leavings of great vats after the best vintage had been casked.

Poor little lad! One's heart wells and there is a catch in the throat to picture him sitting there in his linen jumper, dusty small feet dangling above the floor he could not reach, and, for once alone and unadvised, facing with wide, brave eyes the very certainty of violent extinction from an existence he had but lately begun to appraise and value. "One will do anything to live," he goes on in what he called his "alcoholic memoirs." The little chap downed a second and what seemed countless succeeding draughts of liquid fire to his unaccustomed membranes, for the loudly amused Pete had called his friends one and all to witness the valiant infant. Little the boy recked that he was inviting strangling death otherwise than from the assassin's knife. That he did not smother, then or in the following hours, is the everlasting marvel. Out of the house and on the heavy gray road again, with his own girl like the other sweethearts sober and solicitous of him, in a tottering haze he solemnly imitated the antics of the wild Irish and Italians in the zigzagging procession that wound among the sandhills. And finally, still imitating, he brought up in a roadside ditch, although he had not intended to overstep its dizzy edge. Out of what might have been his open grave, his sisters and several badly scared older girls fished him, and like one roused from his last sleep in the snow, they tried to keep him walking, walking, those interminable miles home. But when Mrs. London opened the door, it was from their arms she received her raving, unconscious son.

"It is a wonder that I did not burst my heart or brain that night," he says in "John Barleycorn," detailing the experience in such way as the searing horror made possible at so long range of time. And in spite of the heroic reputation his prowess gave him amongst the aliens roundabout, very clear was his "resolution never to touch alcohol again." "No mad dog was ever more afraid of water," and "I didn't like the damned stuff," he recalls his subsequent childish perspective, for there was not much living language in the neighborhood that did not enter into the processes of his pliant, growing brain.

Before he was eight, this sweetly gullible boy with his remarkable contrasting outlook had somehow come into possession of an incomplete copy of Ouida's "Signa," which his mind absorbed like an unspotted, depthless blotter. In the spring of 1912, Jack London, one day browsing in a dingy second-hand shop in Harlem for books to add to our traveling library on a voyage around Cape Horn, came across a cheap reprint of "Signa." Home to our Morningside apartment he carried the small-typed story which, he had all his life declared, had had more influence in the shaping of his carrer than any other, not even excepting Herbert Spencer's "Philosophy of Style." Upon the lurching poop-deck of the big four-master "*Dirigo*," off the unseen coast of Brazil, I listened, not always with dry eyes, to the rhythmic, caressing voice as Jack reread the loved romance which had opened to his groping intelligence the gates to unsurmised beauty.

"He was only a little lad," was Signa, the warm-souled Italian peasant child who attained to heights of fame. With these very words the roseate tale commenced. And so was he, schoolboy Johnnie London, only a little lad. Therefore he speedily constituted himself a peasant likewise, in whom there might reside untold marvel of genius, even if imprisoned within a gray landscape that required closed eyes and concentration to clothe with the splendor that was Signa's Italy.

"Beading the story, "the grown man gazed down his years, "my narrow hill-horizon was pushed back, and all the world made possible if I would dare it." And he dared, at least to contemplate greatness for himself. Like the tawny, golden-eyed bambino, he would become a musician, and a superlative one; only, his mother's unforgotten lessons led him to think music in terms of ivory keys and certain not unpleasing harmonies he had stumbled upon. There was no piano in the farm house, and the breathy strains in dance-measure, from accordions manipulated by tipsy volunteers on that shuddering Sunday of Holy Week, were the sole music he had heard for nearly two years.

Eliza's budding practical foresight had not hitherto made toward planning artistic achievement for her dreamy half-brother. But when he had coaxed her to read his book, with mutual infatuation they discussed it upon every possible occasion—while he dried the dishes, or they helped papa sack his smooth-coated, regularly symmetrical potatoes, or in quiet corners where she helped him with his examples. Ouida herself would doubtlessly have regretted the established denouement of her own novel, could she have listened to the hazards these two made concerning the missing last quarter of it. However, they did come to share it in the long run of their futures.

CHAPTER IV

LIVERMORE VALLEY

Ages 8 to 10

LIVERMORE VALLEY, where lay the last of the string of farms in John London's diminishing fate, never glowed in Jack London's memory any more rosily than the preceding San Mateo countryside. A fertile enough district it was, and undeniably torrid in midsummer, as I can attest; for here, again, our paths crossed when I as a child camped in the low hills not far from this same farm. "Livermore Valley was very flat," was his retrospect, "and even the hills around were then, to me, devoid of interest. . . . They and their valleys were eyesores and aching pits, and I never loved them till I left them."

"Signa," pored over for numberless hours here, from his eighth to tenth year, and still lacking the forty tragic final pages, had ruined him for the commonplace. "Even then there were whispers, art-promptings; my mind inclined to things beautiful." Life on a ranch became to his awakened ambition "the dullest possible existence," while every day he "thought of going out beyond the skyline to see the world." He was on his bright way to a soaring idealism, which later, combined with an enduring practicality, made of him an extraordinary entity both as Doer and Thinker.

Despite the dreary image of it which he henceforth carried, the eighty-acre Livermore holding was really the liveliest and most promising of all—and further distinguished as the first California land John London had been able to call his own. As a grown citizen, Jack would have been charmed by the fact that it was portion of an old Spanish estate, and thus bound indissolubly with the glamorous forties. As it was, the farm could not have been actually unattractive. There was a nine-acre orchard in full bearing, and what boy does not welcome an orchard? And pigs there were, chickens, and cooing pigeons galore—to say nothing of remunerative rabbits, fluffy, snow-white, pink jewel-eyed bunnies that could not but stir the boy's animal loving bosom as well as his innate sense of beauty; while the proud cocks and their harems were of no mean breeds. The farm house was comfortably large for all needs of family and the extra men hired in harvest time. To be sure, everybody worked—Flora and her husband here and there and everywhere. Eliza, barely fifteen, cooked for the whole hungry establishment, and besides aided her papa with the rabbits and pigeons and the three incubators in the brooding houses—John was right up to the minute in modern appliances,—not to speak of her work in the vegetable areas. As with Jack London, there was never anything small or restricted in John's projection of an ultimate achievement. It was in judgment of character, and of investments for his hard-gained money, that he seemed wanting. He had failed to discover in civilized society the undeviating honor shown to honor by the otherwise crafty aborigine of the Middle States. Perhaps, too, he was leniently weak in the matter of capitulating to counsel even less prudent than his own. Just when he might be considering a halt in expenditures, his wife's vehemently expressed insights would make appeal, or, listening to her exposition of the way out of a difficulty, he would be overborne. Thus a mortgage was laid upon the Livermore land in order to erect a twenty-five-hundred dollar barn for his Blackhawk and Morgan horses; and proud as he was of this handsome feature of the farm, he was not content under the burden of debt. And yet, just as he had gambled on new scenes in his youth, this fresh risk was not without its allurement; and the pair of them took other long chances—poorly handled investments, irresistible lottery tickets, and God knows what else.

John's aspirations were far-seeing and clean. It was more than a decade after the good man was laid to rest that Jack London's own agricultural experimentation began to open out. And he grieved for the broken dream and endeavor of this honorable, straight-aiming spirit. John's best satisfaction, even at toll of grinding labor, lay in pursuing an ideal which the younger man, guided by his cumulative data, came to regard as unerring and incalculable in its economic benefit toward humanity.

Sometimes their mysterious affairs caused Mr. and Mrs. London to drive up to San Francisco. And he, reins taut over the polished backs of the best trotting-blood in America, probably was happier then than at any other time in his middle life. Later, the beautiful Blackhawk stallion, with his mares as well as the Morgans, went to liquidate the livery stable bills incurred on these trips. Once they had remained away for two months, leaving Eliza in sole charge. She must have pondered, young thing that she was, while she worked indoors and in field, grasping what little social fun there was to be had in the sparse neighborhood, if life were all of a workaday piece. Her half-brother pondered, too, when he trudged home from school and found her hard at it, in season and out, and himself called to help at chores. Yes, everybody had to labor, it seemed, women and all. There must be some way out. And while he performed his day-long task of watching for the bees to swarm, he registered the vow that when he became a man, no women-folk of his should toil like this.

How they got into the house he never knew, but one day he came upon a "Life of Garfield," also a worn copy of "Paul du Chaillu's African Travels," in which he retained belief and admiration all his life. The school teacher lent him Washington Irving's "Alhambra," which he proceeded to bolt whole, and reread and digest for the period spent on the Livermore farm. Once again, always the Builder, he started to build, not a little Inferno as in Alameda, but an Alhambra on the plans of Washington Irving. From the mellow-red bricks of a fallen chimney he reared its towers and laid out terraces and arcades, labeling with his school chalk its various sections. All the while he existed in a world of his own making, that outstripped the humdrum existence of the hot little ranch—a world so real that he could not comprehend why every one, at home or in school, did not share in the wonder of his creation. He seemed set aloof from the beginning, by means of the uncommon knowledge he acquired.

"My other reading matter," he surveyed that portion of his childhood, "consisted mainly of dime novels, borrowed from the hired man, and newspapers in which they gloated over the adventures of poor but virtuous shop-girls." Through reading such trash, he goes on, his outlook became ridiculously conventional; and so, when a stranger arrived from the city, very proper as to manner and boots, with fine clothes and stylish hat, the famished idealist conceived this to be the manner of man who would know all about the Alhambra and be able to discuss the enchanting subject. He possessed himself of the visitor's unwilling hand, led him to where the little red-brick Alhambra lifted its proud turrets, then stood looking up with shining expectation of an oracular approval. None was forthcoming—nothing but a laughing sneer; and the pitiful small seeker, abashed and comfortless, fell back upon the inevitable if perplexing conclusion that there must be but two clever persons in the whole desolate scheme of things—himself and Washington Irving. This "gentleman" guest from the city, heaven knows why, deliberately and with malice stole and hid the hallowed volume far underneath the house, in company with a cherished rubber ball. I have seen Jack almost weep when reviewing the tragedy it was to his trusting little self, puzzled, blameless of offense—for he was not a boisterous or troublesome child. None but a creature of distorted impulses could have tortured a young thing for days and nights as this one was tortured. Superacute as pain always was to his body, never did he suffer as keenly from physical as from mental hurt. Only an inherent normality preserved him from spiritual ruination by his non-understanding environment. I cannot recall distinctly how he recovered the book, but have a dim impression that he told me the tormenter finally guided him to the point whence he had thrown it under the house, and laughed mockingly at the scrambling bare legs of the youngster as he dived unafraid among cobwebs and ordinarily dreaded crawly things, in eagerness to clasp his treasure.

Johnnie's first acquaintance with death came during this phase in his undirected development, and furnished matter for exercise of his speculative trend. He was helping his father reset some pasture fence posts that the cows had bent down. Digging deep, John London unearthed a corpse that had not altogether returned to dust. The boy remembered it as a fearsome mess that had lain a long time. They never learned how it came there.

That he was beginning to formulate some sort of logical sequence out of the chaotic mass of observations which bivouacked in his brain, and suspect a different and improved existence, is evidenced by a well-ordered plan he outlined to Eliza for their common future. They were to live in a large dwelling almost entirely filled with books. He would not marry until he was forty and his mind stored with the knowledge he craved; for matrimony did not present itself as conducive to studious repose. Meantime Eliza would make a home for them both, and more especially stand between him and the annoying people he yearned to avoid.

It may be that I have Eliza to thank that this became my own devoted task, instead of hers. At the age of sixteen she exchanged one life of unrelieved care for another, by uniting herself to a widowed veteran of the Civil War, one Captain James H. Shepard, nearly thirty years her senior and with several children, the eldest about Johnnie's age. Captain Shepard, desiring to place his motherless brood in a country home, had written to a friend in San Francisco, who in turn inquired of Flora London if she could accommodate them. Some correspondence passed, and through misunderstanding Captain Shepard arrived at the farm with the children when John and Flora were away. Eliza drove to the station to meet the guests, and entertained them to the best of her conspicuous ability, captivating the middle-aged ex-soldier as much as anything else by her maternal ways. In three months her little brother's dream was smashed and he left desolate, for she married and went to live in Oakland. Her devotion to the stepchildren was provocative of much good-natured raillery amongst the neighbors, to the effect that she had fallen in love with and married the children.

Through a combination of disastrous investments, and poor management, things had been going from bad to worse. A few months after Eliza's departure the farm was abandoned and as much realized as possible from the sacrifice of improvements. John and his wife with their boy and Ida removed to Oakland, where they put what was left from the farm proceeds into an eight-roomed house at East Seventeenth Street between Twenty-second and Twenty-third Avenues, near where Eliza lived. Not far off dwelt Mammy Jenny Prentiss, whose joy it was to spoil more passionately than ever her "white child," for his foster-sister and -brother were both underground by now. When Prentiss died some years later, Jenny sustained herself a long time by nursing and a slight income from a bit of inherited "property" she always proudly referred to. Chided for working so hard, when she might rest upon her foster-son's bounty, she would indignantly snap: "They think I'm in my *dotey* (dotage), and can't take care of myself alone!" This pride cost the adult Jack more trouble than her "property" was ever worth, for she looked to him to make it pay. He often advised her to sell her lots and spend the money on herself—"Buy silk dresses and theater tickets with it, Mammy Jenny," he would implore. "You know I'm never going to see you in need, now and forever, whether I live or die; and I want you to quit worrying and have a good time with your money while you can"—all the while appreciating her desire for economic independence.

In his eleventh year, the dreaming lad awakening to the gripping, harsh realties, began to perceive the under side of things. He was enrolled as one of the first pupils of the four-roomed Garfield School on Twenty-third Avenue, between Sixteenth and Seventeenth Streets, and soon progressed to the Franklin School at Eleventh Avenue and Fifteenth, where he came abruptly upon his first radical clash with another's personality. The teacher did not understand him nor even try. He, phenomenally quick in mastering lessons, which gave him more time for the ever-handy story book, could not learn from her, and failed of promotion. More than once his perturbed mother was obliged to call at the schoolhouse to straighten out alleged insubordination. He was an eminently teachable creature, but from the very first he seemed to gather that teachers were not placed on a rostrum to *think*, but merely to teach. Whenever he tried to elicit reasoned opinions upon his vivid ideas and their relations one to another, he faced a stone wall, and was thrown, as in the Alhambra incident, back upon himself and his lonely particular ego. Evidently the system was such that a child could not learn to the extent he was able, but must limit his most divine searchings to a gray curriculum that was, for him, only too readily compassed. He did not represent the difficulty in just this way, but clearly grasped that he was embarrassingly different from the patterned children around him, and that his gropings and probings were interpreted as impertinences. He had not yet happened upon the felicitous word "mush" to describe the interior substance of certain persons possessed or unpossessed of teachers' certificates.

But what he did or did not gain from association with so blind a treatment, drove him, as did his first and very brief university education, to the ramshackle public library that leaned against the old City Hall on Fourteenth Street, for collateral reading. The little boy, hunched over the worn library table, so long deprived of all literature except the four books at Livermore, devoured print until his eye-muscles twitched and burned and he saw black spots everywhere; while his almost prostrated nerves jumped into the preliminary stages of St. Vitus' dance. He became so irascible and rickety that he would cry out when spoken to or touched, "Don't bother me—go away, you make me nervous!" Somewhere he writes: "I filled an application blank [with "The Adventures of Peregrine Pickle"], and the librarian handed me the collected and entirely unexpurgated works of Smollett in one huge volume. I read everything, but principally history and adventure, and all the old travels and voyages. I read mornings, afternoons, and nights. I read in bed, I read at table, I read as I walked to and from school, and I read at recess while the other boys were playing." It was at the ripe age of twelve that he came to read Wilkie Collins's "The New Magdalen," and greatly shocked a nice young lady by trying to discuss it.

Presently he attracted the notice of the head librarian, Miss Ina Coolbrith, and fell shyly in love with this to him new type of womanhood—so lady-fine, and a true poetess. Hers was the first intellectual guidance under which he benefited, and he never ceased from his loving gratitude and admiration.

Straightway the boy's two families, his mother's and Eliza Shepard's, must apply for library cards, which he kept so busy that he crossed and recrossed the library threshold more often than any other subscriber. It was from this same public library that, when he joined the Klondike Rush, he calmly walked off with two volumes, upon Eliza's pledge that she would reimburse the library—a pledge which she kept, whether or not she approved of the somewhat irregular transaction. "The fact that he wanted it done, was enough," she tersely comments upon the incident.

Luckily for physical well-being, Johnnie soon realized that he must bestir himself toward his own upkeep, and the first move was on the street, selling newspapers. Home life was soon a thing forgotten, if ever it had been a normal one for this spiritually lonely creature. His mother had now determined that a boarding-house for the Scotch women-workers at the California Cotton Mills near by would recover her shrunken fortunes. At times when a cook was unobtainable, Eliza came over and helped out as a matter of course. With the boarding-house earnings in hand, Flora's project spread into a lot next door, which she mortgaged so that she might erect a rooming-house upon it. Her idea was Utopian, for was it not a fine thing for these factory women each to have her own private apartment? But her altruism did not go hand in hand with ability to see it through, and scheme as she and her good husband might, in the end both properties were forfeited to the mortgage.

Jack London's tenderest and most sympathetic memories of his father centered about occasions when the two went boating and fishing on the "Creek," an estuary lying between Oakland and Alameda. His unchained, mobile imagination had begun to take hold upon the dull tragedy of this man with the merciful lips and hands who had asked so little of a perverse destiny which had withheld success from him in even that little. He made no outcry; but from under the thoughtful heavy brows the kind gray eyes gazed forlornly enough across the green waterway to the low ground that was once blessed with his rows of corn and potato hills and succulent rosetted lettuces, and the coral stalks of rhubarb that had been Eliza's especial care and pride. The minds of John London's few acquaintances who still live, are tinged by the lifeless impression carried from those years when the merry-hearted one had become a broken thing, hiding an aching sense of failure beneath his fine reticence. It is but a spiritless image of the warm and lovable character that they can reconstruct.

The average man or woman does not easily learn to search beneath the restrained exterior, the bearded visage, for the tender mouth; or behind the quiet, retrospective eye, for the gentle strength and humor—qualities that were more and more hidden as the elder London bowed to disillusionment. But Jack, being Jack, was by now able to extract more knowledge of his goodness and personal charm than at any time in their years of daily intercourse. This was enhanced by the semi-adventurous experiences they shared on that attractive body of tide water which washed the keels of idle whalers and the ornate sterns of vessels of all rigs and builds from all the world, laid up at the edge of the Alameda flats. Most of them never budged until the Great War required them. Whether digging clams in the oily, cool blue mud, or fishing for flounders and rock cod and "shiners" from wharves or anchored skiff or the old sea-wall that bounded the Creek on the north, or rowing and sailing curiously amongst those painted hulls that had thrilled to the onslaught of the Seven Seas—it was all of a fabric of romance with the books. And in those rare days of quiet communion or interesting hap and mishap, the two came to love each other in true comradely, unquestioning fashion, as they had never before loved any one. Only their eyes, blue to blue under California's blue sky, spoke the deep and holy sentiment that stirred them. Each was better and happier, back in the clattering boarding-house, for these comprehending hours out upon the waters.

Here, tugging at anchor in flood or ebb, or at the oars plunging bow-on to the glossy gray-green rollers cast by John L. Davie's big side-wheel ferry steamers, or yet learning the why and wherefore of eating into the wind under a tiny sail, the little born seaman's heart was claimed by the wave. In all his vivid life, never was he so at rest in spirit as upon the water—be it deep sea or inland stretch.

A railroad accident to John at about this juncture, which laid him up with several fractured ribs, did not improve the prospect; and the succeeding house where the growing boy passed his sleeping hours—for home to him had become a place where one slept and ate—was a small one in the "West End," on Pine Street below Seventh, near the familiar "Point." This man Davie, who had established the new five-cent ferry route to San Francisco from where Broadway ended in the estuary, cutting the octopean Southern Pacific's rate two-thirds, gave the recuperating John London a job as night watchman. In the daytime he added to his slender means by canvassing and collecting. Presently, when John L. Davie rose in Oakland politics, he appointed his dependable friend as a special officer on the Police Force. It was the same Davie, at this writing, Mayor of Oakland for the third time, who, backed by the City Council, in 1917 transplanted from Mosswood Park a seventeen-year-old oak, twenty-four feet high, to the City Hall Park, where it was dedicated to the memory of Jack London, son of his old friend. Only a few yards from this thriving young denizen of the open, now towers the impressive building that superseded the old City Hall and public library where Jack London "opened the books" and began the omniverous reading he pursued unabated for the thirty years that followed.

Under Officer London's protection the newsboy was convoyed about in the "tenderloin" night life of the town, and new and lurid were the reflections that flitted across his expansile mental mirror. In such conditions the two resumed their ever sweet if fragmentary companionship. Squeezed behind the door-keepers of public dance-halls, or of dives, the boy strained his eyes upon the curious performances of the underworld, as well as those of the relaxing working classes. Here again, he could not but be struck by the fool-making effects of too much alcohol; and when these effects exceeded foolishness, and drinkers were jangled off to jail in "hurry-up wagons," he was confused by the fact that drinking was a licensed pastime for the young as well as the matured, and not frowned upon by the men who sat in the high places. On the contrary, in saloons he actually beheld such exalted personages also imbibing the potent drafts, little recking that their joviality was often but a cloak for ills that drove them to the inhibitions of alcohol.

Another circumstance that throws light upon his mental strife was the recurrent enigma as to where the dollars went that his father and mother earned. He knew roughly what constituted living expenses; but where disappeared the surplus, and his own little hoardings? For Jack's inner hurt, at the time, I have recourse again to his letter to the sweetheart of his early twenties:

> "I was eight years old when I put on my first undershirt made at or bought at a store. Duty!—at ten years I was on the street selling newspapers. Every cent was turned over to my people, and I went to school in constant shame of the hats, shoes, clothes I wore. Duty—from then on, I had no childhood. Up at three o'clock in the morning to carry papers. When that was finished I did not go home but continued on to school. School over, my evening papers. Saturday I worked on an ice wagon; Sunday I went to a bowling alley and set up pins for drunken Dutchmen. Duty—I turned over every cent and went dressed like a scarecrow."

Delivering the afternoon paper led him into queer places and deeper bewilderment. In Temescal, at that time the "tough" northern boundary of the city, when he handed the "Enquirer" to Josie Harper, mistress of a road house at Thirty-ninth Street and Telegraph Avenue, he marveled that so immense and unladylike a female should be less forbidding in her manner than certain more refined subscribers. He could not help liking her rough-and-ready jollity, and one day when she asked the barkeeper to pour a glass of wine for him, he was powerless to refuse the honor. But it tasted no better than the "red paint" of Italian Pete, and in future he tried to pass the paper to the barkeeper rather than to that dignitary's hospitable employer.

One happening in his news-purveying always stood forth sharply if laughably in memory, an additional item that gave him pause with regard to the strangeness of human destiny. An appetizing odor of coffee drifted through the doorway of a squalid hallway where he had just shot the hard-folded morning sheet out of his dexterous hand. Now Jack was at all times a lover of coffee, and nothing would do but he must follow his twitching nose the length of the narrow passage, and stick that same nose into a kitchen to the right.

"Good morning," he remarked pleasantly, with no idea that his friendly mood would be met otherwise than friendlily; for there was about him a naturally engaging expectancy of fair treatment that neither the buffeting of childhood nor maturity could quench from his spirit.

A grizzled slattern, prey of God knows what ill-usage and despair, whirled from the hot stove, butcher-knife in hand, and made one leap for him as his foot was raised to step inside. Only the genius for keeping one jump ahead of all sentient life on his familiar planet saved his face, literally speaking, not to mention his skull. But one correlation deserted him—or was it that she beat him to the outer egress? He found himself blocked from the street entrance, with no avenue but an uninviting stairway at the rear of the hall. Up this he tore three steps at a time, barely escaping the slashing blade wielded by the crazed, panting harridan.

Doubling back along the parallel upper hallway, he broke through the door in which it ended, into a room where an unoffending elderly couple flew awake at his abrupt entry. Before they could protest, he had swept off their entire bedcovering, and faced right-about to meet the onrush of the raging bedlamite, who had been halted but an instant by the door he had not forgotten to shut. Flinging over her head the smother of blankets, he tripped and laid her impotently struggling on the floor, and made good his escape; and sweet music to his ears were her muffled shrieks.

Ida London had married. From this union was born Jack's nephew, John Miller. So, Jack's family had dwindled to three. In the little Pine Street cottage, for some cause that was justified in his mother's mind, he received his first, and last, whipping from her reluctant husband. John rebelled, but finally submitted. He and Jack, the latter far more concerned for his father than for himself, went where they could earnestly discuss the punishment from every angle. Each tried to hide from the other his own belief in the joint disaster that was to befall them, but agreed that in all the circumstances it would better be gone through and done with. And when the onerous duty had been performed, man and boy, they abolished habitual reserve and wept unashamed in each other's arms.

"But what possessed her, do you suppose?" he wound up. "Whom do you think I must have reminded her of—what dark vengeance did I suggest?—I'll never be satisfied until I know, and I'll never know!"

Jack London always retained the conviction that his original impetus toward literary leanings was supplied by a teacher under whom he sat during the last of his grammar school education, in the Cole School at Twelfth and Alice Streets. Jack had the gift of a pure and musical voice, and the spinster in authority "flatted" abominably. Ergo, Jack presently demonstrated his mettle by firmly declining to join in the offending discord, stating his reasons when asked. The lady, by nature incapable of admitting her failure, wrestled with the obdurate pupil, but was finally obliged to send him to the principal. Mr. Garlick, instead of thrashing the lad, and so trying to force him toward the destruction of a notably true sense of pitch, listened attentively to his reasoning, and talked over the question at some length. Being what he proved during many years in the Oakland halls of learning, both judicial and commendably politic, Mr. Garlick delved into the predispositions of the young brain, informed himself where the student stood highest, and returned him with a note to the schoolmistress. Therein she was tactfully instructed, under the guise of advice, to command Jack to occupy the vocal periods in writing compositions. And thus he, who dearly loved music and singing, was deprived of one outlet only to pour another talent upon paper, which he did with considerable gusto and resultant good, if grudged, marks.

It was upon his entry into the Cole School that he made his stand for the simple and effective name of Jack London. "Your name," the teacher asked. "Jack London." "No," she admonished, "you mean *John* London." "No, ma'am," respectfully but with finality, "my name is Jack London." Some further discussion ensued, but the name Jack London went upon the roll intact, as it has stood upon a greater roll this many a year.

There were other boys in the Cole School at the same time with Jack London, who made successful names for themselves—James Hopper, first as football "giant" at the University of California, later story-writer and war correspondent; Elmer Harris, well known playwright; and Ed Boreen, since illustrator and artist. But, as "Jimmie" Hopper once said, they were "pretty tough kids, I think, who would have shied a brick at any long-nose who might have suggested we write or draw."

Another situation Mr. Garlick worked out in this manner: Jack and a classmate, balked mid-battle in a soaring exhibition of fisticuffs, were called upon the carpet. An interrogation satisfied the Principal that Jack had had cause for starting the row, but he fancied chancing an experiment. He left it to the pair of flushed and itching combatants to continue the engagement to a finish, then and there in his office, or, calmly, like "little gentlemen," to consider all sides, and kiss and make up. "I will," promptly offered the other boy, who had tasted the bitter impact of Jack's small, agile fists. The latter, not wholly unscarred, though not relishing such caress from one whom he was sure he could "lick" in fair fight, hesitated but a moment. Then, with heaven knows what correlations of pride, defeat, consideration for his admired superior, and his latent sense of humor, all flashing across his subjectivity, with a half-abashed grin he stuck out a grimy paw and met his late enemy's lips.

John London, once summoned to stop a fray in which his son was successively taking on the members of an entire family of brothers, each one taller than the latest vanquished, inquired as he strode to the scene: "Is my boy fighting fair?—if he is, I guess there ain't any call for me to interfere." And he puffed his pipe with earnest appreciation sitting in his eyes, until the biggest of all the brothers of the smitten line tried to deliver a foul blow to the infuriated bantam, when John called a halt. He insisted only that his boy, playing the game in clean sporting fashion, should be met by sporting methods, even by one twice his adversary's size.

Who can overestimate the blessing of the influence upon Jack London, exerted in their different fields by men like Mr. Garlick and John London? It endured as a prominent factor in the youth's wisely-timed emergence from the vicious environment that presently claimed him, and that would in short order have destroyed him as it destroyed many of his companions. The effect of these two was priceless in the expanding mental operations of the boy, as he evolved a working philosophy that enabled him to deal intelligently with boys and men of strange breeds and outlandish practices. And terribly soon it was to be almost solely from associates physically his seniors that he was to learn "the worst too young."

CHAPTER V

BOYHOOD TO YOUTH: OAKLAND ESTUARY, SAILORING, ETC.

WITH an inherent aristocracy of both mental and physical being, sometimes Jack London indulged in speculation upon the effect, had this significant term been passed under cultured and leisured conditions.

"I should most likely have become a poet," he would reflect, "or a composer. As it was, an equal urge came to me later from both poetry and music. Somewhat of an exquisite, I'm afraid, if only from my excessive physical sensibilities—but I am surely not a sissy!" with a whimsical look at me. "If I had turned to sociology at all, it would have been merely in an intellectual, impersonal way, not because I felt kinship with the submerged. Curiosity, rather than sympathy, would have led me to investigate here and there out of my elect caste. You know how I love to prowl anyway—no interval is long enough to make me forget the lure of it." And to Cloudesley Johns in March, 1899. he wrote: "It is well you appreciate the virtue in lack of wealth, and you seem to be all the better for it. Here's what wealth would have done for me: it would have turned me into a prince of good fellows, and, barring accident, would have killed me of strong drink before I was thirty."

By nature a leader, a master, Jack would probably have grown up elegantly autocratic, even despotic in a benevolent way, had the conditions during his adolescence been more sympathetic. As it was, there was implanted in him a second nature of protest and rebellion. However, except in so far as he bludgeoned with that puissant intellect, there was no cruelty in him. Once, and once only, in childhood, he had tortured an animal, a frog—the only assignable motive being curiosity. He never forgot this, nor ever forgave himself. In the year of his death, I happened to be present when a young fellow related humorously, and with apparent relish, how in boyhood he had suspended a puppy by its paws and enjoyed its yapping when he struck it. From the phenomenon of his face I glanced at Jack's, which moved no muscle, yet recoiled with every nerve, while his eyes became welling pools of darkness. He had liked this man. By land and variant waterways I have travelled with Jack London: by steamer—tramp and liner; windjammer, sampan, pleasure craft of all sorts; in railroad trains of many countries; by automobile, bicycle, saddle, and horse-drawn vehicle, from cart to tallyho; even on foot, which was least to our mutual liking; and we but awaited opportunity to take to the blue together—this chance coming to me alone after he had gone beyond that blue. But it was upon the liquid two-thirds of earth's surface that I saw him the most blissfully content. Dawn or twilight, he loved the way of a boat upon the sea. His bright inquisitive spirit might have sailed to its human birthing, so native was he to the world's watery spaces. The sea nurtured a gallant and adventurous spirit that made us all watch his banner. His influence was felt like a great vitalizing breath from the West—wide land of red-veined men—in which he lived and died. "Seamen have at all times been a people apart," curiously so, from the rest of their kind; and the sailor Jack London was a man apart from the rest of himself. Imagination, nerves, work, pleasure, all ran in smoother grooves when his feet stood between the moving surface and the blowing sky, his own intelligence the equalizing force amidst unstable elements. Seldom in waking hours without books or spoken argument exerting upon his wheeling brain, yet at the helm of his boat, braced for day-long hours, he would stand rapt in healthful ecstasy of sheer being, lord of life and the harnessed powers of nature, unheedful of physical strain, his own hand directing fate.

Graduation from grammar school came at about his thirteenth year. Pathetically enough, the poor boy did not appear at the graduation exercises, because he was ashamed of his shabby clothes. It may interest the harsh critic of Jack London's chosen careless attire, to learn that he was once slave of convention in the matter of clothing. I have heard him laugh softly, with a dimness in his eyes, at the pathos of the shrinking little figure he had cut in earliest schooling days, when his mother resolutely clad him in some garment he thought different from his schoolmates' clothes, and he died a thousand deaths of shame.

It had come to the ears of busy Eliza that her brother intended to forego being class historian at the ceremonial, to which honor he had been elected. She made an effort to locate him, that she might buy him a new outfit, and left word for him to come to her. But for some cause her plans miscarried.

School finished, what playtime remained after "hustling" newspapers and performing odd jobs was spent in a fourteen-foot, decked-over skiff, equipped with centerboard and flimsy sail. Questing a new world beyond the tide-ripped mouth of the estuary, out upon the treacherous water of the bay proper he ventured to Goat Island, more formally Yerba Buena, now conspicuous in all the array of a naval training station. The fish he bore home gave him economic sanction for his favorite recreation. Very important he felt with those still dimpled fists closed about the rickety little tiller—captain of his ship and soul, salt spray upon his parted lips, and the free west wind sweeping through his young lungs, that came, unlike other blessings, without price. Sitting high on the windward rail, sheet in hand, feeling out the strength of the breeze, with wistful eyes he watched great vessels tow Golden Gateward, breaking out their gleaming canvas, and longed to run away to sea. Or, slipping along with slack sheet before a light zephyr, one eye on the sail, one hand at the helm, he devoured countless tales of voyagers, the covers of which he first protected with newspaper against injury by dampness or salt spray.

In this wise he applied himself to master the manners of little craft until their management should become automatic to hand and brain. Here he laid foundation for the consummate small-boat sailor to whom I, yachtswoman long in advance of our meeting, entrusted my life seventeen years later in ocean voyaging on a forty-five-foot ketch. "The small-boat sailor is the real sailor," was his opinion, although he courteously prefaces the remark with "barring captains and mates of big ships." And he goes on: "He knows—he must know—how to make the wind carry his craft from one given point to another given point. He must know about tides and rips and eddies, bar and channel markings, and day and night signals; he must be wise in weather-lore; and he must be sympathetically familiar with the peculiar qualities of his boat which differentiate it from every other boat that was ever built and rigged. He must know how to gentle her about, as one instance of a myriad, and to fill her on the other tack without deadening her way or allowing her to fall off too far." As for the captains of liners as well as officers and able seamen, I have heard them frankly admit: "No,

I can't swim; and I don't know the first thing about handling small sailing vessels." It is an art by itself, and Jack London became a past master of it during his early teens.

Never did he forget his astonishment upon encountering his first modern deep-water sailor—runaway from an English merchantman. He sat in breathless wonder-worship of this sea-god who discoursed lightly of hair-raising hurricanes and violent deeds in strange lands and oceans. One day the superior being consented to sail with him. "With all the trepidation of the veriest little amateur I hoisted sail and got under way. Here was a man, looking on critically, I was sure, who knew more in one second about boats and the water than I could ever know. After an interval in which I exceeded myself he took the tiller and the sheet. I sat on the little thwart amidships open-mouthed, prepared to learn what real sailing was. My mouth remained open, for I learned what a real sailor was in a small boat.

"He couldn't trim the sheet to save himself, he nearly capsized several times in squalls, and once again by blunderingly jibing over. He didn't know what a centerboard was for, nor did he know that in running a boat before the wind one must sit in the middle instead of on the side; and, finally, when we came back to the wharf, he ran the skiff in full tilt, shattering her nose and carrying away the mast-step. . . . A man can sail in the forecastle of big ships all his life and never know what real sailing is."

Sometimes a boy companion was his on the thrilling traverse to Goat Island, athwart the churning wakes of leviathan ferry steamers. But most often he occupied unshared his domain of free fair solitude, milling out his own problems, empirical or spiritual—the former rooted in one sure test, "Will it work—will you trust your life to it?"—the latter resolving into an equal conviction that the existence he escaped on shore was sordid and meaningless compared with this. Unaided by man, he was engaged in identifying himself with the universe as it unfolded to his unboyish perspective, establishing his separate ego, and making toward the polymorphic entity he was to become.

And here, fleeing from the crowded turmoil ashore, thrilling with beauty and wonder of sea and sky, in the "vast indifference of heaven and sea," he fell into a cool gravity of contemplation that few realized of him in his manhood. I knew; for with him, speeding away from cities, in peace and truth I was

"... as one that leaves
The heat and babble of a crowded room
And steps into the great, cool, silent night."

"No one has helped me vitally—name me one," he has challenged in bald moments when the struggling past arose. Indeed, in reviewing what I know from him and of him, it does seem that after eliminating all who tried to help, one finds the history of a success that was won almost in spite of proffered assistance, which was for the most part misdirected. This because in the main the effort, through misconception of his superb free quality, made toward conventionalizing, holding him back and down. The only souls who may rest in joy of having helped are those (to whom my gratitude!) who gave him moments of happiness.

Dreamer though he was, and dream though he did, the boy learned withal that a boat would capsize and he be brine-soaked, or worse, if he did not apply practical system in handling her. While his ardent boyish heart was conscious of beauty and pleasure, he respected the means of their attainment. "I have been *real*," he adjudged his mental method, "and did not cheat reality any step of the way."

Those who choose for the foundation of their judgments the sensational aspects of his career, are surprised that his approach by water was not heralded by much noise of steam or gasolene-driven enginery, or, upon terra firma, by dust-rimed, red devil touring-car. Once, indeed, during a period of dangerous depression, he had contemplated the big red devil, biggest and reddest, for the outrunning of his blue fiends. But he never owned an automobile, although, when in 1916 we planned a world-around voyage after the War, the finest purchasable car was to be an item of dunnage in a remodeled three-topmast schooner such as we had seen in the Alameda Basin.

"We shall be anachronisms, you and I, Mate Woman," he would prophesy gleefully, "for when we are seventy and beyond, still shall we be riding and driving horses on the highways, still shall we be sailing boats. I do believe that boat sailing is a finer, more difficult art than running a motor. It wouldn't be right to insist that any one can run the newest fool-proof gasolene machinery, but most of us can. This is not true of sailing a boat. It takes more skill and intelligence, and certainly more training."

Picturing the embryo sailor steering the frail fabric of wood and cotton, clinging almost a part of this workable thing of his dreams, curls blown back from the uplifted face with its marveling smile, I am reminded of what Edwin Markham wrote me in the shadows:

> "I think of him as part of the heroic youth and courage of the world."

One fails to discern where he passed from boyhood into youth. Paradoxically, we might say, as he so often said, that there never was a boyhood for him. Hardly did he experience even a youth. From first to last it was as boy-man and man-boy that he came face to face with life. "I never had a boyhood," were his own words, "and I seem to be hunting for that lost boyhood." One passion of my wife-hood, was, that to son of his and mine, I might have part in making up for that ineffable treasure of childhood that Jack London had missed.

Now see how, in physical immaturity, striving as always for fuller scope, he foregathered in all lawlessness with youths and men. With a rare apperception of their foreignness, soon he was able so to coordinate with it as to bridge incongruity of years and step forth indistinguishable,—to them,—from their own essential quality. Not with foreign bloods, however, was his initiation into the man-game. It took place in the familiar "creek," aboard the large sloop yacht, *Idler*, lying not far from the wide-waisted unused whalers. To the romancing eye of the youngster, head crammed with enticing stories of seafaring, she was shrouded in fabulous mist. Rumor had it that she was interned for a questionable but dare-devil transaction known as opium smuggling in savage isles on the western sea-rim, none other than the Sandwich Islands of glib geography recitation. On more than one occasion his skiff had tacked at respectful distance about the slim white hull and raking scraped mast, and he had vaguely envied the husky, bronzed caretaker, who kept the elegant craft shipshape.

One day came the golden opportunity to meet with this brawny man of nineteen, who was reputed to be a harpooner, waiting his chance to put to sea in professional capacity on one of the whalers, the *Bonanza*. Her tumble-down sides even now resounded to the tinkering incident to outfitting for a new voyage. It was the before mentioned runaway English sailor who made possible the event, by asking Jack to put him aboard the *Idler* for a "gam" with the harpooner. The boy, inwardly trembling with delight, hoisted his tiny sail and directly they were zipping across the estuary. He and the sailor were bidden hospitably on deck by the caretaker. Jack, before going below, in precise seamanlike method dropped his boat astern on a long painter, "with two nonchalant half-hitches," that there might be no scratching of the yacht's shining white paint. Then he followed with bated breath down the brassy companionway, and filled his lungs with the musty, damp odor of the first sea-interior he had ever entered.

If we may trace any definite line betwixt his youth and manhood, it leads to this cabin of the opium smuggler, *Idler*, where, though he lapsed for a time thereafter, he became indissolubly bound with the affairs of men. And such men! "At last I was living. Here I sat, inside my first ship, a smuggler, accepted as comrade by a harpooner and a runaway English sailor who said his name was Scotty." Preserving discreet silence, that he might display no jarring immaturity, he was taken for granted.

Newly conscious of his uncouth land-lubberly garments, he regarded the clothing that gently swayed on the cabin walls to the roll left by passing tugs: ". . . . leather jackets lined with corduroy, blue coats of pilot cloth, sou'westers, sea boots, oilskins." It all gave out a musty smell, "but what of that? Was it not the seagear of men?" And the cabin—it and its appointments were photographed on his retina for all time, and their like registered as the dearest and most desirable of surroundings; " . . . everywhere was in evidence the economy of space—the narrow bunks, the swinging tables, the blue-backed charts carelessly rolled and tucked away, the signal-flags in alphabetical order, and a mariner's dividers jammed into the woodwork to hold a calendar."

The swift-evolving lad of fourteen, shrewdly observing by aid of the usual allotment of senses and that extra one of fitness which was the flower of the other five, renewed acquaintance with the oblique concomitant of manhood's prowess and comradery. Where could they get something to drink? Nothing aboard, and no licensed saloons anywhere near. The harpooner knew; and with flask in pocket disappeared overside. The flask was full when again the click of his rowlocks was heard, and the smallest member of the law-scoffing company was deeply mystified concerning the relation between "rot-gut"—euphonious name by which the adulterated fire-water was known by these swagger adventurers—and certain sightless swine. But it was not many moments before the significance of "blind pig" burst upon him.

Vinegar and gall the liquor was to his lips and throat; but he "drank with them, drink by drink, raw and straight, though the damned stuff couldn't compare with a stick of chewing taffy or a delectable 'cannonball.'" And to spend fortunes of cents on such debatable nectar! He carried twenty in his man-length jeans, and could not do less than contribute them with offhand smile toward the many refillings of the square-face bottle, "though with regret at the enormous store of candy" they represented.

As the hours flew, and the fumes rose and worked within his hard young skull, he became aware of the virtue of the potion that unbound diffidences and true modesties. Absorbing the unloosed confidences of these suddenly established cronies, his ego began to loom like a genii within its narrow house, realizing an unsuspected stature side by side with taller egos. All attention to a self-glorying tale of valor from Scotty, and its lurid fellow from the harpooner, he came to think that he had not done so badly either, in his solitary wanderings. Waiting for a pause, he launched into bold narrative of how he had sailed his skiff across the bay in a big southeaster that held deep-water tonnage at none too safe anchorage in port. Spurred by the respect he seemed to command, a step further he dared, charging Scotty with being a "bum" hand in a small sailboat. Only another round of whisky disengaged the inflamed pair, who, now outside of all reticence, vowed in maudlin embrace, that, inseparable, they would navigate the round world around. Jack beheld himself one of the *Bonanza*'s crew in the North Pacific, thence in other keels to Far Ind. They all three roared sea chanteys, and boasted to the pitying skies.

"The fortunate man is he who cannot take a couple of drinks without becoming intoxicated," was Jack London's opinion. "The unfortunate wight is the one who can take many glasses without betraying a sign." Though the young Jack had betrayed signs a-many on this day of infinite consequence, it was he, the virgin carouser, full to the guards, who put the two seasoned sinners to bed. Yearning to lose consciousness in another of the tempting mattressed bunks, he yet felt called upon to demonstrate, new-made giant that he was, that no tottering weakness moved within him. Again at his tiller, sail set, he plunged the skiff's bow into the crisping channel and angled, madly careering, across to the Oakland shore. "I was now at the pinnacle of exaltation. I sang 'Blow the Man Down' as I sailed. I was no boy of fourteen, living the mediocre ways of a town. . . . I was a man, a god, and the very elements rendered me allegiance as I bitted them to my will."

The water was at lowest mark, and hundreds of feet of greasy grey mud intervened between its lapping edge and the boat landing. With centerboard lifted, he drove full speed into the ooze, and when the skiff lost headway, stood up in the sternsheets and punted with an oar. And here outraged mind and flesh refused to function in common. As the one gave in to the poison, the other crumpled overboard into the unspeakable slime; and the poor little man-of-the-world knew painfully, as his skin tore against the barnacles of a broken pile, that he was nauseatingly drunk. But not as the others were drunk, he still contended as he scrambled to his feet, for in the sinuous maze of his struggling wits there stirred a lofty satisfaction that he had beaten two strong men at their own game.

Once more, as in San Mateo six years before, he swore "never again." Not even the limitless vision he had been vouchsafed, in addled ecstasy, of the glories of a conquered world, could compensate for the come-back of miserable days of sickness and depression. Purple as had been the dream, it and the means of it he repudiated, spent his next savings on taffy and "all-day suckers," and returned to his odd jobs and life on the streets. The inexhaustible trove of the library seemed ample foreign adventuring for the nonce.

CHAPTER VI

CANNERY. BUYS SLOOP "RAZZLE DAZZLE." QUEEN OF THE OYSTER PIRATES

15 to 16 years

ALTHOUGH the hero of this book more than once ran away bodily from manual labor, before final desertion of it through conviction of its conflict with his remote ends, a sense of responsibility never released him for long, if at all. He was destined to become a sort of patriarch to a group of dependents.

Barely fifteen, shore life for him had begun to reveal itself as a serious and manacling thing, and from the needs of the household there were left but few cents of his slender earnings, and fewer hours of leisure, for amusements and taffy. His first steady servitude was in an Oakland cannery, established in an insanitary old stable which was ventilated by drafty interstices in its ramshackle frame. Here he became an unconscious example of child-exploitation—that most incredible of all the shames of civilized society. His broadening shoulders that had shaken free under the open sky, or braced squarely against the shock of brave west wind and drenching southeaster, were now rounded above dangerous machinery for an average of ten hours a day, with as many cents compensation per hour. Roofed from their divine right of sunshine, boys and girls alike they sat and stood before their unprotected machines, the safety of tender young hands and fingers depending solely upon deft mental correlation. Some, slower by nature than others, were beaten in the unfair contest, accidents were frequent, and the victims went mutilated for the rest of their lives; the girls more sadly in proportion than their male companions.

"We could not spare a look or a qualm from our own wariness of the machinery, when one of us was hurt," Jack has visualized the scene for me. "A frightened look aside, a moment's letdown of tensest attention to the thing in hand, and *slap*! off would go your own finger. I guess I was just lucky," he disclaimed credit for his own keen correlations.

Those fittest to cope with the work could talk back and forth down the bowed rows, boys and girls chaffing one another and making "dates" for noon-hour and street-corner trysts; but even this intermittent social chatter was confined to the forenoon and for a short time after lunch. The later of the ten actual working hours were passed under almost unendurable strain of taut nerves.

Even if in spirit of blindly humorous yet grim reprisal against fate in general, one sort of revenge for their toil and pain seems to have been taken by the overdriven employees. From Jack's reminiscences to me, I have gathered that other extraneous matter than tears of weariness and rebellion was often closed and soldered into the shiny tin cans of tomatoes and peaches, berries and corn; and none felt called upon, in absence of the overseer, to skim off dust blown into the toothsome contents by streams of wind that forced through the apertures of the old barn. One of the filth-collecting ledges on the wall that faced the workers was almost on a level with their eyes, and now and again contributed its quota of menace to the health of others than the cannery's workers. And thus the public, also, was ill served by the masters of labor—all valuable mental pabulum for the fiery reformer Jack London was soon to become.

To him perhaps alone of these slaves of the old cannery was given a capacity to react in good time, and make himself heard in no uncertain voice, for the education of the mole-minded workers toward protest and demand for protection and adequate compensation, even to the seizing of the very machinery of production. That his mind was set astir even in the thick of the gruelling experience, one reads from his own view of that drab period:

> "I asked myself if this were the meaning of life—to be a work-beast? I knew no horse in the City of Oakland that worked the hours I worked. If this were living, I was entirely unenamored of it."

And the girls: here again, those beings he heard referred to as the "weaker" sex, and therefore to be cherished, were being despoiled by the same iron lot that befell their brothers. At the same time, for some reason which he had not fathomed, they were denied the relaxations and robust recreations allowed these brothers; else they were not considered "nice" girls. Maintaining pace with awakening sex-consciousness, curiosity urged him to speculate widely concerning these pretty, fun-loving creatures of more delicate frame than himself. More marvelous became contemplation and reality of his trysts with the little maids of the cannery whose lash-veiled affirmative glances in stolen instants from work answered the questioning lift of his own brows. Whatever knowledge his curiosity and their complacence yielded in time, he never forgot the exquisite spiritual quality of the aura that surrounded his first love, a couple of years later.

The while he remained a slave, an irreproachable slave he was. None could criticize his faithfulness nor the product of his effort. But when his moment struck, through he was with restraint and all its works. Insurrectionary he stood forth; though along with a radical shifting of viewpoint, an amazingly careful estimate of values coordinated with the flinging off of bonds. Up to a certain stage, the marshalling of values must have been unconscious; but his bursts of action in any premise were as if well-considered from every angle. That he did not function without some measure of deliberate thought, there is ample evidence from his own reminiscences.

What I am trying to present is this: Out of a free range of conscious or unconscious thought-material, garnered as consciously or unconsciously from his already varied experience, he abruptly formed concepts that led him as abruptly to rise and throw off any complication that proved unendurable and unprofitable to his logic. Back in his small but independent flat-bottomed shallop on the wicked currents of one of the greatest and most treacherous of harbors, he suddenly came to reckon with the absurdity of the groveling, destructive existence he had let himself sink into. Which held the meaning of life?—the turbulent waters with their "careless captains," alcohol and all, or a "viewless, hueless deep" of dehumanizing labor? Perhaps his thrilling heritage of physical ardor determined the issue. At all events, selfhood asserted overnight, and heaved the burden from off his spirit. And the only outlet that was shown to him was the waterway he so loved. Money he must bring home—there was no discussion about that, and no idea of evading responsibility crossed his mind. But why not combine his heart's-desire with bread-getting?

He "remembered the wind that blew every day on the bay . . . all the beauty and wonder and the sense-delights of the world denied . . . the bite of the salt air . . . the bite of the salt water" when he plunged overside. The pulsing colors of forgotten sunrises and sunsets flushed in his jaded brain.

Still again, I draw on that "duty" letter to his later sweetheart:

" . . . worked in the cannery for a short summer vacation—the reward was to be a term at college. I worked in the same cannery, not for a vacation but for a year. . . . My wages were small, but I worked such long hours that I sometimes made as high as fifty dollars a month. Duty—I turned every cent over. Duty—I have worked in that hell hole for thirty-six straight hours, at a machine, and I was only a child. I remember how I was trying to save the money to buy a skiff—eight dollars. All that summer I saved and scraped. In the fall I had five dollars as a result of absolutely doing without all pleasure. My mother had to have the money—she came to the machine where I worked and asked me for it. I could have killed myself that night. . . . Duty—had I followed your conception of duty, I should never have gone to High School, never to the University, never—I should have remained a laborer."

Once more at the sun-warped tiller of his barnacled skiff, leg o ' mutton sail trimmed, frayed sheet slipping deliciously through his fingers as he blew down the ebb tide before the wind, tremulous with joy of returning to what appealed as his natural habitat, the clear-eyed young viking of the West expanded long-cramped lungs and gave himself over to taking inventory of his assets: One good, average think-box, he calmly flattered himself, and one good average body that could, at need, surpass in resistance others of its age and size, not to mention certain older and bulkier physiques. And his priceless asset, of which he was then ignorant, was the cogency of that brain which enabled him to focus swiftly and surely upon an aggregation of data and set each item where it best would serve his ends.

I think it must have been right here, aligning his equipment for immediate benefit of all concerned in his province, that the budding philosopher forever renounced idle dreaming. Henceforward he appeared to range his conclusions with more or less logical application to practical solutions.

Reviewing the months just past, during which he had availed himself of law-abiding means of making, not his way in the world, but mere bread and butter, he was "unenamored" of the process. Body and soul had been outraged by the sodden, bestial dullness, and he was ripe to swerve into an equally pernicious if more attractive abyss.

The seabreeze bore him tidings of incommunicable lure, and his would have been the bliss of blindly answering the call, had he not felt the cords of duty. It was not in him to flee from the failing ones at home. A sturdy, law-respecting quality that ran in his composition would best have been sustained if the water had offered some honest method of livelihood. Plainly he could not contribute his share toward family expenses by mere angling from a skiff.

What wonder, if his reading had limned the charmed word "pirate" in illuminated characters? Suppressed boyhood and adventure-lusting youth rose to the word and all its glamor. "Why not? What boy is withheld from "playing pirates," or "burglars" or Indian or white-man atrocities, with their lurid imagery? The fancied evil of it leaves no more mark on the playing-child's perceptions than did the actual evil cling to this working-child. Besides, drudgery had not impressed him as innocent and unharmful. The sin of filching oysters at the risk of limb and liberty, enmeshed as it was with exaltation of adventure, appeared a lesser harm. Besides, were there not plenty of oysters for everybody. Again, that threshing mind flayed out the "irrefragable fact" that lurked in all seeming contradiction, and went on finding itself through agency of empirical research. Who was to tell him what was right and what wrong? He must discover for himself—and the exploration promised delight in its manful hazard.

"I wanted to be where the winds of adventure blew," his desire ran. "And the winds of adventure blew the oyster pirate sloops up and down San Francisco Bay, from raided oyster-beds and fights at night on shoal and flat, to markets in the morning against city wharves, where peddlers and saloon-keepers came down to buy. Every raid . . . was a felony. The penalty was state imprisonment, the stripes and the lockstep. And what of that? The men in stripes worked a shorter day than I at my machine. And there was vastly more romance in being an oyster pirate than in being a machine slave. And behind it all, behind all of me with youth a-bubble, whispered Romance, Adventure. "

"French Frank," a man of fifty, a notorious "oyster-pirate," had stirred Jack's interest in the water-front circle. Slight, graceful, debonair, a dandy with the brave ladies of his hot-headed class, French Frank's very foreignness surrounded him with romance. Young Jack heard that French Frank had a boat to sell, a nifty sloop with the dizzy name of *Razzle Dazzle* zigzagged across her saucy stern. Three hundred dollars was her price—three hundred cart-wheels! But he did not take time to gasp, for his ramping fancy entertained no obstacle. Upon his vision, roving for possibilities, impinged Mammy Jenny's thrifty purse, that purse which ever sagged open-mouth toward her "white child." What of the social exigencies of his new profession of swashbuckling, he was a long time paying back that three hundred dollars of her wages for nursing the sick; and it was a happy day when at last he laid the final instalment in her soft, dark hand.

The Sunday when he dropped his skiff on a long painter astern of the *Razzle Dazzle*, and stood on his "two hind-legs like a man" talking business with a real pirate, albeit of defenseless bivalves, carried Jack across the moat into man's estate. A twenty-dollar gold piece ratified the agreement, which was to be drawn up on the morrow. Then the prospective owner, treading almost reverently the deck of his first boat worthy of the name, moved in a dream down into the stuffy little cabin that reeked of tobacco and the flowing "red paint" of abhorrent memory.

In "John Barleycorn" is given an euphemistic account of the affair and how it terminated. The sloop was anchored near the Alameda bank of the Creek, not far from Webster Street Bridge. French Frank, scintillating with joy of much wine and feminine companionship, made Jack acquainted with his friends—"Whiskey" Bob, a hardened character only a year older than himself, "Spider" Healey, "black-whiskered wharf-rat of twenty," and, for the most approved piratical garnishing, though not the spoils of sea-raiding, two young and attractive females whom Jack has named Mamie and Tess. Mamie, unbeknown to the boy, was the object of a frantic French passion; but the honorable offer of wifehood from the elderly if dapper Frank had not proved sufficient prize to make her forswear free-lancing as Queen of the Oyster Pirates.

When the bulgy demijohn of red wine tipped to another tumbler, Jack, with the eye of the gay Queen upon him, all his childish bridges crashing, swallowed first his rising gorge and then with befitting sang-froid the tumblerful—and kept it down with a set smile that he hoped was natural in its seeming. The others had been drinking for hours and, with the exception of the Queen, were soon paying all their attention to the singing of popular ditties, at first in uninterrupted solos and presently in discordant medley, each singing on his or her own account.

"PIG PALACE"

Jack found himself "able to miss drinks without being noticed or called to account." Also, "standing in the companionway, head and shoulders out and glass in hand," he could cool his head and fling the wine overboard. "My manhood," he reasoned, "must compel me to appear to like this wine . . . I shall so appear. But I shall drink no more than is unavoidable . . . And we sat there, glasses in hand, and sang, while the demijohn went around; and I was the only strictly sober one . . . And I enjoyed it as no one of them was able to enjoy it," he illustrates his growing wisdom and observation. "Here, in this atmosphere of bohemianism, I could not but contrast the scene with my scene of the day before, sitting at my machine, in the stifling, shut-in air, repeating, endlessly repeating, at top speed, my series of mechanical motions. And here I sat now, glass in hand, in warm-glowing camaraderie, with the oyster pirates, adventurers who refused to be slaves to petty routine, who flouted restrictions and the law, who carried their lives and their liberties in their hands."

He did not try to resist the Queen, wise beyond her years. Before the native pentration of this girl, who was less commonplace than the average run of her sisterhood, well as he succeeded in merging with her social stratum, he could not altogether dissemble his almost pristine freshness. Disregarding any peril to him from her hot-headed suitor of nearly four times Jack's age, she swept the handsome boy into her train. Oh, no—he did not lose his head; show him the petticoat who could bring about such lamentable disaster, indeed! No Mark Antony he, but an Augustus capable of taking feminine wiles at their proper worth in his career. He knew his history books, and Augustus had earned his distinct approval.

As always, a woman's-man, still women never interfered with his playing the man's game. I do not think any woman ever made him miss an engagement with a man. In short, passionate lover though he might be, he was no follower of petticoats to the extent of clouding his manly attitude toward his own sex. It might be said, reviewing his rise to prominence, that he succeeded in spite of petticoats.

The Queen abstracted him from the maudlin crew, and more especially from her not uninterested sister, and made love to him where they sat on the cabin roof; while the boy, entirely unaware that he was poaching upon Frank's preserve, added the charm of her presence into the crucible of his perfect hour. Even at that, her charm was negligible in comparison with the thrill he knew at prospect of endless days that had no business with routine, but were concerned with life, more life. That was it—too long he had made one with the unburied dead; and the renascent desire for life, boundless life, bore him out beyond the reef of old clock-watching, whistle-obeying standards.

His capacity for happiness had no horizon on that day of days. Faultless was the round blue universe, he was its conscious center, and his princely ego paced out upon its conquering way. "The afternoon breeze blew its tang into my lungs, and curled the waves in mid-channel. Before it came the scow schooners, wing-and-wing, blowing their horns for the drawbridges to open. Red-stacked tugs tore by, rocking the *Razzle Dazzle* in the waves of their wake. A sugar bark towed from the 'boneyard' to sea. The sunwash was on the crisping water, and life was big. . . . There it was, the smack and slap of the spirit of revolt, of adventure, of romance, of the things forbidden and done defiantly and grandly. . . . To-morrow I would be an oyster pirate, as free a freebooter as the century and the waters of San Francisco Bay would permit. Spider had already agreed to sail with me as my crew of one, and, also, as cook while I did the deck work. We would outfit our grub and water in the morning, hoist the big mainsail, and beat our way out the estuary on the last of the ebb. Then we would slack sheets, and on the first of the flood run down the bay to the Asparagus Islands, where we would anchor miles off shore. And at last my dream would be realized: I would sleep upon the water. And next morning I would wake upon the water; and thereafter all my days and nights would be on the water."

CHAPTER VII

OYSTER-PIRATING

"I NEVER told you, did I, Mate Woman, the essential reason for my title 'Prince of the Oyster Pirates'?" This from Jack London to me twenty years thereafter. And here I warn that the story may seem unpretty to those who pharisaically shrink from the facts of life.

"Why, you see when I, the youngest of the pirates, commanded my own *Razzle Dazzle*, the Queen went along with me! I was the only skipper in the fleet sailing with a woman aboard, and it made a sensation. Spider had told me French Frank was 'crazy jealous' the night she asked me to row her ashore from his boat; but I couldn't believe that a man of his age could be jealous of a boy like myself. So I dismissed the matter from mind until one night he tried to run me down in a black squall on the oyster-flats.

"Spider I paid to do the cooking and help me generally, and I did the deck-work and sailorizing—I had already learned pride in a boat. I guess the Queen had an easy time enough.—*Why* did I take her? It would be hard to say it all," he retrospected, an odd bashful expression flitting across his face. "I was making a career for myself, after a picture I had created out of the books I always kept on exchanging at the old library. I was in revolt from the beastly hopelessness of the labor I had been performing, and had not yet seen ahead to the other kinds of beastly consequences of the life I was entering—inescapable to any one who stayed in it. All I saw was glamor of conquest, of scarlet adventure and yellow gold—which latter I needed badly.—Men did these reckless things; only, I would do them better than I saw them done around me: I would preserve the romance and leave out the brutality if possible.

"The Queen again?—you'll never know her real name, my dear. . . . It was largely a hard-headed manifestation of myself as a man among men. And she wanted to go with me. But in all my life, in its roughest, toughest aspects, surrounded by brutal men and brutal acts, I never laid my hand on a woman except in gentleness—I hardly need tell you this. But my personal feeling—why, I liked the girl. She was good-looking, and warm and kind, and best of all she made a real home in that little bit of a cabin. It stirred my imagination—I glimpsed, beyond adventure, dim visions of a future in which wife and children and home figured. Besides, she was a sort of waif herself and we had that unspoken sympathy between us. Then, too, I could not help admiring a certain pluck she had about her, good fellow all through, unafraid of God or man or devil. But along with a prestige that obtained from holding my own woman against all comers, I knew the handicap of being considered tied by apron-strings; and there were times when the Queen knew better than to show her head above deck.—And then you must take into account," he referred to the human passion of a body that ever remained incorruptibly normal, "I was a husky man at sixteen, and already knew girls—my first wondering knowledge had been presented to me by one much older than myself; and the Queen met more than one need I had come to recognize."

The real comradeship that existed between them partially redeemed the precocity of the affair. There was nothing of the moral imbecile about the Queen. In her make-up was no weakness of "squealing" at danger, nor for hurt feelings nor even the desertions incident to her chosen adventurings. She took the world as it came, and this remarkable new friend's very unsentimentality appealed to her along with his vital charm. That he did not spill over nor deceive her as to the shallowness of his ultimate regard, was to her in his favor. She asked no more than he gave, and she appreciated his humanity.

As one wise woman has remembered him: "Sincerity was the greatest trait of his character. He never made pretensions and he built neither his work nor his life on sophisms and evasions."

"I'm a funny sort of fellow, I guess," he pursued the self-revelation. "Because I have sung the paean of the strong, and despite the whole heart I threw into showing the weak how to become strong, as I saw it, the world has given me the personal reputation of a cave-man! How much of a cave-man have you, or has any one, found me? . . . Sometimes I *almost* wonder if even you would not have more respect for me, love me more if I'd beat you up soundly once in a while"—laughingly whirling me into an embrace. "You know my opinion of woman in general, and that it's not all flattering by any means; but even in my 'violent youth' a woman was always to me something to handle tenderly. Oh, I'll rough-house with a bunch of romping boy-girls and give as good as I take, and then some. But that's different." And once he mused: "I cannot understand the type of man who, having held a woman in his arms, thinks less of her. Girls have told me of such 'lovers,' and I was aghast. To you I say solemnly that no woman, howsoever little dear to me, whom I have ever held in my arms, but has been dearer to me for it."

And so, the Queen of the Oyster Pirates, now herself long dead, clasped the shadow of the lover he was in ripeness of time to discover himself. Indeed, she clasped but the shadow of what he then was, for he gave her no more of himself than was expedient, not even yet having been touched with the shy madness of first love.

The maturing philosopher would perform no uncongenial work, so long as there were others willing to receive his pay for the same; yet he would rupture a blood-vessel or rip off his sensitive nail-quick, jumping into a breach or doing what appealed to a whim, or to accomplish an end. And he asked no man to do what he could not himself do. That he did not break his neck or cripple himself for life, was due to his exquisite balance. Waste motion was a crime against common sense. Master of life that he intended to become, he would eliminate every effort that did not bear directly upon his success. And success in what? Merely living to the full while he earned something over and above his bread and butter. The cannery masters worked with their heads—why not he? Seven years later, and a year before his precipitate first marriage, he wrote to Cloudesley Johns:

"I, too, have worked like a horse, and eaten like an ox; but as to work—while no comrade can ever say Jack London shirked in the slightest, I hate the very thought of thus wasting my time. It's so deadening—I mean hard labor. . . . While I have a strong will, I deliberately withhold it when it happens to clash with desire. I simply refuse to draw the curb. When I was just sixteen I broke loose and went off on my own hook. Took unto myself a mistress of the same age, lived a year of wildest risk in which I made more money in one week than I do in a year now, and then, to escape the inevitable downward drift, broke away from everything and went to sea."

During school days and afterward, he had been an indefatigable trader and collector of everything under the sun. There were his painstakingly hunted and labeled bird-eggs; a treasure of marbles—finest collection of agates he had even seen, won by skill in schoolyard or street games; and his cigarette-pictures and posters and albums had been the envy of associates. Not having had the spending of his own money, he had made use of duplicate papers in trading with the newsboys. Foreshadowing what was to become a perfect system in larger matters, he amassed a series of pictures complete from every cigarette manufacturer, "such as the Great Racehorses, Parisian Beauties, Women of All Nations, Flags of All Nations, Noted Actors, Champion Prizefighters." And each series he had in three different ways: "in the card from the cigarette package, in the poster, and in the album." After which, he set out to gather sets for trading purposes. In addition, through barter he had accumulated an excellent album of postage stamps, a fair shelf of minerals, and some good curios that whetted his instinct to rove in far countries.

Because this hoarding depended, not upon money, but upon his wits, he achieved a name as a sharp trader, and trading became to him a game. "I could make even a junk-man weep when I had dealings with him," he refers to one branch of operations that lasted into his pirate days. "Other boys called me in to sell for them their collections of bottles, rags, old iron, grain and gunny sacks, and five-gallon oil-cans—aye, and gave me a commission for doing it."

And now, determined fledgling in a cutthroat crowd who sneered at boyish sports which to some of them were indeed unknown, he steadily strengthened his pinions among "birds" vain of titles like "Whiskey" Bob, Joe Goose, Nicky the Greek, "Scratch" Nelson, "Soup" and "Stew" Kennedy, "Clam" Bart, "Irish" and "Oyster" Kelly, Patsy Haggerty, "Harmonica" Joe, "Hell and Blazes." He wrote to his dumbfounded mother to distribute his wealth according to the choices of his erstwhile cronies. Here it must have been that he commenced to foster that distaste for looking behind him with which I came to reckon early in our friendship. "We are now concerned with to-day," was his familiar adjuration. "Forget the mistakes of yesterday, except as warning against making the same mistake twice." He would have no commerce with what he termed "the rule of the dead. "The living present was the thing.

Inimical he knew this new world to be: therefore he would concentrate upon becoming one with it only insofar as it gave him pleasure and profit. Oh, he did not reason it in so many words; but his cerebration was to that effect. The old shackling sense of poverty he resolutely disowned, and with free fist spent all of eighty cents upon detested liquor when it served the purpose of educating himself in mastership of the human elements that surrounded him. Abandoning a measure of caution, drink for drink he tossed them down. And he marveled and gloated upon the patent fact that he could as before win laurels from the well pickled villains with whom he had cast lot. If the whiskey route was the only one by which he, the rank tyro, could overtake his book-heroes, the whiskey route for him—on the surface at any rate. But there were stolen occasions when the *Razzle Dazzle*'s snug cabin, locked from the inside, was the scene of blissful secret orgies of reading and sucking "cannon-balls" and taffy. For "dollars and dollars, across the bar, couldn't buy the satisfaction that twenty-five cents did in a candy store."

"I was aware that I was making a grave decision," he declared. "I was deciding between money and men, between niggardliness and romance. Either I must throw overboard all my old values of money and look upon it as something to be flung about wastefully, or I must throw overboard my comradeship with those men whose peculiar quirks made them care for strong drink."

The very embodiment of the thrilling baresark of the boy's Norse mythology was "Young Scratch" Nelson—one day to be the mightiest-shouldered cadaver that the Benicia undertaker ever laid out. That he could neither read nor write, far from diminishing, rather enhanced the figure he was to Jack. What had his Viking ancestral drift to do with type and ink? "Squarehead" did not suit the younger boy as a just or beautiful appellation for this blond beast of unconsidered rages that flared in terrible, admiration-compelling deeds. The first of these which came under Jack's observation was a mad freak in a nasty blow one starless night, when the Scandinavian sailed his piratical sloop *Reindeer*, dredging a record burglary of oysters, around and around the other boats that fearfully clung at anchor in the pounding shallow waves.

As for "Old Scratch," young Nelson's sire, blue-eyed and yellow-maned, owner and master of the great scow schooner *Annie Mine*—what wonder Jack's most exalted pinnacle seemed reached on the day when Old Scratch accepted quite as a matter of course his shyly-dared invitation to have a drink! Treat by treat, mere "beer-bust" though it was, the session was protracted until the distended brace of salts succumbed. But what of that? Old Scratch was as helpless as he, the novice—more helpless than he, was the one thing of which the latter felt sure. And before the hops and the heat of the summer afternoon had reduced him to slumbrous defeat, out of his book-lore and the connivance of his and the bartender's combined tact in supplying beers large and small, he had led the old sea dog into unbelievable reminiscence of his youth in northern seas. The telling sobriquet of "Scratch," by the way, had been won by virtue of a tigerish mode of clawing off the faces of opponents in his Berserker brawls. And when the rumor came to Jack's ravished ears that he had been "soused all afternoon with Old Scratch," his cup of self-esteem brimmed.

Little had he dreamed, that day aboard the *Idler*, filled as he was with idolatry of the runaway sailor Scotty and the harpooner and the whole neighborhood, that he would so soon be his own fearless buccaneer. But here he was, causing the waterfront of his home town, that once had been his awe, in turn to feel the shock of his dare-devil exploits, and beholding his one-time hero, Scotty, and the impish "Irish," and "Spider," successively taking orders aboard his own ship. For government was in his veins, unguessed by the very ones who submitted to his vital charm and admirable ability to make good in the matter of their wages. The very air whispered deviltry, and the whimsy of his altered relation must have shaken thoughtful moments with silent mirth. Gone were parsimonious days, flung to the four winds. I can see the glint of eye and firm clutch of jaw, when he ranged the sloop alongside the wharf with the biggest load of stolen oysters of any two-man craft in the raffish fleet. I can see him with a cocked double-barreled shotgun in his small salt-grimed hands, crouched feet-on-wheel holding the plunging *Razzle Dazzle* on her course under a racing dark sky, that exciting night French Frank failed to ram him.

"And there was the time when we raided far down in Lower Bay," he recounts, "and mine was the only craft back at daylight to the anchorage off Asparagus Island. . . . And the Thursday night we raced for market and I brought the *Razzle Dazzle* in without a rudder, first of the fleet, and skimmed the cream of the Friday morning trade. . . . And the time I brought her in from Upper Bay under jib, when Scotty burned my mainsail." (In 1909, among those seeing us off on the steamer *Loongana* from Melbourne to Launceston, Tasmania, was Scotty of the *Razzle Dazzle* days. Jack, grinning at the recollection, could not forbear a reference to the burned mainsail. "But you burned the mainsail," Mr. Scott disputed stoutly, whereupon argument waxed. But after we had waved our last to the receding quay, my ex-oyster-pirate smiled, "Well, after all, if it makes him happy to think I burned that main-sail, why shouldn't I let him have it that way!")

As for fear of the law and its enforcement, read this: " . . . lying at the wharf disposing of my oysters, there were dusky twilights when big policemen and plainclothes men stole on board. And because we lived in the shadow of the police, we opened oysters and fed them to them with squirts of pepper sauce, and rushed the growler or got stronger stuff in bottles." Jack would ruffle with pride at remembrance of the "A. No. 1" oyster-cocktails he had mixed.

"Mayn't I meet Johnny Heinold some time?" I once asked Jack, learning that he had been into the "First and Last Chance" Saloon on Webster Street, to see his old friend. The stamping-ground of the waterfront habitues, where the boy's intrepid foot had rested upon the brass rail, bore this two-faced pseudonym by reason of its accommodating relation to comers as well as goers across the drawbridge. "Why, I'd *like* you to see Johnny," he acknowledged pleasedly. "I'll ask him up to the Ranch some time. It would be pretty difficult to manage so you could meet him in the old place," he hesitated at my suggestion. "It's a rough crowd that congregates there—though I might slip you in at a slack hour." But the time never was decided upon in our busy lives, and Heinold never found his way up to Glen Ellen; so that I have yet to shake his hand.

Jack first crossed Johnny's threshold on that fateful Monday morning he turned up missing at the cannery. French Frank, dissembling his choler toward the lad for the unwitting theft of his inamorata, had met him here by appointment to receive the price of the *Razzle Dazzle* in exchange for a bill of sale. The transaction completed, the new-made skipper of the tidy sloop underwent initiation, unsuspected save by the proprietor of the bar, into public-house etiquette. French Frank, once with Jack's funds in pocket, proceeded to demonstrate the wastrel progress of camaraderie amongst men of his loose profession. Readily could Jack grasp the logic of the seller, which caused him "to wet a piece of it [the money] in the establishment where the trade was consummated." But on top of this, Frank "treated the house." The boy speedily concluded that the saloonkeeper made a profit on the drink he accepted—which reasoning was upset when Johnny treated in return. He could also see why Spider and Whiskey Bob were included in the invitation, along with Pat, the Queen's brother. But why in the name of sense should every one else standing about the sawdusted floor be bidden to help squander the Frenchman's money—Mammy Jenny's hard-won savings?

Although it was early morning, the entire company ordered whiskey. So "whiskey for mine," the freshman outlaw registered indifference. But his soul sickened that he must make of himself a martyr to this silly custom of pouring a nauseous and expensive draught down his throat, when his desire was to be off to his new command.

With his thoughts upon the sloop, he failed to notice an awkwardness that crept into the manner of the others, though he did vaguely sense a growing antagonism in French Frank, which also seemed to tincture the Queen's brother. All waited for him, the boat-buyer, to treat as the seller had treated. And here Johnny Heinold rendered the first of many kind services to the youth, whom he alone of the foolish gang understood in his ignorance of drinking usages. "Watch out for French Frank," Heinold breathed, bending close as he reached for the soiled glasses. On many another occasion, closely following the amateur drinker's unwilling matriculation into the brotherhood of the saloon, Johnny took it upon his elastic conscience to save Jack from himself by warning when he had had enough small beers or other liquor, by which magic potions the student of raw human nature beguiled its traditions from this same human nature.

Whiskey Bob, and Spider, too, softly articulated, "Keep your eye peeled for Frenchy," or "Frank's ugly, take my tip and look out." To their friendly signals he nodded comprehension where comprehension was not, and perhaps this very bepuzzlement preserved him, what of his apparent cool poise in a tense and vibrant situation. How was he, hardly sixteen, who had worked sordidly for his living and gleaned his romance from the books, "who had not dreamed of giving the Queen of the Oyster Pirates a second thought, and who did not know that French Frank was madly and Latinly in love with her—" how was he to know? "And how was I to guess that the story of how the Queen had thrown him down on his own boat, the moment I hove in sight, was already the gleeful gossip of the waterfront?" When he presently learned the inwardness of his celebrity as a bold gallant, he could not help feeling elation "that French Frank, the adventurer of fifty, the sailor of all the seas of all the world, was jealous . . . and jealous over a girl most romantically named the Queen of the Oyster Pirates. I had read of such things in books, and regarded them as personal probabilities of a distant maturity. Oh, I felt a rare young devil, as we hoisted the big mainsail that morning, broke out anchor, and filled away close-hauled on the three-mile beat to windward out into the bay. . . . Such was my escape from the killing machine-toil, and my introduction to the oyster-pirates. True, the introduction had begun with drink. But was I to stay away from it for such reason? Wherever life ran free and great, there men drank. Romance and adventure seemed always to go down the street locked arm in arm with John Barleycorn. To know the two, I must know the third. Or else I must go back to my free-library books and read of the deeds of other men and do no deeds of my own save to slave for ten cents an hour at a machine in a cannery."

Even after losing one hundred and eighty dollars in one glorious night of inchoate induction, ashore with Nelson, his sobered aching head still deduced: "Better to reign among booze-fighters, a prince, than to toil twelve hours a day at a machine for ten cents an hour. There are no purple passages in machine toil. But if the spending of one hundred and eighty dollars in twelve hours isn't a purple passage, then I'd like to know what is." But he would avoid over-drinking when drink was thrust upon him, he forewarned himself, and there should be no alcoholic beverage of whatsoever description aboard his own sloop except in port at anchor when it devolved upon him to entertain. Alcohol and his austere ideal of seamanship had nothing in common.

Ashore, however, one of his proudest moments after he had adjusted to the necessity of "boozing" with those whose temper he must discern, was when Johnny Heinold, quite as a matter of course, reached down his book and opened a charge account for the young reveler's convenience, his name at the top of a clean page. A trusted customer he was established, as behooved one in this man-world wherein he had elected to distinguish himself.

The vicissitudes of several months' living, earning, spending, landed him metaphorically high and dry one comfortless foggy dawn after a wild orgy on the sand-flats, with empty pockets, a burned mainsail, and a breach with Scotty resulting from an overnight fistic engagement. Young Nelson in similar fashion had forfeited his crew, and bore one wounded hand in a sling to boot. Their mutual plight and a consultation terminated in a pact whereby Jack and Nelson cast together their fortunes as partners in rakish crime on the smart *Reindeer*, and forthwith departed for the oyster-beds. But first Johnny Heinold was approached for a loan with which to buy stores, and he, knowing their ethics in such matters, trusted them without misgiving. Reviewing that night, Jack London makes an appeal for sympathy of understanding of the unsatisfied boy-soul that was his:

"And now, of all this that is squalid, and ridiculous, and bestial, try to think what it meant to me, a youth not yet sixteen, burning with the spirit of adventure, fancy-filled with tales of buccaneers and sea-rovers, sacks of cities and conflicts of armed men, and imagination-maddened by the stuff I had drunk. It was life raw and naked, wild and free—the only life of that sort which my birth in time and space permitted me to attain. And more than that. It carried a promise. It was the beginning. From the sand-pit the way led out through the Golden Gate to the vastness of adventure of all the world, where battles would be fought, not for old shirts and over stolen salmon boats, but high purposes and romantic ends."

His own boat was raided by a rival gang of pirates, dismantled and set adrift. By the time Jack found the battered hulk, she was hardly worth the twenty dollars he got for her.

"Never have I regretted those months of mad deviltry I put in with Nelson," Jack always averred. The Norseman was a blind genius in affairs nautical, and luck played its part in that the pair escaped with their lives. "To steer to miss destruction was his joy. . . . Never to reef down was his mania, and in all the time I spent with him, blow high or low, the *Reindeer* was never reefed. Nor was she ever dry. We strained her open and sailed her open continually. "

The odd thing is that far from the making of Jack a reckless sailor, he became an exceptionally cautious one. The only tangible harm that seemed wrought by association with Nelson was the ruination of his vocal cords and his ear, and by the same process that had been worked on him by the teacher in East Oakland. Nelson had no sense of pitch, and bawled endless rowdy songs and sea chanteys regardless of key. Jack, doing his valorous best toward augmenting the unmelodious din, bereft himself of what he has told me was a "golden voice." (His speaking tone remained pleasant, even musical; but the mellow timbre was gone, to return wholly, but once. When he was about twenty-five, on the lecture platform one evening he discovered himself listening to a voice that had been asleep for nearly a decade. "It was the 'golden voice,' Mate—I'd give anything if you could have heard it," he said long afterward. "I don't believe it—but I heard it, I'm telling you. I reveled in it, turned it over on my tongue, sounded its clarion for all I was worth. When I stopped speaking—just to show you this is no fairy tale—people came up the hall and told me what a beautiful voice I had! And that was the one and only time, since Nelson finished the spoiling of my ear. It's the only thing I've got against Nelson!")

To the madcap masters of the *Reindeer* the lower-bay haunts soon became inadequate. In the opposite direction they ranged over the vast and devious waters behind the Golden Gate, and eastward into the terrific narrowed tides of the tributary San Pablo and Suisun Bays. "Well Jack fixed in mind the Forbidden Anchorages of the traffic routes of the main harbor, and the violent habits of Raccoon Straits, between Angel Island and Tiburon. And high and quiet his happiness, the time they first voyaged northwest across the big waters of the inland sea, Golden Gate and Angel Island sliding by on the left; on past that sunset cabochon jewel, Red Rock, so long coveted from afar; northerly skirting The Brothers, with Marin Islands to port; thence entering San Pablo Bay. Then the joy of running into anchorage in the purpling dusk on the flats; heaving over the sturdy hook; watching the vessel swing to the proper length of cable that slipped through his measuring hands; while the heavenly odor of frizzling bacon and strong, rich coffee floated up the companionway from the hot little galley stove, and the wild geese honked overhead. Life was sweeter than honey on his tongue, and he dreamed dreams of seeing the whole wide world some day, in a boat of his very own. How well I know it all—ah, do I not? who have done it with him in that very boat of his own!

Steadily, through the muck and ruck that mixed with the healthier material of his experience at this time, there burned the pure flame of adventure's passionate enchantment: the falling asleep peacefully to the rocking of the sloop to the rippled ebb and flow of tides along

THE GREAT GATE OF REDWOOD LOGS INTO THE "BEAUTY RANCH"

1905. "JACK'S HOUSE" AT WAKE ROBIN LODGE

her sleek sides; the opening of happy eyes each morning upon a different spaciousness of sky and water; the adjusting and stabilizing of himself in relation to undependable mankind and the rolling planet, victory resting upon his acuity in gauging the capriciousness of all things.

Intermittently within this succession of months between the ages of a little under sixteen and up to say twenty-one, the incipient sage, adding to his knowledge of mankind and its singular way upon the earth, must have committed nearly every *natural* crime in the calendar, save disloyalty and murder. Nothing, in his view or temperament in any period, was meet to invite him to the taking of life, little as he came to respect life; and even when it was merely the question of honor among thieves, his instinctive ethic, if an ethic may be instinctive, was that disloyalty was the only real sin. And he died reverencing this self-made axiom. To me he has confessed:

"If I should serve sentences on end for pranks I did in sheer pursuit of the tang of living, from time to time during the scattered months I was busy finding myself on the Bay, or tramping, or ashore with the 'Boo Gang' and the 'Sporting Life Gang' that terrorized Oakland, I'd languish behind prison bars for a hundred years!"

As for *unnatural* crimes, these were not admissible in his magnificently balanced body and mind. No inbred fastidiousness was weak enough to unfit him for eating and sleeping, playing or working, with the unmoral and the unwashed, to their complete befoolment as to his intrinsic difference from them. He could love with them, and fight with them; for he had "kissed his woman and struck his man," although he did not know the lusty old phrase. But in all his days, let the unnatural, the abnormal, creep near, and his trigger-like recoil of sense and perception and swift reaction left no uncertain impact upon the aggressor, be he brutal or subtle. Except in one or two defensive incidents, such as when French Frank was out hunting for him on the oyster-beds, either with the pirates or the subsequent fish-patrol contingent, Jack went unprotected by other arms than an ordinary table-fork. The sole provocation under which this ridiculous but effective weapon was drawn, was in the case of a degenerate Greek fisherman he had aboard in capacity of sailor. The happening does not lend itself to polite literature, and should be treated by some one compounded of a Balzac and a Havelock Ellis.

CHAPTER VIII

FISH-PATROL.

17th Year

WHERE Jack London differed most essentially from his roughneck associates was in the divine unrest that forever withheld him from content with any static condition. One thing or a group of things mastered, he was done with it so far as it represented an end, and hot on the trail of the unexplored. Each experience, or succession of experiences of a kind, was automatically retired to its due niche in a mind that had become surfeited with that particular phase, laid by for reference when needed. With him, only in minor details did habit replace definite thought; whereas his comrades, as time passed, reflected less and functioned more through blind habit.

Vital in his phychology was that law-respecting tendency which drew him to realize, under all paint of romance, the unsavoriness, the rotten structure of this "pirate" society. It had looked so bright on the surface. Even Nelson, through blood if not brain the truest, maddest adventurer of all whom Jack had overtaken and passed in their own game, even he, young Scratch, urged by his eager partner to new fields of exploit up country, wavered. He was unenthusiastic from sheer lack of capacity, and melted back into the Oakland waterfront life that was now outworn of value to the superior youth. Jack had touched at all points upon its restrictedness—exhausted the most intricate processes of its once mysterious denizens, as well as become familiar to boredom with the hundreds of miles of indented shore line of the lower and main harbor and the peculiar currents thereof. Wider activities were calling to be shared, and far-stretching water lanes to be investigated, some of which he and Nelson had sailed but not lingered upon.

And so, the two parted in all friendliness.

Almost a foreign port seemed the quaint interior town of Benicia. From its great wharf the *Solano*, the largest ferry steamer in the world, conveyed transcontinental trains of imposing railway carriages, with their leviathan locomotives, to and from the main-line tracks at Port Costa across the risky Carquinez Straits. On the voyage from Oakland, nearing Benicia, Jack had passed Vallejo, and Mare Island Navy Yard with its fascinating old training-ship that was none other than the historic, many-decked hull of the 1812 battleship *Independence*.

Once at Benicia, he proceeded to become at one with the fisherman element which housed in a floating suburb of little arks moored or half-grounded in the rustling tules. And never far from this bachelor purlieu flickered the scarlet night lights of one or another of the pleasure barges that swung to anchor on the fringes of such communities. Sometimes, as in his initiation with the lower-bay people, he was struck afresh with the belief that he, newest in their midst, was having a much better time than these older, more experienced men, whether workers or vagabonds. Their obtuse sensibilities were in greater or less degree numb to the very romance of which they were part. Sheer animal spirits might be theirs; but to Jack's glorious and contagious animal spirits that brought to him admiration and affection from the most unlit of the roystering inhabitants, was added comprehension. Not only did he envision the romance of the present, but further romance for which the day at hand was a preparation, a stepping-stone.

Missing no smallest sheaf of joy-gleaning by the way, he still must keep a circumspect eye to business chance; and surely it tickled his fancy that the most lucrative employment in sight should be with the Fish Patrol service. Combing for possibilities, he had fallen in with a trio of deputy patrolmen, one Charley Le Grant, Billy Murphy, and Joe Boyd, who put the idea into his head. The patrolman proper, under whose orders they worked, was a salaried employee, while the deputies depended for their pay upon a certain percentage of the fines collected from violators of Fish Patrol rules.

Knowing so well the illicit side of the shield, Jack naturally found the other face of it keenly interesting; and being anything but retrogressive in his bent, the restraining of a felony was more to his liking and logic than the committing. His all-round nature at the same time responded warmly to a pity for even the most insubordinate Italian and Greek and Chinese desperadoes he must assist in holding down. To these, who had to abstract their living from the waters, the half-understood Fish Patrol laws and the drastic punishments for trifling with them seemed captious and unjust. To Jack this eternal strife for existence, by land or sea, often appeared a dog-eat-dog matter at best. As he says: "We menaced their lives, or their living, which is the same thing. . . . We confiscated illegal traps and nets, the materials of which had cost them considerable sums and the making of which required weeks of labor. We prevented them from catching fish at many times and seasons, which was equivalent to preventing them from making as good a living as they might have made had we not been in existence. . . . As a result, they hated us vindictively. . . . They looked upon the men of the Fish Patrol as their natural enemies."

Following his calling, he knew hazards many and hair-breadth. Sometimes it was a perilous contest outmaneuvering a clever Greek or Italian or vicious oriental fisherman whom he was trying to apprehend; sometimes it was a battle with the shouting waves when terrific Northers from across the illimitable valleys whipped the frenzied incoming and outgoing ocean tides into mighty upstanding tide-rips; sometimes it was all together. Pitting his seamanship against enemies and elements was to him the acme of high living, and he won praise for both that seamanship and his cunning from the smartest of his companions as well as from the outwitted law-breakers. His capacity for enjoyment is expressed in a tale of that time:

"I was as wildly excited as the water. The boat was behaving splendidly, leaping and lurching through the welter like a racehorse. I could hardly contain myself with the joy of it. The huge sail, the plunging boat—I, a pygmy, a mere speck in the midst of it, was mastering the elemental strife, flying through it and over it, triumphant and victorious. . . . Conflicting currents tore about in all directions, colliding, forming whirlpools, sucks, and boils, and shooting up spitefully into hollow waves which fell aboard as often from leeward as from windward. And through it all, confused, driven into a madness of motion, thundered the great smoking seas from San Pablo Bay," through which he "roared like a conquering hero." He knew of deep-sea vessels that had confidently made their way here and ignominiously capsized, drowning their astounded captains. There would be no capsizing for him.

Leaving out the factors of his robustness, luck, and common sense, Jack's survival of this taxing period in his growth is due to two things: outdoor, active days, and his unconquerable aversion to the taste of alcohol, which prevented him from being a regular tippler. Even so, it is a marvel that the quantities of whiskey consumed at intervals did not wreck him beyond nature's repairing. He had not glimpsed the delicate esthetic of imbibing artistically for the sake of stimulating wit and other social graces, nor yet for the purpose of inhibiting sorrow and the disillusion of merciless truth. He cast off from his moorings of caution for a time and, in the frequent leisure spaces between raids on the fishermen, abandoned himself to becoming congenial to the men with whom he made headquarters. Gradually he "developed the misconception that the secret of John Barleycorn lay in going on mad drunks, rising through the successive stages that only an iron constitution could endure to final stupefaction and swinish unconsciousness." Wherever he walked, saloon doors swung open to him, the "poor man's clubs" that drew together those who knew no higher amusement and relaxation. On the way home to ark or sloop, the youngster would accumulate enough "snake poison" to deprive his bed of its occupant; and when, of a morning, his "unconscious carcass was disentangled from the nets of the drying frames" whither he had "stupidly, blindly crawled," and when the waterfront buzzed over it "with many a giggle and laugh and another drink," he quite excusably regarded his inebriation as something to be vain of.

An eminent American writer who, desiring to be a realist, yet recoiled temperamently from observing realism at first hand, once appealed to Jack London in this strain: "Must I, in order to describe a saloon, myself become familiar with saloon life?" Jack, true apostle of the real, was uncompromising in his counsel. "But," quavered the would-be realist, "do you mean to say that *you* ever have been actually drunk?"

"Man, I have not only been drunk, beastly, hopelessly drunk unnumbered times," Jack assured him, with inward cheer at the jolt he was delivering, "but once I was drunk for three weeks on end. I mean, literally, that I did not draw one single, sober breath for twenty-one days and nights."

It was this very debauch, coupled with a fearful incident which grew out of it, which first, if not permanently, aroused the decision that he was making little progress toward the fair ideals he had set for himself. He discovered, when it was almost too late, "abysses of intoxication hitherto undreamed." His was too fine an organism to trifle, unscathed, with this insidious destruction of mental as well as physical fiber. He, who loved life so vitally, to whom the idea of suicide had always appeared an abnormal ferment in the cowardly and unfit, suddenly came to consider death. Poisoned through and through, it seemed to his undermined vision that he had lived life to the last, lowest ebb, and the dregs, plainly to be drunk with the bums and loafers at world's end, should not be for him.

It came about by his stumbling overboard from the sloop where he had reeled to sleep. In his stupefaction, the best the shock could do for him was to show up the worthlessness of this mundane existence. A powerful channel run-out laid hold and swept him seaward, while he, keeping afloat effortlessly as any untutored young animal, developed a dream of going out literally and figuratively with the tide, yielding his useless sordid self to the all-embracing sea that was his mother o' dreams. With contradictory fervor he luxuriated in tipsy sentiment and the silken flood that enveloped him, exalted in deliberate, kingly choice of a romantic passing that proved him, after all, not entirely devoid of definite will and ambition. Then, as is the way of alcoholic sentimentality, he broke down and reveled unctuously in tears.

Greatly fancying the courage of his non-resistance, he began to chant heaven knows what funereal song, as the still tide carried him past the town. But he was not yet clear of Dead Man's Island, around the end of which he knew the strong suck and sweep of the tide under the long steamboat wharf. Abruptly remembering the menace of barnacled piling, he worked off all clothing and swam for his life so that he might better court death according to program. Only when he had left behind the last of the wharf-end lights did he cease to swim, and rest on his back under the stars. Again in mid-channel, with none to hear and interfere with his disposal of his fate, the enthusiastically lugubrious death-song was resumed.

But the worst alcoholic fever must give way to hours in cold water, and the ever-moving currents hereabout are far from tropical. Before dawn the boy was thoroughly chilled, soberly wretched, and in a fine panic at thought of drowning, which was now imminent enough by reason of weakness. Swinging resistlessly into the ugly tide-rips between Vallejo and the Contra Costa shore, he was becoming exhausted and already swallowing salt water. And he would indeed have been lost, unwillingly doomed, except for a Greek salmon fisherman who chanced along in the smother.

One last raid, he concluded, and he would move on. In that raid, he nearly forfeited his life at the hands of a murderous Chinese shrimp poacher who marooned him gagged and bound, on one of the Marin Islands, and returned alone to kill him. How Jack outwitted the would-be assassin, he tells in "Yellow Handkerchief," one of the stories in "Tales of the Fish Patrol."

The "vast good luck" in which at all times he liked to think he believed, preserved him then and thereafter in all his cool chance-taking. He made himself acquainted with other towns on the straits and bays and rivers, towns with alluring names—Martinez, Black Diamond, Antioch, Rio Vista—knocking about seeing what he could see, and finding as always, look where he would, that the swinging portals of "poor man's clubs" were the only doors to companionship for such as he. In a short while he had drifted back to Nelson and the old Oakland crowd, although only socially. He had quit pirating for good.

But he never referred with much pleasure to this period. Gone was the zest he had known when the Estuary and the public-house and the gilded sin of pirating shellfish were untried domain. Nothing new presenting itself, he loafed between sporadic jobs ashore, spending far more time carousing and running with the hoodlum gangs than was good for his best self, especially in lack of the outdoor life he had become used to. Occasionally there was chance to cruise for a few days as an extra hand on one of the scow schooners peculiar to this region—great, flat-bottomed, square-ended hulls that carry cargo and sail incredible, and that have made more than one fine yacht, built for speed championship, lose her laurels in the racing winds and seas of the harbor.

He went on drinking, sometimes to excess; and it took another knockout jolt from this source to set his face toward deep water, the thought of which had at no time been entirely buried. It was during a free-for-all saloon rouse, incident to electioneering in Oakland. He awoke one evening, quite alone, with aching jaw and head, from nearly twenty-four hours of unconsciousness, in a strange room in a dingy lodging house where Nelson and the boys, for whom he had been fighting, had put him to bed. All of the details of the ridiculous but dangerous exploit he had figured in, and which had so effectually put him out, were not clear in his mind. He could not remember whether it was a Democratic or a Republican parade he had joined, in another town whither the politicians had given a train-ride gratis to as many loafers as were willing to assume a fire brigade helmet and red shirt and carry a torch to the glory of the party. He recalled that the saloons had been reported as bought for the day by the merry politicians, and that he and his clique had not been backward in testing the validity of the rumor. There was a head-splitting memory of smashed train windows on the return trip, when the maniacally-drunken anti-Nelson and pro-Nelson factions locked in a fray that wrecked the interior of the coach. And his last conscious impression was of the start toward him of an anti-Nelson fist that had sent him, too whiskey-suffocated to defend himself, for a night and a day, into the black as of death. He was sickened with the unlovely spectacle of himself and the meaningless madness of the conditions that had laid him so low. Body and soul, he was very, very sick.

"So I considered my situation," he writes, "and knew that I was getting into a bad way of living. It made toward death too quickly to suit my youth and vitality. And there was only one way out . . . and that was to get out. . . . Whiskey was dangerous, like other dangerous things in the natural world. Men died of whiskey; but then, too," his wide-awake philosophical twist asserted, "fishermen were capsized and drowned, hoboes fell under trains and were cut to pieces." At the same time, while in a moral sense he did not consider drinking wrong, he reverted to a former conviction that it must be done with discretion.

"It struck me," he sums up, "from watching those with whom I associated, that the life we were living was more destructive than that lived by the average man." He could see no fun in becoming a helpless, dependent sot, nor yet in giving up the ghost. His one experiment had cured any desire, even in his silliest cups, for suicide. There was something ahead—he felt it in his bones. Also, he could never quite disabuse himself of that old pride in the captaincy of his own powers.

In line with this, "Everywhere," he reasoned, "I saw men doing, drunk, what they would never dream of doing sober. . . . Saloon mates I drank with, who were good fellows and harmless, sober, did most violent and lunatic things when they were drunk. And then the police gathered them in and they vanished from our ken. Sometimes I visited them behind the bars and said good-by ere they journeyed across the bay to put on the felon's stripes. . . . *'If I hadn't been drunk I wouldn't a-done it.'*" He listened to their pitiful and unavailing plea as they reviewed the cause of their undoing. The boy did a world of thinking about these, for in those days a criminal was a criminal,—whether he was or not, so he was convicted of crime. Jack London lived to see a glimmer of the light that psychologists are increasingly permitted to sift into the courts and punitive institutions. But in the years of his untrained observation of the sightless legal disposition of misguided human souls and bodies, he was puzzled and distressed at the very apparent contradictions that outraged his embryonic logic of justice.

So it will be seen that this second unmistakable warning dealt by John Barleycorn was but one item in the mass of data which pointed a conclusion that he was on the road to destroy his efficiency as master of his own destiny. Realizing, beyond all loyalty to his late congenial heroes and friends, that he was unendurably bored with them and their standards, he shook the mislaid dreams of conquest into the forefront of his curly head. He began without delay, although of course in the saloons, to affect the society of the seasoned personnel of a sealing fleet then wintering in San Francisco Bay. Mingling freely with them, from boat-pullers and -steerers, up to the keen-eyed hunters, the chesty mates, and the to him imposing captains, grown men all, he felt his way to the big adventure. A friend he made of one of the seal-hunters, Pete Holt, who was looking for a likely schooner, and in a half-dozen glasses they pledged that Jack sign on as his boat-puller for the next cruise to the coast of Japan and Bering Sea. So possessed with relief and recrudescent joy was the boy at cutting loose from the old life which now gloomed so dun to his retrospective eye, that he fell victim to momentary fear lest its ginny "death-road" might trip him before the day of departure. "I lived more circumspectly," he confesses, "drank less deeply, and went home more frequently. When drinking grew too wild, I got out."

"Home" at this juncture meant a plain, unattractive cottage at Clinton Station, one of several built from the materials of torn-down recreation buildings on the site of old Badger Park, where once Jack had set up ninepins and swept out lemonade booths, and which he subsequently employed under the name of Weasel Park as setting for a scene in "Martin Eden." From this house he went forth to see the world. With a regret in his heart that he could not share this supreme adventure, he noted the wistful look in John London's gray eyes at parting.

Never, since the day he paid over the *Razzle Dazzle*'s price to French Frank, had he known quite such thrilling contentment as upon his seventeenth birthday. On that date, January 12, 1893, before a real shipping commissioner, he signed as boat-puller on the articles of a real sea-going vessel, the beautiful three-topmast schooner *Sophie Sutherland*, bound for Japan and Bering Sea. And in his being swelled the lofty purpose of making good in all respects with man-size men in a man-size universe.

CHAPTER IX

"SOPHIE SUTHERLAND," SEALING

17 to nearly 18 years

WHENEVER Jack London set foot upon deck-planking, he left behind more than the solid earth. Whatsoever load of soul-sickness or care he had borne to the water's edge fell from him, or, more fitly, shrank to its true scant measure under the springing arch of life. Any embarcadero was a wharf of dreams where, glad face to sweeping river or to open sea, he felt the burthen upon his shoulders transfigured into blithe immateriality as of wings.

Even so early, the dollar had ceased to stand as an unqualified goal; it was but a means to an end, or to many ends. Money bought larger life, and life to the full, was all his goal. Good indeed it was to know that he possessed ability to earn gold and silver which in turn was good to spend in playing the game as he saw it, the game wherein duty and pleasure were two of many points to win. The concept which had caused that clean break with a miserly past when he gave away his boyish treasures, had rendered it unlikely that mere money-getting should ever again hold him from the joy of living. "And somehow," he puts his case, "from the day I achieved that concept . . . I have never cared much for money. No one has ever considered me a miser since, while my carelessness of money is a source of anxiety to some that know me."

Descending the steep companionway into the fresh-paint air of the *Sophie Sutherland*'s renovated forecastle, he deposited his bulging canvas sea-bag, packed the previous night at Eliza's, in a bunk selected for the best lighting from the hatch. And in that moment he relegated to its expedient limbo all worry as to finances. Fixed wages would be accumulating against the day of his return, and in that day the coin should be applied where it would benefit the most. Meantime thought of the same need not vex his head, a head which must be bent upon the study, moment by moment, of fitting himself into his exact place, be it audacious first or humble twelfth, among the round dozen deep-sea veterans in this deep-sea bottom. There was no call for currency in the fo'c's'le, and thank heaven the last round of drinks for many a month had been bought. The schooner carried no liquor of any sort.

Do not conceive of him as reflecting at any length with idle hands. A "busy child" he had been; a busier man he now was. Child-dreamer or man-dreamer, he worked while he dreamed, he "thought on his feet," to use his words, and with him action was quick as the thought. Throughout his complex mechanism there resided that unity which defied either misapplied effort or unproductive inertia.

"While the handsome schooner's crew was typical of its rough Scandinavian class, Jack was immediately struck by an incongruity higher up. The sealer's owner, a somewhat unusual circumstance, sailed in her for personal reasons unfathomed by the ship's company, unless it was to make a sailor of his son, who was also on board. Apparently the father was a land-lubberly soul in a quiet, pensive way—his exterior, to their simple judgment, even suggesting piousness. Little he seemed to know or care about seamanship, always preserving an air of detachment from the management of his vessel, which was left entirely in the hands of the sailing master. "He thinks he's on his yacht," one of the men guffawed below deck a few days out.

Jack, one eye on sailing-master and mate, the other alert to his companions of the forecastle, kept tongue between teeth as he had done with unprofessional ones of their stripe, and walked warily. Things were different now—no longer was he master of his own keel, nor even partner, as on the *Reindeer.* No authority of any kind was his, except over his inner self, and that was a confidential matter. He had had the "nerve," as Pete Holt had grinned, to sign on as A. B., he, who had never been more than a mile outside the Golden Gate. But what of that?—he was able-bodied if any of them were, and he was a seaman or he did not know what the word meant. He would see to it that he was an able one.

"I *was* an able seaman," he asserts. "I had graduated from the right school. It took no more than minutes to learn the names and uses of the few new ropes. It was simple. I did not do things blindly. As a small-boat sailor I had learned to reason out and know the *why* of everything. It is true, I had to learn to steer by compass, which took maybe half a minute; but when it came to steering 'full-and-by' and 'close-and-by,' I could beat the average of my shipmates, because that was the very way I had always sailed. Inside fifteen minutes I could box the compass around and back again. And there was little else to learn during that seven-months cruise, except fancy rope-sailorizing, such as the more complicated lanyard knots and the making of various kinds of sennit and rope-mats."

It must be remembered that, while he realized he was measuring against better-informed sailors than those he had known, his undue reverence for deep-water men had been shaken when they came to managing small sailing craft. Scotty's fiasco with the little old skiff of tender remembrance was not the only one he had witnessed.

Of him there should be no complaint from captain or officers. Simultaneously he appreciated that any difficulty in making good lay in relation to the forecastle rather than to the deck. He sensed a sneering antagonism, in certain able-bodied salts for'ard, toward the mere undersized bay-sailor he indubitably was, and his chest rose and his eye darkened with the zest of strife against odds. Oh, not strife with his hands, unless forced; he would make no hasty nor false moves. But the conquesting of minds of their caliber he well knew was easily possible, though only by keeping one jump ahead of them. One did it with animals, and he had found the same method practicable with most boys he had known and with some men.

Swiftly "sizing up" the seamed visages of the elder A. B.'s, he divined without error the ones he must deal with from the word go. Not for nothing had he pondered the weird unreckonable quality of the order of Scandinavian intelligence that had come his way in the past. And here he uncovered the same mental quirks, although not one of these "squareheads" could boast of the physical beauty or charm of either of the "Scratches."

He must make no blunders. These seasoned tars would make capital of the raw material they deemed him, as they were traditionally accustomed. He would degenerate to a mere cabin-boy, a door-mat, and worse, if he were not cautious and more than cautious. Obliging he would be, of course; but he must firmly entrench himself short of being imposed upon. He gave them credit for a primitive cunning that would pounce upon an unguarded weakening. Difficult clay this for a youngster to mold for his own survival, but malleable clay nevertheless, which he must steel himself to thumb without fumbling. Here he laid foundation for the tactician without hypocrisy which in time he came to be.

Reviewing his problem, he writes: "These hard-bit Scandinavian sailors had come through a hard school. As boys they had served their mates, and as able seamen they looked to be served by other boys. I was a boy . . . I had never been to sea before—withal I was a good sailor and knew my business . . . I had signed on as an equal, and an equal I must maintain myself, or else endure seven months of hell at their hands. And it was this very equality they resented. By what right was I an equal? I had not earned that high privilege. I had not endured the miseries they had endured as maltreated boys or bullied ordinaries. Worse than that, I was a land-lubber making his first voyage. And yet, by the injustice of fate, on the ship's articles I was their equal.

"My method was deliberate, and simple, and drastic. In the first place, I resolved to do my work, no matter how hard or dangerous it might be, so well that no man would be called upon to do it for me. Further, I put ginger in my muscles. I never malingered when pulling on a rope, for I knew the eagle eyes of my forecastle mates were squinting for just such evidence of my inferiority. I made it a point to be among the first of the watch going on deck, among the last going below, never leaving a sheet or tackle for some one else to coil over a pin. I was always eager for the run aloft for the shifting of topsail sheets and tacks, or for the setting or taking in of topsails; and in these matters I did more than my share."

While he adjusted and outlined further adjustment, he was sensible of being very much alone; but he was always that, in almost any group. It was his fate to be isolate, owing to a faculty for anticipating, which left him little to learn from the average run of individuals. And in his predicament aboard the schooner, as usual there seemed to be none to help him; he must work everything out for himself. Although he did not know it then, this was because he was actually preeminent in judgment of the fitness of things. Seldom did he come in contact with persons who could discriminate as quickly as he, due to that supreme awareness which quickened his every wakeful moment. His keynote was awareness, consciousness.

Making this appraisement of the *Sophie Sutherland*'s complement and his relation to it, meanwhile exerting his mightiest in setting sail and making fast and coiling down, he retained capacity to glory in the fact that he was at last clearing the Golden Gate on the beautiful, lifting highway to Heart's Desire. When the tug had cast off outside the Heads, and the trim sailer breasted the Bar and filled to her course on "the sea's blue swerve," surging past the rocky Farallones and slowly burying the high coast line, the young voyager filled his lungs with the flowing seabreeze and realized with enormous relief that he was also clearing the moral morass ashore that had threatened to engulf him. "I shudder to think how close a shave I ran," once he referred to his escape. Never again, he promised himself, would he more than skim the surface of that morass—for the sake of old times and friends to whom he felt and owed loyalty.

But there was another and very important factor that entered into his calculations, namely his own temper, which was itself "on a hair-trigger of resentment" in face of "any abuse or the slightest patronizing." And the men were not unnoting of the warning advertised by an involuntary setting of that square jaw or a tightening curl at one corner of the full mouth, nor of the sudden omen of darkening eyes behind their long crescent lashes. Several times he "mixed" hotly with one or another of them, in sudden flares that as suddenly subsided; but "I left the impression that I was a wild-cat and that I would just as willingly fight again," he recalls. "I proved that the man that imposed upon me must have a fight on his hands. And, doing my work well, the innate justice of the men, assisted by their wholesome dislike for a clawing and rending wild-cat ruction, soon led them to give over their hectoring."

Comparatively seldom, considering the way of his life, had he hit out with his fists. There had been the usual school and street "scraps," in the course of determining his status among the boys. Once, when he was running with the hoodlum crowd, one real battle royal between the two bad Oakland gangs, had taken place on a bridge which spanned the neck of water separating Lake Merritt from the Bay. The waterfront brawls had drawn him in on more than one occasion. He never forgot the day he made good his threat, twice repeated, to knock the daylights out of a stupid lunk-head of a sailor on the *Reindeer*, who had as many times let go the main-sheet in a delicate maneuver Jack was essaying in a tight corner. Practically, these were the only times he had used his hands in this way. And he was punctilious always in a determination never to threaten unless he intended to make good. "I hope I'll never have to draw a gun," I have heard him say, "because, if I did, I'd have to use it!"

On the *Sophie Sutherland*, however, it remained for one decisive victory to clarify the atmosphere for all the voyage.

Red John, a huge-boned Swede, had not yet ceased looking for trouble with this smooth-cheeked boy who declined to be mere boy, nor heeded the signs that boy hung out in plain sight from time to time as the other tried to incite him to protest. But one day, when Jack, on watch below, was sitting in his bunk engaged in the unoffending task of weaving a rope-yarn mat for sister Eliza at home, the inevitable moment presented, and he recognized and dealt with it for all it was worth.

It was Red John's peggy-day—his turn at cleaning house in the sailor's quarters; and Red John's eagerness to impress the greenest hand into personal service cost him his caution and a distinct loss of dignity. Some rough order he flung at Jack, who woke from pleasant reverie and bristled and tensed, but paid no other attention to the bully, while he went on making his love-gift.

Red John mumbled and cursed without noticeable effect on the mat-weaver. Suddenly boiling over, the incensed giant let go the coffeepot he was carrying, and gave the boy a back-handed blow across the mouth. Like a flash Jack landed on the other's eye, dodged the return swing of the sledge-hammer fist, and the combat was on—the strangest ever seen by their mates, who scuttled into bunks to be out of the way and enjoy the show. With that cat-like swiftness he later ascribed to his "Sea Wolf," Jack had outflanked the foe and sprung upon his shoulders, where he clasped powerful short legs in a strangle-hold about the roaring bull-throat, while his fingers sought eyes and windpipe of the confounded, raging brute under him. The only recourse left the Swede was main strength, which he used, perhaps by mere instinct, in butting his captor against the deck beams. This inflicted bloody and painful damage to the young tiger's scalp and crouched shoulders. But those excruciating pointed digits in larynx and eye-sockets settled the issue, and the tormented Berserker was forced to give in by hoarsely bellowing assent to Jack's breathless repetition of "Will y'leave me alone, now? Will y'let up on me for keeps? Will y'leave me be?—*Will* yuh? *Will* yuh?"

Once more on his feet, quivering and weak amidst the wreck of the forecastle, but wrapt in the solicitous congratulations of admiring colleagues, he cemented their respectful regard by an utter lack of swank over his victory. "That's all right, boys," and a "Thank you kindly," was all they could get out of him as he grinned through the blood that dripped from his lacerated scalp, and went about cleansing it. Hardly needful to mention, Red John became the staunchest admirer and champion of this valiant cub whom he had failed to whip. As for the others, "It was my pride that I was taken in as an equal, in spirit as well as in fact. From then on, everything was beautiful, and the voyage promised to be a happy one." Quite opposed, it will be seen, to accounts from inexcusably careless biographers, that the friendly schooner was a hell-ship in which Jack London had a fight on his hands, or provoked one, every day of the voyage!

And very happy it was. While he could get along comfortably without approbation, his content was enhanced by it; and the pleasure of camaraderie with his fellows below or on deck, or aloft in the shrieking rigging in a gale, was not to be calculated. No exhausting strain could dampen the ardor of holding his own with the best in sheer muscular rivalry. Even in middle age, for him to be able to say, "I have toiled all night, both watches on deck, off the coast of Japan," meant more to him than the best passage he had ever written. It should be remembered that eye-to-eye, strain-to-strain, blow-to-blow, with these rougher forces, he overbore the unjust handicap of supersensitiveness—making no allowance for small-boned wrists and ankles that were foredoomed to injury. But whatever his disgruntlement may have been as regarded those fragile extremities, he could be secretly pleased with the augmenting bulge of muscle on back and shoulders, legs and biceps, although it may be the strenuousness of his hit-or-miss education in hardship cost him an inch or so of stature.

He was never apathetic to the beauty of the world about the pretty schooner he took prideful hand in sailing. His trick at the wheel, ably and faithfully discharged, brought him inexhaustible delights, not the least of which was the satisfaction of holding his own as a helmsman among helmsmen. The chronometer, that "least imperfect time-piece that man has devised," and the nautical instruments, were things almost of enchantment, and again he dreamed dreams of some day working his own ship by their aid under sun and star. The wide sea and dome of sky, with all their moods of color and motion, pervaded him with a never-palling joyance of eye and spirit. In the night watches, swinging majestically under the wintry steel-blue stars, or fighting through big seas beneath low scudding moonlit cloud-masses, with only the pale-glimmering binnacle for company, he knew again those lofty, cool levels of contemplation wherein his vision was extended into ever-receding distances of thought.

Because of the extravagant and unappeased hunger of his mind, sleeping hours he divided with the books he had smuggled aboard. At the nearest possible inch to the inner wall of his confined bunk, he crept with a tiny improvised light, fitted with a shade so that he might not disturb the men. I think he has described the contrivance as a saucer of slush-oil containing a floating bit of wick, which "lamp" he was obliged to hold in his hand. To such lengths he went to feed that mind-hunger. Two reasons there were for this stealth—a decent consideration toward the men, and, still more important, an unmistaken intuition that good fellowship depended upon hiding propensities they might construe as "airish." There was too much at stake.

It was some years since this inquisitive pilgrim, with his disturbing aptitude for looking aside into the amazing byways of cause and effect, had begun to outstrip the childish methods of argument common amongst sailor folk. He concealed his advanced opinions, thrashing out in busy solitude the questions that arose in him, and nursing an increasing wonder at what Dana has called "the simple psychology of the forecastle." Hour upon hour he harkened to these huge men argue prodigiously and earnestly, and even come to blows, over the most obviously infantile details, splitting hairs ad infinitum and ad nauseam. He had to play down to their intelligence—caught himself time and again anticipating their conclusions, with leisure to indulge in speculations of his own while automatically following their talk.

Nevertheless certain simplicities of code were beneficial, and perhaps in the *Sophie Sutherland*'s crowded forecastle were fixed in him economies of habit that stayed with him always, such as orderliness with personal belongings, and a notable scarcity of the same. It was only right that one's private possessions and convictions should not get in the way of others. There were places for both groups, and they should not be misplaced to the harassment of persons one had to live with and vice versa. Besides, such encroachment was promptly resented in no uncertain terms and actions.

Though they were really children mentally, he noted vital differences of character. Victor and Axel, Swede and Norwegian respectively, were the youngest and most congenial to the antic side of his own personality, and after the wild adventure of the first landfall, they became known as "the Three Sports" aboard ship and ashore. Pete Holt, the hunter, Jack always liked to work with in the boats. For the vanquished Red John he felt good-humored tolerance along with ungrudged admiration for his gigantic proportions. And Long John was a fair sport. The senior member of the crew, poor fat Louis, old at fifty, was in Jack's sailor psychology that most unfortunate of wrecks, a broken skipper. He was deeply impressed to learn that drink had been the cause of Louis going to pieces and losing his papers. There it was again—drink had "thrown" a good man, "and he was winding up his career where he had begun it, in the forecastle." The worst of this, the boy was almost convinced, was that it had not killed the reduced skipper outright, but had done "much worse . . . robbed him of power and place and comfort, crucified his pride," and sailor-pride remained to Jack a superfine quality. And now the luckless Louis, once master of a ship, was "condemned to the hardships of the common sailor."

But when this youngest A. B. discovered himself repeating that solemn vow of Never Again, there would leap behind his eyes the rollicking high times, the "purple passages" that went hand in hand with lusty drinking. "Often, of course," he relates, "the talk in the forecastle turned on drink, and the men told of their more exciting and humorous drunks, remembering such passages keenly, with greater delight, than all the other passages of their adventurous lives." The eternal riddle propounded by alcohol took place in his thinking as a cosmic contradiction.

Then, when he had failed to reach any congenial solution, he would turn to another sort of derelict, the man in their midst whom he always thought of as the twelfth and last of the dozen. No one knew his name. The only personal items he had let slip were that he was a Missouri bricklayer, and had never seen salt water before. That would have been enough to disqualify him; for not only in this respect was he an insult to the forecastle—"he was vicious, malignant, dirty, and without common decency." Apparently he was strong, and perpetually he looked for a fight, though an unfair opponent. The first day out, he had reached for Jack's table knife to cut a plug of chewing tobacco. Jack "promptly exploded," and the first row of the voyage ensued. Subsequently, the man came to blows with every one of the other ten men. Combined with personal nastiness, his uselessness fomented the hatred of the crew, whom he bullied by indirection. "Try as they would, they could never teach him to steer. . . . He never mastered its [the compass's] cardinal points, much less the checking and steadying of the ship on her course. It was mentally impossible for him to learn the easy muscular trick of throwing his weight on a rope in pulling and hauling. . . . He was mortally afraid of going aloft. He managed to get under the cross-trees, and there he froze to the ratlines. Two sailors had to go after him to help him down."

Fifteen years later, the subject of "praying to death" by the Kahunas (witch doctors) one day came up when we were in Hawaii. Jack declared a wholesome respect for the belief, soberly enough recalling the uncanny ending of the "Bricklayer" in the forecastle of the *Sophie Sutherland*, in the sealing grounds off Japan. "He was a beast, and we treated him like a beast," I find him saying. "It is only by looking back through the years that I realize how heart-less we were. . . . He had not made himself, and for his making he was not responsible. Yet we treated him as a free agent and held him personally responsible for all that he was and that he should not have been. As a result, our treatment was as terrible as he was himself terrible." The man was ill of some mysterious ailment, but he had long since forfeited kindness from any one. Nor did he want kindness. Instead, he repelled any tentative offer. "For weeks before he died we neither spoke to him nor did he speak to us. And for weeks he moved among us, or lay in his bunk in our crowded house, grinning at us his hatred and malignancy. . . . He encumbered our life with his presence, and ours was a rough life that made rough men of us. And so he died, in a small space crowded by twelve men and as much alone as if he had died on some desolate mountain peak . . . He died as he had lived, a beast, and he died hating us and hated by us."

Strange mental food for one so young and so thoughtful as Jack. But whatever remorse he may have felt was neutralized by the inevitable memory of the man's awfulness. Yet after the body had been flung overboard from the ice-rimed vessel, he did what no one else dared do—calmly moved his belongings into the thoroughly cleansed deserted bunk, mainly for the reason that it was dryer than his and commanded a better light for reading. By now the boys had accepted his little row of books as an amiable idiosyncrasy. "My other reason was pride," he explains. "I saw the sailors were superstitious, and I determined to show that I was braver than they. I would cap my proved equality by a deed that would compel their recognition of my superiority. Oh, the arrogance of youth! . . . Then they begged and pleaded with me, and my pride was tickled in that they showed they really liked me and were concerned. . . . I moved in, and lying in the dead man's bunk, all afternoon and evening listened to dire prophecies of my future. . . . Also stories of awful deaths and grewsome ghosts that secretly shivered the hearts of all of us."

Although not recorded that the Bricklayer's obscene wraith was cognizant, it had its revenge upon at least one hated survivor. That night, hovering just above the identical spot where the unsavory corpse had been consigned to the deep, followed by his belongings, which the most avaricious had no stomach to appropriate, Jack saw wavering what seemed a long, gaunt ghost, and himself stood not upon the order of his going, but "leaped like a startled deer and in a blind madness of terror rushed aft along the poop, heading for the cabin." His "arrogance of youth and intellectual calm" deserted him cold, and he was "panic-stricken as a frightened horse." Through him "were vibrating the fiber-instincts of ten thousand generations of superstitious forebears who had been afraid of the dark and the things of the dark." He excuses or explains his abrupt terror on a biological basis: "I was not I. I was, in truth, those ten thousand forebears. I was the race, the whole human race, in its superstitious infancy."

He came to himself descending the cabin companionway, "suffocating, trembling, dizzy. . . . I clung to the ladder and considered. I could not doubt my senses. . . . But what was it? Either a ghost or a joke. . . . If a ghost . . . would it appear again?" and pride rushed to his rescue: if it did not appear again and he awoke the ship's officers, he would become the laughing stock of all on board—which, of course, was unthinkable dishonor. Even more unthinkable would be his plight if the officers turned out to witness a practical joke. So he figured, "If I were to retain my hard-won place of equality, it would never do to arouse any one until I ascertained the nature of the thing."

"I am a brave man," he asserts. "I dare to say so; for in fear and trembling I crept up the companionway and went back. . . . It had vanished. My bravery was qualified, however," he temporizes. "Though I could see nothing, I was afraid to go for'ard to the spot where I had seen the thing . . . As my equanimity returned . . . I concluded that the whole affair had been a trick of the imagination and that I had got what I deserved for allowing my mind to dwell on such matters . . . and then, suddenly, I was a madman, rushing wildly aft. I had seen the thing again, the long, wavering attenuated substance through which could be seen the fore-rigging. This time I only reached the break of the poop. . . . Again I reasoned . . . and it was pride that counseled strongest. . . . And for a third time I resumed my amidships pacing." Growing angrier and angrier with the idea that he was the butt of hoaxers who had seen him twice run, at the third demonstration he drew his sheathe-knife and started for the Thing, though almost curdled with fear. "Step by step, nearer and nearer, the effort to control myself grew more severe. The struggle was between my will, my identity, my very self, on the one hand, and on the other, the ten thousand ancestors. . . . "

"And then, right before my eyes, it vanished . . . faded away, ceased to be. . . . I swear, from what I experienced in those few succeeding moments, that I know full well that men can die of fright. . . . In all my life I never went through more torment and mental suffering than on that lonely night watch."

Of course, he never mentioned the incident aboard the schooner, nor how, in despair at the impossibility of running away from "the malevolent world of ghosts" to which he had suddenly given credence, he had as suddenly discovered the cause of the apparition in the shadow of a rocking topmast against the cloud-dimmed moon radiance on the fore-rigging. "Once again I have seen a ghost," he admits, and he was done with ghosts forever. "It proved to be a Newfoundland dog, and I don't know which of us was the more frightened, for I hit that Newfoundland a full right-arm swing to the jaw."

It may have been it was the happiest period of his whole life, that voyage in the *Sophie Sutherland*; for then even his disillusionments were healthy, and the compensations ample. Within him, as the active days of the exceptionally fine passage rolled by, was the delicious anticipation of his first foreign port, which was to be in the Bonin Islands, a cluster to the southeast of Japan, once known as the Arzobispo group. And they would be wholly foreign. Thus he foretasted the bliss of lifting their heads above the sea-rim, for he had read that since recognition of their Japanese ownership over thirty years before, American and English settlements had been deserted. And even though dead, these were volcanic isles, which was another thrilling consideration—albeit not the first he had seen. For the *Sophie Sutherland* had navigated the southern route, skirting Hawaii, the highest island in the world; and he had gazed spellbound upon the night-glow and day-smoke of the world's greatest active crater, Kilauea, in the foreground of a snow-capped mountain nearly fourteen thousand feet high.

The young Argonaut was deeply affected when at last the blue-distant peaks of the Bonins pierced the horizon, steadily growing less mirage-like, until he could make out the heavy green forestage, and smell what no voyager ever forgets, that scent, borne on the ocean breeze, of a tropic garden-isle of fruit and flowers and cocoa-palms. And presently the schooner was threading the surfy reefs and sounding her way into a landlocked harbor. Here were anchored twenty-odd sail of the American and Canadian fleets, put in for repairs and replenishing of water supplies, in readiness for the seal-hunting to the north. All about were sampans and queer native canoes paddled by oriental aborigines, who made for the latest arrival and swarmed aboard as Jack had read in old chronicles.

"I had won to the other side of the world," he rejoiced, "and I would see all I had read in the books come true. I was wild to get ashore."

He could hardly wait, when on leave they rowed across the clear green water above a fairy jungle of branching coral, to beach on the gleaming coral sands. Such fishing as they would have on that reef, from those outlandish sampans, after all that was possible had been seen of the palmy, blossomy heights. Somehow he did not think so much about the village itself. He wanted to stretch himself out of doors, on that mountainside, and perhaps find other villages, much more strange and picturesque than the one on the beach, which was alive with white-skinned mariners anyway. And so, he and Victor and Axel "walked across the fringe of beach under the cocoanut palms and into the little town, and found several hundred riotous seamen from all the world drinking prodigiously, singing prodigiously, dancing prodigiously—and all on the main street, to the scandal of a helpless handful of Japanese police."

Victor and Axel proposed that they have one drink for old sake's sake, before starting on their long, warm hike. Jack did not want the drink—but what should be his troubles to them? "Could I decline to drink with these two chesty shipmates? Drinking together, glass in hand, put the seal on comradeship." Fifty-one days had worked all the alcohol out of his system, and he swears he had not known the desire for it, doubting if he once thought of a drink. But apparently "It was the way of life. Our teetotaler owner-captain was laughed at, and sneered at, by all of us because of his teetotalism. I didn't in the least want a drink, but I did want to be a good fellow and a good comrade." He thought of poor old Louis's case, but his own swamp was far behind him, and he felt too strong, from the splendid conditioning of the voyage, to be fearful. "My blood ran full and red," he was healthily conscious; "I had a constitution of iron; and—well, youth ever grins scornfully at the wreckage of age."

The feet of the Sailors Three never trod that flowery path into the perfumed fastnesses of the mountain isle. The pitfalls of the town were too numerous to step over or around. Their long-deprived eyes were captivated by the flower-faces of the impossibly tiny, doll-like girls, dressed in bright kimonos with their reversed *obis*. "Little bits of things off a fan," Jack once described the Japanese women to me. And provokingly unreal they appeared to his young fancy, the little butterfly courtesans. So Jack and Axel left the turbulent village only in order to carry Victor, a lunatic from vast quantities of adulterated whiskey and the pale-golden native *saké*, back to the schooner, which he proceeded to "clean up." Balked in this, he threw himself overboard. The other two followed to the rescue, for though the keenest of the older crew, Victor evidently was one of the notorious able seamen who could swim little. Jack and Axel were not so tipsy but they wanted to return to the delights ashore, which they did after getting the subdued Victor into his bunk. "It was curious," Jack reflected later, "the judgment passed on Victor by his shipmates, drinkers themselves. They shook their heads disapprovingly and muttered: 'A man like that oughtn't drink.'"

Jack seems to have kept his head long enough to capture his meed of the saturnalian orgy that ran wide open that night. "Ashore, snugly ensconsed in a Japanese house of entertainment," he and Axel had several quiet nips of saké, first alone together, then with succeeding ship-mates who dropped in. Just as they were luxuriously settling on their native wooden head-rests to enjoy the novelty of music made on samisens and taikos they had engaged, "came a wild howl from the street . . howling, disdaining doorways, with bloodshot eyes and wildly waving muscular arms, Victor burst upon us through the fragile walls." It developed later that Victor had dreamed that a pretty Japanese girl whom he had known earlier in the afternoon was appropriated by Jack, and he forthwith ran amuck. "The orchestra fled," Jack recounts; "so did we. We went through doorways, and we went through paper walls—anything to get away." They returned, however, to pay for the demolished house.

"The main street was a madness. Because the chief of police with his small force was helpless, the Governor of the colony had issued orders to the captains to have all their men on board by sunset." This was the signal for a "general debauch for all hands." The men "went around inviting the authorities to try to put them aboard." Jack, still sober enough to take it all in, "thought it was great. It was like the old days of the Spanish Main come back. It was license; it was adventure. And I was part of it, a chesty sea-rover along with all these other chesty sea-rovers among the paper houses of Japan."

Many pictures he remembered, in which he unconsciously posed, the last one "standing out very clear and bright in the midst of vagueness before and blackness afterward." He and several angel-faced apprentices of his own age from the Canadian sealers, "are swaying and clinging to one another under the stars . . . singing a rollicking sea-song, all save one who sits on the ground and weeps; and we are marking the rhythm with waving square-faces. From up and down the street come far choruses of sea-voices similarly singing, and life is great, and beautiful, and romantic, and magnificently mad."

As in his babyhood beer-bust, returning intelligence was under the anxious eyes of some one, this time a strange Japanese woman, the port pilot's wife, where Jack, stripped of everything but his trousers—money, watch, shoes, belt, everything—had been left upon her threshold as a joke by the angelic blond apprentices.

For ten days it was the same story, except that the Three Sports "caroused somewhat more discreetly." Even Victor, repentant of excesses, saw the wisdom of discretion. But why regret that one adventure went wrong? Jack undoubtedly figured, then and after, that because he missed exploring the island he perhaps lived more than he would have in all the mountain climbing on earth. Of him I have observed, when on occasion one arrangement was interfered with by some other, that he forgot regret, or at least replaced regret, with wholesouled interest in the substitution. Eventually he summed up the entire Bonin incident in his customary philosophical way, though in this instance pointing the immorality of alcohol's accessibility to the young.

"I might have seen and healthily enjoyed a whole lot more of the Bonin Islands if I had done what I ought to have done. But, as I see it, it is not a matter of what one ought to do, or ought not to do. It is what one *does* do. That is the everlasting, irrefragable fact. I did just what I did. I did what all those men did in the Bonin Islands. I did what millions of men over the world were doing at that particular point in time. I did it because the way led to it, because I was only a human boy, a creature of my environment, and neither an anemic nor a god. I was just human, and I was taking the path in the world that men took—men whom I admired, if you please; full-blooded men, lusty, breedy, chesty men, free spirits and anything but niggards in the way they foamed life away.

"And the way was open."

Each daybreak on the northward run brought its fresh excitement of locating the positions of other vessels in their race for the sealing grounds. These reached, for twelve weeks they saw the sun hardly as many times. Jack, boat-puller, did his man's work at the oars, and skinning as well as packing the fabulously valuable pelts which he could scarce credit were the same furs that made the lovely, plushy coats he had seen on fine ladies who could not forego wearing them even in California's mild winters. With habitual thoroughness he had soon informed himself of the process of plucking and softening the unbeautiful slimy hides he was instrumental in securing.

"The deck was a slaughter-house, week in and week out," he has told me. "There wasn't a malingerer left among us since the Bricklayer slid overside; and we kept up a lively competition to see who would have the biggest number of skins salted down at the close of the season. It was wild, heavy work off the coast of Siberia, with no letup weeks on end. We had our fun, though—savage fun it sometimes was, but wholly good-natured. One horrid practical joke I remember," he exploded in that giggle which every one about him always enjoyed, "—oh, it was silly, and dirty and disgusting and everything else—and it did nearly cost us Long John's friendship; but he got back at us in some way, I forget how, and all was forgiven.

"Maybe it was Long John's length that put the idea into some one's mind, or his custom of sleeping naked—there'd be so much of him to shock! Now a skinned seal is not a pretty object nor nice to touch—all grease and blood, and colder than hell. We had a time getting it into the forecastle unknown to Long John—it was a whale for size—and into his bunk, where we laid it close to the ship's side, and covered it all up. When we went to bed those nights, we were so dog-tired we turned in all-standing, never looked first but just grabbed up the bedclothes, flopped in with them on top, raised our feet to swoop the blankets under and around, and were dead to the world. No reading for me those nights.—You can follow, can't you," he interrupted himself, "how I got the habit you've noticed, of spoiling my nicely made bed, pulling the blankets out with my feet and rolling up in them. I'm a savage anyway, in spite of my tender skin!

"But anyway—we were all on hand for the show; and some show! It went like a charm. Long John ripped off his oilskins and woollens, everything, and in one big movement landed under the covers full length of his bare, warm body against that horrible, blood-slimy, half-frozen corpse. God!—but he let out the most soul-curdling yell I've ever heard, and shot out of that bunk a hundredfold quicker than he went in. I'll bet his first thought was of the Bricklayer—but his next was no slower, for he tried to lay out the whole fo'c's'le. When a slow man does get mad. . . . I can tell you no one of us ever turned in again on that voyage without examining the bed!"

About the only relaxation the crew got was an occasional "gam" aboard the other sealers, scattered widely over the face of the gray sea, One of these, the schooner *Herman*, in 1907 under the name of the *Roberta* trading in the South Seas, put into Taiohae while we were visiting the Marquesas Islands in the *Snark*.

The sole indisposition I know of, that claimed Jack on the *Sutherland* voyage, was a sudden and severe attack upon his sensory nerves by the excruciating "shingles" (herpes zoster)—an intercostal manifestation that came near to proving fatal.

One more adventure Jack was promised, and they would be bound home with a big catch. Into the capacious Bay of Tokyo the *Sophie Sutherland* made her way, and let go anchor off Yokohama's imposing docks. Those docks, with the modern public buildings, invested the Far East metropolis with a-disappointingly European character. It was the largest city he had ever seen, its population totaling upward of 200,000, and incredulously he referred to one of the history books he had brought on the voyage, which stated that Yokohama had been a mere fishing hamlet less than thirty-five years earlier. Ever afterward he nourished an admiring respect for these short-legged, canoe-bodied, brilliant-minded sub-Mongolians and the shorter-legged, gentle-voiced, flower-faced mothers of the wonderful race. The preceding generation of average Californians is apt to be slipshod to a degree not understood by citizens of the Atlantic seaboard, concerning both Chinese and Japanese immigrants of whatsoever station. This because the familiar cook and coolie, house-servant, laundryman, and vegetable peddler, of western pioneer occupation, were usually Mongolian. Jack, in his hoodlum antics, had undoubtedly not been guiltless of teasing a Japanese or Chinese boy or two. Still, I have heard him indignantly descant upon how he had seen a ruthless gang jump off a moving Seventh Street "local" in order to besmirch and tear to bits the clean laundry on a wagon, first binding the helplessly chattering Chinese driver by his long queue to a telegraph post. "Teasing" of this criminal sort seems not to have been funny to Jack.

In skiff-voyaging on San Francisco Bay, then populous with lofty-masted ships of all the world, toward which his eyes had yearned so worshipfully, he had dwelt upon the scented cargoes which he imagined lay in their holds—rarest teas and glossy silks, perfumed fans of carven sandalwood, lacquered furniture and bamboo wares. And now he was making ready to land upon one of the massive piers of the very emporium of Japan's silk industry.

The sailors were kept aboard at ship's work all the first day; and none more anxious than Jack London that *his* American vessel should be the most immaculate and trim in port. That ship-pride kept pace with his years, and became as natural as his efficiency or his sense of the beautiful.

Evening came at last, and spic and span the young mariners disembarked from their rowboat upon a warf, and pursued their laughing way in 'rickshaws directly to a Japanese public-house. There they were to meet the hunters, to whom the Captain had given their pay. The hunters were already in full possession of the gay, paper-partitioned building and its engratiating entertainers.

When the fortnight was ended, and he bent to the windlass to break out the schooner's hook, and braced to her heeling pace before the homing West Wind of the northern passage, he knew what his undeviating course was to be when he landed in Oakland: steady work of some sort and what schooling he could cram in. As the thirty-seven days of the voyage neared completion, each of the crew conceived a plan of sheerest virtue for himself. They were all going to cut out this drink stuff for good, and make up for wasted time and money. A good payday was still due, despite those wastrel Japan nights—they could live, if they lived decently, until next year's sealing, on what was coming to them. And warmly they vowed to sail together the following season.

"They refused to buy anything more from the slop-chest. Old rags had to last, and they sewed patch upon patch, turning out what are called 'homeward-bound patches' of the most amazing dimensions. They even saved on matches, waiting till two or three were ready to light their pipes from the same match."

When they had reentered the Golden Gate and were towing slowly past the San Francisco wharves, the crew in profane language warned off predacious sailor-boarding-house runners who flocked aboard from Whitehall boats. Once ashore, and the owner departed for his home, all the *Sophie Sutherland*'s family, from sailing-master and mate to her youngest sailor, Jack, agreed that they must have one drink to pledge friendship and safe return. There were nineteen all told, and each of course must treat. And so it went. Every good intention of the older men was shattered that night, as it had been shattered on former returns. "From two days to a week saw the end of their money and saw them being carted by the boarding-house masters on board outward-bound ships."

Jack, lucky enough to have a home, did not spend all his payday nor get shanghai'd. In the early morning he withdrew and crossed to Oakland.[1]

The following year, Pete Holt reminded Jack of his promise to sail another voyage with him as boat-puller, this time on the schooner *Mary Thomas*. But Jack declined on some pretext, for his reading had by then fired him to inspect quite a different part of the world—the South Seas. The *Mary Thomas* never was spoken after she passed the Farallones. Her disappearance, remains, in so far as I know, a mystery to this day.

[1] Referring to his first sea voyage, in the "duty" letter to his girl in 1898, he says: "Aye, I at last kicked over the traces; but even then, did I wholly run away from duty? Many a gold piece went into the family when I returned from seven months at sea. What did I do with my pay day? I bought a second-hand hat, some forty-cent shirts, two fifty-cent suits of underclothes, and a second-hand coat and vest. I spent exactly seventy cents for drinks among the crowd I had known before I went to sea. The rest went to pay some debts of my father and to the family."

CHAPTER X

AUTUMN INTO SPRING, 1893-1894—JUTE-MILL; COAL-SHOVELING; BOY-AND-GIRL LOVE

17-18 years

SOMETHING was wrong, very wrong. There was a sense of confusion, and he could not see the light. Here he was, man-strong with mighty shoulders and chest and biceps developed in fair competition with veteran seamen. He had measured up in work and endurance with the best, and felt entitled to all the arrogance of individuality that welled up at thought of his "hard-won place of equality" with the professionally able-bodied; he had experience of the world—a being far removed from the mere boy of less than a year before who had worked in a cannery for ten cents an hour. And yet, the best job that offered to him, big sailor with a rolling gait, was at "humdrum machine toil" in a jute-mill—at the same old ten cents an hour for the same old ten hours and more a day. He was thoroughly persuaded by his mother that he had roamed enough; that his allotment of dreaming and blond-beasting had ended; that he must acquire a trade and settle down. But for the accident of a restless intellect which could not tolerate unrelieved routine, Jack London might have lived and died an artisan instead of artist and greatly more.

No outrage was so ill-entertained by him as outrage to his common-sense. And this thing was ridiculous. Like Kipling's tramp-royal, "Me that have been what I've been"—and still ten cents an hour, "me!" Notwithstanding, he must get to work, and immediately, for his parents needed his strength to lean upon. So he dismissed the unresolved and confused issues, and buckled to in that single-minded way he could assume which made him such an exemplary asset to employers of unskilled labor. Once going straight in the shafts, being an artist he took pride in his work, and became quite a conventional member of the proletariat, pleased with his own capability. "As for the unfortunates, the sick . . . and old and maimed," he reviewed his position, "I vaguely felt that they, barring accidents, could be as good as I if they wanted to real hard. . . . Further, the optimism bred of a stomach which could digest scrap iron, and a body which flourished on hardships, did not permit me to consider accidents as even remotely related to my glorious personality."

He has also declared that to him at that time the dignity of labor came to be the most impressive thing in the world, and he evolved a "gospel of work" that put Kipling's and Carlyle's in the shade, though he knew it not. "The pride I took in a hard day's work," he marveled, "would be inconceivable to you. It is almost inconceivable to me now as I look back upon it." For him to shirk on the man who paid him wages was a sin second only to that greatest sin, disloyalty; indeed, it *was* a disloyalty. In short, as he says in an essay, "my joyous individuality was dominated by the orthodox bourgeois ethics. I read the bourgeois papers, listened to the bourgeois preachers, and shouted at the sonorous platitudes of the bourgeois politicians." Such a virtuous conformist did he become that he could not understand his old infatuation for the waterfront. "I didn't care for the drinking, nor the vagrancy of it," he affirms.

Back he wandered to the Free Library, and read and reread the books, with eyes made wide by experience. Boyish enthusiasm had been satiated for a time and he felt superior, steadied. He had done some of these slashing and romantic things himself—and could tell a few more that were not in the books if he were so minded.

This several months' interval between the sealing voyage and his next abrupt breakaway from Oakland is notable especially for producing his first literary effort viewed as such. In a letter to a friend he says: "When I was working in the jute-mills, I received forty dollars pay and at the same time twenty-five dollars from a prize in a literary contest. I bought a ten dollar suit of clothes and got my watch out of hock. That was all I spent. Two days afterward, I had to soak my watch to get money for tobacco."

It was his mother who noticed the prize-offer from the San Francisco Call for the best descriptive article submitted within a given time. Jack was slaving for thirteen hours a day, finding it difficult to get enough rest as it was. Finally he gave in to her urge that he try for the prize. "Only, what shall I write about?" he complained. It was evening, and in his wearied eye was the prospect of rising at half-past five. "Oh, why not tell about something you did or saw in Japan, or at sea," Flora pricked his memory. This he mulled with knit brows. All at once, with a grin, he swooped down upon the kitchen table with an old school tablet, where he wrote furiously without note of the clock until breakfast. Two thousand words was the limit fixed by the Call, and he had already exceeded this, with his idea but half worked out.

"The next night, under the same conditions," he says, "I continued, adding another two thousand." And the third night, in a wakeful trance from exhaustion, he revised his story into the proper length. The manuscript, signed "John London," published in The Morning Call, Sunday, November 12, 1893, and entitled "Typhoon Off the Coast of Japan," to his amazement, carried off the first prize, probably because it had been whipped out hot from the mind of one who possessed exceptional powers of observation and instinct for beauty. Still more amazing, the contestants who took second and third awards were students of Stanford and the University of California respectively. Jack's father was so elated that he bought up every copy he could lay his hands on, to distribute to friends.

Jack himself, greatly excited, harking back to dreams in the days when he had pored over "Signa," could hardly wait to catch up with sleep before putting his hand again to such fascinating and lucrative work, which had been mere amusement so far. But what he next sent to the Call editor he designates as "gush." It was promptly rejected, and he contented himself with his regular employment.

But some sort of recreation beside reading did the subdued and amiable young factory hand naturally crave. He did not drink. He did not want to drink. He never in his whole life wanted to drink for drink's sake. He devoutly wished, from beginning to end, that drinking never had been invented as a social function. "I wish there had never been any alcohol in the world." I have heard him say, "it is all to the bad."

And here lies the pity of his preceding youthful experience. It had for the most part unfitted him for the healthful, normal youngness of fellows of his own age. He knew of the opportunities for athletics as well as education in the Young Men's Christian Association. All his future, indeed, he spoke warmly in appreciation of the work and scope of this organization.

The Y. M. C. A. was all right, he conceded; it was he who was at fault, or, more concisely, so unfortunate as to be too worldly-wise to find its atmosphere congenial. To him, the sophisticated, it proved juvenile to boredom. It had come too late, even though he was for the moment the perfect conformist in a bourgeois environment. "I had bucked big with men," was his regret. "I knew mysterious and violent things. I was from the other side of life so far as concerned the young men I encountered in the Y. M. C. A. I spoke another language, possessed a sadder and more terrible wisdom"—although it seemed far from "terrible" to him then. And he "got more out of the books than they. . . . Their meager physical experiences, plus their meager intellectual experiences, made a negative sum so vast that it overbalanced their wholesome normality and healthful sports."

Still, though he could not command social advantages that would have helped, these months formed a clean and pleasing period, singularly innocent and satisfying to one so lately roughing his way over the world. He always recalled the purity of his first love and the idyllic way of its pursuit, idyllic despite its setting; and his companionship with Louis Shattuck, who led him into its sweet paths.

Louis Shattuck, blacksmith's apprentice and dandy, considered himself quite a devil of a Lothario. Nevertheless it was through his tutelage in town ways of their class that Jack happily regressed to boyhood's simple consciousness, and overtook somewhat of the pristine ecstasy which had not come to him in the usual order of adolescence.

Remember, in their stratum, there were no chaperoned calls in cozy parlors of the working class homes, no formality of any sort in the mode of getting acquainted, no dancing schools other than the dubious and expensive public dance-halls and picnic-park Sunday whirls. And neither Louis nor Jack could afford these. At sunset and twilight of Sunday afternoon, in linked pairs the young girls strolled the sidewalks, the boys likewise. The head-gear of the boys tilted at angles esteemed smart: the smarter the angle of "tile" and glance, the greater impression upon the demure or tittering female of the species in her "fresh print gown."

Jack was suddenly devastated of the pride he had nourished in his manhood's prowess toward man and woman. He discovered himself without knowledge of the guileless methods of boys like Louis, who was "without one vicious trait . . . handsome, and graceful, and filled with love for the girls." In Louis's manner, alas, Jack did not know girls at all. He "had been too busy being a man" in all departments of his buccaneering life. "And when I saw Louis say good-bye to me, raise his hat to a girl of his acquaintance, and walk by her side down the sidewalk, I was made excited and envious. I, too, wanted to play this game."

Recalling personal ways of my husband, it seems to me I often lingered pleasantly upon the movement with which he lifted his cap or hat—almost diffidently, with an expression as if it were a practice newly sweet and consciously lovable. When he was Louis's chum, of course he already knew that hats were "tipped" to ladies, but with him it was far from having become an involuntary gesture. Louis, modestly charmed that he could teach anything whatsoever to such a traveled hero, planned how Jack should "get a girl." Which was more difficult than it sounded, Jack found: "We both lived at home and paid our way. When we had done this, and bought our cigarettes" (Jack had smoked steadily since his newsboy days) "and . . . clothes and shoes, there remained to each of us . . . a sum that varied between seventy cents and a dollar for the week. We whacked this up, shared it, and sometimes loaned all of what was left when one of us needed it for some more gorgeous girl-adventure, such as carfare out to Blair's Park and back—twenty cents, bang, just like that; and ice cream for two—thirty cents; or tamales, which came cheaper and which for two cost only twenty cents." He, who as pirate had squandered nearly two hundred dollars in one night! And right here he reiterates that disdain of his for money; but characteristically, in his philosophy he completed the circle, finding himself "as equable with the lack of a ten-cent piece" as he had been in the lurid months passed by.

Listen how they went about it: "Louis's several girls he wanted for himself. . . . He did persuade them to bring girl-friends for me; but I found them weak sisters, pale and ineffectual alongside the choice specimens he had." So Louis had to initiate Jack, who was bordering on panic worthy of a lad of thirteen, in the accepted manner of getting acquainted with some one whose looks did appeal to him. All spruced up, the two boys met of evenings in a little candy shop, where they bought their smokes and sometimes a nickel's worth of "red-hots." Louis was as frankly fond of sweets as Jack.

Consider this quondam lover of cannery maidens; Prince of the Queen of the Oyster Pirates; gay reveler of red-lanterned barges on the winding rivers; squire of more than one lowly Madame Chrysantheme on her native heath: it would seem that he was yet undespoiled of delicacy and virginity of imagination. Struggling with diffidence, he entered into what he has termed the "Arcadian phase" of his career, and learned how to overtake with a jaunty lift of his hat the pretty young things who did not look unapproachable; and how to walk and joke lightly and make speeches that commanded approving glances and laughter. But the infatuation he craved, as he saw it working in Louis, did not immediately descend upon him, although he "pursued the quest." Looking back upon it all, he wrote: "Some of Louis's and my adventures have since given me serious pause when casting sociological generalizations. But it was all good and innocently youthful."

At length it came, "All the dear fond deliciousness of it, all the glory and the wonder" of boy-love and girl-love. I almost think it was the most wonderful, beautiful, uplifting thing in his whole life of learning how the world was made. One evening he had found himself, out of curiosity, at a Salvation Army meeting, and the little woman of under sixteen, there for the same reason, sat next to him beside her aunt.

He has called her Haydee, and never divulged her true name. She was somehow different from the other good little girls he had flirted with; and he caught himself thinking the shape of her face and delicate coloring, her brown sweet eyes and tip-tilted nose, her pretty brown hair and petulant rosy mouth, were the loveliest he had ever seen. I can see now why he always favored a tam o'shanter. Haydee wore a tam o'shanter. It must have been about this time that he bought for a nickel, at a rummage sale, an old brown "tarn" which made an item of his wardrobe aboard the *Snark* into the South Seas, from Australia to Ecuador in the tramp collier *Tymeric*, upriver in California on the *Roamer*, and around Cape Horn on the *Dirigo*; the which I darned, darn upon darn, and which finally with regret he pronounced too far gone for further service, and had laid away in the attic with other beloved old "gear."

To this blond, awkward-bashful sailor, already tanned for life, face and hands, it was a "great half-hour" they spent in the Salvation tent, the while they "glanced shyly at each other, and shyly avoided or as shyly returned and met each other's glances more than several times." Indeed, so great was that half-hour that he was solemnly ever afterward "convinced of the reality of love at first sight."

As stern fate would have it, when he followed the girl and her aunt from the tent, that he might learn where they lived, he in turn was followed by quite another sort of woman, and accosted by her. She was not unknown to him—I wonder if it was the Queen herself?—and wished to tell him of young Nelson, who when he was shot had died in her arms. But when he had listened to all she had to relate, he pulled himself back from a host of undesired memories of his rampaging past, bade her farewell and hurried on after his love. Although he lost her that evening, Louis was able to tell him something of Haydee: she was a Lafayette School pupil, he knew girl friends of hers, and an introduction would be easy. Jack could not wait, and begged one of the girls to carry a note to her from him.

His experience with regard to Haydee is almost incredible. That he, "who could sail boats, lay aloft in black and storm, or go into the toughest hangouts in sailor town" and be quite at home, "didn't know the first thing I might say or do with this slender little chit of a girl-woman whose scant skirt just reached her shoe-tops and who was as abysmally ignorant of life, as I was, or thought I was, profoundly wise"! He came to know, in brief meetings, sitting on a bench under the stars, with "fully a foot of space" between them, "all the sweet madness of boy's love and girl's love." He goes on to record that "so far as it goes it is not the biggest love in the world, but I do dare to assert that it is the sweetest. . . . Never did girl have a more innocent boy-lover than I who had been so wicked-wise and violent beyond my years."

He could not believe, as in all ages, first-lovers have failed to believe, that so exquisite a creature as his worship made her could be merely human; that she really had to eat to live—though once she daintily shared with him a nickel's worth of red-hots; that she could be similar in any mere human way to other humans. I have heard him tell it! He did not know how to act. Should he kiss her? She, the chrysalis Eve, tapped his lips with her glove. Hear this: "I was like to swoon with delight. It was the most wonderful thing that had ever happened to me." Then followed an "agony of apprehension and doubt." Should he imprison that little hand along with the glove? "Should I dare to

JACK AND CHARMIAN LONDON

kiss her there and then, or slip my arm around her waist? Or dared I even sit closer?" But he dared nothing. "I merely continued to sit there and love with all my soul."

They never met more than a dozen stolen half-hours, and "kissed perhaps a dozen times—as boys and girls kiss, briefly and innocently, and wonderingly. "The quality of his adoration was so mysteriously holy, passionless, clean—as if for an angel or a bird. This is the way he closes the incident:

"I have always fondly believed that she loved me. I know I loved her; and I dreamed day dreams of her for a year and more, and the memory of her is very dear."

When winter came on, social recreation perforce terminated. It was too wet and shivery to promenade, and Louis and Jack, unable to buy overcoats, were driven to search for the most quiet saloon where they could keep warm whilst playing cards—they were deep in the intricacies of two-handed euchre. They did not want to drink, but self-respect pressed them each evening to indulge in a small beer apiece, as tacit rent for the table and the boon of the big stove. Sorely they grudged the two nickel pieces, wishing they could be spent on red-hots. But Louis's girl friends who waited on customers in the little candy shop were not allowed to entertain in the sitting room where their idle moments between customers were lived.

The saloon least distasteful in its crowd was the old National, at Tenth and Franklin Streets, where the two young men met some of their childhood schoolmates. But the inevitable consequent treating "skinned" them of forty to fifty cents a "clatter," and the two were "broke" until next payday. The National was too speedy for them; and meantime their thin coats were buttoned higher at the necks while they played euchre and casino in a livery stable. Sometimes discomfort made them cast tentative glances at the Y. M. C. A. reading and social rooms, and their speculations even strayed as far as Sunday-school socials, where girls whom they knew told of jolly good times. But Jack for one felt distressedly alien, the very delicacies of his diffidences standing in the way.

Unskilled labor, reason presently unfolded to Jack, was getting him nowhere—in a favorite phrase, "buying him nothing"; even a promised increase to $1.25 a day was not made good. He looked about, and with his usual deliberation selected a trade he believed would give him the chance to rise. As an electrician he could go far; and ambition, which never was denied for long, swelled afresh.

"He saw me coming, all right," Jack reminisced a bit grimly, telling the story of his call upon the superintendent of the power plant of an Oakland street railway. This man, by name Grimm, was of a towering patriarchal presence, his face winged with huge, snowy burnside whiskers. "How could I know he was mad that morning at the quitting of two coal-passers who didn't like their pay, and that I looked good to him merely from the standpoint of coal-passing! I, young fool, intent on learning electrical engineering from the ground up, listened entranced to his suave elucidation of the necessity of beginning on the lowest floor, literally, in this case; and I calculated I could shovel coal with anybody. I could, too, it seems, for until I learned through an admiringly compassionate fireman that I, a youth of eighteen, was doing by day, for thirty a month, with only one day off, what two horny-handed laborers, working day-and-night shifts and getting eighty, had thrown down as too stiff for them—well, until I found out this, under binding seal not to give the fireman away, I staid with it though it nearly laid me out."

I have listened to his account of how he had to strap the swelling of those small-boned, sprained wrists that were so ill-suited to obey the driving muscles of his overdeveloped sailor shoulders; of how he would eat his daily-larger packet of lunch ere the forenoon was half over, and be famished and almost done before quitting-time; how he would fall asleep on the car going home, and when the conductor shook him at his corner he had already stiffened so that other passengers helped him to the ground, where he almost fell; and how, struggling in a dual nightmare agony of hunger and drowsiness, he would drop asleep "wolfing" bread and butter while his mother put the hot dinner on the table, rouse to partake of it, and almost immediately fall into slumber so profound that Flora and John carried him to his room, night after night, undressed him and put him to bed.

"He would have told me sooner, the fireman said, except that he thought I would soon get enough of it and clear out. I was just about killing myself, I admitted; and he pointed out that I was keeping two men out of a job anyway, and cheapening the price of labor. This sounded reasonable; but I was proud of my ancestors who had fought in all the wars of the U. S. A., and I wasn't going to give up the job till I showed I could hold it down without breaking. So one day, when I had concluded my purpose was accomplished, I spread myself getting in the last of the night coal (you see I'd already got in the day-coal!)—and resigned. And I did some thinking, too, after I had slept for twenty-four hours without waking."

CHAPTER XI

TRAMPING —"THE ROAD"

The Sailor on Foot and Rod—1894

19th Year.

MANY become tramps, not through a reasoned mental attitude, but because their bodies rebel against the maiming from overwork that precludes natural gladness of being. Not so with Jack London. When hard toil was a game, winning its own delights, as he found it on the water, all was fair enough. But long-continued and underpaid grind that left neither time nor strength for recreation, not even for reading, held no reward that he could see, no matter how earnestly he had gone in for "settling down." The cooperation of logic and adventurousness worked a revolt in thought, which went hand in hand with revolt in action. He was intelligently resentful toward what he felt was merciless exploitation of his manifest and enviable muscle. As far back as the cannery episode, despite the pretty picture he had been struck unpleasantly by the luxury of the carriage in which a daughter of one of the cannery-owners rolled about the city. It had almost seemed that his own muscle had something to do with the pulling of her elegant equipage.

The revulsion was now more portentous than ever before, coming as it did near the end of that state of flux which precedes full growth, when youth's beliefs are likely to crystallize for bad or good, and what he did or did not do exerted an increasingly grave bearing upon his ultimate manhood. For the time being he cared little if he never "settled down." It was an irritating phrase, now he came to think of it. Settling down did not look good to him. "Learning a trade" could go hang. He would break loose, at least until rested in body and spirit, and that would be a long way off. After all, he owed a little something to himself. So even duty went by the board for once. The result of his orgy of work, brief though it had been, was to sicken him of toil. The memory of the overdose of hard graft he had let himself in for was actually nauseating. When he presently ran across, and approved, Milton's "Better to reign in hell than serve in heaven," more firmly than ever was he persuaded, as in the case of Washington Irving and others, that great minds ran in the same channels.

Probably this was the most critical juncture in his life. Only that magnificent balance preserved him from ruin. He had had sense enough to stop before any vital physical deformity had been wrought. Even at that, when he shook those unharmed shoulders defiantly once more, his very liberty was tainted with disgust at his inadequate wrists, bandaged with tight straps that for a year he was never without.

He strolled along the waterfront and considered going to sea. He was not tired of the water. Never did he tire of going down to the sea in ships; "the savor of the salt" could not stale. And here he might from sheer bleakness of soul have slid along the weakest line of resistance that stretched before his uncaring vision. As it was, out of a complex of temporarily dulled desires there glimmered the undying one that had influenced him to decline another sealing expedition. He had only one life: there were more varied experiences than he could ever get around to in that one life; therefore no hour was too soon to get about the business of pursuit. Anyhow, as he said of himself, "I was so made that I couldn't work all my life on one same shift."

In his final decision there was no intention other than for adventure and surcease from deathly routine, no notion of gathering data for sociological conclusions. In all the vivid plannings of his adult years, adventure was the prime factor. The fact of his office being located under his hat was a secondary, if important, consideration. Any port would incidentally provide grist for his lucrative literature-mill; but the port, in relation to personal enjoyment—the port was the thing. That his present unmitigated lark of loafing across the continent made him into a socialist philosopher was but an inevitable sequence in a passionately adventuring intellect. As he put it: "Sociology was merely incidental. It came afterward, in the same manner that a wet skin follows a ducking."

What Jack's next move might have been if the notorious "Kelly's Army" had not just then been forming in his home town, one can only speculate. It was shortly before Easter, in the year of 1894. "Industrial Army" he heard it called, and this unvarnished phraseology would not have enticed one in his irritated mood toward industrial connotations; but certain sneering remarks that accompanied the words in connection with the unique organization had fixed in him the picture of a tatterdemalion crew of bums and hoboes and other wearied rebels like himself. He would join the thing and have whatever fun there was to be got out of it, and Coxey's Army farther east. He would "just as leave" wind up at Washington, D. C., as any other city; besides, once that far on the way, he stood a chance to see other big Eastern centers.

When he went to bid Eliza farewell, it took her but a moment to find out that he had only a few cents in his pocket. Concealing under a bright demeanor any disapproval she may have harbored for this new wild-goose chase, briskly she stepped to the bureau, and lifted her snowy pile of best handkerchiefs from the top drawer, beneath which reposed a ten-dollar gold piece.

"Run out and get this changed," she said, "and I'll give you half. I'm afraid, if you have it all, some of the bunch of do-nothings will get it away from you." But when he came back with the change, conscience smote her that he should depart with only five dollars, and she pressed the entire sum upon him. And I have not a doubt that when upon Easter Sunday she put on the last Easter's retrimmed straw, it made her twice as happy as would the coveted new one she had set her heart on previous to her brother's leave-taking.

On a Friday morning—to be accurate, April 6, 1894—Oakland's city fathers were to forward the "Army" by free-rail conveyance to the unappreciative capital, Sacramento; but when Jack arrived at the stated hour of seven, to make one with the "push," he found they had been packed incontinently off two hours earlier. The only thing to do was to spend part of his precious ten dollars in following by fast passenger-train.

According to his penciled diary, he and a companion he calls Frank arrived in Sacramento at eight P. M., and supped at the Mississippi Kitchen. On the trip from Oakland, whirring by the old scenes of wild times he had known on land and boat, his somber mantle of discouragement had fallen from him as it had fallen when he boarded the *Sophie Sutherland* on that morning of dawning world-adventure. Again he felt "the prod and stir of life," not to go back into the debilitating commercial treadmill—heaven forbid; but to conquer life in the open once more, to "royster and frolic" over the face of the earth.

Sacramento had been too quick for him; she had not delayed in passing the hungry hundreds on to an unreceptive Nevada. Jack and Frank drifted to the arks and fishing-boats on Sacramento's river-front, where they came upon a scanty remnant of indigent young riffraff left behind for lack of rolling-stock.

"The water was fine," Jack remembered, "and we spent most of our time in swimming." The men "talked differently from the fellows I had been used to herding with, . . . and with every word they uttered the lure of the road laid hold of me more imperiously."

Every moment, with alert ear and eye, this latest recruit was absorbing each scrap of information that would instruct him in the idiom of the road. No, not the idiom, but the language; for a language it surely is, living, picturesque and foreign. And this he had to do while learning the fine art of dodging horrid accident to body and limb on stolen rides by way of the whirling, clanking machinery underneath "limited" railway coaches.

The wanderlust had returned to flame as fresh as on that day he sat in the *Idler*'s cabin with Scotty and the alleged harpooner; as lawlessly as the evening he took the Queen with him aboard his own *Razzle Dazzle*, broke out anchor, and hoisted sail for the oyster flats. Although the learning amassed when he had been one with hoodlum and pirate and common sailor stood him in good stead in the present emergency, it was only to a quickly reached and limited degree. The "road-kids," by misfortune of birth or later mischance, seemed a lower sort of human animal, unemployed by choice or physical inability, on their backs and in their pockets only such clothing and money as they could beg or pilfer.

These reckless ones regarded life from a contrary angle to the independent, carelessly free-handed spenders he had known, who made a generous, if sometimes haphazard, livelihood upon the waters. Revolutionary that he was, Jack slammed the brakes upon previous norms, took a square look at himself and the eccentric crowd, then eased into their rate of going. The road-kids did not like his hat. Neither did he. So they showed him, just off K Street that night, how to remedy matters.

"But you did not join that raid years before when the Oakland gang destroyed the poor Chinaman's laundry," I demurred to his confession of the hat.

"The laundry," he declared, "was not *that* Chinaman's property; he had to pay his customers for their lost raiment. The Chinaman from whom I lifted the hat owned the hat, and he was not a poor 'Chink,' for the hat was a beauty, and he was otherwise well dressed. You will admit there is a difference, *no*? Yes?" And to me, I having meekly admitted the difference, he melted.

"It was not nice; it was wrong and wilful. Yet I did not do it in sheer viciousness. It was part of the new game that I must learn in a hurry. I'd like this very minute to pay that frantic, jabbering Chinaman the five dollars he must have spent for that beautiful Stetson." He giggled at the comical fracas that had ensued. "What? Wearing a Chinaman's hat? Oh, it was never my habit to let squeamishness stand in the way when expediency was sufficiently pressing. And I've worn more suspicious articles than Chinaman's hats! A tramp cannot be an exquisite, my dear. I washed my face and took a bath of some sort whenever there was opportunity, which wasn't every day, because chances for swimming were scarce. Don't forget, I'm pretty much of a savage when amongst savages. Yes, I've slept with them and eaten with them and begged with them—and *loused* with them, which was the awfullest. And you, thank God!" he broke in with beaming eyes,—"you, tender woman in your pretty gown, you don't blanch in my face at the raw facts. What a lot most women miss by shuddering from playing some part of their men's adventure-game or even from trying to understand it. Wait a minute—where did I say it?" He reached for his shelf of first editions. "Here it is; listen, 'It is not given to woman to live in sweet-scented narrow rooms and at the same time be a little sister to all the world.' You, Mate Woman," he concluded, "I don't ever want you to know real hardship at first hand, and you have never known it yet; but I do want you to know and face facts as they exist. Shrink your closest from the thing itself, and no blame to you; but not from the fact that the thing exists."

Still, he himself was never physically inured to the hardships youth put upon him. Irritation of burning cinders, grit, exposure, strains on wrists, jarrings of unexpected long jumps on slender ankles—all such hardships showed a rare endowment of beautiful elasticity. What I mean to make clear is that wherever he excelled in this and that arduous game, the price he paid was greater than that of the average man.

On the riverfront that April day he was very busy under an amiably nonchalant exterior, acquiring the qualifications of a proper "blowed-in-the-glass" hobo. Since he had elected the road, nothing less than tramp-royal would he aim to be, and by the shortest cut possible.

What he did not take to himself of the tramps' oblique psychology would make very small additions to the literature of America's mighty army of Weary Willies as the country knew it before the Great War.

So well did he listen and apply that under his own "monaker," Sailor Jack, presented by his mates, he, the absolute tyro, was the only one of the crowd except Frank, who acted upon his example, to make a clean getaway on the late *Overland* Limited train of the Central Pacific. The "shacks" (brakemen) accounted for all the rest, and one luckless road-kid lost both legs in the scuffle. Of course, Jack registered automatic brain-notes upon the incompetence of the poor dubs at their own calling.

Sailor Jack had been warned beforehand to stay on the mail-car's deck—this being its roof,—to which he had clawed like the seaman he was, until a certain junction had been passed where the constables were especially unpopular with the "stiffs." Afterward he would descend to a less unsheltered nook on the platform of a blind-baggage. But this particular stiff made security from shacks doubly sure by holding down his precarious upended bed clear over the "hill," as the Sierra Nevada summits were styled by the "profesh," all through those smoke-stifling miles of snow-sheds. These somehow reminded him of the beamed ceiling of the *Sophie Sutherland* when he had bestridden Red John's heaving shoulders. He let himself down, almost congealed with cold, gritty, and scarred with hot cinders, only when Truckee was reached. Having beaten the railroad "over the hill," he had won his spurs as a proper road-kid, and he never owned up to the "bunch" when they overtook him at Reno, watching some Piute Indians gambling, that he had spent the night on the "deck." He arrived at Reno in a "side-door Pullman," which is a box-car, and was thrown off a passenger-coach he tried to ride out.

"It was no time at all," he told me, "before I was riding the rods on a 'ticket.' Oh, no, not a pasteboard one; but a little bit of a piece of wood, with a groove across the middle to hold it on the rod." One day he came across the old "ticket" that had been part of his slender equipment, and at my request labeled it. How different from most lavendered mementoes a widow may cherish! I step to his huge fire-proof safe and take it out—a weather-grayed section of four-inch board less than an inch thick, irregularly six inches long, with the shallow crosswise groove hacked out by his jackknife long ago. And how eloquent is the high polish on the originally unplaned surface! The tag reads, in his own hand:

> My "Ticket" used by me, in 1894, when tramping.
> The notch rested on the rod inside the truck of the
> four-wheel passenger coaches.
>
> Jack London, Aug. 12, 1914.

His agility in ducking under rapidly moving cars and invading the internal mechanism of four-wheel trucks always remained a matter of pride to him, calling as it did for the smoothest coordination of nerve and muscle. This meant the grasping of a gunnel and swinging his feet under to the brake-beam, thence crawling over the top of the truck to let his body down inside to a seat on the cross-rod, made somewhat easier by sitting on the "ticket"—all this in darkness and deafening noise of grinding, revolving wheels. How he, or any tramp, could dare even drowse in what one may be excused for calling an extreme predicament, is an enigma. Yet I have Jack's word that he was able so to drowse, although many a time he "burned" his boots or trousers-legs, and even his flesh, on a whizzing steel periphery.

I have heard him swear with exasperation at the incorrect descriptions of this nimble feat—an exasperation which reached its just climax when his own description, in "The Road," was wrongly illustrated by photograph.

Together with his big sincerity, sometimes of the bluntest, in Jack London there dwelt a prominent trait of the play-actor, and this served him well in beating his way across the States. Unwilling cooks and housewives, loath to part with "handout" or "set-down," burly policemen, temporary employers, with all classes he practiced his wits to see how far this play-acting gift would carry him into their hearts for the attainment of his ends.

Owing to his natural penchant for independence, however, one sharp disinclination he had to overcome was this very begging, whether on the street for a "light-piece" or from door to door for the "hand-out" or "set-down." His first lesson in the gentle art was undergone even before he saw the last of Eliza's ten dollars, and it was almost beyond him to bend to the humble posture. But very shortly he adjusted his focus, and thereafter encouraged that latent histrionic talent, much to his own amusement. Time and again he nearly landed into trouble when a glib use of invention led him too far into piteous fiction that unfolded the circumstances which had reduced his estate. Or else his originality was too much for the gravity of some appreciative, if less talented, companion whom Jack was also bent upon victualing. Having cast himself for this purposeful mummery, he hesitated not to make capital of all the seraphic facial advantages he was heir to. Still, he never ceased to feel a half-serious guilt regarding certain kind-souled women who, as reward for the best their larders afforded, fed upon the almost unbelievable misadventures that had brought this guileless child, with the innocent mouth, to the dire strait of begging food. However, he was able to offset this uneasiness by considering that there had been no palpable harm.

"If those ladies had been less trustful . . . they could have tangled me up beautifully in my chronology. Well, well, and what of it? It was fair exchange. For their many cups of coffee and eggs and bites of toast I gave full value. Right royally I gave them entertainment. My coming to sit at their table was their adventure, and adventure is beyond price, anyway."

Many editors and publishers have wondered how they came to sign certain contracts which, to his own enrichment, Jack London had defaced with initialed amendments on their margins. During one of our visits in New York I said that I would give anything to hear him talk business with these men when he was discussing new contracts or renewing expiring ones. But he would never consent.

"I will confess to you that I do a good deal of play-acting at such times," he said, salving my disappointment. "It's a game or a play. We're all acting. The best actor wins most. If I were under your scrutiny, it would spoil my play-acting, and thereby lose money for us both, you and me. You know me too well." And once, referring to the subject, he said: "Somehow, I don't know exactly why, but I don't seem to want you to see me in this role. Maybe I'm not especially proud of it."

Many were his chances to learn what it really meant to go hungry, but in his case even clawing emptiness of stomach did not discourage. It was part of the big play in which he was more or less a puppet; and, too, his was the consciousness of stored efficiency so lacking in the bulk of his associates, which kept him atop the heap of the more dispirited and the hopeless ones. While it still made him curiously uneasy to contemplate steady work or routine of any sort, he was highly enjoying this great picnic of irresponsibility. Occasionally, too, he was in funds of a few dollars that dribbled along his lengthening trail from the hand of Sister Eliza; while several times his mother, terrified lest vagrancy land him in jail, spared him small sums.

No loveliness of mountain or desert or prairie-land, morning, noonday or night, escaped his ranging eyes. No morning too cold, no aching muscles too painful after a night on the unprotected blind-baggage, no headache too violent from sleeping over a round-house boiler, to deprive him of the beauty of the new day that was the herald of unguessed variety.

"Sweet plains of Nebraska" they were to him, and it was not until he had made his way across them as far as Council Bluffs that he came up with the elusive, more or less orderly mob under command of General Kelly. That undisappointing figure on "a magnificent black charger" fired Jack's imagination with the human romance of the exploit of this man who had marshaled an augmenting force of the dissatisfied clear from the Pacific coast. Nor had they walked, but proceeded upon captured trains to the double-intentioned cheerings of citizens of a West only too anxious to see the shape of their backs. Jack's, by the way, was adorned by a huge blackened rent caused by fire from a cinder that had caught his overcoat one night of ride-stealing.

The Eastern railroads took a sterner view, and the Army hung up at Council Bluffs. Jack dropped into the last rank of the rear-guard as the procession, stepping to martial music, swung out on the several miles of road to the town of Weston. There its advent tied up two important railway lines that declined on principle to operate any trains whatsoever rather than oblige the invaders. A state of mild anarchy prevailed, for Council Bluffs, to obviate a return of the divisions, prepared to commandeer a train and run it to Weston for General Kelly's use. In the end the Army arrived at Des Moines on foot, and never rode again, except when it lifted its feet on river boats. Jack's dislike for "hiking" increased rapidly, for the soles of his shoes wore into holes until, I find in his diary, he was walking on "eight blisters and more coming." No shoes were to be had from the commissary, and finally his feet were in so "horrible a condition" that he dropped out and waited for a chance to ride with some farmer. The process of reducing the Army to the pass of tramping by foot cost the railroad companies "slathers" of money; but they established what they knew was an important precedent. In the end the Army arrived in Des Moines, and on Monday, April 30, I read in Jack's faded penciling, he "walked 15 miles into Des Moines, arriving in time for supper." That diary, incidentally, is absorbing reading, and his boyishly conventional comments on the good people who came to camp are delicious, though it is too long to quote entire.

Jack forever nursed a soft spot in his heart for the Iowans, who, though not wholly with disinterest, welcomed, banqueted, and bade Godspeed to the "two thousands stiffs" that composed General Kelly's following. Jack voted it the time of his young life.

"It was a circus day when we came to town, and every day was circus day, for there were many towns. Sure; they enjoyed it as much as we. We played their local nines with our picked baseball team; and we gave them better vaudeville than they'd often had, for there was good talent left in some of the decayed artists in the Army." Years afterward, from our drawing-room on the Limited, pulling out of Des Moines, Jack pointed out to me the old stove-works where he with the Army had camped and invited the city either to furnish six thousand meals a day or to make the railroads come across with unremunerated accommodation. They continuing to decline, the riddle was solved by General Weaver's brilliant idea of building, at the city's expense, enough ten-foot flatboats to float the whole two thousand "soldiers" down the Des Moines River to Keokuk, on the Mississippi, and good riddance at the price.

Sailor Jack selected nine of the likeliest fellows from Company L, of which he was a member, known as the "Nevada Push," and contrived to get his boat out first of the string. Thence on, the ten graceless scamps proceeded to raise Cain for everybody along three hundred miles of the shallow stream, helping themselves to the cream of the provisions collected by farmers in advance of the main Army's descent. In the diary I note a recurrent phrase, "living fine." Jack was not impressed with the dignity of the Army's management, looking upon the whole scheme as bound directly toward failure, which it eventually reached.

Meanwhile, having been outwitted by General Kelly in the continuance of their high-handed methods of preceding the main body, Jack and his contingent returned and disbanded one division, reorganizing it pretty much to suit themselves; after which they resumed and enlarged upon the scope of their cussedness. It is to be hoped that General Kelly and his sorely tried officers, for the sake of their own remembered youth, reaped a little fun out of the incorrigible pranks of these prodigals, whose ringleader was the irrepressible and resourceful John Drake, an alias under which Jack received some of his mail. As for the latter's own sober retrospect, he wrote:

"I want to say to General Kelly and Colonel Speed that here's my hand. You were heroes, both of you, and you were men. And I'm sorry for at least ten per cent of the trouble that was given you."

From Quincy, Illinois, to Hannibal, Missouri, Jack had opportunity to become acquainted with twenty-odd miles of the Mississippi of *Tom Sawyer*, and enjoyed it as much as was possible from the questionable vantage of an enormous raft formed by lashing together all the flat-boats. Somewhere along the way there caught up with him a letter from his mother, addressed to John Drake, Quincy, Illinois, and variously forwarded, as the scrawled envelop attests, to St. Louis, Cairo and Louisville.

Oakland, Tuesday, May 22, 1894.

"Dear Son—

"I sent you a few lines this afternoon as soon as I received your postal of the 16th and mailed it immediately that you should know immediately that there were some 8 or ten letters at Chicago waiting for you each one of which contained stamps, paper and envelopes, two of which contains money in greenbacks, one 2 dollars and the other $3.00, which you must stand very much in need of. John just as soon as we know whether you have got what we have already sent, we will try and send you some more. John take good care of yourself, and do not under any circumstances fight, if it should come to that. Remember you are all I have and both papa and I are growing old and you are all we have to look to in our old age. . . . When we did not get a letter for three weeks I worried so that I could neither eat or sleep, but Papa would always say 'never mind Jack, he knows how to take care of himself, and he will make his mark yet.' John, Papa builds great expectations of your future success. . . . John under no circumstances place yourself in a position to be imprisoned, you have gone to see the country and not to spend your time behind the bars. Be careful of fever and ague that is the bane of the East. Keep your liver and kidneys all right and you need not fear it. If you succeed in getting your Chicago mail, be careful not to fall into the water with what money we have sent you, for as it is in greenbacks it might be spoiled like your writing paper. Now my dear son take good care of yourself and remember our thoughts and best wishes for your success, happiness and safe return are always with you. With lots of love, Papa, Mama and Sister."

On Thursday, May 24, arriving at Hannibal, Jack remarks:

"We went supperless to bed. Am going to pull out in the morning. I can't stand starvation." Truth to tell, he and several others had gleaned all they wanted of this particular class of adventure. So they hit out in a borrowed skiff, thence by hand-car and blind-baggage, with many vicissitudes, for Jacksonville. Jack was the only one of the party who was successful in staying aboard a "K. C. Passenger" to Mason City. On the twenty-ninth, at seven in the morning, he slipped circumspectly off a cattle-train in Chicago. First, at the general delivery window of the post-office he was handed the letters referred to by his mother, and the five dollars in greenbacks which he found therein were partly spent "amongst the Jews of South Clark Street," where, "after a great deal of wrangling," he fitted himself out with "shoes, overcoat, hat, pants and shirt." Thus equipped, "with a shave and a good dinner," he started out to "see the sights. Went to the theater in the evening, and then to bed," the first bed, he records, that he had lain in since leaving home nearly two months before. The next day he passed at the White City of the World's Fair, and "in the evening went to the Salvation Army and then to another fifteen cent bed."

"Your mother's people" had always been a familiar phrase to Jack's ears, enunciated by Flora London; also "my sister Susie," or "your Aunt Mary." So he had been specially exhorted to make a side-trip to "St. Joe," Michigan, that Aunt Mary Everhard and her sons might have a look at Flora's shoot of the family oak. Mrs. London must have lived in some trepidation as to the appearance he would present after tattering weeks on the road. Evidently Jack's shopping in South Clark Street had only slightly improved his appearance, for I have it from one of Aunt Mary's sons, Mr. P. H. "Harry" Everhard, that his

1894. PICTURE OF AN ENCAMPMENT OF KELLY'S INDUSTRIAL ARMY

cousin Jack "landed in St. Joe in somewhat ragged condition, but in good health and spirits, having enjoyed his experiences. . . . Mother," he goes on, "was greatly pleased at his coming. Took him down town and rigged him out in a suit of store clothes, and gave little parties for him, inviting those of his age or a little older."

Somehow the spectacle of this world-wise, weather-seasoned sapling sunning himself in the mild social atmosphere of Mrs. Everhard's carefully selected companions of his years or even "a little older," is delightfully comical. Chances are, however, that her not ungrateful nephew's deportment toward her and her friends was above reproach, for his instinctive manner, from earliest childhood, had been one of responsive gentleness. While he was hail-fellow-well-met in all sympathy of understanding when the going was rough, refined surroundings, with affection in the balance, always saw him sympathetic, even anticipatory of well meaning and courteousness. Hence, far from being shocked by what she may have learned or guessed of his bold past, in Aunt Mary's eye he was, according to her son, "a 'hero,' and she just worshiped him."

Undoubtedly owing to the quality of her love for Jack, which was responsible for certain unintentional injustices that she wreaked upon her own affronted offspring, he "did not make any hit at all with my brother or myself," Harry Everhard recalls. He adds that this want of appreciation by himself and Ernest was repaid in kind and with interest by their guest. Jack was enjoying his bespoiling for all there was in it as a brand-new sensation, save for his lifelong indulgence from Eliza. It is easily possible, too, that he had let loose upon these well-raised cousins a few salient sketches of his tour, and that their mother would not listen to not nice reports of surreptitious introductions into various sorts of "blind-pigs" in prohibition Iowa, accessible to any wide-awake male of any tender age; nor unthinkably loathsome campfire meetings of "alkistiffs" (those dregs of tramphood who imbibe druggists' alcohol undiluted, "stuff that would take the bark off your throat.") And Jack, even allowing for the latent artistry in him, probably did not greatly exaggerate his doings with the outcasts he had, in passing, made good with.

One incident alone told me by Harry Everhard will absolve the wrathful brothers from the onus of inhospitality.

"There was a good-sized lawn or yard of possibly an acre of ground with big elm trees, well covered with timothy and clover. With the exception of the grass close to the house it was allowed to grow high enough to make hay. . . . My brother on the day covered by this incident had the hay all cut and in small stacks and called to Jack to help him load it on the wagon.

"It was a pretty hot day and with a rain in sight that would have spoiled the hay. Jack jumped to the work and was pitching hay like an old hand when mother got sight of him and called, 'Ernest, don't you know better than to expose Jack to that hot sun?' And she forthwith made Jack go in the shade and protect himself. Now he had been sleeping in box-cars and had crossed the desert where the sun roasted one as if in an oven, but according to Mother's view of it our summer sun of St. Joe was too strong for his literary habits. Anyhow, I had to finish out helping to get in the hay and Jack got a shady place under the trees."

The beautiful name of Ernest Everhard always dwelt in Jack's memory, and he used it for one of his own favorite characters—hero of "The Iron Heel." It is not to be marveled at, however, that his cousin, inoffensively pursuing a serener pathway in life, was not markedly pleased with this bestowment of his name upon even the noblest conceivable of labor agitators and revolutionists, no matter how much a pet of his creator.

Little wonder that Jack lingered several weeks in the easeful environment of the roomy, vine-trailed brick home; and it would seem that he had not entirely abandoned thought of writing, which made decided impression upon his fond aunt. Mr. Everhard remembers him "sorting up notes he had taken during his trip," and that he "had a sort of ledger and journal system of keeping his data. He did not call these books by that name, but they had the same relation to keeping account of his thoughts as a book-keeper uses in keeping account of business transactions." This was an outcropping of a future relentless system with his myriad notes, and further pointed an ingrained brain-saving executiveness that goes side by side with government.

Two strong motives appear to have been struggling for possession of the genius that was in Jack. One, of art-expression, was controlled by a conventionality he had not yet been impelled to pluck from out his consciousness, as shown by his diary, as well as a number of amateurish stories he wrote of knights and ladies and such hackneyed themes, submitted the following months to Aunt Mary for her criticism. The other motive, quite apart, was based upon his expansive lore of the underworld of down-and-outs. It was, still unrealized, his desire to coalesce ideal and reality into tangible art.

CHAPTER XII

TRAMPING

From St. Joseph, Mich., to Washington, D. C., New York, Boston, Canada, and Home—1894

"ANY day of all the days is a day apart, with a record of swift-moving pictures all its own," Jack has said. Still charmed with the absence of monotony in a peripatetic existence "for such as cannot use one bed too long," he, being one of these, pulled out upon the brake-beams again some time in July. He was now wearer of the proud nom-de-rail of "Frisco Kid," and would "go observin' matters" first in Washington, D. C., thence up the Atlantic railroad lines to other cities.

I have before me an eloquently battered notebook of cheapest imitation red leather. It contains names and addresses of friends at home, including Louis Shattuck and a Mr. Darnell; and there is a string of girls—Lizzie Connolly, who figures as a character in "Martin Eden"; Katie, Nellie, Dollie, and Bernice; and a few eastern names, among them Eugene J. McCarthy, 69 Barton Street, Boston. One item reads: "Mrs. Logan's house—her house used to be the old stone hospital during the war." Captain Shepard and Eliza, both for some time past engaged in the business of prosecuting pension claims, had been guests of General Logan's widow during the Grand Encampment of the G. A. R. in Washington two years before Jack blew into the city, and Eliza wished Jack to meet her friends. Her brother's annotations reveal the intention of seeing everything possible relating to the war in which John London had fought Abraham Lincoln's fight to preserve the Union.

Follows an itinerary of sightseeing, such as "Alexander, Va., by steamer, fare 15c," and short historical references to Arlington, Mount Vernon, and other suburbs. And of course this was his first chance to see the Atlantic ocean and dream of further travel. The first deciperable data in the scrappy little journal is Thursday, August 9, 1894, on which he made a tour of the United States government buildings, the name of each crossed off as done with.

A couple of tiny pages are devoted to prose on the subject of "Beauty," which, though without grace of quotation marks, he credits to Frank D. Sherman. Evidently Jack had been dipping into wells of theological speculation, for several sheets are covered by a dissertation on Deism and Theism based on the query: "Which came into the world first, the chicken or the egg?" One may judge from his remarks that biologically he was far from satisfied with the Bible story of Adam and Eve and the succeeding generation or two.

There are copies of quite commonplace sentimental songs of the day, with their refrains; and his current notion of humor may be guessed from this:

"Johnny! Johnny!" said the minister, as he met an urchin one Sunday afternoon carrying a string of fish, "do these belong to you?"

"Ye-es, sir; you see that's what they got for chasing worms on Sunday."

Fragments of dialogue that struck him as worth preserving, perhaps for use in the yarns submitted to Aunt Mary, are interspersed with copies of poems, good and bad, conundrums lacking answers, and streaks of tramp vernacular. And midmost of this living stuff one meets a quoted verse that speak's the boy's awareness of life's unrest:

"'Twere best at once to sink to peace
Like birds the charming serpent draws,
To drop head foremost in the jaws
Of vacant darkness, and to cease."

Some years ago, sorting over keepsakes he had stored in the Oakland residence where Jack London housed his mother and his Mammy Jennie, he came across that little worn memorandum-book. "Look, Mate—here's one of the diaries I kept in my tramp days," he cried, and fell to running over the penciled notations. Presently he looked up with a moist luster over the profound gray of those deep-fringed eyes, and the expression of untried chastity upon his mouth which made him into a beautiful boy-child hesitant to divulge his deeper emotions. "It brings up my groping ideals of that time," very softly he went on, "and I want you to mark especially how I recurred to my old ambition for fatherhood and stability in life, in spite of my vagabonding tastes.

Listen to this." And what he read quite solemnly to me, I now give from the same source, reverently word for word:

"In Washington, D. C., Thursday, August 9, 1894, in the afternoon, suddenly there came over me a great longing for paternity. A longing for children; not a sensuous longing for the accompanying pleasure of begetting them, but a pure spiritual longing for something in this world to look up to me; to depend on me; trust me, and be akin to me, as I must have been to my father and mother. Now I must confess that this is rather foolish of me, a lad of eighteen, to think of. It was brought on by contemplating the hopeless, friendless condition of a tramp I had been talking with in particular, and of the whole of mankind in general. I always said that I would not marry till 26 or 27, and I still think that holds good. But I will look around me in the meantime and try and profit by the experience, obtained by others through the lottery of marriage."

Evidences of his awakening interest in economics are to be found in scattered quotations, as well as through observations of his own. Having attached himself to a job that he might make a better appearance whilst seeing the metropolis and his sister's friends, it is inconceivable that he did not spend some of his spare hours at the libraries. He was plainly studying for a vocabulary, as well as facile punctuation, attested, as one reads on, by a strict following of the latter in quoting authors.

At some period of his stay in Washington he seems to have put up at the "Hillman House, at 226 North Capitol St." Hard upon some comments on immortality and the merits and demerits of a man's taking his own life, by Jas. E. Barker, a number of narrow pages are filled by Hamlet's Soliloquy, followed by a couplet from Longfellow's "Golden Legend" that might have been the suggestion for Jack London's disposal of the hero in "Martin Eden":

"A single step and all is o'er.
A plunge, a bubble, and no more."

The job above referred to might be classified as janitorship in a livery-stable, where he also made his sleeping quarters. In line of relaxation and easement of his gambling proclivities, he was not averse to sit in at various highly exciting and illicit crap-games by gaslight with negro horse-boys and their friends. A concerted police raid upon a session one evening, when as luck would have it, he was only a "broke" onlooker, was the cause of Jack's resigning his position. This he did by way of a window, first dodging on all fours between the irate legs of an officer with that catlike quickness of his. That he could put up a better sprint than the star-breasted "bull" who decorated with the window-sash, lit out upon his heels, was the reason Jack did not sleep behind bars.

Indeed, he did not rest at all that night. Added to the fact that the "cops" were on his track, he had seen and done all the things for which he had come to Washington, and now seemed the fateful moment for him to quit the beautiful city. So he worked his discreet flight around toward the railroad yards, where he caught the first "blind" out on the Pennsylvania Express. At Baltimore a railroad bull reached for him before he had swung off the platform, and the night's second Marathon was on for many confusing blocks in a strange "burg." His prided sense of direction helped him back to the tracks, where successfully eluding "bull" and "shack" he ensconsed himself damp and winded on a baggage platform. But that sense of direction suffered a grievous setback when, after forty shivering miles, he discovered himself again in the bright station at Washington. He had squandered the whole night in a fatuous round-trip to Baltimore. Mad as a wet hen, spraining even his robust Western vocabulary, he rested not or breakfasted until, late in the morning, again in Baltimore, he "threw his feet for grub."

Thence up through Pennsylvania he adventured, always overtaking the variety upon which his nature feasted. Little he asked of the world, it seemed to him—just the privilege of going and coming quite harmlessly at his own sweet will, with gift of an occasional meal, infrequent loan of cigarette "makin's," and a place under roof or stars to "pound his ear," meaning to slumber.

One day when he was swimming alone in the Susquehanna, some one went through his clothing. He bewailed the loss of his tobacco more than the small change. But "I leave it to you," he laughed it off, "if being robbed isn't adventure enough for one day." Glad that the thieves had spared his clothes, shortly he had the pleasure of borrowing what he could have sworn were his own "makings" from a bunch of waifs who were not wide awake enough to perceive that he was "on."

There was that fearful afternoon, he, a hobo, suffered mental and emotional torture in a camp of American gipsies, when one of the men dispassionately flogged his children and their protesting mother.

Here Jack, most passionate of champions of the weak of either sex, had to call upon a philosophy out of keeping with his age to control all knightly inheritance of his long line of fighting forefathers, that he might refrain from interference. It would have made the woman's plight more desperate, and undoubtedly brought about his annihilation. Eight or wrong in the abstract struggled in his brain with man's civil- and uncivil-practices. But in his own anguish in the woman's anguish, which made him clench longing fists till a gipsy man, noting, for Jack's own safety warned "Easy, pardner, easy," there came to his succor one face of the uncommon commonsense that reinforced sensitiveness all his difficult life. In her ethic, this woman gipsy among gipsies would not thank a rank outsider for "butting in." Jack had marveled before this upon the notorious ingratitude of certain females, oftenest of foreign blood, when their husbands were deterred, by outsiders, from fistic manifestation of possessiveness. As well might Jack's deep-burnt emotion have justified him in trying to halt with his hands an execution by hanging which later in youth he witnessed at San Quentin. These were not hazards in the open, where the best man or beast wins. Outrageous, hurtful, abysmal wrongs, in his profoundest deeps he felt them to be. But *they were the law:* one, the law of the outlaw, if you please; the other, alas, the strange law of that most free of all civilized nations, for which his father and his father's father and grandfathers had bled.

So he drew himself together with a mighty effort and met, cool steel for steel, the glitter of the gipsyman's narrowed black eye. He could fake an indifferent aspect; but his flesh was clammy and he was sick to his marrow—every crack of the wicked thong laid on the cowering woman's frame striped his soul with red as few experiences ever marked it. It did more; it lashed him to swifter sifting of the tares from the wheat in his abundant thought-harvest.

But Jack was healthy-minded and -bodied, and it would have been a morbidity not to dismiss the occurrence as best he could. The development of that mind had not reached a point where he could even think he knew the remedy for such demonstration as he had witnessed. The searing day was done—" . . . one day of all my days. Tomorrow would be another day, and I was young," he said.

As he "pointed his toes" northward, unknown to himself adventure was undergoing a transmutation into something potentially different from the ideal which had quickened imagination and footstep to the varied gifts of earth. His unquieting perceptiveness was getting in under the skin of things the while he paid a lessening if still bright and discerning attention to the world of landscape and architecture and industry. From these, indeed, he wrested progression and sustenance, alone or in company with specimens of the floating population of incompetents that coasted this same smiling prospect.

Men were so wonderful, he could not fail to be impressed, when he looked about his father's great state and the Quaker City, in a similar way that he had been impressed by any large town since his careless days in Yokohama. When men could be so wonderful, why were many of them such hopeless derelicts? This early he was exhibiting a penchant for inviting secrets from the most furtive and cryptic human sources. In his life's periodical "prowlings," done out of driven curiosity to see how society was managed or mismanaged, many a woman of the street or brothel who earned her price with a surprised willingness, by merely treating the friendly searcher to a correct study of causes she had hidden with a reticence that had been her one pride.

As he held up and turned inside-out before his mind the unlovely confidences to which this sympathetic faculty made him confessor, Jack was blest if he could see where he himself had anything on most men in the matter of opportunity. Some, indeed, had been maimed—they did not count in this strain of reasoning. And yet, and yet, come to think of it, they did count, at least a large per cent. From that night in Sacramento when he, the novice, had left behind him some two-score professional hoboes, one of whom had been cut in two, he had noticed how man after man was beaten by inefficiency at his business of running away from useful efficiency. Jack's own survival could not be all blind luck, he thought. The others must be failures from aforetime, hereditary inefficients. He got the phrase reading of afternoons in free grassy parks, where he loafed and warmed up after a chilly or wakeful night, and invited knowledge from book, or newspaper he had "frisked" by dawnlight off some doorstep. Book or folded paper formed his sleeping pillow. And of course—always of course, it seemed—there was the toll of alcohol's vanquished. His own luck apparently resided in the inheritance of a good body that was informed by a good brain—a brain at least of ability to withhold him from becoming permanently a piece of the floatsam of mankind with whom he now drifted.

Moreover, time and again he met hoboes who were from the first ranks of a culture he had only glimpsed, as when with the poetess-librarian friend of his childhood, Ina Coolbrith. From these abodeless ones, who had lapsed to a plane that seemed scarcely related to the everyday world of men, he learned of the arts or professions that had been their callings, and was stirred afresh to his own ambitions. The majority of the decayed gentlemen who slouched within his radius, he could not reason clearly otherwise, were foreordained wrecks. One had been a Philadelphia attorney, university graduate and the rest, and upon his intellect of many facets Jack sharpened his own while they traveled together. Oddly enough, it was in this companionship that he fell into the only serious difficulty he encountered in trampdom.

Something that had disturbed him for long; something definite, hard and fine, yet palpitating warm and tender, was coming into being in his heart. And though he knew it not, it was Love, the most selfless of all loves—nor love of blood, nor for woman, but the brother-love for the unlovely and unloved forsaken of men, which was destined to break that heart of his in the end.

But not yet was he possessed. It was a hell of a note, to be sure; but what could a fellow do 1 So he went on his way, "a beggar gay," rejoicing in glorious well-being and freedom, in his stomach "that could digest scrap-iron," and in his own fortune generally. He took chances with that luck, in a manner that challenged weary outwitted brakemen and even policemen who had not forgotten their youth or else remembered their sons who were chips off the old block, challenged them to implore him not to commit suicide. This they argued he was bound to do if he persisted in riding two fast-freight cars at once, as a circus rider divides himself between two or more horses in the sawdust ring. Many the officer he drove to incoherent very despair of wrath, until he would give up to Jack's uncapturable agility or the eloquence or humor of his ready slanging. But his supreme wide-awakeness guarded the young wilful from extermination, even upon that night he took out on a freight from Philadelphia in fashion so precarious that for once he "had enough, and then some."

The wonder-city of New York held him spellbound; but no astonishment nor admiration could slow down the heated mechanism of his brain. What he saw only caused its wheels to move faster. If he was impressed by the spectacle of the city's incomputable wealth and power, he was stirred even more deeply by the reflection that so mighty a capital should permit the wretchedness of its own East Side.

What must conditions be if New York's cold of winter were as severe as was this smothering torridity, which drove him to spend long afternoons in a green square that gave on Newspaper Row and the city hall? It was some years before he learned for himself what New York winter meant to the submerged.

He rather enjoyed "battering the main drag" of a morning for nickels and pennies, and found the public not ungenerous. Meantime it was great sport seeing all he could of the promenading *bon ton* of America. With the money solicited, he lived well, largely on milk, never spending a cent upon liquor unless obliged in chance company. In fact, during all his tramp experience, he avoided drink as much as was compatible with the men he picked as the most worthwhile companions. As usual, the crying pity was that the livest and keenest, most individual and adventurous, were the drinkers. It was proved to him an inescapable truth; and he did not let them know the radical point where they and he differed, which was in his personal antipathy to alcohol as a beverage.

He had enough money left over to buy books from itinerant push-cart men, who vended imperfect volumes culled out by publishers. The serious incident before mentioned, that divided his New York visit in two sections, made him more avid than ever for reading matter. In narrational sequence this incident belongs here; but I have reason for moving it to the end of the chapter.

In that shady square, little booths did a cool trade in sterilized milk and buttermilk at a penny a glass, and we have Jack's word that he "got away with from five to ten glasses each afternoon" in the "dreadfully hot weather," which goes to show where his throat's refreshment lay rather than in alcohol. That he did not surfeit that throat for life I have ample evidence. Particularly do I remember a soft-drink "hole-in-the-wall" in Sydney, where, in 1909, strolling home from theater or organ festival in the great town hall, Jack would stop for a long draft, maybe two or three drafts, toward his unslakable thirst for ice-cold milk-shake or buttermilk, in frank preference over any drink dispensed in the mezzanine of the Hotel Australia close by.

Only once in New York did he suffer from contact with the police; and, just as fate would have it, the club thwacked upon his unsuspecting and blameless skull without rhyme or reason that he was ever able to fathom, he being a mere detached spectator of a street-corner row. Was it always to be that way with him—that he would "get away" with real things he set out to do, and then run into punishment when he happened to be innocent? He could only class the riddle of this New York cop's landing upon him along with that of the Temescal harridan who had taken after him with a butcher knife. Tom Sawyer's Aunt Polly oiled her conscience and saved her face by declaring it wasn't a lick amiss, when she once thrashed her nephew undeservedly. But so tireless was Jack in digging to the bottom of human enigmas, that even so trivial elusions as these two bothered him.

The railroad journey to Boston was as full of mishaps as any short trip he made in the East. For one thing, he started in the blaze of a hot Sunday afternoon, catching a freight at Harlem, after bidding farewell to the Bowery and the friendly City Hall Park. I have before me an article entitled "Jack London in Boston," written in Oakland about 1904, and never published in book form. It was the Old Colony Railroad, he thinks, and he was systematically thrown off section after section by zealous shacks, until finally he came to rest inside one of a load of huge iron pipes on a flat-car, "gondola" in tramp parlance, where he "curled up and read the New York Sunday papers, and, as the light waned, dozed off and regained the sleep lost the previous night in the company of a pessimistic printer out of a job." But the stow-away had been observed by a busy shack who awaited his own convenience to strike the ringing iron and forcibly invite the trespasser to "hit the grit." Jack goes on:

"As behooved a tramp of parts, my mastery of intensive adjectives and vituperative English was such as invariably to move men in my direction. This was what I desired, and this the shack proceeded to do by crawling in after me. On the outside he controlled both exits (a pipe having two ends), but once inside he surrendered this tactical advantage. So I withdrew by the opposite end, while I bandied words with the man, criticized his general make-up, and dissertated upon the vascular action of the heart and the physiological cataclysms caused by intemperate anger. I also commented upon his ancestry and blackened his genealogical tree.

"I found the town in which I had alighted, on my own feet, which is a nicer way to alight, all things considered, to be Attleboro, a place where the inhabitants solved the scheme of life by manufacturing jewelry. As a traveler and a student of economics and sociology [he had become both by now], it was perhaps my duty to visit those establishments, but I preferred going around to the back doors of the more imposing residences. After breakfasting with a pretty and charming matron, to whom I had never been introduced and with whom I failed to leave my card, I returned to the depot. It was raining, and I sought shelter on the covered platform and rolled a cigarette. This action, being essentially Californian, at once aroused attention, and forthwith I was surrounded by a group of curious idlers. This was in 1894, so I suppose they have in the interim grown sufficiently degenerate to roll their own cigarettes. Nevertheless, I often wonder if any of them recollect the lad with the gray suit and cloth cap, smooth-faced and badly sunburned, who taught them how to do the trick.

"I must be treated leniently if it chanced that I saw but the surface of Boston. Remember, I was without letters of credit or introduction, while my only entree was the police station. Entertaining peculiar tenets regarding cleanliness," he describes the reputation of Boston jails of the period, "it is not to be wondered that I avoided this place and sought a park bench instead. I wandered hit or miss till I came to the Common." He comments upon the raw September wind that blows in The Hub around 2 a. m., and says that he shivered and shook, collar pulled up the cap down, vainly trying to sleep, till a policeman tapped him. "Always placate the policeman," he advises the penniless wanderluster. "He is at once the dispenser and obfuscator of life, liberty and the pursuit of happiness. He shapes the destinies of lesser creatures, and free air or dungeon lurk in his gruff 'Move on,' or 'Come on.'" Jack drew upon his histrionic abilities, and simulated mumbling in his sleep. "What?" the officer peremptorily demanded, and Jack answered, "Oh, never mind. I wasn't awake yet, and I was dreaming about Ueno Park." He asked, "Where's that?" and Jack replied, "Japan." Then he tells how for two hours he led that policeman's interest up hill and down dale, in Yokohama and Tokio, or Fujiyama, through tea houses and temples the narrator had never seen, bazaar and marketplace, till his listener forgot the municipality he served and the malefactors who feared him. "At the end of that time he discovered that my teeth were chattering, said he was sorry he hadn't any whiskey about him, gave me a silver quarter instead, and departed—he and his club."

Having feasted upon the juicy steak and "Java" the silver quarter made possible, the young rascal spent the rest of the night in the winding streets, trying to get back to the Common, which eluded him for two days. Meantime, he found himself on the bridge to Charlestown, and fell in with one of his fraternity, looking for a residence section that would furnish breakfast.

"'You're no gay cat,' he remarked, after a comprehensive glance.

"I signified in the appropriate terms that such was not my rating, and we unified our pace.

"'New to the town, eh?' asked. 'How'd you find the floppings? Petty crimpy, eh! Well, I know the old jerk like a book, and I'll put you wise.'"

Yet this tramp was an erstwhile gentleman, Jack soon found out, "with more knowledge and culture under his rags than falls to the average man who sits in the high places." Two days they spent together, and, "discovering an affinity of tastes and studies, discussed the possibilities of a reconciliation of Kant and Spencer, and talked Karl Marx and the German economists, until, in a sort of bashful way, he announced the possession of antiquarian propensities. Thereat I was haled across the bridge to the North End, where he resurrected all manner of architectural antiquities and fairly bubbled with the histories of the old buildings. Needless to speak of my delight in all this, for I was fresh from the 'new and naked lands' of the great West. But I lost him one day, as men will lose comrades on the Road, and next picked up with a Dissolute Plumber's Apprentice of Celtic descent and cursed with the Curse of Reuben. He had read Arthur McEwen's 'San Francisco News Letter,' and my heart warmed to him. He was possessed of the modern spirit, exulted in modernity in fact, and bent his efforts toward showing me the latest achievements and newest improvements. I remember he took me to the public gymnasiums. And he it was who led my erring feet back to the Common."

But winter was coming on, and Jack's eye was fixed on Montreal and Ottawa. One night Boston turned bitter cold, so he "beat it" for Lawrence, where he forsook his tenets "and slept in the police station" for warmth and shelter.

Tramping for recreation in summer weather was all very well, but once he was in autumnal Canada, neither gorgeous scenery nor new cities could restrain the thinly clad homing vagabond from making the best westward speed consonant with prudence. At Ottawa he succeeded in partly outfitting with an eccentric assortment of winter garments, but the difficult process and unsatisfactory yield filled him with disgust and haste to be gone from so uncharitable a "burg." It was, he declared, second city to Washington, D. C. where he had for a fortnight vainly begged a pair of shoes. The day in Ottawa he swears he walked forty miles, the reward of his "work" being "shy" of a shirt; while the pair of trousers acquired was tight to absurdity and showed "all the signs of an early disintegration." It was equally hard for a "bo" to extort food; but finally this one obtained a surprisingly large parcel. When hungrily opened in a vacant lot, it turned out to be inexplicably composed of more kinds of cake than he had ever thought possible of man's—or woman's—ingenuity. Cake being the pet aversion of the blowed-in-the-glass stiff, he owns to fairly shedding tears over that "multitudinous pastry." Not yet having cut his eventually large and cavernous sugar-tooth, he declined in choicest idiom to partake of the saccharine muchness. However, at the very next house, his appealing orbs bought him an entirely edible setdown from a beautiful French woman.

Across from Canada he stole passage, the determined train crews granting little margin of repose. It amused him, those thousands of miles of the ten thousand he computed that he covered that year, to attempt overtaking one hobo whose "monaker" of "Skysail Jack," carved with its latest-passing dates along the route, aroused sleeping sea memories. Himself now long since a "comet" and "tramp-royal" in his own right, Jack managed one night to pass the other and keep ahead all across Manitoba, carving or painting his old monaker of "Sailor Jack" for the other's benefit. Then "Skysail" went by also at night, and led across Alberta, always a day in advance. Again our Jack, in company with a member of the old Boo Gang of Oakland who had fallen upon evil times, nearly caught the fleeing "Skysail" somewhere along the Fraser River, in British Columbia; but when he reached Vancouver the jaunty, elusive sailorman had taken ship across the Western ocean, and never did the two meet.

"Truly, Skysail Jack," his brother-tramp Jack London rendered honor, "you were a tramp-royal, and your mate was 'the wind that tramps the world.'"

A week after Jack had crawled out from under a passenger coach in Vancouver, British Columbia, he, too, took passage on his home-land coast waters, stoking his way southward on the *Umatilla* to San Francisco.

And now for the account of the interruption in his New York sojourn. I place it here in order better to illustrate Jack London's outlook upon his return to California, in relation to immediate issues as regarded their telling weight upon his whole future.

This happening was but the climax to inductions he had already made as corollaries of his entire history to date. It set immovably certain malleable stuff of his being, impelling him to synthesize, out of an extraordinary practical knowledge for one still so young, a simple, forthright philosophy of economics. At least, it appealed to him as the most applicable of any he had found to the anarchic social scheme that had arisen and persisted through Capitalism, and which he could contemplate only as man's shame to man under the free light of heaven.

Jack and the aforementioned fallen member of the Pennsylvania Bar had left Gotham together for a side-jaunt to Niagara Falls. And no one was ever more rapt than Jack London over the incomparable cascade. "Once my eyes were filled with that wonder-vision of down-rushing water, I was lost," he says. Afternoon and sunset, he could not tear himself away. "Night came on, a beautiful night of moonlight," and still he lingered upon that sounding glory of waters. Near midnight, dinnerless except for the feast of beauty, he pulled himself together and looked about for a place to sleep. The night being warm, without covering he slept in the grass of a field. Waking at five, too early to "batter" for breakfast, still mazed with the splendor of what he had seen overnight, he thought to return to the falls for a couple of hours. In the silent town of Niagara Falls he saw walking toward him three men, apparently hoboes. Two of them were so, and one of the two at close range he knew for his lawyer friend, who had separated from him at the falls in the evening, in the (to him) larger interest of "grub."

Alas for the close range that brought Jack within recognizing distance of the rueful ex-attorney. It was also within nabbing reach of the central figure, an industrious "bull" who, because Jack was unable to name a hotel in a town unfamiliar to him, promptly took him into custody, despite his glib lie that he had just arrived. Into the city jail the trio were marshaled, and searched and registered. Jack's case was the most dubious, for the name he gave, Jack Drake, did not tally with some letters in his pockets that happened to be addressed in his true name. He was never able to recall which was recorded on the blotter.

So far so good, he thought—the town was strict in the matter of vagrants, and he had been hauled in through his own carelessness. He felt a bit sheepish to recollect his mother's warnings. But in court, where he made one of sixteen prisoners, there were no official personages save a judge and a pair of bailiffs—no counsel, no witnesses, NO CHANCE. Simplicity of procedure was all very well; but this clockwork execution of justice outdistanced his utmost dreams of efficacy. The judge called a name. A hobo stood up. A bailiff droned, "Vagrancy, your honor." "thirty days," enunciated the court, and the hobo sat down while another rose to his name.

And Jack, even he, no milk-and-water stripling innocent of the careless injustice of the world at large, could not believe his ears that were still ringing with the thunderous organ music of Niagara River. He thought of his American school history; of Sir William London's sacrifices in the cause of freedom; of all his male progenitors down the fighting line for democracy. He reviewed what he could remember of the Constitution of the United States as he had studied it for recitation; and then he dropped back with a thud to the cold, irrefragable fact that his turn was approaching in this chamber of relentless practises. . . . Bosh, he brought himself up presently; these hoboes were dubs, and deserved all they'd get of the city jail. Hell! he'd show them a few. His ideals recrudesced warm and bright. One of the liberties those ancestors of his had scrapped for was the right of trial by jury. A demand for this could not be denied in any court of law in the Republic of America. Could it not? Why, his own "trial" was ended and the next hobo's begun before Jack could realize that the judge's peremptory "Shut up!" had cut short the blossom of his first sentence that had burst simultaneously with the court's utterance.

He was dazed. "Here was I, under sentence, after a farce of a trial wherein I was denied not only my right of trial by jury, but my right to plead guilty or not guilty."—*Habeas corpus*! there, he knew about that. So he asked for a lawyer. They laughed at him in the jail corridor. Well, they had him—that judge was the quickest man he had ever tried to talk against. But wait till he got out of jail. He'd be good as gold while inside—it paid; and he was a diplomat, even if he did sometimes nap. But let him once get out, and there'd be the biggest noise and odor of a scandal that ever was let loose in the uninformed press of the U. S. A.

Jail! It turned out to be not mere jail but Penitentiary stripes for all the sixteen, the only offense of the most of whom had been homelessness. Jack, erstwhile patriotic son of a patriotic veteran, was handcuffed small white wrist to big black paw of a huge, happy-go-lucky negro, equally guiltless of felony, and placed in the very vanguard of the beaten procession that marched to the train for Buffalo.

Please, I beg, picture it, just once and honestly, any one of you who fought to impede Jack London, man and artist, every hard-won, invincible inch of his way until your tardy homage only bent at last to tired eyes and lips closed in death. Just once and honestly, I beg, put yourself in the fine skin of that burning young patriot being unmade because men were needed for the rock-pile. Then, just once and honestly, do you marvel that patriotism took on new lineaments in his ideal? For the rest of his life, until Mexico and Germania threatened his country, Jack London's only tender connotation of the word patriotism as applied to capitalist civilization was the fact that his father and mine were single-minded veterans of Abraham Lincoln's victorious forces.

Talk about sudden conversions at the Mercy Seat! He had pretended them, even striven to experience them, more than once at revivals, but had emerged spiritually untouched. But here in New York State there was no mercy. And the ruling class of America, finally, upon that day of ultimate outrage to his logic and his sensibilities, through its own uncaring stupidity forfeited that which might have become an ornament to itself, what of Jack London's temperamental leaning toward the excellence of strength. It was of such a being as this exuberant, protesting boy, that one who has been acclaimed Dean of American Letters, many years afterward, even in the face of favors received, declared: "Jack London is a self-confessed felon, and ought to be behind the bars to-day."

That he was not made into a dangerous criminal, as were many of his chance mates, was not due to the masters. His brain and eye missed no iota of cruel wrong of the penal institution in itself and in its administration. His common sense that made him from moment to moment follow the lead of the wiser convicts to the playing of politics that in short order created him a trusty—these faculties enabled him to convert the month of durance into a powerful ally of mental growth. With customary abandon he gave himself to the game, and went observing instant by instant.

Here, to be sure, he might have been deflected into a consideration of the wisdom of eliminating the unfit, which would have led him to the pursuance whole-souled of oligarchy's high awards. It was the hot heart of him that interposed before the cool weighing of his reason, and he would make no terms with the enemy of the underdog. But true to his quality, that abiding saneness just as uncompromisingly determined that he scale the social shambles he saw butchering the careers of unprophetic or indolent comrades. Although he honored the martyrs of old, their method could never be for him. He would himself first climb out of the pit, that he might live to reach a hand to the fellow who could not rise by himself.

One may thank that princely ego of Jack London's which triumphed to serve, that there was any boyhood left in him when he had doffed the stripes and emerged shaven headed from the great gray house where he had been consigned by the majesty of Niagara Falls police court. And he had learned how best to serve both himself and those still incarcerated, which was by making himself, upon his release, very small in the matter of immediate protest. Loud mouthed ones discharged during his own occupancy of a cell, had shortly returned very silent and very sore. So he walked exceeding soft; exceeding quietly he stole under the first New York and Pennsylvania train bound southeast. More carefully than all else did he avoid coming within tagging reach of any cop in Buffalo, for amongst other teachers in the "pen" were the men who had served their thirty days for vagrancy and run forthwith again into the winnowing arms of the same or other officers. Some had been committed a second and third time, according to their degree of stupidity.

Remembering the monstrous cruelties of the penitentiary in the course of administering criminal "justice," Jack not unnaturally concluded all State prisons were alike. It became almost second-nature for him to take to nimble heels whenever a policeman hove in sight. In the "pen" he had soon ceased from cursing his failure to jump out that morning in Niagara Falls, because of the tremendous eye-opener the prison was to him upon the nether-scenes of society. Nothing could better exhibit the rottenness of the social structure than this mad manhandling of human potentialities, in need rather of wise physicians for mental as well as physical deficiencies. Jack, being essentially healthy, shook himself free as of yore from the unnormality of the thing, and went on his way rejoicing in escape. But this time it was with a deeper difference than ever before. Read in "The Road" his two sections entitled "Pinched" and "The Pen," for a hint of what he calls the "unprintable" details of what with his own eyes he saw in the Erie County Penitentiary in 1894. "They were unthinkable to me until I saw them," he avows, "and I was no spring chicken in the ways of the world and the awful abysses of human degradation."

When Jack this time passed homeward through the Golden Gate of the West, it was eyes front to the exigencies of his future; and there was a new look in those eyes—wide, grave, imperious. He had figured it out, once and for all. He had been wont to glorify his beautiful youth's muscle and "silk." Where had it got him? What had it bought him? Where would it land him? Tell him that! Each time he had tried it out, he, fit among the fit, had been exploited for a paltry wage—or none, when it came to a penitentiary rock-pile. Being obsessed with love of life that should go with such a physique, he confessed terror as to what would happen when he grew older and had lost his silk, whenas he should be "unable to work shoulder to shoulder with the strong." The vaunted dignity of manual labor, as he had heard it expounded by teacher and preacher and politician, suffered a total eclipse. He had informed himself as to the doings in the cellar-pit of society. These had shown him that the men without trades were helpless, and the ones with trades were obliged to belong to unions in order to work at those trades. Unions were forced to maintain constant war with employers' unions, which came back at them in turn. Therefore, no trade for him—and no criminality either. He would work up out of the pit, but not with his muscle. In short, brains paid, properly used, and not brawn. His economic interpretations sanctioned the decision, for himself, that brain, and brain only, would he sell.

Here he might have switched to the track taken by the hero he created in "Martin Eden," and become technically an aristocrat, with little care for those he was easily superior enough to leave in the shambles. But no; he would use his potent intelligence to double purpose. His choice, and the use he put it to, are the most eloquent illustrations of his nobility and integrity.

CHAPTER XIII

HIGH SCHOOL

19th Year

WHEN Jack London, too late to enter at the beginning, jumped midway into his first High School term, he was "driving many horses," to use a favorite expression. One was Book Education, another Socialism, a third the requisite Job, the fourth Social Usage, and so on, with all their intricate harness.

With very unorthodox views on labor and capital, he was still orthodox enough to believe that the success he craved must rest upon classical learning. Even before the Lily Maid brought her refining influence to bear upon his training, he was soaring along in his High School classes toward Berkeley's academic eucalyptus groves. It will not do for any woman, or man, either, to rise after Jack London's death and say, "It was I who educated Jack London, or started him to educate himself toward college; I put the idea into his head. I taught him the English that made him famous. In short, I made Jack London." There has been a tendency on the part of a few self-advertising souls to hint such claims; but any one truly acquainted with any part of Jack's make-up must in all honesty realize that, no matter what the helping hand, he "made himself," upon rigid lines that he had established for himself, until of his largeness he spread the lines to embrace all attainable life and erudition. He was by far too unique to be influenced vitally or permanently by any single restraining or even propelling touch.

Relentlessly, as the illuminating months went by, head high he repudiated convention after convention of belief as it proved non-essential to his advancement; still, he held to the belief that "education" was indispensable. Fellows who did things, big things, must finish their schooling first; he heard it on every side. Schooling it should be, from its first word to his last degree at the University. He had not meditated the apt query as to why some of mankind's brightest adornments had neglected to march up the grades in the way properly constituted individuals are supposed to march; nor had he then spurned what he came to scorn as "the bourgeois valuation put upon the university pigskin." This I take from a letter written to a schoolgirl two years before his death. But in the year 1894, to be called "a college man" was his ambition as guaranty of unquestionable excellence. So far there had not dawned upon him the priceless worth of his first-hand experience to a writing career; or, if this treasure did suggest itself as part of the equipment, it was in secondary measure. At least, it must pass through the alembic of rule-of-thumb culture.

Upon Jack's return to Oakland from The Road, his good luck it was to find John London improved in health and holding down his situation as special officer on the police force, with pay sufficient for the little household. This left the boy, all on fire to study, at liberty to concentrate.

He set about forming work-habits that clung all his life. In the pretty white cottage on Twenty-second Avenue, between Sixteenth and Seventeenth Streets, his mother fixed up a roomy bed-chamber for his "den." In the matter of a bed, he asserted himself in favor of a large and comfortable one—"Because I shall spend much of my time in it, keeping warm while I study," he planned. Since good beds were a weakness of his mother, the wish was gratified without protest. "I always have good beds in my house if I haven't anything else," was her boast.

Opposite the big bed, squarely against the window-sill, Jack set a plain table large enough for study books and writing materials, to buy which Eliza had advanced him money; and by the bed a small stand to carry a reading-lamp, one of the "student" variety, with books, scribble-pads, and pencils. In one corner a dresser, of the style with a long mirror, two large drawers, and several small ones rising on the right of the glass, took care of his meager wardrobe and shaving outfit.

The furnishing was completed by a chair at the table which at night supplemented the small bedside lamp-stand to hold a dish of fruit and his cigarettes and matches. And woe to any who should from a motive of whatsoever virtuous orderliness misplace an item of his paraphernalia. After his mother had been possessed of one of her "cleaning streaks" in his absence (who of us has not agonized from this uncomprehending and indefensible madness in one's elders!), Jack would rage through the cottage, storming that he couldn't find a damned thing. Flora, in self-defense, learned to intimate mildly that "Eliza was over, and thought she'd tidy up a bit," because, forsooth, he never dared storm at Eliza. As he admitted: "I knew better than to yell at Eliza, for she'd talk back at me twice as hard."

Here in the den, air blue with smoke of cigarettes, he made his smashing offensive on the books, and prepared himself for "exams," picking up where he had left off when he had been graduated years before from Grammar. When exhausted from bending unheeded hours over the table, he retreated to the wide bed where, propped on huge pillows, he continued to "dig" until dawn. Night after night, a well meaning neighbor, Mrs. Aldridge, seeing the light, worked herself into a state of pity for Jack's mother, poor worried soul that she must be, sitting up all hours waiting for a wastrel son to return. Finally she and her daughter walked over one evening to make Mrs. London's acquaintance and, if agreeable, to sit up with her, only to be informed by Flora that the lamp illumined the pages of her student son.

But he must have some sort of exercise, and the loan of a bicycle by another neighbor gave him something to cope with bodily. It was one of those fearful and wonderful pioneer objects comprised of a wheel of expansive diameter with another and tiny one behind—the old "ordinary" of painful memory. Before an early breakfast, that he might practise unseen of delighted passers, Jack proceeded to master the thing with vigor and dispatch. "At first," Eliza relates, "he was most of the time sprawled about the ground; and he'd come over to my house for breakfast—bruised, dripping wet and red in the face, his curls all tousled, fighting mad, and explaining carefully what slow work it was getting the best of the 'infernal machine!' Then he'd burst out laughing at the idea of how he must look when he tangled up and went down in a heap with it."

When he started going daily to the "Oakland High" on Twelfth between Jefferson and Clay Streets, Eliza presented him with a latest model of the low "safety wheel." Speeding to and fro, bent above the handle-bars, he sometimes looked aside wistfully to the estuary that several blocks down paralleled the Avenue, wishing he had leisure for a sailboat. But the days and nights were all too short for the multitudinous activities he had engaged in. There were shadows beneath his eyes from lack of sleep and pallor under the vagabond brown. In addition to class work, he wanted to contribute stories to the High School paper, *The Aegis*. One of these, done in the medium of colloquial road-kid diction, appeared in a February 1895 issue, entitled "Frisco Kid's Story," and its fresh tone and touch of sincere pathos created a breeze in school circles. "The yarns I wrote at that time drew little upon my imagination, but were more relations of real incidents than anything else," he described them.

With an instinct for live diction, the dead, formalized instruction worked a bepuzzlement in him. Miss Mollie Connors, instructor in languages, gives the following example:

"One morning," she relates, "I noticed Jack sitting at his desk with a gloomy, heart-breaking look on his face. In front of him lay a manuscript that had been so marked with a criticizing pencil that it was difficult to read the original. 'It's no use, Miss Mollie,' he said in reply to my inquiry as to what ailed him. 'I'm going to quit. I came here to study English because I thought I could write; but I can't—look at this!' I managed to read the article, corrected by a teacher to whom pure English meant so much more than talent: 'Never mind, Jack,' I said. 'I'm going to tell you a secret: 'The only trouble is that you can write, and she can't. You keep right on.'"

He had deliberated earnestly upon a pursuit for which he should qualify, and it seemed that he must definitely abandon music, and poetry, and other alluring ways of what he had thought of as "the wide joyfields of art." The more he pondered, the more convinced he became that fiction writing would pay the best, bringing to him the means of good living for himself and others. In writing he would still be creating art, which seemed necessary to a full realization of himself. It would not take him long, he figured, to get where he could incorporate art and beauty into form that would sell for several dollars a column, if rumors were dependable.

From one ancestor of his mother at least, Jack London inherited stern fixity of purpose and perseverance. This Wellman had "blown in" his own bank and all others of his interests for the construction and maintaining of what was in its time the largest blasting furnace in the iron districts; but, like some of Jack's ideas, it was in advance not of its need but its recognition. I cannot refrain from wondering if he had not set up for his motto Washington Irving's "Great minds have purposes; others have wishes."

"And no brother of mine is going to take any chewing tobacco into High School in *my* town," Eliza announced her disapproval of an unsavory habit he had brought home from his tramp society. Whereupon Jack submitted the excuse that he had to keep chewing incessantly, when he was not smoking incessantly, to prevent his teeth from aching. Suiting action to his defense, he opened his square jaws and exhibited an array of cavities, in every tooth that the Kelly's Army dentist had spared from his forceps.

"You ought to be ashamed of yourself—you needn't have had a mouth like that if you'd taken half-decent care of it," Eliza scolded full righteously. He owned she was justified, and then proffered the bargain that if she would get him some new upper-fronts, and have the cavities filled, he would abandon the abhorred "chewing." Which he did, except on one or two surreptitious occasions when, sailing and fishing up-river for a rest, alone or with some unregenerate compatriot, he renewed acquaintance with "plug cut."

"Well," he remarked when the plate had been adjusted, "here I am with my first store teeth and my first toothbrush I ever bought—I got them both at the same time, at nineteen years of age."

"Well, it's nothing to be proud of," his sister flashed back with rising color. "It's your own fault, because you knew better. I didn't bring you up that way! And I wouldn't brag about it before anybody. It's no credit to you."

For quite beyond her it was that he, always shouting for bath and towels, "nice woolly ones, you know," or brush and comb and razor, and who used a whiskbroom assiduously on his shabbiest suit, should have slipped up in this matter of caring for his teeth. He had no excuse save "Oh, I was always busy, or reading, or interested in something, and forgot it! "

Jack's first mishap while he and the new plate were becoming accustomed, was upon a day when he rode the spic and span "safety" to call upon a girl schoolmate. Coasting down hill, a violent sneeze ejected the teeth, and in his lightning effort to catch them midfall, they and he and the wheel went down together. Although his sensitiveness was acute, he would hide it at such times under a bold brusquerie. Once, I remember, at the Piedmont Swimming Baths in Oakland, he

JACK LONDON

lost his plate in the tank, and failing to recover it by crawling along the bottom in eight feet of water, he finally gave up secret methods and offered a dollar to the boy who would find it for him. Great hilarity ensued, in which he as noisily shared, and there followed a mighty splashing and engulfment of small divers. And when one strangling brat had emerged successful, the owner concealed his blushes under water while he slipped the teeth into place. "Be a good sport, no matter how it hurts," was the word.

Already Jack was conspicuous in propaganda work for the old Socialist Labor Party. Yes, he had some time back discovered the name for what he had become: *Socialist*—though he had been made aware from his fearless start that the word was a grief in the ears of "nice" persons regardful of bourgeois peace and order. But, born rebel against anything less than a square deal, and personally ambitious into the bargain, he subscribed in effect to the maxim that "Satisfaction with existing things is damnation." Eager though he was to benefit mankind, early in the game, to the questions "You hope to cure social ills with socialism! Do you think it will be long in coming?" Jack replied: "I don't know; the student quits prophesying early in the action."

Now this particular steed in his speeding team, Socialism, did not seem to step precisely with sedate ethics in the High School; but he had much information to plunder, and would not worry. Blithely would he remove obstacles as they arose, and it should be easy enough. He would reduce all difficulties to their simplest forms—which indeed often abolishes difficulty—and proceed to handle the same as simply. In a fine degree Jack had that consciousness which Wells has said is discord evoking the will to adjust itself.

No Laodicean, Jack. His facing to the world must be direct and unmistakable, though composed of many and mobile features, for the countenance of his soul was not created rigid except in the basic integrities. Rampant individual was he, in every fiber. But how about the next fellow, his brother or sister individual? Evidently, from his observation about the world, just the right chance was not accorded them all. He happened to be husky and could make his own berth, though even he had to strain unduly to survive, and he had come to see that countless ones were unable to endure the race. He thought of child-labor as he had known it and as he saw it progressing in the land. And the mangling mercilessness of commerce—the industrial accidents, the scrap-heap of cripples and mendicants; for the unprotected machine, since he had worked at it, had not been improved upon. He did not have to take the say-so of others: he had his own experience to tally by. The boy's heart beat for poor blind humanity; and perhaps, after all, the higher-ups did not know how wrong things were, just as the cannery owner's daughter, lying in the cushions of her rumbling victoria with its silver-clanking high-steppers, could not possibly have dreamed of the conditions in the converted stable cannery.

So he founded his early and persistent hopes upon the latent nobilities he felt were leaven in the human of all classes. These classes should be got together. He groped for the best way of helping. The spreading of Socialism was the best solution that presented as he reared in protest against the injustice of life—and of nature, too: never did he cease to marvel at the slight consideration of nature toward her children. There seemed to be so much wrong all down the line. Justice appealed as such a simple thing, if only everybody could agree on ways and means. Why could not every one perceive what was right and what wrong? Surely, any veriest boob could see that it was not fair or even sensible for an unformed child of school age, or an invalid female of whatsoever age, to be obliged to do hard work for bread and meat! It was worth fighting for, to try to bring things right. He would do his part in showing them what he had found. But why should he, particularly he, who was so very busy, have to do the fighting? Why were not those with leisure and money doing the work of balancing things? Why could not they see for themselves, without being shown? And, worse, he found that some who were convinced, actually took the opposite tack, and fought against the obvious right. It was not as if the down-and-outs he had known had originated from the slums. Quite the reverse; in his travel he had learned that more often they were drafted from the more sensitive ones, well above the slum class, while many were far above it, and then some. Besides, there ought not to be any slums.

So it should be Socialism for him. "And socialism, when the last word is said," he saw it, "is merely a new economic and political system whereby more men can get food to eat. In short, Socialism is an improved food-getting efficiency." One must have food, and plenty of food, to attain to other kinds of efficiency. From his first socialistic conceptions, there was never anything of the soft-headed genus of humanitarian about the boy. His small feet were rooted in the soil of practicality, the while his young head plotted emancipation of the common man who was his blood-brother under the red banner of democracy. The anarchists made him laugh—every man for himself, and devil take the hind-most; anarchy would abolish law, and mankind could not thrive socially without law and obedience to the same, for the good of the many. He had played ducks and drakes with some pretty good laws himself, laws he had known were fairly just even in his trifling with them. That had been in youth's free prankishness, and in protest against laws that had already been broken over his own back; so he could not take his past evasions too seriously.

Very well, Socialism, as flatly opposed to Anarchism, stood for law, more law, better law, and law enforced as it should be—for everybody, employer and employed, for man, and woman, and child. His old diffidence cropped up, and he did not then or ever like to speak publicly; but he would enter the lists in the holy cause of propaganda for this lofty religion that had come to him.

With eloquent tongue preaching, and eye, rejoicing in the smack of the game that entered into his every activity, slanted on the listening, closing police, he was promptly arrested for street speaking. Thus he scored the first telling notoriety that accompanied bringing his politics into prominence.

And then he, clarion trumpet of law-building Socialism, was contrariously and ignominiously dubbed by the capitalist papers as Anarchist, red-shirt, dynamiter, and what not! He could only foam at the mouth over the impotence of justice and the unfairness of destiny. Oh, well—it was all right; he had expected too much at the beginning. Anyway, he had done something toward waving the sacred blood-red flag of the Brotherhood of Man, and would keep on waving if he died for it!

Jack's efforts on curb and soap-box did not make for any especial popularity with Mr. McChesney, principal of the High School, nor with the teachers; any more than did certain baffling fallacies he introduced into algebraic problems for his own entertainment and their undoing. His general progress was meteoric enough to command their respect and forgiveness, however. Those photographic retinas of his wide eyes, together with an alert brain that missed nothing, and long-pursued omniverous reading, made most of his studies mere play and granted much time for further reading which a half-dozen family-cards helped the old public library furnish him. He has told that it was possible for him to repeat almost word for word a column once gone over, say of a newspaper; but except insofar as it served to facilitate recitations or entertain socially, he soon gave up developing the faculty. "That sort of thing, carried to excess, is a detriment to larger functioning," he once explained me his view. "I made use of it for skimming the cream from pages, as you see me do. Before long, I had fixed the habit of making written notes of details, in order to save my brain for general principles. If one forms and retains principles, the details can be reconstructed easily enough." When Jack London's elder daughter, Joan, entered High School precociously early, remembering his own youth he modified a disapproval he had harbored as to cramming young minds too full and fast:

"If her brain works as rapidly and effortlessly as did mine," he capitulated, "it's all right for her to go ahead this way if she wishes, so long as her body is being properly nourished and cared for. I learned so quickly that I had time on my hands at my school desk, and if I did not have a book handy, I fretted and fumed at the sinful waste of time."

Another interest during his first term was the stimulating one of argument, not only with the instructors but with the members of a club that met under the name of the Henry Clay Debating Society. There he also became acquainted with girls who did their hair high and who wore longer skirts than those of little Haydee. He found himself invited into some of their pleasant and cultured homes, for these young women did not make casual street friends with men. While he oriented himself, he often thought of his wild and woolly past on land and sea. And in the long run of his days, there in Oakland and in more glittering ranks of society about the world, he founded his agreement with Kipling, that "The Colonel's lady and Judy O'Grady are sisters under their skins."

Some of the well-raised maidens' brothers were prone to look askance upon the "Boy Socialist" who was attracting altogether too much unflattering comment about town. But in spite of prejudice, they and their sisters could not fail to admire the arresting personality of the bright, incessant young student, the beauty of whose well-set-up body with its free sailor-shoulders could not be hidden even under ill-fitting, shiny-seamed cloth. Still, I have met one elegant matron who remembers him principally by his "untidy clothes."

He kept them "guessing" every minute by the poignant charm of voice and manner, even if it sometimes lapsed in polish, for it was hard to discern where self-confidence gave place to a suspected clever bluff born of old sensitiveness and timidity; and his adroit tongue was apt to prove a wily snare to their best laid arguments.

But let him once come under the empery of serious thought, and he was transformed into a commanding figure. I have seen Jack London enter a room full of people, wearing that half-diffident smile of lips and eyes that so disarmed them all—just a human boy, all human, all boy—until some question set the keener mechanism of his brain in movement. Instantly! the whole man changed, a mind appeared to take the place of the human personality, a mind sure, insolent with surety, a very autocrat of minds. He impressed the onlooker as removed, set above, exalted over common thought and thing. The usual engaging expectancy of his justly featured face changed into lines of stern imperiousness, the very repose of which seemed to mark him as a consecrated vessel of some austere purpose.

To return: He "dallied with little home clubs wherein were discussed poetry and art and the nuances of grammar." The socialist local kept his wits on razor edge with study and oration upon philosophy, political economy, and politics state and national. He wrote letters to the Oakland *Times, The Item*, and other papers, which were published under leaded titles such as: "Is against single tax; Jack London disagrees with John McLees: claims it will not regulate present difficulties." And again: "Socialistic views on coin. Jack London takes issue with the Populists. Where he thinks them weak. The small capitalists trying to ride on the backs of laborers." When the People's Party in Oakland offered a prize for the best essay written by a pupil of the schools, Jack's was the winner. It was entitled "Direct Legislation through the Initiative and the Referendum," and was given publicity in *The Item*. Two stories, "Old Baldy," and "An Old Soldier's Story," were printed in a magazine, *Evenings at Home*; and a Socialist article in *The Amateur Bohemian.*

As if he had not already assumed enough to wear down that Titan energy which made possible his fame, want of money urged him into an assistant janitorship in the school. That position was an eminently convenient one though it did strain even his breadth of beam and buoyancy of endurance, when added to myriad other tasks and interests.

"Poverty made me hustle," he wrote long afterward, and included this among the items of what he called his "vast good luck"—others being "good health; good brain; good mental and muscular correlation." So he turned his beautiful muscle to stoking the furnace, and his blithe walk to account upon wooden miles traversed in the course of cleansing floors and wainscot and furniture of the educational pile that was a stepping-block to college. Still furthere to eke out his earnings, he kept an eye for unmown lawns and dusty carpets, putting in chance holidays and spare evenings at this kind of exercise, to a further lessening of closely-scaled sleeping hours.

The securing of the janitor work came about through his sister. Soon after entering High School, Jack had noticed that the janitor, Jacob Winkler, seemed to have more duties than a veteran of the Sixties could well accomplish. He had once been the Commander of Lyon Post Number Eight of the G. A. R., and Eliza Shepard simultaneously having been President of the Woman's Auxiliary Relief Corps, Lyon Post, Department of California and Nevada, Jack went to her. In his behalf she manipulated such strings as she could, and despite her brother's political leanings, got him the berth. It was slyly whispered that Winkler's advancement to a "better and easier place" in another school was coincidentally an expression of the School Board's disapproval at the appointment of the handsome young firebrand in unmodish garments over the head of a boy previously named. Years later, after delivering a lecture on Socialism at the old Dietz Opera House in Oakland, Jack was approached by the selfsame Jacob Winkler, who wrung his hand with the assurance of his warm sympathy with the Cause.

To his daughter entering High School, again Jack wrote, in order to circumvent possible ill-advised snobbery due to his renown, adjuring her never to forget that her daddy once swept the very woodwork upon which she was now treading.

One afternoon, to her stepdaughter Jessie Shepard—she with whom Jack had played piano duets at school and church concerts in earlier East Oakland years—Eliza declared:

"There! I know I've just seen that girl Jack's been raving about lately, for she exactly fits his descriptions. She's a pretty little wisp of a thing—big blue eyes, hair yellow as spun gold—you know, the perfect blonde. Pale, though, and looks delicate. She was all tricked out in fluffy white things, with a wonderful picture-hat, and had an English bull-pup on a chain—and she was laughing at the way it was leading *her* . . . I know she's the girl!'

(The occasion of Eliza's introduction to the young lady, however, was somewhat undignified, if gallant. Jack had taken the Lily rowing upon the estuary. Anchored off the Derby Lumber Yards, while she read aloud he fell asleep in the bottom of the boat. He awoke to find the tide had ebbed until they were high and dry; and so, removing his footwear, he "packed" his friend through the oily ooze to the shore, where Eliza met them.)

Eliza had made no mistake. It was she, Jack's Lily Maid of Britain. He thought of her as the Lily Maid, although he had never read "Idyls of the King." And she might have hailed from Astolat or any other romantic hamlet in her English isle, for all he knew or cared. In the exquisiteness of her appeal she was the Haydee of his riper youth, a patrician Haydee, imperious of homage in her dainty femininity, and he was all a-fevered to compass the ways of chivalry that would command her smile and the touch of her well-groomed white hands. He acknowledged no frailty of chin or of that pale profile against the Rembrandt velvet brim she wore. Frailty, in her, was delicacy. She seemed set apart from all the other girls in the Henry Clay Society—so lofty-cool sweet, so superior, so spirituelle compared with his rougher masculine clay. It was her complementing unlikeness to him, in whatsoever the unlikeness consisted, that made him lift worshiping eyes to her fairness, white woman of his own breed, clay of his clay, though clay sublimated.

Her brother had invited him to dinner. In her home he found no snobbery, no slanting glances at his well-worn ready-made suit that pulled into wrinkles across swelling muscle of shoulder and back—only helpfulness and a likable courtesy. They were real people, he decided, the sort he had dreamed about in his aspiring ideals. Before he had grown intimate enough to pit his mind against their minds, he betrayed some awkwardness, especially when it turned out that the daughter of the house was in the University. The experience began in pleased wonderment, for little did he credit any sense which might have whispered that he himself was of closer-fibered integrity than she or her family, more subtly fine than any woman he had yet gazed upon or perhaps should ever meet. He adored her culture and herself who guided him so sympathetically to the books she loved, who opened for him sublime gates to a higher world of poetry and art. He was wrapped in a new gladsomeness of existence that kept him company while he dusted, swept, and scrubbed the big schoolhouse or beat germ-laden breadths of brussels and monstrously floral carpeting in obscure back yards.

When there showed weaknesses or thinnesses of quality he had glamored as almost virtues in her porcelain delicateness, he still brushed them lightly aside; they should not be estimated as faults, but rather components of a temperamental daintiness—somewhat in the way certain tiny pellets and potions out of slender vials seemed part of her fragility. Why, maybe she was right—he was eager to grant when they had clashed, as clash they did—and he, from his mere clayness, coarsely in error. Thus he felt his tentative way into the labyrinths of culture, from the niceties of table etiquette to a mental etiquette he presently hesitated to employ, sensing its restrictedness.

Meantime the Lily Maid's drawing room was his oasis of refinement where intellectual converse, or so it then appeared to him, with well-bred deportment was carried on in modulated tones. Here he laved his thirsting soul in the best poetry, and was at liberty to take away with him any book he wished. He fell deeply interested in the science of chess, playing with the Lily's brother, though he noticed it was hard to concentrate if his lady were near. She and he were as different as the poles and their very difference charged the atmosphere with sparks of living fire. She could not have told why she vibrated so thrillingly in the presence of this unconventional boy who was apt, in any moment of mental excitation, to throw to the winds the example set him of gentler conduct, and "talk with his hands," rumple wildly his adorable sun-gilded curls and fling himself about all over the place. And only too often he was showing a tendency to flout with merry tongue and baffling, teasing eyes, her most cherished ikons that she had chiseled as changeless deities. But the sheer inexplicableness of his magnetic attraction preserved its charm, and she ceased from troubling to reason "about it and about," but gave herself true womanly to her due of the palpitant sweetness of loving, blushing herself warm with the secret and unmaidenly desire to lay her two hands about that muscular tanned neck which in its smooth round shortness was like a tender baby's, notwithstanding its power.

How distant glimmered the days and deeds of the old waterfront and river life. Occasionally Jack ran into one or another of the men, and these could detect no alteration in his breezy comradeliness, although he confessed to having "cut out the booze, you fellows—water-wagon for me now—got too much to do; no, not even one!" For a year and a half on end, he never took a drink. Drink did not enter his mind. A different thirst had taken hold, a purely mental appetite. With his studies, janitor-duties, and "innocent amusements such as chess," he had no moment for unprofitable idiling in saloon society. Such was the passion of his exploration into the new world he had entered, that the former destructive one held no inducements even to trifle on its margin. In fact, the only public-house threshold he stepped across was that of The Last Chance, and this to solicit a loan from the ready friendliness of Johnny Heinold, against payday for janitor-work. Not a single drink did he take to "wet the transaction." Heinold was an understanding man; and the ringing gold eagle Jack borrowed on several occasions was the only article that passed across the reflecting polish of the bar into the hand of the resolute disciple of concentration upon large issues.

The dreams of his father and mother, that made them invest in irresponsible "securities," knew no abate as the years waxed. The money went somewhere—"God only knows where," Jack and Eliza would disclaim all comprehension. To the Lily Maid, referring to High School struggles, in 1898 Jack in a fit of despondency wrote:

"Do you know what I suffered during that High School and University period? The imps of hell would have wept had they been with me. Does any one know? Can any one know? Oh the hours I have eaten out my heart in bitterness! You say Duty? I fought it off for two long years without cessation, and I am glad. You knew me before those two years—did they do me any good?"

Excess of application is an exhausting process, and Jack nearly broke beneath the load, added to the nerve-strain of inadequate sleep and financial cramp. At the end of a year he sat down by himself and mulled his progress and prospects. There were two full years of High School yet to go before he could be graduated into the first of four long years at college. Six years!—and he was close upon twenty. It couldn't be done. He must devise a short cut. An obvious drollery occurred to him—that fate should matriculate certain hare-brained, financially carefree and equally uncaring fellows into the university; while for himself, with a self-recognized serious future at stake, the way was made so difficult. But he wasted no time in repining, for he must be up and doing.

He had heard of a "cramming joint" over in Alameda, Anderson's I think he said it was, that bridged the spread-out years of High School. Unfortunately, it was an expensive academy, and where was the money to come from for the advance fee? Eliza—but could she spare so much at one time? She had multifarious uses for the money she earned in partnership with her husband. He would find out. She did have the needed amount, and was glad he had come to her.

Jack bade farewell to his classmen and women who were going into Junior High School without him, and daily pedaled his wheel back and forth over the Webster Street bridge to Alameda, too introspective to grant more than a reminiscent glance to the passing show of the pictureful estuary he spanned.

He began in the senior class of this "prep" school, "scheduled to graduate right into the university at the end of four months, thus saving two years." In other words, he had a third of a year in which to do the final two years' work of High School. Night and day he crammed for five weeks. And then, out of a clear sky, a curious and hurtful blow fell. The reason was that his speed had become a matter of dissatisfaction in the classes, and it would raise a scandal for any preparatory establishment to permit a student to enter college who had annihilated two years' learning in twelve weeks. The master of the academy said he was sorry to lose so splendid a pupil, but the universities were growing more severe in their accrediting of prep schools, and he had to consider the reputation of his own.

The shock to Jack was not dissimilar to that inflicted by the city visitor to the little old Alhambra at Livermore. But he was proud and angry now, and departed without a word. His face in such crisis, when recourse was out of the question, was masked with a baffling sweetness, a trifle pale, the pain so withdrawn behind quiet unflinching eyes that an onlooker was conscious of it only after he had passed from sight.

Eliza's money was paid back intact, and the boy shut himself in the den, where without laboratories or coaching of any sort he dug and clawed with renewed ferocity into chemical formulas and simultaneous quadratic equations, so as to be ready for the entrance examinations at Berkeley. His vitality was taxed almost to bursting. His muscles twitched as once before they had nearly twitched into St. Vitus' dance. Even those dependable sailor-eyes wavered and quivered and saw jumbled spots, but as always through life, he won out.

Twelve weeks at nineteen hours a day, with rare moments off, he maintained the killing pace. Reviewing the period, he thought that he may have been a bit "dotty" toward the last, for he caught himself believing he had unearthed the formula for squaring the circle, though he would defer advertising the fact until he had passed the exams that were to put him inside the college portals. When the day of handing in his papers had come and gone, he collapsed with brain-fag, at least to a degree where he "didn't want to see a book . . . or to think nor to lay eyes on anybody who was liable to think," too utterly tired to be even interested in waiting to learn the report on his examination sheets.

The next he knew he was drifting upon a morning ebb in a loaned Whitehall boat, toward the great free medicine of that island sea beloved of all his years. Quintessential seaman that he was, his ills fell from him when the clean white spritsail sphered in the outside breeze. I have had to ask about that canvas—whether it was a spritsail or a leg o'mutton. One friend who had sailed with him, tells me either canvas is used in a Whitehall, but adds: "Jack always liked a spritsail." So much for the seaman who may read.

The first of the flood up the main bay set him fairly on his course into the San Pablo waters, where Carquinez Straits were ripping against the incoming tide; and now the released burner of daylight and candlewick sang hail and good-by to this and that reminding landmark, left astern in his white flight. The sea was up and the wind was whistling and he would keep right on across Suisun Bay and up the San Joaquin. Nothing could stop him except a drop in the wind in league with turn of tide—when he could anchor or tie up to the river-edge tules, songful with blackbirds.

As Benicia grew larger on the port bow, he got to thinking of Young Scratch and his dreadful death that in this very town had stretched out the giant shoulders for the last sleep. He wondered were any of the old Patrol crowd there now. It seemed as if he had been upon another planet a weary space in eternity, and had heard no tidings of the good comrades of other aeons. What was the matter with stopping off for an hour or two and hunting them up? The wind showed no sign of easing, and he could resume the drive and surge through the smoking combers he wotted of in Suisun Bay. And what he needed was an old-fashioned glass of whiskey. For once it would do him nothing but good to invite a mild jingle—you know, just to let down tension after that awful overdraft of study he wanted to forget. Besides, he was close to twenty now, and not an infant blind to consequences.

By the time he had opened the bight of Turner's Shipyard, the notion of the drink had intensified into a real desire—the first instance of such in his not unbibulous youth. As his Whitehall rounded the old *Solano*'s long wharf, he grinned at the recollection of his suicidal death-chant on that inebriate midnight in the not so long ago, and surged along abreast of the patch of tules and the clustering fishermen's arks" where he had cronied and reveled deep with the bunch. Lord! Lord! what a lot he had seen and done since then. How could any man work always at one job?

He sailed in, made fast, and poked about among the arks. Good it was to find them there, all the survivors of the "old guard," and gladdest of all to welcome him, Charley Le Grant himself, who positively embraced his old friend, assisted by a capacious and motherly wife. And when Charley hit across the railroad tracks for Jorgenson's Saloon of dizzy memory, Jack yelled gaily after, "No beer for me this time, Kid! Whiskey's my tea for this afternoon!"

Quite deliberately, with purpose throughout, Jack proceeded on a thoroughgoing "jag," drinking every treat and his own treats in return. Many old acquaintances dropped in, among them Clem, once partner of Young Nelson of the unreefed *Reindeer*, and Jack listened, weeping, in the too-sudden slackening of his nerve-cords, to the tragic account of the violent passing of his Berserker friend. There were sorry tales of other friends who had passed or even worse. "Nearly all my oyster-pirate comrades are long since hanged, shot, drowned, killed by disease, or are spending their declining years in prison," he once pointed what he insisted was his own good luck in escaping disaster.

While Jack held high jubilee with the old "push," Charley went out and worked hard shifting the Whitehall outfit into a roomy Columbia River salmon boat that *was* a boat, and stretched boom and sprit scandalously for such a breezy day; but Le Grant knew his friend "could sail as long as he could see." No urging succeeded in staying the migrating bird over night, not within hearing of the clash and slash of the upstanding seas of that fierce strait-confined run-out which hurled against the brave west wind now filling his ears with its shouting. And this time the receding tule-marsh echoed to a different music from his funeral song of years gone, as now he voiced unmeasured disdain for the bitted elements and all books and institutions of learning. Together with maudlin spoutings on higher mathematics, economics, philosophy and art, he rendered such airs of his riotous, swashbuckling memories as "Black Lulu," "I Wisht I was a Little Bird, Little Bird," and a dozen more, including a rare medley of sea chanteys.

Much fun he had in later years, attempting the old ditties for my benefit, two fingers to his temple, or vertically on his scalp-lock—a little mannerism when cudgeling memory under embarrassment. The verse which came easiest was something as follows:

"O treat my daughter kind-i-ly,
And keep her safe from harm;
And I will leave you
My house, my farm, and -all-the-little
chickens in the garden."

The pulse of his life roared like a gale in the rigging. He nearly sailed the salmon boat under in his renewed enthusiasm of battling with wave and wind. When at even-tide, sobered with the beauty of the lagoon-like river delta and the velvet rose and fawn of the Montezuma Hills across a pearl-gray flood, he laid alongside a friendly potato sloop at Antioch, above Black Diamond, he was kneedeep in sloshing, washing brine. And his was a glorious sharp appetite for black bass fried in olive oil, meaty stew redolent of fresh garlic, and crusty Italian loaf that taxed his precious "front plate" near to cracking. Aboard the sloop, in a dry bunk that was pressed upon him, he and the boys "lay and smoked and yarned of old days, while overhead the wind screamed through the rigging and taut halyards drummed against the mast.

With his unexcelled resiliency of brain and body tissue, a week of cruising in the staunch salmon boat restored him to where the fearful toll he had exacted of himself for a score of months was as if it had

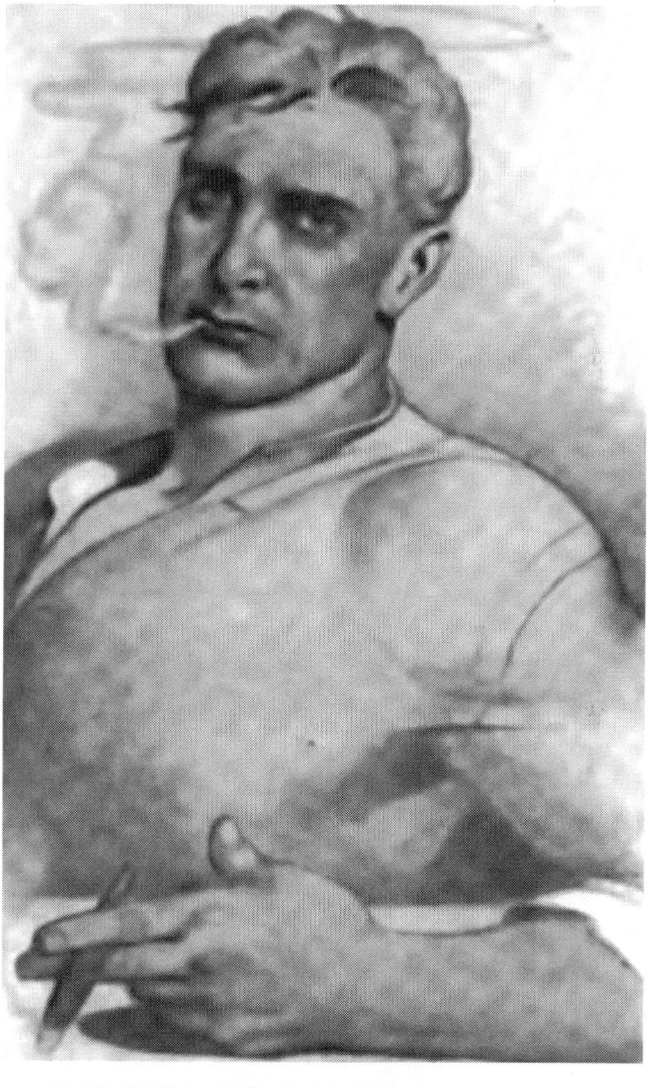

CAPTAIN LARSEN WONDERS ABOUT THINGS

"I evolved this face from the marvellous description of it.
Here's to you—Jack!" O. C.

never been, or so it seemed. Who is to prove that supernormal effort does not weaken the whole structure of a growing lad?

That one revel he had permitted himself was the last; but the determination to keep it so cost him much in that he must avoid looking up any more old chums. That was the perfect hell of sobriety—just the live, "breedy, chesty" men one wanted to mingle with as a tonic for brain-fag were the ones with whom it was necessary to practise this injurious custom. So he held, all his student days, to an almost puritanical abstemiousness, through expediency coupled with want of desire when among people who were strangers to alcohol.

CHAPTER XIV

AT THE UNIVERSITY OF CALIFORNIA

1896-7

AND here he was, in the fall of 1896, after all his struggling, two years ahead of his High School classmates, at last "a college man," fellow to the Lily Maid's brother, and James Hopper, and a Henry Clay Club friend, Fred Jacobs, with others he had known previously, albeit they were Juniors and he but a verdant "Freshie." High time, too, for in January he would be twenty-one, though to save his soul he could not figure how the four years were to be managed on the slim and uncertain income he had little leisure to pick up outside of study and lecture and reading hours. But he was a-thrill with having won to a paramount desire. It was worth all the striving and scrimping.

James Hopper, '98, and Jack met one day on the Campus, for the first time, knowingly, since they had played marbles, and scrapped together in the Cole Grammar. Mr. Hopper's notes on the meeting, written the day after his friend's death, compose one of the most sympathetic pictures I know upon the radiant subject; and from them I draw a few lights:

"He possessed already then a certain vague reputation among us boys as one who had done man things and wild things and romantic things.... His latest exploit—that of passing the University entrance examinations after three months vigorous cramming while stoking the furnace of the Oakland High School—was in many mouths. His already was a colorful personality, and when the boy who had been telling me about him said suddenly: 'There he is, see? Coming down the steps,' I moved up and 'braced' him.

"But—but—well, I hate to say it. Perhaps if I explain carefully people will understand. You see, he was a newly-entered freshman . . . and I was a full-fledged junior, and on the football team and editor of the *Occident*, also holding a well-defined place in a very regular organization—a bit of a bourgeois prig, in fact. So that when I went to Jack London, I did so—God forgive me—thinking consciously how nice and democratic this was of me!

"If he felt my condescension—and he must have, for under his sturdiness ran a fine net of fine nerves—he did not show it. I may say right here that the dominating quality of Jack London's character was bigness. 'Attend to the big things and let the little things go'—if he ever made for himself a motto it must have been that. He let the little things go that time, and met my advance with an open frankness that was like a flood of sunshine.

"Sunshine—the word leaps of itself to the end of my pen. . . . He had a curly mop of hair which seemed spun of its gold; his strong neck, with a loose, low, soft shirt, was bronzed with it; and his eyes were like a sunlit sea. His clothes were flappy and careless; the forecastle had left a suspicion of a roll in his broad shoulders;"—and here Mr. Hopper appreciates the notable beauty of the man: "he was a strange combination of Scandinavian sailor and Greek god, made altogether boyish and lovable by the lack of two front teeth, lost cheerfully somewhere in a fight."

As for Jack's irrepressible enthusiasm: "He was full of gigantic plans—just as, indeed, I was to find him always whenever I came upon him later in life. . . . He was going to take all the courses in English, all of them, nothing less. Also, of course, he meant to take most of the courses in the natural sciences, many in history, and bite a respectable chunk out of the philosophies.

"And as he unfolded his intentions to me, there in the sun in front of North Hall, radiating himself at least as much light and warmth as the sun, I, all of twenty years old and hence disillusioned, frozen (lightly frozen) in a gentle pessimism, polished with a worldly skepticism, I listened to him and smiled, and tried to make my smile just a bit ironical and withal kindly. You see, I had taken some of the courses of which he was going to take all, and I found there—well, not all I had sought. Three or four times I came near telling him that. But his enthusiasm was so intrepid, so young and touching, so pure and vibrant—that I didn't have the heart."

Jack concentrated especially upon the English branches and biological sciences, and took other things by the way, one of them

French; but I retain the impression from a reference he made to me that for some reason he did not continue long with the latter "extra." Probably, in the super-urgency of his state, he weeded it as a nonessential if graceful perquisite toward the English literature he felt he was to father into being. In fact, he never seems to have laid stress upon the value of etymological intricacies. Rather the reverse, it strikes me, as I recall uncompromising utterances on the wisdom of eliminating Latin and Greek and Sanskrit and what not, made to his own offspring and to other youth of both sexes who flocked in quest of advice for the shortest cut to a career of letters. This is the more surprising because of his strong predisposition toward investigating basic components of whatsoever interested him—from subduing to saddle or harness an incorrigible "outlaw," to overcoming on the high sea loftier mathematics of navigation seldom disturbed from musty repose by professional masters, or in possessing himself of the colorful why and wherefore of opals bought in the Antipodes for his wife.

For all it had absorbed, his brain was as a perpetual dry sponge—impossible of saturation in its myriad folds. The instruction he sat under, far from appeasing, impelled him to the library, where he read volume after volume, each leading indefinitely on to other volumes over and above recommended collateral reading. "I can do the work quicker than they can teach me," he once put into the mouth of an autobiographical character; and I have heard him seriously hold forth that the method and content of university education were of slight benefit to him. This estimate and library cramming were the chiefest bestowments of the university upon his particular ego. His abiding belief was that he could have done as well without those months of attendance. To be sure, he did not always try to discourage others from seeking their training in this way; but in his own case he claimed he had "succeeded in spite of it, rather than because of it," what of the to him untenable formalizing process upon "the wheel of university subservience to the ruling class," as he wrote his daughter. And of course he came to respect Experience as the Teacher of Teachers.

The following exploit has been told, as instance of Jack's clearheadedness and daring: The college advertised for a steeplejack to furbish up the flagpole which stood midcenter of the campus. Weeks elapsed, and none volunteered. Then, one morning, students on the way to early classes were amazed to behold their curly-headed freshman slowly working his way earthward from the lofty golden ball, meanwhile plying a paintbrush dipped in the pail on his left arm. He had grown impatient at the sight of the weather-soiled eyesore on his campus, and with the breed of youth that had not learned to "shinny" heights. There was a norther blowing, but his experience as sailor made the work real play—it felt good to wrap his long-unaccustomed legs about the swaying land-mast that had once been a storm-swept living pine, like the sturdy stick of the *Sophie Sutherland*, and to feel the high breeze humming through his hair. When the thing was done to his taste, he rolled his paint-soaked overalls in a bundle, and unlimbered his cramped legs quick-stepping to classrooms.

In the month of his twenty-first birthday, the first half of the freshman year at his back, despite the growing if grudged apprehension that college was not yielding quite all he had hoped of it, Jack went about preparation for the second term. And if it had not been that he was unable to spare enough time from study to coin the wherewithal for a living, he would doubtless have seen through at least the one year of university work before finally discarding it as to him a telic nonessential.

Hunched over the inky, ashy table in his den, with might and main he cut loose and embarked upon the career of fiction he had chosen. I have heard him laugh to recall the madness of desire to arrive at a style that would serve his ends. "Never was there such a creative fever as mine from which the patient escaped fatal results. . . . I wrote everything—ponderous essays, scientific and sociological, short stories, humorous verse,"—and all other metrical and irregular poetic matter from triolet to lugubrious blank verse and "elephantine epic in Spenserian stanza." Steadily day by day he composed at the rate of fifteen hours out of the twenty-four.

During these weeks of nerve-wracking application, in his brief family contacts Jack was about as soothing a housemate as a ruffled porcupine, and irascible at the racket of his sister Ida's two-year-old boy, whom Flora was tending for a consideration while its mother, now separated from her husband, went out to work. But at last, neat sheaves of manuscript were mailed with importance by the expectant author to eastern editors, who made use of Jack's return stamps with a celerity that modified his hot confidence to a not uncheerful hope. Not one single line of all the output of devoted days and nights elicted one single line of approbation from the stony-hearted men who, tilted in swivel chairs back in New York, Boston, and Philadelphia, controlled the food supply of literary aspirants. It was incredible. He wondered what an editor really was like. He had never seen one and felt a colossal awe that was in inverse ratio to the regard with which only too soon he began to favor the phenomena of their own disappointed intellects.

Almost his only recreation was an occasional game of chess at the Lily Maid's house. Although he continued resolutely to pluck his deportment and tongue of roughnesses in her presence, he could not be "good" *all* the time, and out of immediate earshot relaxed vigilance. For example, one afternoon, he was deep in a game with her brother in the garden. Oversure, Jack suddenly realized as the other quietly reached for the next move, that he had tripped in his calculation, and faced disaster. Tipping back in his chair, he coolly and dispassionately gave unhurried vent to a selection of eight words, choice, succinct, most unsaintliest of his unsaintly sea-and-road expletive.

As the last syllable issued close-clipped but deliberate from betwixt his teeth, a horrible certainty overtook him that the two men of them were not alone. A queer smothering look spread upon his opponent's face, in which embarrassment struggled with mirth. Then all doubt vanished as a stray zephyr from behind Jack wafted a wisp of white mull within eye-tail vision. Let us drop the curtain as the balancing front-legs of his chair come slowly to the grass.

What really hurt most, though, in this blank failure of immediate victory over grateful magazine staffs, was the associated failure to shower upon his father the shining gold returns; for he had allowed this beloved and patient friend of all his singular fortunes to feed him, which had been done with a willingness that John could ill afford, and in natural expectation of the needed reimbursement.

One ray of light that always struck athwart Jack s darkest hours, was his father's quiet, persistent faith in him. "Don't you worry about Jack, mama," he would say to his wife. "He'll win out, I tell you—he was built to win, and nothing can stop him from winning, nothing at all," firmly he met Jack's own dependence upon his ability to pull through in the big way.

At first appalled by untempered condemnation from every invaded sanctum on the Atlantic coast, coldly expressed by prompt rejection slips, the author then reexamined his prolific pages. This was not done alone in appraisal of their quaint appearance resulting from his brother-in-law's old "boiler factory" that typed only in capital letters, but from the severest critical standpoint of rhetorical construction; and finally, and what should be of gravest importance, thought and subject matter that would be acceptable to panderers of a misguided public. He could not help laughing at the first consideration—the unrelieved capitals were weird enough to put the most amiable editor in panic fear of losing his eyes and reason. As for the other two, Jack suddenly came to see a lengthening road of endeavor to be traversed ere he could hope to command attention. He thought of the easy money earned from that prize-story in the San Francisco *Call*, but realized that he had won out then by an unvarnished narrative of events eye-witnessed; whereas, in his present difficulty, he had tried to be erudite, to infuse his own subjective processes, without sufficient preparation. He was fair and modest enough to feel shame that he had ever had the nerve to try putting over such amateurish practice-stuff upon men old in the game. He would not again be so hasty in his judgment of them.

On the other hand, no acknowledged rawness could shake a divine trust in himself, for he knew his thinking and his writing were not all worthless. He refused to be discouraged. Success was merely delayed for further preparation, and he went about it, reading and studying mightily. But all too soon there was no blinking that things could not go on this way. John London, while uncomplaining, was not well—that war-ravaged lung gave increasing trouble; and the mother was oppressed by temperamental foreboding. Jack surrendered to pressure of necessity and innate affection, and capitulated to manual labor, little as he favored it since he had harnessed his wagon to a star. He must eventually make his brain pay, and pay well. Others did it; he must and would do it. Therefore it was an aching distress to waste precious, fleeting time for the small wages to be gleaned by bodily strain—all for the want of a few niggardly dollars that the predatory rich could so easily spare and never miss. Notwithstanding, he asked no alms of them. Fair field and no favor for him—no matter how unfair he esteemed the race to be.

A young man of his acquaintance, an expert launderer who needed an assistant, opened the way to a job in the country—oddly enough, down on the "Peninsula," not many miles from the old San Mateo County ranch. This unfamiliar work was in the model steam laundry of a military school—Belmont Academy; and for "long sizzling weeks," all day and part of many a night of rest for all the institution except these two, Jack sweated as laundryman for the munificent sum of thirty dollars per month. Just the same, it was a sort of vicarious pleasure to work hard, when the prize hung high, at even so uncongenial a shift as cleansing other people's dirty linen. Indeed, for all that his ideal of university value had been partially undermined, it was of the laundry experience that he wrote: "This was the only time that I worked because I loved it," in view of continuing at college. When he should have earned enough money to go on, he would have to shorten time in making up what he had lost by enforced absence from the classes of 1900.

As summer came on, the space in eternity consumed ironing the white ducks of the students nearly broke him body and spirit. So heavy was the work that even the up-to-date appointments of the laundry and the combined expertness of the two boys in cutting out waste motion scarce made possible the handling of it. "What I don't know about mangling, and handwork, bluing and 'fancy starch'—which was what we called the faculty's wives' thin waists and fine embroidered and lace-trimmed linen—would make you weep," Jack told me; "and so help me God, no circumstances could ever make me touch an iron again if I died for it! The only ray of fun we two sweating fools got out of the whole brutal toil was a silly vengeance we took on all creatures of unearned luxury. This was by starching stiff the dainty linen of the women—and of course the comicalest appeal of the naughty prank was that we could securely depend upon their hide-bound conventional modesties to seal their lips from complaint against us. Lord, Lord, when I think of the boards we made of those garments . . . "he exploded into a wicked giggle.

The worst of this work-orgy, as with former harmful outlay of strength for an insufficient living-wage, was that no snap was left in him to respond to the trunkful of books he had begged and borrowed, and which formed his main luggage. By the deferred bedtime he was so played out that try as he might his eyelids would not stay propped open. He would drop asleep from exhaustion, cigarette on relaxed lips, until some profound falling sensation, or singeing forelock or insistence of the electric light burning through closed lids, jumped him awake. Then he bestirred to fasten again upon the blurring print, and repeated the performance of falling unconscious a couple of times—habit of long-enforced concentration—until finally, with a swearing sigh, he laid down the futile volume, turned off the irritating bulb, plumped into the air with the loosened covers wrapped about him, and sank into dream-driven slumber which was interrupted for the new day's steaming task that began under artificial lighting.

He gave over trying to cram the heavier subjects—biology, jurisprudence, political economy—and substituted history as lighter and more arresting to a drowning attentiveness he could not fix. No use—he would just read the novels; they would hold him awake longer and at the same time guide to what was expected of an author in the manufacture of fiction. This method failing, in blue disgust he threw the books back into the trunk. I know the deep-dented "picture corners" of his mouth that sagged with a pathos he could not hide from his own soul and the smolder of hurt and disillusion that darkened the depths of his tired eyes. Why were things made so difficult for a fellow who really wanted to get ahead?

Damn it all! It was the same old fight over again—the slippery rock wall that reared before a man who submitted everlastingly to manual labor. It was a long time since he had coal-shoveled himself into a state of cool irresponsibility on the Road. Meanwhile money and time had been spent upon equipping himself for a profession . . . but now look at him!—once more a stupid human animal bound to longer hours than any horse, too wearied to exert his superior intelligence for compensations much above those of the horse.

But he was no quitter. His time would come. Better and better socialist all this made him. And there should be no more vagabondage, he thought, though the rosy hands of adventure waved temptingly toward the wide free highway that he knew slanted ever downward. He must stick it out, earn enough to tide over another period of writing-practice and digging which would fit him to produce that which should make editors sit up and take notice.

Then one day it occurred to him that no alleged perfection of labor-saving apparatus but could be questioned and improved upon. Here was tonic for one's inventive ideas that might lighten the back-breaking, torrid afternoons of ironing or running articles through the revolving mangle. I wish I had made notes at the time he explained to me his device to relieve some of the more arduous laundry tasks. It was so simple he laughed to think he had not sooner happened upon it. When attached to whatever mechanism it was intended to control, he could regulate it by one foot from the chair where he rested and read, with an occasional eye to the accelerated progress of work theretofore done by hand.

A tyrannical ancestor of my own, no shirker himself and a rabid dissuader of leisure for others, whenever a child of his made bid for praise in the quick accomplishment of a set duty, would sardonically grin: "Well, that's fine, now; and I guess, since you're so smart in saving time, you can do about twice as much to-morrow in the time saved."

Which is by way of illustrating how Jack lost his place, or at least declined to lapse into time-squandering methods. Vaguely I recall his intimating that his superior in the laundry, though rendering a grudged appreciation of the invention, got word of it to whosoever had upper charge of the department, but who seldom meddled so long as there was no complaint about the work turned out.

Either Jack was "fired," or else his logic was too outraged by the demand that he forego this progressive social contribution to mechanics. At any rate, incontinently he left, rode his neglected "bike" to San Jose before wheeling northward for Oakland, and in a large bottle drank confusion to all sightless subservience to stupid custom. The bottle furnished a relaxation that was indulged in by choice—as others take drugs for their ills—before he should bury himself in another sober stretch of hard graft whatever it be. He acknowledged no harmfulness in this day's mellow forgetting, alone under a grand old oak in a pasture with the China-blue valley sky overarching, where he was not even setting an example to weaker brethren. And of course he did not for a moment reckon with any insidious foe that might lurk behind this unusual desire to recuperate *in solitude.* He hated to think what that bottle had cost; but a man must "pay for his fancies," and he had denied himself fancies of all sorts for a long, long time. Indeed, that altogether delightful, comradely jingle in Charley's ark was the sole instance when he had punished the booze since he could clearly remember.

He scorched up to Oakland, and dug himself once more into the den, writing furiously.

CHAPTER XV

INTO KLONDIKE

1897—21st Year

IF Jack London's roving feet had failed to be drawn into the Klondike stampede of 1897, his future audiences would have ceased not from asking why. But of course he could not fail of response to the lure of this golden adventure—accent on adventure. With all the naivete of previous self-justifications when yielding to his passion for boating, the material treasure-trove in itself formed but an adjunct that made all at ease with his conscience.

It was Klondike or bust. But how, *how*, HOW?—he beat at the obstacle poverty. The steamer *Umatilla*, of recent memory, carrying the great jam of mad gold-seekers, was to sail in four days on the irresistible tide of the enterprise. Klondike or bust—oh, he would somehow get to go; but there was not a cent in sight for grub and gear, and his practical sense warned of meager welcome for the unprepared in the bleak Northland.

Two days moved swiftly by, while he hustled about Oakland to find some one reckless enough to grubstake him into the Arctic. He even called upon Joaquin Miller;—block-head! why hadn't it occurred to him sooner! *There* was a man, a true sport who would understand. *Would* he! He had understood so well that when Jack reached the door, the Sweet Singer of the Sierras had already pulled out on his own hook—"The son of a gun!" Jack ruefully appreciated.

As the hours lessened, he grew reckless; he would depend upon strength and luck, and chance the thing, outfit or no outfit. Unavoidably, he had thought of his sister; but this was an expensive undertaking, and she had done much for him of late without his having proved he could make good. For once he could not bring himself further to burden her.

Yet it was from her household that help emanated, although from an unanticipated member. Jack was stricken dumb when his brother-in-law fell as sudden and hopeless—or hopeful—victim to the gold-fever as any youngster in his unlicked teens, boldly announcing his own intention of Klondike or bust. He furthermore declared that if Jack would trade the benefit of his youth and experience and see him through, he should be grubstaked in partnership. Jack, with shrewd judgment born of bedding with hardship by land and sea, was markedly unenthusiastic in view of the slender and ailing veteran's age and other disqualifications. Still, he was up against a disappointment he could not brook; it was Klondike or bust, and he could ill balk at such last-moment opportunity. Upon the instant he decided, as was his habit in crises.

The elder man's generosity of a grubstake consisted in sinking his own earnings of the firm of Shepard & Company, along with his wife-partner's in addition to the hundreds she promptly realized by mortgaging the home, which was her own. Then, having bowed her sensible head to the impregnable fusion of their juvenile insanity—"both as crazy as loons, one no worse than the other!"—she abetted with might and main. Since they were minded to make idiots of themselves, they should have the best outfit that could be purchased with money; moreover, she would shop with them to see that it was complete in every detail. And the following year her brother was able happily to assure her that nothing to beat it went over Chilcoot that fall of 1897.

Jack shot back across Lake Merritt bridge on his wheel, to start rustling the books he would not sail without, Eliza and her husband to meet him in town a little later. On the way, Captain Shepard's senile excitement precipitated a heart-attack that brought on a deadly faint. The conductor of the street car helped Eliza lay him on a lawn, and some passerby ran for a doctor, who ordered the patient to bed for two weeks. But next morning he was up and away to San Francisco, with his wife and Jack on either side supporting him through a shopping tour that revived all their spirits.

Such a buying jamboree Jack had never enjoyed. Eliza's hundreds flowed like water: fur-lined coats, fur caps, heavy high boots, thick mittens; and red-flannel shirts and underdrawers of the warmest quality—so warm that Jack had to shed his outer garments packing over Chilcoot Pass, and blossom against the snow a scarlet admiration to

Indian and squaw. The brace of gold-seekers agreed upon the advisability of raw materials for the construction of dog-sleds—runners, thongs, and tools. The average outfit of the Klondiker also must include a year's supply of grub, mining implements, tents, blankets, "Klondike stoves," everything requisite to maintain life, build boats and cabins. Jack's dunnage alone weighed nearly 2,000 pounds.

I have no way of knowing how the Lily Maid regarded this latest goose-chase of her strange swain who refused to forfeit the independence of his soul for sweet love or pity or any other meek consideration. There is no record of protest; but if her mother's letter to Jack is any criterion of the girl's opinion, it shows the reverse of a high estimate of his wisdom. I cannot refrain from quoting the cheerful document—and she called him John:

" July 22nd, 1897.

"Dear John:

"We have just received your letter with the awful news that you are about to start for Alaska. Oh, dear John, do be persuaded to give up the idea for we feel certain that you are going to meet your death and we shall never see you again. What your object can be in going we cannot even think, but we feel as though we should never see you again. John, do give up the thought for you will never come back again, never. Your Father and Mother must be nearly crazed over it. Now, even at the eleventh hour, dear John, do change your mind and stay. With lots of love to all and hoping to hear better news, I remain, your sincere friend."

The day following the buying orgy, July 25, 1897, two hours late because of the heavy traffic, the *Umatilla* carried the ill-assorted pair away through the Golden Gate and set her northwesterly course. Aside from a feeble and vaporing "sidekicker," there was but one drawback to Jack's perfection of bliss—his father's condition, which was very poorly. He had lain for weeks in what proved his death-bed several months later. With unshed tears in the patient gray eyes, he had even begged Jack to take him along; he could go into Alaska on a sled as well as not—"Why, if you could only get me up there in the snows, Jack, I'd get strong right off." And Jack with a sob in his voice cried to Eliza: "God!—if I could only take him!"

They never saw each other again, those two good pals. By the first mail in after the spring thaw of '98, word came to Jack of John

"THE LAKE THAT JACK BUILT"

Mrs. London on Horseback

London's death on October 15, and how to the last he had hoped that he might be spared to see Jack come home triumphant from the gold-fields. Faith in his boy still burned with unwavering flame. "He'll come out all right, you watch his smoke," he would beam with quiet surety upon doubters; "and come out big, mark my words." After Jack had gone North, his father foretold not once but many times, "Jack is going to make a success out of the Klondike—*whether he digs it out of the grassroots or not.*"

Only in the last fortnight did his mind blur to a hallucination. Before that he bravely held to it that he would soon be up and about. But later on he would beg Eliza to sit the first-night spell with him, since he could depend upon her unsleeping help in that nightly tug-of-war with the man at the other end of the stick. If he could fall to sleep by one o 'clock, before she went home, the danger would be over—the man could not get him, and he could live through till morning; anyway, till Jack came home.

Captain Shepard, after one good stare at Chilcoot Pass, had turned his back on all such rigors, leaving his stuff for Jack to dispose of. Much improved from the vacation, he arrived in Oakland shortly before the death of his wife's father, and resumed his part in the pension-claim work, which during his absence Eliza had borne. And now, out of her own earnings, she paid the bills of her father's funeral.

At Port Townsend, the *Umatilla*'s hordes had been transferred to the steamer *City of Topeka*, which arrived at Juneau on August 2. Forty-two miles farther northwest, they reached the end of their crowded voyage and stretched themselves on the beach at the Indian village of Dyea, a mere cluster of huts above the reach of high tide on the Chilkoot Inlet of Lynn Canal. The party—now swelled to five, for Jack and Captain Shepard had formed a partnership with Fred Thompson, "Jim" Goodman, and one Merritt Sloper—found the beach a shouting bedlam of gold-rushers amid an apparently inextricable dump of ten thousand tons of luggage. Many of the arrivals were like lunatics, fully as responsible as newly headless fowl in this scramble into an unpitying frozen land. (It was in this same Lynn Canal, in 1918, that the steamer *Princess Sophia* foundered, with the loss of all on board—miners and their families coming south for the winter.)

Although a-tingle with his own excitement, a large share of which was from the stirring spectacle on the beach, Jack's level head had counseled speedy withdrawal of himself and his elderly charge from the mass of humans that appeared to be falling over one another. With open eye and ear to every hint from the knowing ones, he applied his faculties to getting hold of the outfit and pushing onward toward the Chilkoot trail. The more he listened, the better he realized that there was no moment to lose if they were not to be left behind all winter in the impending freeze-up. Only the most alert and fittest could obviate such unthinkable misfortune. How his sister's husband could make it through was the question. Not unnaturally the young man was in terror of losing his own chance through the other's insufficiency.

But that night they slept on the Flats five miles above Dyea, at the head of canoe navigation where the Dyea River narrows to a torrent bursting from a snowy canyon, fed by far glaciers. For once Jack was willing to own that he was dead tired. Captain Shepard, of course, was of negligible worth as a draft partner, and Jack, soft from the inactivity of long days on shipboard, ached in every muscle and in his scarified shoulders, from towing their thousands of pounds of belongings upstream.

Every one had been confident, from reports, that the loading uptrail would be done by Indians for sums within reason. Imagine the chagrin, consternation to many, when the Indians, awake to their own idea of a gold-rush, imperturbably demanded thirty cents a pound shoulder-portage for the twenty-eight miles between Dyea Beach, across the Pass to Lake Linderman. Six hundred dollars a ton! Beaten at the outset, vast numbers of the cruelly chilled enthusiasts watched the few physically equipped, born to victory, attack the first stage to Happy Camp. Sheep Camp, some miles upward, was the next stop; thence on, scaling the whole of Chilkoot's tragic trail, along whose margin the weaker ones fell and expired. One sourdough assures me Chilkoot is "the worst trail this side of hell."

It was one of the happiest moments of Jack's life when Captain Shepard of free choice abandoned the venture, and the two parted in good feeling. Now he was quit of encumbrance other than the deadweight of luggage. He has told me how he experimented with adding to and shifting his pack, readjusting straps, and padding the raw-sections of his strong but tender-skinned back and shoulders until he outpacked in honest pounds any white man who made it through to Lake Linderman, and surpassed many an Indian. Indeed, such feat was a boon to the men who could afford Indian assistance to the summit, as could Fred Thompson; for Jack's example put the sly aborigines on their mettle not to be outdone by this puffing, steaming, white human engine in scarlet flannels. I give his own version:

"This last pack into Linderman was three miles. I back-tripped it four times a day, and on each forward trip carried one hundred and fifty pounds. This means that over the worst trails I daily traveled twenty-four miles, twelve of which were under a burden of one hundred and fifty pounds."

The men had to ford swift and icy rivers, and a swamp that some sardonic wit had yclept Pleasant Valley, where the weight of a pack would drive one to the knees in freezing ooze and muck. The earlier stretches of the trail ascended a long mountain slope largely covered with tundra, which did not afford solid footing. This was superseded by sharp and broken shale. Reaching "The Scales," at the actual foot of the steepest aspect of a mountain wall which looked to topple over backward, Jack found himself preparing for the most grinding test of endurance. For sheer as was the terrific rise, it was yet not sheer enough to prevent huge boulders from finding lodgment in the path, which formed serious obstacles. "A man's job" it was, and Jack London could do no other than make good as a real man among real men.

Of all the anecdotes of this bitter climb that he told in my hearing, only one stands out—the incident of a man bearing a great load, who, in sitting down upon a fallen tree to catch breath, had been overweighted and fallen backward, head and shoulders deep in the snow so that he could make no outcry. Jack, plodding painfully upward, happened to glance aside to where his keen eyes saw a pair of feet above the log. In curiosity he turned and backed up to the log where carefully, slowly, lest he be outbalanced, he rested his pack and freed arms and chest of the straps. Then he plucked the victim, red and spluttering with gratitude, out of his unprogressive posture which, though comical, was of extreme danger; for it was by merest chance that any heavily-laden miner, bent only upon topping Chilkoot's rise, should have spied his snow-crusted boot-soles.

At the summit, the young men faced a fierce driving rain, then negotiated a glacier that descended to Crater Lake; after which a chain of small lakes compelled detours over rugged hills, or the hiring of boats, of which they availed themselves. The last lake, however, before reaching Linderman, was shallow alongshore and could be waded, soft deep mud on the bottom adding to the difficulties of travel. Little marvel that Jack London ever afterward eschewed protracted walking. (I think it was Frederick Palmer, writing of the hardships of soldiers on the Flanders front, who said that one who had crossed Chilkoot in the fall of 1897 would have a fairly comprehensive idea of what the Tommies were up against.)

Eight or nine miles up-river from Lake Linderman, where the timber was good, the boys whipsawed their own lumber and in company with another party constructed two boats, *Yukon Belle* and *Belle of the Yukon.* In this capacity Jack and Sloper were in their element, for the latter knew ship-carpentering and building from keel to maintruck. It became the pride of the owners that never were their well-stored cargoes of supplies removed, though they shot every rapid on the perilous route. Jack, ready shoulder-to shoulder in any sort of emergency, was yet especially invaluable when aqueous portions of the way were encountered. He loved to tell the story of how he navigated the infamous Box Canyon and White Horse Rapids, that sank and drowned crew after crew of doomed men.

By unabating zeal the boys kept just ahead of the forbidding freeze-up that set a bar of iron to the progress of the less forehanded. Lakes froze on their flying heels, so slim was the margin. Jack learned what it meant to pit one's raging impotence against the imperturbability of nature. Never a waking moment did they lose, and allowed no more time for sleep than was absolutely required. At the head of Lake Bennett, news from before was of famine, and that the Northwest Mounted Police stationed at the foot of Lake Marsh, where the gold-hunters entered Canadian territory, refused to let past any man not fortified with seven hundred pounds of grub. The rest were sent down river and interned at Dawson.

Their sternest battle was across Lake Le Barge, the freeze-up of which threatened in the gale. Three days they had been thrown back by cresting seas that fell aboard in tinkling ice. On the fourth Jack said: "To-day we've *got* to make it—or we camp here all winter with the others." They almost died at the oars, but "died to live again" and fight on. All night, like driven automatons they pulled, and at daybreak entered the river, with behind them a fast-frozen lake. And their pilot, from what I know of him, I can swear did not realize half his weariness, so elated must he have been to be thus forward—one of the very few who had made it through.

Undaunted, without wasting precious minutes in discussion, the trio pushed on as one man. The blizzard luckily moved into the south, and they ran before it under a huge sail Jack had devised. With the heavy ballast of outfit, he dared to crack on sail Nelson-fashion when moments so counted. Luck was with him when they came to Caribou Crossing, for a shift of wind at the right time sent them humming down the connecting link between Lakes Taggish and Marsh. Nothing could stop them, and Jack, his experienced mittened hands nearly frozen to the tiller he had rigged, held on in high fettle across the menacing Windy Arm, where in a stormy twilight he saw two other boat-loads of men turn over and miserably perish. It was sickening to be unable to lend a hand; but the very law of life in this inimical cold-crystal sphere of the Northland was to keep one's head in just such temptation. And three other souls beside his own depended entirely upon his sailor competence.

Sixty Mile River, really a head reach of the Yukon, flows out of Lake Marsh, its greatest breadth a quarter of a mile. Deep and swift, it suddenly narrows with a curve into Box Canyon, only eighty feet in width, rocky walls towering on either side. The suddenly confined volume of water gathers terrific speed, marked by great boilings and stiffly upthrust waves, and its action against the canyon walls causes the water to rise in a sort of hog-back in the center.

It was owing to a blinding headache, for liquor had been cut out of his calculations except for medicinal use, that Jack had accepted a drink of whiskey before undertaking to shoot the bad water. Tying their boat, *Yukon Belle*, in the eddy above the Box, the four partners walked ahead to investigate, meanwhile consulting a book written by Miner W. Bruce, Alaskan pioneer. They discovered that hundreds were portaging outfits on their backs. "Nothing doing," Jack scorned. If he took the chance and ran through by water, in two minutes they would save two days of severest toil. According to their custom, a vote was called, which was unanimous for the two-minute route. Jack, as captain, placed Merritt Sloper in the bow with a paddle. Fred Thompson and Jim Goodman, confessed landlubbers, sat side by side amidship at the oars. The boat, twenty-seven feet in length, carrying over 5000 pounds in addition to its human freight, did not possess the buoyancy desirable for such an undertaking.

Jack's head whirled from the unwonted alcohol upon an empty stomach, and he caught himself wondering if that head would serve in his need, where again lives hung upon the perfect coordination of his faculties. But the instant the bow swung downstream into the jaws of the Box, and his lashed steering-oar bore against the cork-screwing anarchy of waters, something went cool and calm through him, and he rose to the work. Afraid that the rowers might "catch a crab" or otherwise fumble disastrously, he ordered in the oars. "Then we met it on the fly," and he went on to picture how he caught a passing glimpse of spectators fringing the brink of the cliffs above, and another glimpse of serrated walls dashing by like twin express trains. Then his undivided energy was centered upon keeping atop the racing hogback. The deep-laden boat, instead of mounting the waves, went dead into them. Despite the peril, Jack could not help giggling at poor Sloper, who, just as he let drive for a tremendous stroke, would quite miss the water as the stern fell in a trough, jerking the bow skyward. "But Sloper never lost his grit," he praised.

In a transverse current Jack threw himself against the sweep till it cracked, and Sloper's paddle snapped short off. They nearly filled, yet went flying downstream breakneck, less than two yards from the rocky wall. Another instant, and they took a header through a smoking comber and shot into the whirlpool of the great circular court that widens midway of the Box, thence spilling over into the second half of the race.

Jack and his crew then walked back and brought through the outfit of a man and his wife, a Mr. and Mrs. Ret. That done, they baled out the *Yukon Belle* and essayed two miles of ordinary rapids to the head of the White Horse, passing several of the Box Canyon wrecks in which lives had been lost. Save for a few who had been drowned, no one had tried to run the White Horse in late years; but our quartette looked it over, and then, with an audience of a thousand souls, went down. Jack nearly lost his boat when he tried to buck the whirlpool, not knowing he had come within its coils; and again Sloper had his paddle snap off. When they had reached the friendly eddy below the Rapids, they returned as before, and piloted down the Rets' boat.

Not until October 9, when the Stewart River was reached, did the invincibles halt. I have obtained the date through the courtesy of Mr.

Fred Thompson, of Santa Rosa, who has lent his Diary. On Upper Island, one of two islets off the eastern bank of the Yukon, halfway between the Stewart and Henderson Creek, and eighty miles above Dawson, they set up housekeeping in one of a group of log cabins that had been abandoned by the Bering Sea fur traders. The fact of empty quarters is indicative of Jack and his crowd being among the first over Chilkoot. Lower Island was inhabited mostly by Swedes, and Jack jocularly referred to it as "the slums."

I think it must have been within the restricted four walls of this little fortress against the Arctic cold, that there was born in Jack London that vision of hospitality which animated him all his unpenurious days. It could not consist of wastefulness as regarded food, but of warmth and shelter, and, inestimable comfort to a certain few who gathered about the red-hot stove, converse of long nights that was the sole entertainment of the frozen-in gold prospectors from all points of the compass.

Studying Mr. Thompson's journal, I find that on the 12th Jack and several others went up Henderson Creek, and staked their claims. Four days later, the party was on its way to Dawson City in the *Yukon Belle*, to record claims and freshen up with news of the country. Camped near the cabin of Louis W. Bond, of Santa Clara County, California, they made the acquaintance of the dog Buck, subsequent noble hero of "The Call of the Wild." They did not leave Dawson until December 3, on the 7th arriving back on Upper Island.

Dawson City—Metropolis of the World to the World's Adventurers!—its snow-packed thoroughfare crunching under the muclucs of the motliest crowd that ever congregated from the remotest arcs of the planet, and splendidly policed by the heroic "yellow-legs," as the Mounted Constabulary was called from the hue of its leggins. And what Jack London's ductile mind took unto itself of the gorgeous romance enacted under the Union Jack that dominated the log-built capital of the Northwest Territory, is free to all who will read between the boards of one or another of a dozen-odd books he devoted to its diverse picturings.

A prize has come to me for the asking, in the recollections of one sympathetic mind that measured blades with Jack London's in the log-cabin on Upper Island—Mr. W. B. Hargrave, of Colfax, Washington—"Bert" Hargrave, or "Kid," as the younger with winsome irreverence bridged a disparity of years. Mr. Hargrave has also furnished me a chart illustrating the geographical situation of the camp, upon which he has jotted: "You must imagine high hills sloping back from the river banks, buttressed by an occasional ridge that had been cleft by the stream, leaving precipitous walls. Forests of spruce, of dense growth in the ravines and along the streams. The islands flat and also covered with spruce timber. A mantle of snow of the average depth of four feet in the lower latitudes." From his letters to me since the death of his friend, not only have we a valuable presentment of both the physical but the mental Jack London of that season:

"It was in October of 1897 that I first met him . . . No other man has left so indelible an impression upon my memory as Jack London. He was but a boy then, in years . . . But he possessed the mental equipment of a mature man, and I have never thought of him as a boy except in the heart of him . . . the clean, joyous, tender, unembittered heart of youth. His personality would challenge attention anywhere. Not only in his beauty—for he was a handsome lad—but there was about him that indefinable something that distinguishes genius from mediocrity. Though a youth, he displayed none of the insolent egotism of youth; he was *an idealist who went after the attainable*; a dreamer who was a man among strong men; a man who faced life with superb assurance and who could face death serenely imperturbable. These were my first impressions; which months of companionship only confirmed.

"He was one of the few adventurers, of the thousands whom the lure of gold enticed to the frozen fastnesses of the Klondike, whose hardihood and pluck scaled the summit of Chilkoot Pass that year. His cabin was on the bank of the Yukon, near the month of the Stewart River. I remember well the first time I entered it. London was seated on the edge of a bunk, rolling a cigarette. He smoked incessantly and it would have taken no Sherlock Holmes to tell what the stains on his fingers meant. One of his partners, Goodman, was preparing a meal, and the other, Sloper, was doing some carpentry work. From the few words which I overheard as I entered, I surmised that Jack had challenged some of Goodman's orthodox views, and that the latter was doggedly defending himself in an unequal contest of wits. Many times afterward I myself felt the rapier thrust of London's, and knew how to sympathize with Goodman.

"Jack interrupted the conversation to welcome me, and his hospitality was so cordial, his smile so genial, his goodfellowship so real, that it instantly dispelled all reserve. I was invited to participate in the discussion, which I did, much to my subsequent discomfiture.

"That day—the day on which our friendship began—has become consecrated in my memory. I find it difficult to write about Jack without laying myself open to the charge of adulation. During the course of my life . . . I have met men who were worth while; but Jack was the one man with whom I have come in personal contact who possessed the qualities of heart and mind that made him one of the world's overshadowing geniuses.

"He was intrinsically kind and irrationally generous. . . . With an innate refinement, a gentleness that had survived the roughest of associations. Sometimes he would become silent and reflective, but he was never morose or sullen. His silence was an attentive silence. I have known him to end a discussion by merely assuming the attitude of a courteous listener, and when his indiscreet opponent had tangled himself in the web of his own illogic, and had perhaps fallen back upon invective to bolster his position, Jack would calmly roll another cigarette, and throwing his head back, give vent to infectious laughter—infectious because it was never bitter or derisive. . . . He was always good-natured; he was more—he was charmingly cheerful. If in those days he was beset by melancholia, he concealed it from his companions.

"There were not many of us that winter in the little mining camp on the Yukon; but the isolated group of cabins housed some lovable and adventurous souls. I will tell you about them, because it was about them that Jack London wrote, and because there is hardly one of them whom he has not immortalized in his writings.

"There was Louis Savard, a French-Canadian. So reticent was he that it was almost impossible to get him to utter more than a monosyllabic answer to a categorical question. He had a pronounced French-Canadian accent, the drollness of which so delighted London that he never ceased in his attempts to draw Louis into conversation. It was Louis who owned 'Nig,' a dog that showed a striking Newfoundland strain, and I have thought it was Nig's antics that gave Jack his inspiration to write 'The Call of the Wild. Louis once took the dog on a 'hike' up Sixty Mile, and when Nig saw his master preparing for the return journey he deserted and came back to camp alone, leaving to the indignant Louis the task of hauling a loaded sledge some thirty or forty miles. Savard was so incensed that he threatened to kill the dog, and it was only Jack London's eloquent appeal that saved Nig from a dishonored end. One of Savard's partners was Elam Harnish. [Elam Harnish's nickname was "Burning Daylight," and he formed the basis of the hero of Jack's novel by that name.] . . . And there was Carthy (his name was Courthè, I believe!). . . . London mentions him, I think, by name in one story. . . . Peacock was another, a Texan. He was one of the few among us who realized the golden dream of the Argonauts. . . . Then there were John Thorsen, Prewitt, and Keogh, a giant Irishman. . . . And a professional gambler, Hank Putnam by name. . . . And Judge Sullivan—he was one of my partners, as was Doctor Harvey. I must not forget Stevens, because he, perhaps, has been used in Jack's Klondike stories more than any of the others."

"Inasmuch as Louis Savard's cabin was the largest and most comfortable it became the popular meeting place for the denizens of the camp. Louis had constructed a large fireplace, and my recollections of London are intertwined with the many hours we spent together in front of its cheerful light. Many a long night he and I, outlasting the vigil of the others, sat before the blazing spruce logs, and talked the hours away. A brave figure of a man he was, lounging by the crude fireplace, its light playing on his handsome features—a face that one would look at twice even in the crowded city street. In appearance older than his years; a body lithe and strong; neck bared at the throat; a tangled cluster of brown hair that fell low over his brow and which he was wont to brush back impatiently when engaged in animated conversation; a sensitive mouth, but lips, nevertheless, that could set in serious and masterful lines; a radiant smile, marred by two missing teeth (lost, he told me, in a fight on shipboard); eyes that often carried an introspective expression; the face of an artist and a dreamer, but with strong lines denoting will power and boundless energy. An outdoor man—in short, a real man, a man's man.

"He had a mental craving for the truth. He applied one test to religion, to economics, to everything. 'What is the truth?.' 'What is just?' It was with these questions that he confronted the baffling enigma of life. He could think great thoughts. One could not meet him without feeling the impact of a superior intellect. Once in a cabin I saw a man who had presided for many years as the magistrate of a high court, and a surgeon who had achieved more than a local reputation—each Jack's senior by many years—sitting in his presence like children facing their school-master, while he expounded some of Herbert Spencer's complex theories. And I remember that Jack once engaged Dr. Harvey in a discussion on the immortality of the soul. The Doctor was an educated and brilliant man, unorthodox, but absolutely convinced of the certainty of a future life. Jack, with eager and incisive questioning, was demanding from him a positively scientific corrobation of his belief. The Doctor had a logical mind, and his inability to comply with Jack's request vexed him much, although he gave far better reasons than can the average man. On September 23rd of this year [1916], in answer to a brief note I sent to Jack apprising him of the Doctor's death, he wrote on the fly-leaf of 'When God Laughs' and sent it to me: . . . 'Hurrah for Doctor Harvey! He was a good scout, and he's scouting ahead of us now, though he never sends back a report.'

"Many and diverse were the subjects we discussed, often with the silent Louis as our only listener. Our views did not always coincide, and on one occasion when argument had waxed long and hot and London had finally left us, with only the memory of his glorious smile to salve my defeat, Louis looked up from his game of solitaire (which I think he played because it required no conversation) and became veritably verbose. This is what he said: 'You mak' ver' good talk, but zat London he too damn smart for you.'"

It was Jack's irrepressible entertaining that caused friction between himself and Sloper and Goodman. The good and thrifty souls could not look unmoved upon generosity of grub to a "siwash" when flour was worth $120 a sack. It appears that seldom did the three sit to dine in absence of a visitor or two, for when the beans and bacon and "dough-gods "were ready to serve, Jack, who if he had thought about it would have starved himself rather than be inhospitable, would bid every one to join the family at table. This in the face of Sloper's eloquent frown and Goodman's mild expression of disapproval. The boys belonging to the camp usually declined to participate, knowing Jack's weakness—often a weakness of their own—which but endeared him to them. The domestic atmosphere did not clear, and matters came to a head through a laughable incident that involved Sloper's favorite ax, which with other treasured carpenter tools he kept in spic and span order.

Jack, by mistake, one night laid hold of Sloper's ax to chop the ice from the water hole. The chopping of this particular hole had been so many times repeated, with the repeated freezing of whatever water was left from each successive chopping, that the river at that spot was frozen to the bottom, leaving a shaft through the ice from its mean surface to the bed. Jack, unaware in the dark that the hole had been "worked out," drove the nice edge of Sloper's ax full and fair into the gravel. When the fellows in the cabin heard him calling, they ran out to find him peering into the hole. "Say, boys," quoth Jack, "did you ever see ice so hard that it would strike sparks from an ax?" and again he struck fire with the ax. Sloper, suddenly suspicious, sprang into the hole. Sure enough, it was his ax—the apple of his eye. By common, unspoken consent, partners and guests adjourned to the cabin where the row could be held without their freezing to death. On the way Hargrave whispered to Jack: "Why did you do it?" And Jack: "Well—I broke off the edge of that ax before I knew it was his, and I thought that was the best way to let him know it!"

Arrived at the cabin, the aggrieved Sloper started in on a comprehensive job of cursing, which disconcerted Goodman, a religious man, far more than it did Jack, although he felt much worse over what he had done than he was able to express. He lighted a cigarette and listened, almost respectfully, answering nothing. But there was a glint in his eye that warned Sloper to stop just short of the fighting phrase. And that night Hargrave, shortly bound for Dawson, told Harvey he would better "hook up with London." So Jack moved over for the rest of his stay on Upper Island, for the Doctor had told Hargrave: "After you, I'd rather have Jack London for a partner than any man on the river."

Hank Putnam, the gambler, had gone to Dawson, leaving his outfit with Doctor Harvey. Presently a stranger appeared in camp, claiming to be half owner of Putnam's belongings. The claimant, being refused by Harvey for lack of written authority, called a miners' meeting to adjudicate the dispute. Very few sour-doughs were left in camp, their places being taken by "chechahcos" or newcomers. These sustained the stranger by vote, and demanded that the Doctor turn over half the goods to which it later developed he had no right. The Doctor consulted Jack: "What shall we do?"

"Fight!" advised Jack.

So they hastily converted the cabin into a fort by knocking out chinking in several places, for loopholes. The chechahcos descended in a body, but when in response to their summons the two defenders of the fort each shoved a thirty-eight fifty-five through a loophole, they withdrew to discuss a plan of campaign.

Of all persons, it was the unloquacious Savard who settled the bloodless fray. Suddenly his cabin door flew wide, and Louis issued with a wicked looking Winchester.

"By gar! you go!" he barked, covering the enemy. They went. There was no more trouble.

Another there was whom Jack London loved, and admired to the extent that he recurred to the memory of him with the superlative sentiment: "Emil Jensen is one of the very rare persons in this world to whom the word *noble* can be applied. I put some of him into my 'Malemute Kid.' I wish I knew where he is, for I'd give anything to see him again, and have him come to the Ranch." After Jack was dead, Emil Jensen wrote to me, but gave no specific address. I replied to General Delivery, San Francisco, and the letter was returned. I want Mr. Jensen to know how Jack esteemed him. If his eye should happen upon these pages, it is my earnest hope that he will write me once more.

Then there was his friend Del Bishop, whom he has used by name in Klondike yarns; and Sam Adams, and Mason, and John Dillon. Good sour-doughs all, these beardless youths. Illustrators are wont lamentably to adorn the visage of a sour-dough with "sufficient whiskers to stuff a horse-collar," as one long-suffering veteran complains. The public never, at this rate, can be made to realize that the Klondike was no place for old or even elderly men unless they were very exceptional ones, as say Joaquin Miller and a few others who escaped deportation by the authorities. I do not think Jack ran across Miller; but Hargrave, one day, laboriously coaxing a sack of flour over a trail that had melted into a bottomless bog from Dawson up to "Number Five Below" on *Bonanza*, came upon a picturesque figure, long-haired, bearded, resting on the bank of a creek. And Hargrave sat there and listened to his discourse of the far future, when the ice-locked land—they were in the "lower sixties"—would be the scene of great cities, marts of commerce reached by tracks of steel that would conquer the now untrodden valleys and mountains. Not until an hour

1909. PEGGY "THE BELOVED." THE "SUPER-DOG" IN JACK'S LIFE

1905. "BROWN WOLF" OF STORY OF THAT NAME, JACK'S ALASKAN HUSKY

had passed did young Hargrave learn that he had been audience to the Poet of the Sierras.

But speaking in general of whiskers, the less of this sort of incumbrance the better, for the same ensnared dampness, and dampness had a way of freezing. It was bad enough to have one's eyelashes and nostril-fuzz congealed. So a razor and its accessories were given place in every kit, though it was often difficult to put one's hand upon a mirror.

Of course, nothing would do but Jack must achieve bread that would be second to none in his neighborhood, and to his last day he boasted of his prowess in turning out proper sour-dough loaves. But, as with exhausting "fancy starch" of old, or foot-blistering hiking, and other manual efforts that he came to repudiate, in later years he swore he had had enough, and would always travel with helpers who would make his "roughing" smooth, so that he could devote working hours to the brain-toil he had elected to pursue instead. Strange—some of his nearest and dearest could never compass his viewpoint, but persisted, to his impotent wrath, in trying to explain away his statement, about "running away from bodily labor," on the grounds of fictional license.

Many and altruistic were the services of young men thrown so closely together in a common need. One of Jack's acts—and I never heard it from him—was in the spring of '98 before the ice went out, when he broke an arduous trail eighty miles each way, in company with Doctor Harvey, to bring in a moose for "Kid" Hargrave, who had sorely suffered with scurvy from the many months' lack of fresh meat.

There is no telling how long Jack London would have stayed in Klondike, nor what treasure he might have wrested and panned from the detritus of his claims, could he have obtained green vegetable food from time to time. As ill luck would have it, the scurvy undermined him to such extent that he was forced to move out of the country as soon as the breaking ice would permit. He did not leave the region by the way he came in. It was characteristic that he seldom retraced a road, though this did not apply to the water routes of his travel.

It was during May, he and Dr. Harvey, with whom he had been bunking for some time, dismantled the latter's cabin (Hargrave had already gone to Dawson for his scurvy), and constructed a raft from the logs, which they floated down the Yukon to Dawson. Here the two realized several hundred dollars from the sale of the raft to the sawmill. The trip was fraught with incident, for their lives, and the raft which represented their fortune, were momentarily threatened in the break-up of the mighty stream. During Jack's brief visit in Dawson, he and the Doctor made better than miner's wages—$15.00 per day—picking up logs from out the Yukon, and towing them by rowboat to the mill, where they brought a fabulous price. One accident of the raft-voyage had been the grounding of the craft on a bar. During their strenuous efforts to get it afloat, Jack cracked the big sweep they had fashioned with much labor, which provoked this comment from the disgusted sailor: "Doctor—I don't know who made this world, but I believe I could make a damn sight better one myself!"—"which," the Doctor was fond of repeating, "was the most blasphemous thing I ever heard."

Far greater treasure than yellow dust of Eldorado or Discovery or *Bonanza* to Jack and Harvey, were a raw potato and a lemon they shared as medicine for their ravaging ailment. I have heard one of them descant with great feeling upon the miraculously quick benefits from the half of a raw potato—and as for his part of the lemon, words failed. Jack's case became so alarming that he was advised in the little hospital at the foot of the hill that it would be well for him to get out to fresh food without delay. But ill as he was, this did not withhold him from renewing acquaintance with the places he had known and the social life therein. How good it was to see a woman's face again—even if at the bar or in the dance-hall of the "M. & M." Saloon, or in Frank Helen's gambling den, and "Monte Carlo," or in the questionable show houses. Jack admired the "grit of women" who, for any reason, had entered the frozen territory.

There were all sorts, of many lands and breeds and mixed-breeds. Freda Moloof, dancer, and alleged Grecian, touched his imagination brightly enough later to employ her romantic personality as a note of color in this tale and that—and, in a much transmogrified form, probably due to a lavish introduction of Lucille's characteristics, as the astute heroine of the play "Scorn of Women," which is based upon his short story of that name.

Jack once wrote me from Oakland: "And who, of all people, do you suppose I ran into last evening, when Eliza and I was rummaging around the street-fair in Oakland?—Freda Moloof, fat and forty—doing the muscle dance in the Streets of Cairo! It was good to see her and talk over old times when I, all doubled up with scurvy, used to admire her dancing and her plucky spirit in Dawson. I've promised to send her a book I mentioned her in." Which promise he redeemed, and her letter of thanks is pasted in his copy of "The God of His Fathers."

And Lucille, she of patrician features, beautiful speaking voice, and versatile tongue that could converse in his own language with almost any foreigner in Dawson. No one knew her history; but more than one scurvy-ruined unfortunate or lung-frozen pneumonia patient well knew the heart of her. Passing along the main street one day in her magnificent furs, she heard a man tell another that his "pardner" could not last long.

"Some one sick?" she inquired.

"My pardner," replied the one addressed, "dying of scurvy."

Lucille stepped quietly into his house, shed her furs, and fell to mothering the sick boy. When she rose to go, he clung and whimpered like a baby. Just before he died, "May I kiss you?" he said. Lucille, like a merciful death angel, nothing loath, folded him scurvy and all to her splendid bosom. I can imagine that Jack London liked her well.

Not at all, except as they represented their tribal differences, was he entangled by the brown maidens of the Indian peoples, nor, personally, in the half-and-less breeds who were sometimes very and elusively beautiful and unusual. Again, as usual, he drew the line. Once, privily, after hearing his familiar insistence, to some pilgrim, that he wrote mostly of what he knew at first hand, I mischievously queried: "You've written considerably and most wonderfully about the squaw-man and his psychology—as well as that of the squaw herself! How about it?"

"Silly!" he broke into his delicious giggle, "thought you had me that time, didn't the wicked woman, who knew better?—No, my dear, I never was a squaw-man. When I make the statement that I write only of what I know, I must not be taken too literally, of course—an artist must have some latitude to spill over into."

At the close of the first week in June, that year of 1898, Jack bade farewell to Hargrave and Harvey. With two companions, Taylor and big-bodied, big-hearted John Thorson, in an unsubstantial mere rowboat, he left Dawson City for the Outside—a traverse of 1500-odd miles of the Yukon, which swerved northward till it touched the Arctic Circle before bending down toward Bering Sea. The Doctor and Hargrave followed a month later, and though they made diligent inquiry at the few sparsely settled camps on the icy river, no trace of the three who preceded them was picked up until Holy Cross Mission gave information. The priest there recognized their description and gave assurance that Jack's boat had gone safely through.

CHAPTER XVI

OUT OF KLONDIKE

1898

I HAVE often heard Jack say that he had no idea of using the Klondike as a literary asset, until his dream of gold fell through and he was bound out of the country, penniless to all intents and purposes. It must have come suddenly to him that the adventure had been sufficient in itself, for he had been smitten with discouragement, before leaving home, as to any success in the coveted direction of a writing future. But now, floating half-frozen down the river of defeat, as the gray and white Yukon seemed to him in his predicament, his assertive buoyancy of brain could not help reviving what he had seen and done and felt in the year just past. Surely *something* could be realized out of it all, to enhance his chance of making a name, earning a voice in the affairs of men.

The idea grew. Meager as the notes appear, he cheered up and went on with a penciled diary started on the day he and the boys had swung into the current out of Dawson and begun to drop downstream. I can do no better than give the entire Journal, dating from June 8 to 30 inclusive. In view of his vaulting achievement at no far distant day, it is amusing to note that at this time his ambition ventured no higher than *Outing Magazine* and *The Youth's Companion.* Also, that in spite of pitiable suffering those three unsheltered weeks in a frail open boat in the mush-ice, only one reference is made to his scurvy crippled body and limbs. Here is his lean account of the voyage:. The ONLY NOTES he kept on the Klondike experience:

"*Tuesday, June 8, 1898.*

Steamboat anticipation.

We start [from Dawson] at 4 P.M. for Outside—last words—sailor and miner friends—parting injunctions, "see so and so, & such a one"—love and business messages—frankly expressed envy of many who had decided to remain—Dawson slowly fading away.

Pitched camp at 10 P.M.—no bunk in boat—slight rain. Day light & broad day light all the time.

Indian Camp at 12 mile Creek. How we were fooled—"Come back Dawson two days ago."

Wednesday, June 8.

Arranged bunk & pulled out at 11 A.M. Reached 40 Mile at 3 P.M. Place practically deserted. Found that the small river steamer *May Mist—Mayor Woods*—had passed us the night before—with 6 tons of whiskey aboard—hot time in Dawson as a consequence. Fort Cudahy likewise deserted. Saw W. A. & T. store and Barracks.

Thursday, June 9.

Arrangement of watches—Taylor cook—objects to watches as has been accustomed to regular hours.

2 A.M.—my watch on deck, sighted the A. C. Co. Steamer *Victoria*, 9 miles above Eagle City—loaded with hardware—no passengers possible.

3:30 A.M.—arrive at Eagle City—once again in Uncle Sam's dominions. 50 people in town, engaged in bucking faro layout and waiting for some steamer to take them to Dawson—short of grub.

9 A.M.—Moose incident, excitement.

Mountains rugged & sternly outlined—few islands in river—stiff 6 mile (average) current.

4 P.M. Passed steamer *Wears*, W. A. T. & T. Co.

10 P.M. Hailed, hospitality a passenger for C.

Friday, June 10.

6:30 A.M.—Passed Seattle No. One—*Mayor Woods* high and dry on a bar with 170 passengers. How they started last summer—frozen in 100 miles below Minook—etc., etc. Some discouraged & starting for St. Michaels by our method.

Circle City 8:20. Stopped & laid in tobacco—same as 40 Mile, no sugar, butter nor milk. Deserted—Mosquitos make a demonstration in force—now, just inside the terrible (so called) 300 miles of Yukon flats. All mountains, after receding & growing smaller above & to Circle City, now utterly disappear.

Description of Flats—not Thousand Islands of St. Lawrence nor "thousands of thousands," but thousands of millions—mosquito's, woods, sloughs, immense piles of drift, all kinds of life what we had been told about, geese & goose eggs, our experiences, the shot gun, etc.

Saturday, June 11.

11:45 to 12:15 no sun, 23 hrs. 30 min. sunshine, warmth at midnight, intense heat at noonday—sweltering in a tropical temperature under Arctic Skies. Cross the Arctic Circle at 3 A.M.

	148
Governor Stoneman hard and fast.	98
John driven out of bed by mosquitos—episode at A. C. Co.'s Cache.	146
	133
	988

Fort Yukon 4 A.M. *Bella* (W. A. T. & T. Co.) emptying cache. Description of Indians working at stevedoring. Indian Squaws & children. Very warm in the sun, more likely some holiday festival at 3 in afternoon.

Capt. Ray defense of caches incident. Nearly all engaged have sledged to Circle City or otherwise disappeared.

Smudges burning on every hand. Mosquito Rig.

9 A.M. Passed steamer *Hamilton* (W. A. T. & T.) 5 hrs. run from Fort Yukon.

Porcupine enters on right.

Scattered Indian camps, deserted log cabins; woodyards.

(*Outing*) [Must have had the magazine in deliberate mind]

Beauty of the night—drifting down the river, midnight & broad daylight, robins & other song birds singing on the islands; partridges drumming tern, seagulls & loons discordant crys echoing across the glassy river stretches; kildees, plover, ducks, foolish or silly cries of wild geese. Martins, owls, hawks.

Heat of sun, sleeping on top blankets at 12 P.M.

Only country where Indians work; wood choppers, deck hands, etc. Big prices for moccasins, moose meat, furs, etc., at Dawson. River-pilots get from $5 a day to $1800 a gradually all year round. Big husky fellows, &—here and there plain traces of white blood apparent.

Sunday, June 12.

All day, Yukon flats. Fun shooting goose. Loaded 4½ drams, with 15 large buckshot; kicked John's arm.

Water sluggish. Evening burned smudges. Mountains becoming visible again.

Monday, June 13.

A.M. Arrived at Fort Hamilton, none but Indians left, everybody else gone to Dawson 65 miles to Minook.

12 M. Coal mine on right 25 miles above Minook.

R. E. Russell of Seattle & an Ohio (Toledo) man working it—cabin, coal bunker, etc., carried away & mine flooded by high water. Sell to steamers $25 per ton. Faces covered with clay, hard job fighting mosquitos. Bid them farewell amid clouds of the same personified ubiquity.

Arrived at Minook at 4 P.M. The first man to greet me as I climbed ashore was Chestnut & old acquaintance & a university man. Had had a rough time coming in. All about barge, *Gov. Stoneman*, etc., to buying men out $50 a piece. All hands to hoist anchor at 4 A.M. Getting out on bank and lining steamboat & cargo, etc. Minook gold (Little Minook) runs $18.75 per ounce. Probably, at favorable estimate, Minook district will turn out $85,000. Some company faking a number of creeks here and selling stock on outside at $1.00 per share—1,000,000 shares.

Introduced to Capt. Mayo—Thirty years in country. Getting stout—very pleasant to converse with. About 500 people in town.

All along river asking for news—war—football, Sharkey, Jeffries, Corbett, Fitz—Did Durrant really hang—what did he say, etc. Went through Rampart.

11 P.M. Ran Rapids.

Tuesday, June 14.

Passed Tanana River & stopped at Tanana Station just above St. James' Mission & situated at the Indian town of Muklukyeto, at the junction of the Yukon & Toyikakat Rivers. The camp was large and the Indians had arrived from the Tanana & were in full force, waiting the fishing. Dance in progress, white man's dances—low room in log cabin.

Effect—In the crowded heated room, discerned the fair, bronzed skin & blonde mustache of the ubiquitous adventurous Anglo Saxon, always at home in any environment.

5 A.M. & everybody was up, children playing, bucks skylarking; squaws giggling & flirting, dogs fighting, etc. Soon all will be asleep, for they sleep all day, and work and play at night.

Banks lined with birch bark canoes, nets in evidence everywhere, everything ready for the fish. Put up netting & fooled mosquitos.

Wednesday, June 15.

Went on watch at Midnight—mosquitos thick. Chant of Indians from miles down river. Arrive at camp (100 miles below Tanana) at 1:30 A.M. Bucks singing, women dancing, raven hair, etc. Skylarking, etc. Pointing at mountain, "When sun appears, fun ceases and all go to bed."

Lafcadio Hearn & Japanese Half Caste—Beautiful, half-breed woman saw here, Caucasian features, slender form, delicate oval of face & head, describe her environment. How much harder her lot than the Japanese Half Caste.

Ubiquitous Anglo Saxon White man from Sacramento living with them, brother-in-law, etc. They also waiting fishing, chopping cordwood & jumping price of same.

Pull out at 3:30 A.M.

6 A.M. Passed Steamer *Alice* bound up river & much enquired about, & followed by the *Marguerite*. Many thought *Alice* lost in the ice.

2:30 P.M. W. C. Merwin.

8 P.M. White man, starting a store. Indians, camps, etc.

10 P.M. Indian village, only old people left. The perpetual cry for medicine. Stoicism of the sufferers. Traces of white blood among the papooses everywhere apparent.

Thursday, June 16.

3 P.M. Stopped at temporary camp of N. A. T. & T. Co.'s station. Station flooded and people camped on hillside. Bought whitefish.

Party preparing to go up the Koyokuk River.

6 P.M. Indian camp. Squaw three quarter breed with a white baby (girl) (2 yrs.) such as would delight any American mother. Unusual love she lavished upon it. An erstwhile sad expression. Talked good English.

"I have no man."

"Father of child had deserted her." Good natured joking, "I'll be your man—I go St. Michaels, come back plenty flour, bacon, blankets, clothes & grub of all kinds. You marry me."

Ring in saving bead work for Charlie.

"Maybe I be married when you come back."

"You marry Charlie?"

"No, I marry Indian, white man always leave Indian girl."

Mountains from Toyikakat have been getting quite snowy, & now, even those with a southern exposure are no exception. I take for a sign of greater snowfall & that we are nearing the coast with its climatic conditions so dissimilar to those of the interior.

9:30 P.M. Nulato. More men preparing to go up Koyokuk. First heard talk of Koyokuk & Minook. Two small steamers are getting ready also. Is looked upon as coming Alaskan Clondyke.

Visited Roman Catholic Mission during service. Shrill chanting of Indian women combining with the basses of the father and brother—weird effect. Delicate features of the mocassined black-stoled priest officiating at the altar.

Father Monroe, make acquaintance. Cultured Frenchman who has devoted his life to his task. For 5 years has labored at this place zealously.

Indians have better appearance—always do around missions. Educational work of missions.

Between 6 & 700 miles to St. Michaels.

Friday, June 17.

Uneventful. Evidences of the ice run all along the line, but here more plentiful than ever and more striking. Whole islands swept clear of trees. Some of mainland in many places. Early Spring & greatest high water known in many years, as a proof, flooding of old established towns, stations & native villages.

Geese have long since disappeared but ducks becoming quite thick as we near the mouth.

Indian camps fresh bear skins hanging in the sun.

Indians all along the line spoiled by rush. Demanding all kinds of prices for their labor or products. Steamer Co.'s will raise grub in proportion. If this will not do will bring in own men under contract. Indian seems unable to comprehend the fact that he can never get the better of the white man.

Passed the steamer——— at 2 P.M.

IMPORTANT FEATURE—Indian graves along Yukon banks. Do not bury in trees like many N. A. tribes. Older graves more roughly made (palings), later, neatly made, often pointed. Shed rain. Once in a while a curiously carved totem pole. Catholic missions seem to get bulk of converts—else what becomes of protestant graves, as all in evidence have crosses. But the more impressive ritual of the Catholic service, so pregnant with mysticism to the barbaric mind, as opposed to the bare meetinghouse puritanical mode of protestant, may doubtless explain away some of this, but beyond a doubt, much is due to the indefatigable efforts of the fathers.

Saturday, June 18.

Among birds, woodpeckers, swallows, kingfishers, seagulls (many could not classify) Remember "Outing" "*Youth's Companion.*"

Large trees uprooted or literally sawed in two by ice. Small trees tender bark stripped, and stand stretching their bleached limbs heavenward, mute witnesses to the Ice God's wrath.

Drifting the boat along the low, flooded banks during midnight watches while comrades snore under the mosquito netting, gun in hand, & dropping the wild fowl as they rise or metaphorically blessing the crazy gun for snapping. I will always recommend such a gun for amateurs. Always a reliable object at hand to lay bad markmanship to.

Sun rises like a ball of copper.

Mosquitos—One night badly bitten under netting—couldn't vouch for it but John watched them & said they rushed the netting in a body, one gang holding up the edge while a second gang crawled under. Charley swore that he has seen several of the largest ones pull the mesh apart & let a small one squeeze through. I have seen them with their proboscis bent and twisted after an assault on sheet iron stove. Bite me through overalls & heavy underwear.

A deserted malemute dog swam off to us. Injured in hind legs. Gave him away at Anvik.

Indians come off in canoes to trade. Made Anvik at 10 P.M. Town under water. Pressed by Episcopal missionary to stop over & spend "at least one Christian Sunday." Traveling west and setting our watches back. Pulled on to station. Pickett in charge. Hearty welcome we received. Given some fresh potatoes & a can of tomatoes for my scurvy, which has now almost entirely crippled me from my waist down. Right leg drawing up, can no longer straighten it, even in walking must put my whole weight on toes. These few raw potatoes & tomatoes are worth more to me at the present stage of the game than an Eldorado claim—What wots it, though a man gain illimitable wealth & lose his own life?

How they got the potatoes? Quite a sacrifice on their part. White through and through.

Left at 11:30 P.M.

Icogmute next stop.

Sunday, June 19.

At Anvik, Yukon, on 38 ft. Spring rise & 40 miles wide.—Shagluk Slough, etc. Get into a slough ourselves. Hoarse croak of the raven, blackbirds.

In afternoon made Holy Cross Mission, headquarters Catholic Missionary work in Alaska. From here four sisters have just been sent to aid Father Judge at Dawson.

At first sight—make homesick—Grassy hills, etc., fences, farm, etc. (Would give 4% for a cow) Indian girls playing in school yard. Homelike.

Trading with Indians. Ducks, Grouse, Goose & Duck eggs, berries, fish, etc. All busy doing something. Making nets, birch barks, rope, peeling slender rods for fish traps, etc. etc.

How make bark rope. Bark off roots—slit into strings, wetted in water and braided into a three stranded rope, very strong and durable.—How squaws work at all such things, tanning leather, making nets, muc luc, mocassins, etc. etc. Weaving grass matting, minding dogs, papooses, etc. etc. Getting among Malemutes now.

Monday, June 20.

Bad weather, went ashore 1 P.M. Pitched Camp.

Tuesday, June 21.

Native village Malemutes—holes in the ground, fire place in middle, hole in roof, etc. etc. Deck of cards for Russian Cross.

6 P.M.—Icogmute—Russian Mission. Very sleepy, flooded, etc. One Russian, could not understand English. Very miserable place.

9 P.M. Native village king salmon 2 cups of flour.

Wednesday, June 22.

Trading native villiages. Nothing important.

Thursday, June 23.

Long stretches of flats. Once in a while river strikes bluffs of low barren hills—the same lined with Malemute villages—then flats again.—Raven's hoarse croak

11 P.M. Andreasky. 2 miles.

Up Andreasky river. Native villiage at confluence. How miserable their condition yet how happy. How they come out & sit on bank, naked legs, bodies, etc. in chill north wind. Trading for curios, etc. flour for fish and game. Method of trading.

At midnight, Malemute paddling kyak & singing—weird effect. They seem never to sleep, are always up.

At Andreasky last low hills are left, save to the south beyond Kusiluf, a snow covered jagged mountain—a landmark to avoid. And we enter the great Yukon Delta, for a 126 mile run to Kutlik.

Threading the maze, keeping to right, etc. Took no guides at Andreasky, avoiding said custom. Fishing villages all deserted. No signs of human life. No white man since Holy Cross Mission, where sick steward of Str. *Hamilton* was down. One Russian at Icogmute who could not speak English.

Terrible racket maintained by wild fowl between 2 & 5 A.M. Above Andreasky had our last experience with eggs—large goose eggs—Beautiful king salmon, cool, firm flesh fresh from icy Yukon.

Friday, June 24.

Threaded Yukon Delta all day. Aphorn Mouth.

Saturday, June 25. Hamilton Station

Last N. A. T. & T. Station, 11:30 A.M. Learned that we passed the Str. *Healy* lying at Andreasky. Inquired after war news—had the latest.

Up to 16th no ocean strs. had reached St. Michaels.

Indians all absent hunting seal in the south channel.

8 miles on passed Bill Moore's. Settled down with Indian wife (years in country) satisfied to remain—ambition lost—hurry-scurry devil take the hindmost competition of civilization has no attraction—sure thing for the rest of life—but how bleak and blank his existence. Pride of Indian in calling him brother-in-law.

Kutlik in evening—low tide—round bottom sea boats—first smack of old ocean.

5 miles on the mouth of River—Slept with open sea in sight.

Sunday, June 26.

N.W. wind. Point Romanoff in sight. Sailed till on shore. Beached boat. Episode of Taylor & Roubeau. (Also at Eagle City on being awakened.)

Monday, June 27.

Off Point Romanoff pick up Father Roubeau on edge of surf in 3 hatch kyak or as Russians call it, Bidarka. Take him aboard—how unlike a father on first sight. Sits alongside of me while steering—ask him if smoke objectionable—on contrary pipe in bidarka. So all light up and are content.

Quite a linguist. French, Italian, Spanish, English, Indian dialects, etc. A native of Nice. Pleasant anecdotes of Jesuit brotherhood. Obedience, poverty, chastity. Alaska 12 years. Reducing Innuit language to a grammar—pride of his life. Revel for hours in eulogy of same, moods, tenses, genders, articles, adverbs, etc. fill the air.

First coming aboard, argument over day, Sunday or Monday.

Dress—fur cap, coarse blue shirt, muc luc sea boots, etc. etc.

Possessed of fatal faculty of getting lost.

Camp, beaching boat in afternoon.

11 P.M. turned out, etc.

Tuesday, June 28.

Midnight—southeast wind blowing—squally, increasing, splash of rain. Dirty sky to southard. Quite a task of running boat out through surf. Shorten down to storm canvas & rush on before it. Big sea tumbling after. *Bidarka* in tow performs strange feats.

Looking for canal. Spots it. Small boat in mouth. Men asleep. Jibe over sail and run in.

Laugh at us. Keep a-going. Stay so long they finally follow. Fooled. 7 hours lost.

Run on and make canal at 1 P.M.

Father at an oar or on the towline.

5 P.M. Father bids good-by & goes on. Never heard of again—lost in some back slough most likely.

How misleading maps [here torn and cannot make out word—Follows something that looks like Towing now.]

Wednesday, June 29.

Camp at mouth of canal.

Thursday, June 30.

St. Michaels early in morning—*Find it to be Wednesday 28.*

Russian priest seen no sign of Jesuit. Tanned skin, brilliant black eyes, of Italian quickness of speech, vivid play of emotion so different from the sterner, colder Anglo-Saxon.

Leave St. Michaels—unregrettable moment.

Jack stoked his steamship passage from St. Michaels to British Columbia, thence proceeded steerage to Seattle. So it will be seen that his homecoming from the fabulous region of names to conjure with—Eldorado and Dominion, *Bonanza* and Sulphur—was the reverse of spectacular, and with a few twinges of scurvy still within him to remind of the unlucrative year.

He found his widowed mother in a tiny cottage on Sixteenth street between Nineteenth and Twentieth Avenues, and worrying about the rent, although in face of Eliza's assurance that she would help out. Eliza was absent on a much-needed vacation, camping in Monterey; but she hurried home to greet her brother, whom she saw bronzed and bigger-muscled than ever, showing marked physical gain from his rough experience.

CHAPTER XVII

RETURN FROM KLONDIKE
LILY MAID LETTERS

1898-9

WITH John London removed by death, Jack must buckle to in earnest to support his mother and the little nephew in whom she was entirely wrapped up—an infatuation which never abated. There was no question of choice as to what work he should do. There were unpaid bills of his father's which he felt in honor bound to discharge—petty sums in themselves, but hugely troublesome in Jack's creditless plight. He must snap up the first job that came to hand, and that quickly. It sounded simple, if uninspiring; but the fact is there was no place offering to an unskilled laborer for hard times were on.

His only trades were those of sailor and laundryman. The long absences of seafaring did not fit in with his domestic responsibility, and he could not uncover any opening in the laundries of Oakland. Writing was not to be thought of. He must be sure of roof and grub, and a decent suit of ready-mades, before he could raise eyes again, if ever, to the literary heavens.

Five employment bureaus and advertisements in three dailies failed to land a situation of any sort, and he began pawning his few personal effects—the silver watch Captain Shepard had given him for the Klondike, the bicycle Eliza had bought, and a raincoat much prized by his father, whose dying wish it had been that Jack inherit. Some curious newspaper items were followed up, but nothing came of them. He owns to having proffered for studio-model his one hundred and sixty-four pounds of well set up, twenty-two years growth of brawn, but some one of several fine-bodied fellows likewise out of employment won the prize. And of course, as he reminds us, along with such frivolous occupations he was trying with might and main to become wop, lumper, or roustabout. The surplus labor army, with winter not far off, pressed hard upon the scarcity of work. "Also I," Jack adds, "who had romped along carelessly through the countries of the world and the kingdom of the mind, was not a member of any union."

While preforming small odd tasks he took civil service examinations for mailcarrier, and passed in the lead, only to face disappointment in that no vacancy existed. Awaiting his chance he penned an article, "Down the River," describing his Yukon voyage. The San Francisco newspaper on which he tried it, neither acknowledged nor returned it. This was not encouraging; but he set that square jaw and launched into a 20,000-word serial especially designed for *The Youth's Companion.* It was completed, even to typing, in one week. "I fancy that was what was the matter with it," he afterward surveyed, "for it came back." To the Lily Maid he wrote: "The art of omission is the hardest of all to learn, and I am weak at it yet. I am too long-winded, and it is hard training to cut down." But here enters a touch of faith in his star: "As yet, this prevents me from writing perfect little gems, examples of which your brother sometimes sends me."

He shortened his tools, focused more intently, and began hewing unique art forms, of unmistakable purity, cut from the blocks of empirical and idealistic material so long storing in the house of his mind against this inevitable day. Out of the stuff of earth, and flesh, mind, and heart, that he knew of his own contact, with head and hand he wrought the transmutation of the mass, molded it into restrained shapes that he felt were new—at least he had met nothing like them; shapes of beauty, or strength, or truth, as desire and his latent genius dictated. In the dynamic, dramatic power of his creation he dared but a hesitant confidence, because he had been unable to conform to conventional patternings revered by those of his acquaintance not big enough in themselves to reassure him of the worth of their authority. He was still fearful of being on the wrong track, no matter how the gleam of it lured.

Even the Lily Maid, to whose perceptions he still rendered a measure of fidelity, failed him with wholly unintentional cruelty. Passionately anxious to polish his astonishing outlines, though sensing unquestionable beauties and excellences, she was overborne by the spectacle of her friend hollow-eyed and pasty-pale from lack of sleep and beefsteak. Moreover and most important to her possessive and protective femininity, he was unsuccessful financially. And so, by means of a tact that would have deceived and influenced a less perspicacious lover, with veiled promptings toward some "position" that would bring in a regular stipend, she chilled him with hopeful references to the mail-carrier opportunity. For she had distinctly approved of his taking the examinations; he needed steadying—some reliable outlook for the future.

More than vaguely was he now disillusioned. Perhaps his very tenderness increased in proportion as his recoil doubled back from her restricted horizon. She was so softly pretty, white woman of his own race—her eyes so blue and true, her long mantle of perfect golden hair as lovely as Lady Godiva's, when she let it ripple down for the pleasuring of his eyes. And then her delicate health made him shrink from wounding by determination to assert his own ego's imperious challenge. Yet it was in the fiber of him to be honest. Although he drained her culture of its last drop that could further the form of his work, inexorably he cast aside what his unerring senses warned him as weakening to it—leaving the pallid girl breathless with a bafflement due to her fate of not understanding.

She is dead, and he is dead. She did her best. But her mold was too narrowed to confine his best, though all the while Jack appreciated her effort to help. She was strong enough in no possible way either to restrain or to fly with the eagle she would have caged. Even in the days of her warmest attractiveness, he would find himself, quite without forethinking, involved by the magnetism of a woman met in her very company, some one entirely her antithesis. Earlier, he marveled at the phenomenon—perhaps, he searched, the reason lay in his own imperfectness of refinement. But he learned about women from both of them. Then abruptly he would overtake the discovery that the Lily Maid's small, vivacious, quick-tongued mother, herself young, was more compellingly enticing than the daughter he had almost been sure was his accomplished dream of womanhood. He was learning about women from them all. His opportunities were of the best—not only in the drawing room, but out of doors on foot or wheel, even to the notoriously illuminating exigencies of camp life; for he made one of their party to Yosemite Valley, which included her immediate family and some outside relatives, as well as friends. And what Jack learned, he never forgot. If detail were lost, the broad principles remained, to play a timely part in maturing tenets and conduct.

Further, and finally, an apparently slight happening marked the passing of his old ineffable instinct of worship toward the girl. In reality it was a trenchant manifestation of essential fraility and lack of poise that forever lost the man to her.

It was an unconsidered climax of petty irritation to her vanity that he should spend hours of his rare playtime at chess, when they might be out on their wheels or otherwise enjoying each other's society. Right in front of him she flung her fateful bolt, out of a clear sky so far as Jack's mood was concerned. Shoulders hunched, brows drawn, he bent over the checquered board, his whole soul gathered in still ecstasy of calculation, unconscious of any universe beyond the problem represented by the carven images.

The slender, white-robed blonde angel stood beside the unheeding mathematician for one exasperated moment, then swooped, lightly in the flesh but oh! how heavily in spiritual consequences, and swept the table clean with her two small hands.

"What did you do?" I asked with bated breath, when years later in reminiscent mood over the Lily's death he recalled the garden tragedy.

"Nothing—what was there to do?" slowly he reconstructed his bleak state of mind. "I felt every bit of blood leave my face; and from her brother's expression, mine must have been something awful. The thing was unforgivable, don't you see? To me it was sheer, brutal, blind-mad outrage to every decency of human fair play. It was a sin against the Holy Ghost! It was a *vicious* act, to wipe a half-solved problem out of existence in that way—from small jealousy of a bloodless rival. . . . No, I did not say a word—then or ever. But when I looked up at her after what seemed a frozen century, and her frightened eyes met mine, she knew what had really happened." For a fleeting moment the young woman glimpsed the import of her pettish deed—that what she had done reached into the very body of their incompatibility. In the biology of things, no superior human entity of vibrating atoms, no matter how little ill-met, can perfectly complement any other entity of similar superiority. Jack, once at rest as to the fundamental largenesses in a given person, could generously discount incidental light qualities, except as they might indicate some abysmal vacuity. And in the Lily Maid he came to discern the stamp of an incomprehension too vast for the two ever to dwell together in mutual satisfaction of any kind.

By now, for all the tenderness of what was become passionless, if staunch and lasting, friendship toward the loving girl, he still beat against the bars of her inadequacy, bars which she fain would have laid down had hers been the ability to do so.

If ever I knew how he came by the following letters written to the Lily Maid, all memory has fled. It is likely that at some stage of their long acquaintance—perhaps after his marriage in 1900—the pair may have exchanged their old correspondence. Much of the matter in these letters was combed for the creating of Martin Eden's Ruth, as the author's blue-penciling bears witness. This proves what I had forgotten: that he had the letters with him in Hawaii and aboard the yacht *Snark* to Tahiti in 1907, since it was during this interval he composed the novel, which originally he had cynically entitled "Success."

Here is the first of the letters remaining in his files, typed by him at 962 East 16th street, November 27, 1898, and sent to the Lily Maid at College Park:

"Forgive my not writing, for I have been miserable and half sick. So nervous this morning that I could hardly shave myself.

"Everything seems to have gone wrong—why, I haven't received my twenty dollars for those essays yet. Not a word as to how I stood in my Civil Service Exs. Not a word from the *Youth's Companion*, and it means to me what no one can possibly realize.

"You seem to misunderstand. I thought I made it perfectly plain, that those squibs of poetry were merely diversions and experiments; yet you say—'But always the same theme.' Theme has nothing to do with it; they were studies in structure and versification. Though it took me a long while, I have learned my lesson, and thanks to no one. I made ambitious efforts once. It makes me laugh to look back on them, though sometimes I am nearer weeping. I was the greenest of tyros, dipping my brush into whitewash and coal-tar, and without the slightest knowledge of perspective, proportion or color, attempted masterpieces—without a soul to say 'you are all wrong; herein you err; there is your mistake.'

"Why, that poem on gold is one of the finest object-lessons in my possession. I was ambitious in that. With no more comprehension of the aims and principles of poetry, than a crab, I proposed or rather, purposed to make something which would be something. I would strike out on new trails; I would improve on the Spencerian Stanza; I would turn things upside down. So I tried what has been probably tried a thousand times and discarded because it was worthless; one Alexandrine at the end of the stanza was not enough; I added a second. I treated my theme as Dryden or Thompson would have treated it. My elephantine diction was superb—I out-Johnsoned Johnson. I was a fool—and no one to tell me.

"So you see, to-day, I am unlearning and learning anew, and as such things are merely principles, you can readily see why I don't care a snap for the theme. I have played Darius Green once, and if my neck is broken a second time it will be my own fault. I shall not be ready for any flights till my machine is perfected, and to that perfection I am now applying myself. Until then, to the deuce with themes. I shall subordinate thought to technique till the latter is mastered; *then I shall do vice versa.*

"I do not know when I can be down—I may be digging sewers or shoveling coal next week. Am glad to hear you are better. Give my regards to everybody.

"Good-by,

"Jack."

Three days later in blackest mood he wrote to her the letter from which I have already drawn portions from time to time as they fitted into my mosaic. I present the remainder:

962 East 16th St. Nov. 30, 1898.

Dear ————:

"I do appreciate your interest in my affairs, but—we have no common ground. In a general, vaguely general, way, you know my aspirations; but of the real Jack, his thoughts, feelings, etc., you are positively ignorant. Yet, little as you do know, you know more about me than anybody else. I have fought and am fighting my battle alone.

"You speak of going to————: I know how well she loves me; do you know how? or why? I spent years in Oakland and we saw nothing of each other—perhaps once a year looked on each other's face. If I had followed what she would have advised, had I sought her I would to-day be a clerk at forty dollars a month, a railroad man, or something similar. I would have winter clothes, would go to the theater, have a nice circle of acquaintances, belong to some horrible little society like the ——, talk as they talk, think as they think, do as they do—in short, I would have a full stomach, a warm body, no qualms of conscience, no bitterness of heart, no worrying ambition, no aim but to buy furniture on the instalment plan and marry. I would be satisfied to live a puppet and die a puppet. Yes, and she would not like me half as well as she does. Because I felt that I was or wanted to be something more than a laborer, a dummy; because I showed that my brain was a little bit better than it should have been, considering my advantages and lack of advantages; because I was different from most fellows in my station; because of all this she took a liking to me. But all this was secondary; primarily, she was lonely, had no children, a husband who was no husband, etc., she wanted some one to love.

"If the world was at my feet to-morrow, none would be happier than she, and she would say she knew it would be so all the time. But until that time—well, she would advise to not think of it, to sink myself in two score years of oblivion with a full belly and no worry, to die as I had lived, an animal. Why should I so study that I may extract joy from reading some poem? She does not, and does not miss anything: Tom, Dick and Harry do not, and they are happy. Why should I develop my mind? It is not necessary for happiness. A babble of voices, petty scandals, and foolish nothings, should satisfy me. It does Tom, Dick and Harry, and they are happy.

"As long as my mother lives, I would not do this; but with her gone to-morrow, if I knew that my life would be such, that I was destined to live in Oakland, labor in Oakland at some steady occupation, and die in Oakland—then to-morrow I would cut my throat and call quits with the whole cursed business. You may call this the foolish effervescence of youthful ambition, and say that it will all tone down in time; but I have had my share of toning down.

(Here follows the paragraph upon Duty, already quoted, and the incident of the meat at school.) He goes on:

"You say, 'It is your duty, if you wish to hold the esteem of those whose approval or companionship is worth having.' If I had followed that, would I have known you? If I had followed that, who would I know whose companionship I would esteem? If I had followed that from childhood, whose companionship would I be fitted to enjoy?—Tennyson's, or a bunch of brute hoodlums on a street corner?

"I cannot lay bare, cannot put my heart on paper, but I have merely stated a few material facts of my life. These may be cues to my feelings. But unless you know the instrument on which they play, you will not know the music. Me—how I have felt and thought through all this struggle; how I feel and think now—you do not know. Hungry! Hungry! Hungry! From the time I stole the meat and knew no call above my belly, to now when the call is higher, it has been hunger, nothing but hunger.

"You cannot understand, nor never will.

"Nor has anybody ever understood. The whole thing has been by itself. Duty said 'Do not go on; go to work.' So said others, though they would not say it to my face. Everybody looked askance; though they did not speak, I knew what they thought. Not a word of approval, but much of disapproval. If only some one had said, 'I understand.' From the hunger of my childhood, cold eyes have looked upon me, or questioned, or snickered and sneered. What hurt above all was that they were some of my friends—not professed but real friends. I have calloused my exterior and receive the strokes as though they were not; as to how they hurt, no one knows but my own soul and me.

"So be it. The end is not yet. If I die I shall die hard, fighting to the last, and hell shall receive no fitter inmate than myself. But for good or ill, it shall be as it has been—alone.

"And you, remember this: the time is past when any John Halifax, Gentleman, ethics can go down with me. I don't care if the whole present, all I possess, were swept away from me—I will build a new present; if I am left naked and hungry to-morrow—before I give in I will go naked and hungry. . . .

". . . . Frank [Frank Atherton, an old friend] has been playing the violin and Johnny the devil in the room while I have been writing this, so you will forgive its disconnectedness. . . .

"Yours,

"Jack."

The next missive is of December 6, 1898, and records the debatable success of a manuscript entitled "To The Man On Trail," which he had submitted to the *Overland Monthly*. The Uncle referred to in my Prologue as business manager of the magazine, from this time on began speaking of the remarkable work being turned in by "this boy, Jack London."

"Frank is at last gone and I can do a little writing. Why did you not send me what you had written? Were you afraid of hurting my feelings—it seems your previous frankness, extending through several years, had precluded any such possibility. . . .

"Sent out in this mail, 'trailers' after articles I mailed last September, and which have vanished utterly. Received a letter from the *Overland Monthly*. This is the substance of it: We have read your MS and are so greatly pleased with it, that, though we have an enormous quantity of accepted and paid-for material on hand, we will at once publish it in the January number, if—aye, if you can content yourself with five dollars.

"There are between three and four thousand words in it. Worth far more than five dollars, at the ordinary reportorial rate of so much per column. What do you think of that for a first class magazine like the *Overland*? . . .

"We are getting ready to sue the Republican Club for our prizes. No word from *Youth's Companion*.

"If I could only come down. Hope this will find you in better health—I hate to think of you lying sick."

Jack had won first award for an essay in a contest held by the Fifth Ward Republican Club for campaign songs, essays, cartoons and poems, the song prize being taken by his friend Rev. Robert J. Whitaker. The Club seems to have defaulted in payment, and hence was sued by the various winners.

On December 22, he wrote the Lily Maid:

"All this week and part of last I have spent in the superior court of San Francisco. One of my Klondike partners, Sloper, has returned, and because he had not struck it rich, his wife, to whom he had deeded over four thousand dollars worth of property before he left, has sued him for divorce, alleging desertion. I had to serve as witness on various points. It sickens one to find a woman can be so small and cold-blooded.

"No news from Republican Club. *Overland* has not paid five dollars yet. *Youth's Companion* yarn came back—prime cause of rejection they state to be unusual length of each chapter, which length is never allowed, they say, "except in very special instances." In the beginning, in response to my queries, I was told that 3000 words made an average chapter, and in the end, none of my chapters exceeded that amount. I take it to be merely an alleged cause, or else a mistake on the part of the one who first advised me.

"Enclosed, you will find the successful *Examiner* story. [Jack's own contribution to this newspaper's contest had been rejected.] Please keep it, remembering that strength of narrative and originality of plot were demanded by those in charge of contest. Some day, when the MSS. I submitted are published elsewhere, I shall forward to you so that you may compare. Also, in the successful story I send you, please endeavor to find what plot there is, if any, or if it is a study, or pseudo-study."

The Christmas of 1898 was a blue one. He faced losing his typewriter, for want of its small rent, and the day brings up dreams that make him evince a trace of unthinking masculine cruelty to the deprived girl who loves him, in his picture of that ever latent desire for fatherhood.

"About the loneliest Christmas I ever faced—guess I'll write to you. Nothing to speak of, though—everything quiet. How I wish I were down at College Park, if for no more than a couple of hours. Nobody to talk to, no friend to visit—nay, if there were, and if I so desired, I would not be in position to. Hereafter and for some time to come, you'll have to content yourself with my beastly scrawl, for this is, most probably, the last machine-made letter I shall send you. . . . The typewriter goes back on the thirty-first of December. . . . Then the New Year, and an entire change of front.

"I have profited greatly, have learned much during the last three months. How much I cannot even approximate—I feel its worth and greatness, but it is too impalpable to put down in black and white. I have studied, read, and thought a great deal, and believe I am at last beginning to grasp the situation—the general situation, my situation, and the correlative situation between the two. But I am modest, as I say, I am only beginning to grasp—I realize, that with all I have learned, I know less about it than I thought I did a couple of years ago.

"Are you aware of the paradox entailed by progress? It makes me both jubilant and sad. You cannot help feeling sad when looking over back work and realizing its weak places, its errors, its inanities; and again, you cannot but rejoice at having so improved that you are aware of it, and feel capable of better things. I have learned more in the past three months than in all my High School and College; yet, of course, they were necessary from a preparatory standpoint.

"And to-day is Christmas—it is at such periods that the vagabondage of my nature succumbs to a latent taste for domesticity. Away with the many corners of this round world! I am deaf to the call of the East and West, the North and South—a picture such as Fred [Jacobs] used to draw is before me. A comfortable little cottage, a couple of servants, a select coterie of friends, and above all, a neat little wife and a couple of diminutive models of us twain—a hanging of stockings last evening, a merry surprise this morning, the genial interchange of Christmas greeting; a cosy grate fire, the sleepy children cuddling on the floor ready for bed, a sort of dreamy communion between the fire, my wife, and myself; an assured, though quiet and monotonous, future in prospect; a satisfied knowledge of the many little amenities of civilized life which are mine and shall be mine; a genial, optimistical contemplation——

"Ever feel that way? Fred dreamed of it, but never tasted; I suppose I am destined likewise. So be it. . . . The whole thing is a gamble, and those least fitted to understand the game win the most. The most unfortunate gamblers are those who have or think they have systems to beat the game—they always go broke. . . .

"I shall forsake my old dogmas, and henceforth, worship the true god. 'There is no God but Chance, and Luck shall be his prophet.' He who stops to think or beget a system is lost. As in other creeds, faith alone atones. Numerous hecatombs and many a fat firstling shall I sacrifice—you just watch my smoke (I beg pardon, I mean incense).

"I started to write a letter; I became nonsensical; forgive me. I go to dine at my sister's. Happy New Year to all!"

The January, 1899, *Overland* published his story, "To the Man on Trail." I find part of a letter written about this time, containing a reference to the skepticism of the *Black Cat* concerning himself; likewise his discovery of the nonexistence of inspiration:

"I, from a stylistic and constructive standpoint, have wandered afar after strange gods, and find it difficult to get back to the right trails. My conversation is still learning to walk, as you will have observed. . . . Don't criticize punctuation in my letters; I type them off as fast as I can think. . . .

"The only other reason of refusal by *Youth's Companion*, was loosely strung narrative, which I can't exactly see; at least the *Companion* is publishing much worsely strung, balder stuff every issue. So be it. . . .

"I have reached a conclusion: there is no such thing as inspiration. I thought so once, and made an ass of myself accordingly. Dig is the arcana of literature, as it is of all things save being born with a silver spoon and going to Klondike. The only inspiration is that which comes to an orator when addressing a vast multitude which is in sympathy with him.

"Poor child! You took four guesses as to the fate of my wheel and missed it, every one—soaked with my Hebrew uncle. Also other articles too numerous to mention. Lots of fun working under such conditions. You are in luck to obtain this *Overland*. It's the only one I possess, and I had to borrow the dime to buy it. . . .

"The Black Cat writes me concerning an MS. submitted to them. They want references, as I am unknown. Then they wish to know if I wrote it myself, if the idea is mine, if it has ever been in print in part or whole, if it has ever been submitted elsewhere, and if others have or will have a copy of it. . . . Wonder what they'll pay? It is a pseudo-scientific tale, founded on hypothetical chemical, biological, and pathological laws, dealing with the diametric converse of chemical affinity and the mysteries of protoplasmic coagulation. Very sorry, but can't forward definitions.

"I have Cyrano de Bergerac, but no stamps to forward; besides, I would vastly prefer reading it with you. . . . Would like to talk Ella Wheeler Wilcox over with you. You seem to misunderstand her. . . .

"'Magnificent.' No word bears exactly the same significance to any two persons. Barbaric splendor is magnificence to the barbaric mind. Two such specimens as Jack and Lucille, fur-dressed, be-moccasined, etc., may strike you as bizarre—it strikes me as possessing a crude magnificence.

"Yes, some of the qualities of Jensen go into Malemute Kid. But Malemute Kid is still something more. I shall tell more about Lucille, some day."

And here is a lovely fragment, treating of an expectant young mother, a mutual friend:

"I have seen a woman in such condition, but the feeling of wonder, of sacred mystery about it, never stales upon me. It's such a natural event, but somehow, I cannot bring my own practical self to view it exactly in that light—there's a something, a vague and intangible something over and beyond, which eludes the grasp. As reason is excluded, suppose it must be classified under the head of emotion, sentiment. Well, sentiment within bounds is one of the redeeming traits of the world."

Another fragment, January 13, 1899, attests his loneliness and restlessness:

"I doubt if you can understand how disappointed I have been—thirteen days since I wrote you, and no sign. At last I thought, 'Perhaps she remembers my birthday and is waiting so her letter may arrive on that day.' Yesterday morning I thought surely it would arrive. When it did not the afternoon became invested with an infallible certainty. Alas! The postman brought a dun!

"Well, yesterday was my birthday. I did not look for 'many happy returns of the day'; nor did I receive many. My sister was the only one who wished me that, or anything else. Thought I would break the tediousness of my endless prose writing and take a little holiday. . . . So I read the morning papers; answered a couple of pressing letters; stood off the butcher and baker to satisfy the absurd cravings of life; wooed the Muse; and sat down to write poetry. The funniest part of the whole thing is that I did it from a sense of duty."

In the course of the next letter, dated January, 1899, again he takes up arms for Ella Wheeler Wilcox; and singularly enough the paragraph he quotes from the "sweet singer," as he termed her in later life, expresses what he had felt for the Lily Maid to whom he offers the paragraph with a challenge to criticize it:

"Right in the neck—don't mention it. 'Tisn't exactly right to ask for criticism, and then criticize—I understand that, but, well, I wanted to show the point of view by which I worked. I was wrong in doing it, and besides, did it rather rudely. Still, I believe you're none the worse for it. I wish I could talk with you; I might explain better.

"One other thing. I don't know whether you share this belief with your brother, but think you do—that I do not take time enough; do not let a thing cool; do not write and write and rewrite; do not, in short, exhibit the peculiar, or rather, exercise the peculiar methods of the lapidary. To this, I believe, you attribute the weakness of the characters I have drawn. Two other possibilities arise. First, as I stated before, the lack of effect may be laid to your egregious ignorance of such types. Secondly, the fault may lie in me, but not in the trick of the hand or phrase. The latter may do their work very thoroughly, admirably, and through no weakness on their part, produce a puerile result. This then, is due to insincerity of vision on my part; and all the polishing of the MS. will never succeed in bettering it. You see what I am driving at. I am sure what I have written reflects almost perfectly the thought, the image in my mind. I know, if I draw the complete character of Malemute Kid in one short story, all raison de etre of a Malemute Kid series ceases.

"Am very sorry to hear you are worse; and you had been so hopeful, too. Hope my last letter had no bad effects—if it stirred you up, as it evidently did your brother, it was really criminal on my part. Forgive me. Though I guess you know already what a rough-shod barbarian I am, even at my best. At least you cannot say I am anything but candid. Unless your brother mentions it, don't let him know you know I was lectured—it's only Jack, anyway.

"By the way, forgot to tell you in my last letter, that I stand first on the eligible list for carriers. My percent was 85.38. My postman tells me I stand a good show for appointment. At first one goes on as extra man, making about forty-five dollars per month. After about six months of that he becomes regular with sixty-five dollars. But the whole year may elapse before I get anything at all. . . .

"You are unusually prejudiced against Ella Wheeler Wilcox; your brother shares it with you; I am sure your mother does too; and hence, with no further search, you fan each other's distaste. Tell me what you think of the following—style and thought:

> "'The effect of the sweetly good woman upon man is like the perfume of a flower that grew in his childhood's garden, or a strain of music heard in his youth. He is ashamed of his grosser appetites when he is in her presence. He would not like her to know of his errors and vices. He feels like another man when near her and realizes that he has a spiritual nature. Yet as the effect of the strain of music or the perfume of the flower is necessary, so often her influence ceases when he is absent from her, unless she be the woman who rules his life.'

"Speaking of marriage—the following is what Zangwill calls Spinoza's 'aphorism on marriage': 'It is plain that Marriage is in accordance with Reason, if the desire is engendered not merely by external form, but by love of begetting children and wisely educating them; and if, in addition, the love both of husband and wife has for its cause not external form merely, but chiefly liberty of mind.'

"John Keats wrote to Miss Jeffry: 'One of the reasons that the English have produced the finest writers in the world is that the English world has ill treated them during their lives and fostered them after their deaths.'

"What do you think of it? Don't harbor the idea for a minute that I deem myself in that category. I consider myself a clumsy apprentice, learning from the master craftsmen and striving to get my hand in.

"It's midnight, and I'm going to mail this before I turn in. Your brother is over in 'Frisco, gone to the theater I believe. I shall read in bed till his return. If the *Overland*, *Black Cat*, and Republicans pay me next week, within a couple of days of each other, I may be able to come down. Good-night——"

Follows the last of this correspondence in my possession, with its opportune dovetailing as will be seen in the final paragraph; into the Cloudesley Johns series of letters; letters which carry on the evidence of Jack London's unfolding in the crucial beginnings of his rapid elevation to prominence. In the closing paragraph one marvels upon the boy's perspective on his own work, from his heartstick reference to "The White Silence," that masterly story of which George Hamlin Fitch a year thence wrote: "I would rather have written "The White Silence" than anything that has seen the light in fiction in ten years."

"962 East 16th St. Feb. 28, 1899.

Dear ——:

"Yours came to hand not half an hour ago. Am very sorry to hear of your brother's illness, and can appreciate just about how well worn out every one is. Now as to my coming down. If absolutely necessary, telegraph, and I will be there. Yet much as I would like to, my hands are so full and there is so much to be done, that I could not be just to my family and myself did I come when it was not absolutely necessary. You know how we are living from hand to mouth, nothing coming in except what is earned, even yet much of my stuff is in pawn and bills running galore.

"And I wish to turn out some good work in this coming month, for I expect a call from the Post Office in April if not sooner. As to the good work—I will explain. James Howard Bridge, editor of the *Overland*, has at last returned. He at once sent for me. . . . This is the essence of our conversation:

"While advising the majority of candidates for the magazine field to seek other pursuits, he would not do so in my case. I showed the proper touch, only needed bringing out. Different people had been asking about me, Sunday Editors of the *Examiner*, etc. He had bought the Feb. *Overland* on the train West, and was quite taken with my 'White Silence.' Said it was the most powerful thing which had appeared in the magazine for a year; but he was afraid it was a fluke and perhaps it would be impossible for me to repeat it, etc. Now to his proposition. The *Overland* prints forty pages of advertisements at thirty dollars per page, while *McClure's* print one hundred pages three hundred dollars per page; yet printing, plates, paper, mail service, etc. cost just as much for the *Overland*. The only thing the *Overland* could scale down was the writers, and these it had to. While not in position to pay me well, he thought he could give me most valuable returns for my work. If I sustained the promise I had given, he would give me a prominent place in the pages of his magazine, see that the newspapers, reviews, etc. puffed me, and inaugurate a boom to put my name before the public. You can readily see how valuable this would be—putting future employment into my hands from publications which could afford to pay well. Yet the best he could do would be $7.50 per sketch. It would take too long to go over all we said. I may be called over again some day.

"You understand my position, I hope; yet frankly, should it be necessary you know you can call upon me. As I expect it to rain this week, the roads will be impassible and I will have to have recourse to Ferry to Alviso. . . .

"From what I have told you above, you may see that things are brightening, only as yet in the future. I may not fulfil expectations, break down, and have to still further develop before I come out; and if I do not, even present success is a matter of much waiting. Enclosed letter from Cloudesley Johns, return with what you think of it. Don't think I've got the swellhead. I was sick at heart when I read printed 'White Silence,' and I yet fail to see anything in it. Give my regards to all, not excepting a good share to yourself, and believe me ready to come if you cannot get along without me,

"Jack."

CHAPTER XVIII

THE CLOUDESLEY JOHNS CORRESPONDENCE

CLOUDESLEY JOHNS was the first person who ever wrote to me about my work, "I have heard Jack say. Mr. Johns had read "To the Man On Trail" and "The White Silence" in the January and February numbers of the *Overland*, and was unreserved in praise. At the head of Jack's reply is penciled, for the guidance of some one to whom Mr. Johns may have sent it for perusal:

"I prophesied greatness, and told him not to disappoint me. He won't.
"Cloudesley Johns."

Jack's reply is dated at 962 East 16th St., Oakland, February 10, 1899:

"Dear sir:

"What an encouragement your short note was! From the same I judge you can appreciate one's groping in the dark on strange trails. It's the first word of cheer I have received (a cheer, far more potent than publisher's checks).

"If a strong chin and a perhaps deceptive consciousness of growing strength, will aid in the fulfilment of your prophecy, it may to a certain extent be realized. Yes, my name is Jack London—rather an un-American heritage from a Yankee ancestry, dating beyond the French and Indian wars.

"Thanking you for your kindness, I am,

"Very truly yours,

"Jack London."

With his second letter, Mr. Johns sent Jack a manuscript to pass upon. And pass upon it did Jack, with no uncertain touch. It is a pity I have not space to print his critique in full, the advice is so pertinent. As an example:

"It's hard to explain what I mean. Thus, for the Mexican—Statistics are not emotional, when stated in statistical manner. Don't say the Co.

treated the men this way, or cheated them that way. Let the reader learn these facts through the minds of the men themselves, let the reader look at the question through their eyes. There are a variety of ways by which to do this—the most common would be to have them talk with each other. Let them carambo! and speak out the bitterness of their hearts, the injustice they suffer or think they suffer from the Co., the hatred they bear their bosses etc., etc."

He is generous in extolling wherever he honestly can:

"Your style occasionally reminds me of Bierce," or "a true stroke and a strong stroke." And I smile, in view of the clamor that often arose from frightened editorial staffs anent Jack London's offensive redbloodedness, to read his uncompromising advice: "I would not be so ghastly with that intestine; strike out 'and hung down'—(my taste only, yet I appreciate such things for I have seen much of them)."

It will be noticed that Jack had not yet conquered his own over-niceness, for the word "intestine" is used, whereas not so long thereafter he would have employed the shorter and more commanding "guts," in grim defiance of horrified friends and public—who nevertheless continued to read and extoll him.

Jack softens his forthright rending of Johns's manuscript:

"I never did any criticizing anyway; so I just say what I think—hence, you gain sincerity of me, if nothing else."

He continues:

"Thanks for tip to *Western Press;* I have some of my earlier, immature work with them now. Suppose I'll some day call my present work just as immature. . . .

"Will take advantage of tip to Vanity Fair. . . . As to photo of myself. You shall be one of a number of friends who wait and wait in vain for a likeness of yours truly. My last posed foto was taken in sailor costume with a Joro girl in Yokohama. Have but one. But I'll do this: tell you all about me. 23 years of age last January. Stand five foot seven or eight in stocking feet—sailor life shortened me. [He measured five feet nine inches at full stature.] At present time weight 168 lbs.; but readily jump same pretty close to 180 when I take up outdoor life and go to roughing it. Am clean shaven—when I let 'em come, blonde mustache and black whiskers—but they don't come long. Clean face makes my age enigmatical, and equally competent judges variously estimate my age from twenty to thirty. Greenish-gray eyes, heavy brows which meet; brown hair, which, by the way, was black when I was born. . . . Face bronzed through many long-continued liaisons with the sun, though just now, owing to bleaching process of sedentary life, it is positively yellow. Several scars—hiatus of eight front upper teeth, usually disguised with false plate. There I am in toto.

"Tell me what you think of inclosed verse—get your mother's criticism too. Tender my thanks to your mother for her short note." [Mr. Johns' mother, Mrs. Jeania Peet, to whom Jack at intervals refers, is an exceptionally talented woman—writer, sculptress, and "artist of happiness" as Jack expressed it; mother of gifted sons, and once stepmother of our American poet Percy Mackaye.]

"Feb. 27, 1899.

"Dear sir:

" . . . I cannot express the effect of hearing that what I have written has pleased others, for you know, of all people in the world, the author is the least competent to judge what he produces. . . . When I have finished a thing I cannot, as a rule, tell whether it is good or trash. . . .

"My life has been such a wandering one that there are great gaps in my reading and education, and I am so conscious of them that I am afraid of myself—besides, in the course of a sketch, I become saturated with the theme till at last it palls upon me.

"I appreciate, in a way, the high praise of being likened to Tourgenieff. Though aware of the high place he occupies in literature, we are as strangers. I think it was in Japan I read his 'House of Gentlefolk'; but that is the only book of his I have ever seen—I do not even know if the title is correct. There is so much good stuff to read and so little time to do it in. It sometimes makes me sad to think of the many hours I have wasted over mediocre works, simply for want of better.

"I can only thank you for your kindness: it has put new life into me and at the same time placed a few landmarks on the uncharted path the beginner must travel. Would you tell me of the error you mentioned? The compositors made some bad mistakes, the worst being a wilful change in the title, and a most jarring one. It was plainly typewritten 'To the Man On Trail'; this they printed 'To the Man on the Trail.' What trail? The thing was abstract.

"Yours sincerely,"

"My dear sir:

"How I appreciate your complaining of your friends when they say of your work, 'Splendid,' Excellent,' etc. That was my one great trouble. The farther I wandered from the beaten track (I mean the proper trend of modern style and literary art), the more encomiums were heaped upon me—by my friends. And believe me, the darkness I strayed into was heartbreaking. Surely, I have since thought, they must have seen where I was blind. So I grew to distrust them, and one day, between four and five months ago, awoke to the fact that I was all wrong. Everything crumbled away, and I started, from the beginning, to learn all over again. . . .

" . . . I do join with you, and heartily, in admiration of Robert Louis Stevenson. What an example he was of application and self development! As a story-teller there isn't his equal; the same might almost be said of his essays. While the fascination of his other works is simply irresistible. To me, the most powerful of all is his 'Ebb Tide.' There is no comparison possible between him and that other wonderful countryman of his; there is no common norm by which we may judge them. And I see I do not share with you in my admiration of Kipling. He touches the soul of things. 'He draws the Thing as he sees it for the God of Things as they Are.' It were useless for me to mention all my favorites of his; let one example suffice. 'The Song of the Banjo,' and just one line from it. Away in the wilderness where younger sons are striving for hearth and saddle of their own, the banjo is singing, reminding them of the world from which they are exiled:

"'Hear me babble what the maddest won't confess:
    I am memory and torment; I am town;
I am all that ever went with evening dress.'

How often, a thousand miles beyond the bounds of civilization, thirsting for a woman's face, a daily paper, a good book, or better music,—sick for the charms of the old life—have I had that line recalled by the tumpy turn of a banjo, epitomizing the whole mood. . . .

"No; I appreciate how educating my roving has been. At the same time I am sorry that my years could not have been condensed in some magic way, so as to have introduced an equal amount of the scholar's life. That's the trouble of having one's nature dominated by conflicting impulses.

"O yes: I have children constantly footing it to the 'silent sullen peoples' who run the magazines! The *Overland* . . . 'The Son of the Wolf' was sent to them a week ago; they will have it out in the April number, if possible, illustrated by Dixon. I have seen some of his Indian work and think he's just the man for my types. . . .

"Speaking of the *Black Cat*: sometime since, they accepted a pseudo-scientific tale from me. I want to warn you, in case it comes out in the next year or so, that it was written several years ago—so you will forgive it. I hardly remember what it is like. The title is enough—'By a Thousand Deaths.'

"Another friend made the same criticism of 'sole speck of life.' I was saturated with my thought—on the relation of the soul to infinity, etc.—was dealing with the soul of Malemute Kid and did not at the time recognize the dogs. Such slips are liable, since, like you, I can't revise manuscript. My favorite method of composition is to write from fifty to three hundred words, then type it in the Ms. to be submitted. Whatever emendations are made, are put in in the course of typing or inserted with ink in the Ms. . . . Have at last learned to compose first, to the very conclusion, before touching pen to paper. I find I can thus do better work.

" . . . And I warn you, I am as harsh on others as I expect them to be on me. This primrose dalliance among friends never leads anywhere. I once had a friend [this was Fred Jacobs]—we went to college and did much of our studying together—with whom we could candidly discuss each other, holding back nothing. But he lies dead in Manila now. Yet once in a while even he got angry when I expressed my opinion too plainly.

" . . . How are you off for humor? To save my life, while I can appreciate extremely well, I cannot develop a creative faculty for the same."

"Mar. 15, 1899.

"Dear sir:

" . . . I agree with you that R. L. S. never turned out a foot of polished trash, and that Kipling has; but—well, Stevenson never had to worry about ways or means, while Kipling, a mere journalist, hurt himself by having to seek present sales rather than pothumous fame. . . . Kipling has his hand upon the 'fatted soul of things.'

" . . . Speaking of humor—find enclosed triolets, the first, and also the last, I ever attempted. Perhaps there's no market for such things. *Judge* and *Life* refused them and I quit.

"So you have completed a novel? Lucky dog! How I envy you! I have only got from ten to twenty mapped out but God knows when I'll ever get a chance to begin one, much less finish it. I have figured that it is easier to make one of from thirty-five to sixty thousand words and well written, then one three or four times as long and poorly written. What do you think about it?"

Mar. 30, 1899.

"My dear friend:

"Three or four months on the edge of the desert, all alone—how I envy you; and again, how I thank Heaven I am not in a similar position. What a glorious place it must be in which to write! That's one of the drawbacks of my present quarters. Everybody comes dropping in, and I haven't the heart to turn them away. Every once in a while, some old shipmate turns up. With but one exception, this is their story: just returned from a long voyage; what a wonderful fellow Jack London is; what a good comrade he always was; never liked anybody in all the world so much; have a barrel of curios aboard which will bring over in a couple of days for a present; big payday coming; expect to get paid off to-morrow—'Say, Jack old boy, can you lend us a couple of dollars till to-morrow?' That's the way they always wind up. And then I scale them down about half, give them the money and let them go. Some I never hear from again; others come back the third and fourth time.

"But I have the fatal gift of making friends without exertion. And they never forget me. Of course they are not of the above caliber; but I'd just as soon give them the money and let them go, as to have them eat up my time as they always do. Among my feminine friends I am known as 'only Jack.' 'Nough said. Any trouble, tangles, etc., finds me called upon to straighten out. Since Saturday morning I have spent my whole time for one of them, and have accomplished what she and her friends failed to do in five years. This evening I shall finally have settled the whole thing to her satisfaction—but look at the time I have lost. Of course, remuneration is out of the question; but it will have so endeared me to her, that she'll call again the next time she gets into a scrape. And so it goes—time—time—time. How precious the hours are!

"But I should not be unjust. The other afternoon I met an old friend on the car. Delighted to see me; must go back to the 'society' again. I finally promised to go down the following night; but lo, he had spread the news among other friends who had not seen me for two long years. I really did not think they or people in general ever had cared so much for me, and I was ready to weep with sheer happiness at the sincerity of their delight. . . . Couldn't escape; the whole night was lost among them; supper had been ordered, other forgotten friends invited, etc.

"And to me, the strangest part is, that while considering myself blessed above all with the best of friends, I know that I have never done anything to deserve them or to hold them. Mind you, the crowd I have reference to in previous paragraph, has never received a favor of me, nor is bound to me by the slightest social, racial, or perhaps intellectual tie. And so it goes.

"But I have been isolated so much, that I can no longer bear to be torn away for long at a time from the city life. In this particular you will see my thankfulness at not filling your position. Yet you may keep in touch with the world with those trains ever passing.

"I suppose you see many of the genus hobo, do you not? I, too, was a tramp once. . . . I remember, one night, leaving a swell function in Michigan and crossing the lake to Chicago. There, the following morning found me hustling at back doors for a breakfast. That night I made over two hundred miles into Ohio before they finally put me off the train. I wonder what the young lady whom I took into supper would have thought, had she seen me anywhere from twelve to twenty-four hours after.

" . . . How I chatter—all about self! . . . I cannot rewrite; but in turn, I write more slowly. I used to go at it like a hurricane, but found I failed to do myself justice. . . . After sending criticism, and being reminded by the same of Bierce, I dug up 'Soldiers and Civilians.' I notice in his work the total absence of sympathy. They are wonderful in their way, yet owe nothing to grace of style; I might almost characterize them as having a metallic intellectual brilliancy. They appeal to the mind, but not to the heart. Yes; they appeal to the nerves, too; but you will notice in a psychological and not emotional manner. I am a great admirer of him, by the way, and never tire of his Sunday work in the *Examiner*.

" . . . A strong will can accomplish anything—I believe you to be possessed of the same—why not form the habit of studying? There is no such thing as inspiration, and very little of genius. Dig, blooming under opportunity, results in what appears to be the former, and certainly makes possible the development of what original modicum of the latter one may possess. Dig is a wonderful thing, and will move more mountains than faith ever dreamed of. In fact, Dig should be the legitimate father of all self-faith.

" . . . And by the way, what do you think of Le Gallienne? As a writer I like him. . . . I know nothing about him as a man. . . . In his version of the 'Rubaiyat,' I was especially struck by the following, describing his search for the secret of life:

"'Up, up where Parrius' hoofs stamp heaven's floor,
My soul went knocking at each starry door,
Till on the stilly top of heaven's stair,
Clear-eyed I looked—and laughed—and climbed no more.'

" . . . My one great weakness is the study of human nature. Knowing no God, I have made of man my worship; and surely I have learned how vile he can be. But this only strengthens my regard, because it enhances the mighty heights he can bring himself to tread. How small he is, and how great he is! But this weakness, this desire to come in touch with every strange soul I meet, has caused me many a scrape.

"I may go to Paris in 1900; but great things must occur first. I like the story you sent. No sentimental gush, no hysteria, but the innate pathos of it! . . . Our magazines are so goody-goody, that I wonder they would print a thing as risque and as good as that. This undue care to not bring the blush to the virgin cheek of the American young girl, is disgusting. And yet she is permitted to read the daily papers! Ever read Paul Bourget's comparison of the American and French young women?"

To a warning from Cloudesley Johns, Jack had replied:

"I realize the truth in your criticism of ringing the changes on Malemute Kid. . . . But you will notice in 'The Son of the Wolf' that he appears only cursorily. In the June tale he will not appear at all, or even be mentioned. You surprise me with the aptness of your warning, telling me I may learn to love him too well myself. I am afraid I am rather stuck on him—not on the one in print, but the one in my brain. I doubt if I ever shall get him in print."

"April 17, 1899.

"My dear friend:—

"Am afraid you will suffer offense every time I write to you. I never wrote a letter yet without forcing myself to it, and I never completed one without sighing a great sigh of relief. As a correspondent I shall never shine. But how dearly I love to read the letters which come to me from those who little know how I dislike answering. And I never would answer, did I not know they would also cease. . . .

" . . . I see you are opposed to Jingoism. Yet I dare not express my views, for to so do myself adequate justice, would require at least one hundred thousand words. An evolutionist, believing in Natural Selection, half believing Malthus' 'Law of Population' and a myriad other factors thrown in, I cannot but hail as unavoidable, the Black and the Brown going down before the White. I see, after stating that I would not express my views, I have done the contrary. Will shut up at once.

" . . . *Town Topics* has accepted a two eight-line stanza humorous fancy. Have you ever dealt with them? [This was "If I were God One Hour," published May 11, 1899.]

" . . . But enemies—bah! . . . Lick a man, when it comes to a pinch, or be licked, but never hold a grudge. Settle it once and all, and forgive.

"All my life I have sought an ideal chum—such things as ideals are never attainable, anyway. I never found the man in whom the elements were so mixed that he could satisfy, or come any where near satisfying my ideal. A brilliant brain—good; and then the same united with physical cowardice—nit. And vice versa. So it goes and has gone. . . .

"It's a great thing, this coming to believe 'that the universe can continue to exist and operate in a satisfactory manner, without the perpetuation of one's own individuality.' I am an agnostic, with one exception: I do believe in the soul. But in the latter case, I can only see with death, the disintegration of the spirit's individuality, similar to that of the flesh. If people could come to realize the utter absurdity, logically, of the finite contemplating the infinite!

" . . . Don't agree with you regarding your criticism of face torn away by bear. Had forgotten Kipling's 'Truce,' but anyway it does not matter. Many men are killed yearly, up there, and many more fearfully mangled. If we should allow the successful men to copyright any topic they once happen to camp upon, what the devil would you and I and a very numerous tribe do?

" . . . Ran across these lines of Helen Hunt Jackson; have been haunting me ever since:

"'His thoughts were song, his life was singing,
Men's hearts like harps he held and smote,
But ever in his heart went ringing,
Ringing the song he never wrote.'

"Yours, as ever, sincerely,"

"April 22, 1899.

"My dear friend:

"I remember 'Thomas the Doubter.' A friend of mine quoted portions of it one night, but I was just dozing off and failed to follow him. It is very good, and how one can, in the face of it, stomach such things as the infinite mercy of the most infinitely merciless of creators, is more than I can understand. Pardon the double superlative. . . .

" . . . I sometimes fear that, while I shall surely develop expression some day, I lack in origination. Perhaps this feeling is due to the fact that almost every field under the sun, and over it too, has been so thoroughly exploited by others. Sometimes I hit upon a catchy title, and just as sure as I do I find some one else has already used it.

" . . . Ha! ha! You demand comfort in place of conventionality, eh? Ditto here. To-morrow I shall put on a white shirt, and I shall do it under protest. I wear a sweater most of the time, and pay calls, etc., in a bicycle suit. My friends have passed through the stage of being shocked, and no matter what I should do henceforth, would, I know, remark 'It's only Jack.' I once rode a saddle horse from Fresno to the Yosemite Valley, clad in almost tropical nudity, with a ball room fan and a silk parasol. It was amusing to witness the countryside turn out as I went along. Some of my party who lagged behind, heard guesses hazarded as to whether I was male or female. The women of the party were tenderly nurtured, and I hardly know if they have recovered yet, or if their proprieties rather have yet come down to normal. In fact, there was only one I failed to disturb, and he was the rugged old Chinese cook—nothing shocked him except the Mariposa Big Trees. Coming unexpectedly upon the first one . . . he blurted forth 'Gee Glist! Chop'm up four foot ties, make'm one damn railroad!' . . .

"As to evening dress, I think many a man looks extremely well in it. Of course, not all by a large majority. I like that clean feeling of well fitting clothes, etc.—which is strange for one who has passed through as many dirty periods as I have. But there are very few women I care to see in décolleté. . . . As to the breeding of cripples, I shall try to get something uncompressed before marrying, and then, if I have to take her off to a desert isle, I'll see that no compression goes on while she is carrying any flesh and bone of mine. Barrenness is a terrible thing for a woman; but the paternal instinct is so strong in me that it would almost kill me to be the father of a child not physically or mentally sound. Sometimes I think, because this is so very strong in me, that I am destined to die childless. I can understand a Napoleon divorcing a Josephine, even casting aside state reasons. At the same time, I could not do likewise under similar circumstances. I can condone in others what I haven't the heart, or have too much heart to do myself.

"How one wanders on!

"I also send you some of my schoolboy work. Stuff written years ago. . . . Through reading it you may gain a comprehension of one of my many sides, though of course you must take into consideration my youth at the time of writing, if you should try to weigh my presentation of the subjects in hand. People thought I would outgrow that condition and fall back into the conservative ways of thinking. I am happy to say they were mistaken. But believe me, while a radical, I am not fanatical; nor am I anything but normal, and fallible, in all affairs of reason. Emotion is quite another matter. The trouble is so few understand Socialism or its advocates. But I shall cut this short, else I will be delivering a diatribe on the dismal science.

" . . . There is only one kind of infallibility that I can tolerate, nay, I can enjoy it, and that is the infallibility of the good-natured fool. As for cowardice in man: I can forgive the errors of a generation of women far more easily than one poltroon of the opposite gender.

"'In the fell clutch of circumstance
I have not winced nor cried aloud,
Under the bludgeoning of chance
My head is bloody, but unbowed.'

Such, in all things, is what I admire in men. The 'fine frenzy' of the poet can rouse no greater number of tingles along my spine than a Captain going down on the bridge with his ship; the leading of a forlorn hope, or even a criminal who puts up a plucky fight against overwhelming odds. . . . Say what you will, I love that magnificent scoundrel, Rupert of Hentzau. And a man who can take a blow or an insult unmoved, without retaliating—Paugh!—I care not if he can voice the sublimest sentiments, I sicken."

"April 30, 1899.

"My dear friend:—

" . . . I like the form of refusal you sent me. Here you will find a couple I received the middle of this week. Disagree with both as a matter of course. Can't see any other ending, in the nature of things, to the McClure Ms., while Frank Leslie's—well, that poor young American girl who mustn't be shocked, nor receive anything less insipid than mare's milk—she seems to rule our destinies.

" . . . So you, also, are a Socialist? How we are growing! I remember when you could almost count them on one's great toes in Oakland. Job Harriman is considered to be the best popular socialist speaker on the Coast; Austin Lewis the best historical, and Strawn-Hamilton the best philosophical. The latter has just gone to his old home in Mississippi, where he remains until December. Then he will go to Washington to fill a private secretaryship under some legislative relative. He spent 48 straight hours with me a couple of days before he went. He has a marvelous brain, one, I think, which could put that of Macaulay's to shame. He has served no less than twenty-nine sentences for vagrancy, to say nothing of the times turned up on trial, in the several years preceding his joining the socialists. As interesting a character in his way as your Holt, who, by the way, I would like to run across. The world is full of such, only the world does not generally know it. But I don't agree with you regarding the death stroke to individuality coming with the change of system. There will always be leaders, and no man can lead without fighting for his position—leaders in all branches. Sometimes I feel as you do about it, but not for long at a time.

"I see we at least agree about courage. A man without courage is to me the most despicable thing under the sun, a travesty on the whole scheme of creation.

" . . . You misunderstand me. It was the very strength of paternal desire, coupled with the perversity of things, which made me feel doubtful of ever realizing it. The things we wish the most for usually pass us by—at least that has been my experience. He who fears death usually dies, unless he is too contemptible, and then the gods suffer him to live on and damn his fellow creatures.

" . . . See Frank Norris has been taken up by the McClures. Have you read his 'Moran of the Lady Letty'? It's well done.

" . . . My mother also wishes to be cremated. I think it is the cleanest and healthiest, and best; but somehow, I don't care what becomes of my carcass when I have done with it. As for being buried alive—he's a lucky devil who can die twice, and no matter how severe the pang, it's only for a moment. I am sure the pain of dissolution can be no greater than the moment the forceps are laid upon a jumping tooth. If it is greater, then it must be stunning in its effect.

"Do you remember Robert Louis Stevenson moralizing on death in his 'Inland Voyage'? It is a beautiful expansion of 'Eat, drink and be merry, for to-morrow we die.'

"You asked about the age of Prof. Markham: I saw him down at the Section last Sunday night, when Jordan spoke on 'The Man Who Was Left.' He (Markham) is a noble looking man, snow white hair and beard, and very close to sixty. I send you a miserable reporter's account of the meeting, in which nobody or nothing is done justice.

"You really must pardon this letter; my mind is dead for the time being. Have been reading a little too heavily. Just as a sample, I shall give you a list of what I am as present working on, to say nothing of three daily papers, and a stagger of an attempt at current literature:

"Saint-Amand's 'Revolution of 1848.'
Brewster's 'Studies in Structure and Style.'
Jordan's 'Footnotes to Evolution.'
Tyrell's 'Sub-Arctics,'

and Boöhm-Bawerk's 'Capital and Interest'—this latter is a refutation of Carl Marx's theory of values, as determined or measured by labor.

"Good night—By the way, I have forgotten to inform you that an unwelcome guest has annoyed me all evening, and is now getting ready to crawl into bed. This has bothered me not a little. He is such a fool."

This was one of the drawbacks of Jack's quarters—that he must share his bed with no matter what guest chose to remain, invited or otherwise. "And I'd as soon sleep with a snake as with a man," he complained to his sister.

And now I come across an incomplete letter to the Lily Maid, of date May 4, 1899:

"Dear—:

"Yours to hand yesterday morning; caught me in bed, and sick abed for the first time in over three years. But I couldn't stand the pressure, so got up in the afternoon. Feeling too heavy and forlorn to-day to do anything, hence, this prompt reply. Your brother has already remarked that little trait of mine; inflicting letters upon my friends, only at such periods that I cannot do anything else.

"What am I doing? Same old thing. Got a twenty-five dollar offer from *Youth and Age*. Not so bad, or at least better than having the thing die in my drawer. It stands for ten days' work, so I get two and a half per day for it. I notice in to-day's want column of the *Examiner* an ad. which runs to the following purpose: 'Wanted: a bright, intelligent, well educated young man, thoroughly competent at stenography and typewriting, for office work. References required. $4 per week to commence.' He who runs may read—he'd have to work nearly two months to get what I expect to get.

"And there's this redeeming feature in thus getting rid of my earlier work: it cleans up my books; reduces my stamp outlay; and gives me the wherewithal to send new things a-traveling. . . .

"Sea Sprite and Shooting Star: Held the 'Call' up to find out whether they paid or not. Their reply was 'not.' Then I told them to return; they replied by giving me hogwash and sending proofsheets. Subsequent letter from me to them was courteously sententious, and if, on top of that, they dare to publish, I'll sue them.

" . . . Have you seen this month's *Black Cat*? It has my story, written a couple of years ago, revised hastily and then sadly mangled by those at the other end. It can only be taken for a penny's worth of rot. You have not told me of 'The Son of the Wolf.' May *Overland*, have you seen it? Maynard Dixon has done excellent work—excellent is even too weak to do him justice.. . . .

"Then I received a refusal from *Frank Leslie's Monthly*. . . . 'Well written, too risque for our use. We would be glad to consider a short story if you wish to submit one in the Fall.' . . . Encouraging, to say the least. Well, well, plenty of dig, and an equal amount of luck may enable me some day to make perhaps a small livelihood out of the pen. But what's the diff.? I get so hungry sometimes, hungry for all I have not, that I'd rather quit the whole thing and lie down for the good long sleep, did I not have my mother to look out for. This world holds so much, and it takes but such a little to get a fair share of it"—

The remainder is missing.

I take up the Johns correspondence at May 18, 1899.

"My dear friend:—

"Back again at the machine. How one grows to miss it! And you did not mention my scrawl—said scrawl feels slighted. . . .

"I do most heartily agree with you as regards drowning. My stock statement is that I should prefer hanging to drowning. From this you may infer that I, as a strong swimmer, have had some experience. One notable instance was similar to the one you mention as happening to you: that of being dragged down by another, who, perhaps, wasn't worth saving. It happened to me by the dock, with a crowd above but not a boat or boat hook to be had, and the tide very low—twenty feet nearly from the water to the top of the wharf. I was about sixteen, and the lad I was trying to pull out, a wharf-rat of about twelve or thirteen. Really, I saw nothing of my past life, nor beautiful scenes, nor blissful sensations. My whole consciousness was concentrated upon the struggle, my sensation upon the awful feeling of suffocation. Another time, I fought a lonely battle in the ocean surf on a coral beach. Carelessly going in swimming from a sheltered nook, I had drifted too far out and along the shore, and not having the strength to stem my way back, was forced to a landing on the open beach. Not a soul in sight. The seas would swat me onto the beach and jerk me clear again. I'd dig hand and foot into the sand, but fail to hold. It was a miracle that I finally did pull out, nearly gone, in a fainting condition, and pounded into a jelly-like condition." Here he gives a brief account of his attempted suicide by drowning in the Carquinez Straits, ending with "And I was about gone, paddling as the man in the *Black*

Cat paddled, with the land breeze sending each snappy little wave into my mouth. Was still keeping afloat mechanically, when a couple of fishermen from Vallejo picked me up, and can dimly recollect being hauled over the side. No, drowning is not a pleasant shuffle.

" . . . As with you, socialism was evolutionary, though I came to it quite a while ago. You say, 'that to retain a leadership one must possess, or acquire, all the virtues which society and politics demand of their favorites—hypocricy, insincerity, deceit, etc.' Robt. Louis Stevenson was a man looked up to, a leader of certain very large classes, in certain very fine ways. I am sure he lacked those virtues. So it would be in all the arts, sciences, professions, sports, etc. . . . Of course, I realize you mainly applied your statement to politics. But have you ever figured how much of this fawning and low trickery, etc., is due to party politics; and with the removal of party politics and the whole spoils system from the field, cannot you figure a better class of men coming to the fore as political leaders—men, whose sterling qualities to-day prevent them crawling through the muck necessary to attain party chieftainship?

" . . . How concisely you analyzed the lack of unity in the May tale—a lack of unity which you may see is recognized in the very title, 'The Men of Forty Mile.' The subheading was not of my doing, as were none of the others. I wonder what you will think of 'In a Far Country,' which comes out in the June Number, and which contains no reference to Malemute Kid or any other character which has previously appeared. As I recollect my own judgment of it, it is either bosh, or good; either the worst or the best of the series I have turned out. I shall await your opinion of it with impatience.

" . . . We live and learn. With such letters as this, the stereotyped forms of ending have always tortured me. I now comprehend the beauty of yours and make haste to adopt it.

"Jack London."

"May 28, 1899.

"My dear friend:—

" . . . further, believe me, I do not look for the regeneration of mankind in a day: nor do I think man must be born again before socialism can attain its ends. The first motor principle of the movement is selfishness, pure, downright selfishness; the elevation merely an ultimate and imperative result of better environment.

" . . . As you have lost your respect for Roosevelt, so had I long ago lost mine for George Washington, because of the ill manner in which he, too, treated Paine—Paine, who in this case was a contemporary, and who had in his own way done probably as much for the American Revolution as had his immortal traducer. However, I believe you to be less tolerant than I, at least concerning religion. Apropos of Dewey's alleged remark that God superintended the fight in Manila Bay, and your conjecture as to whether he (Dewey) ever took the trouble to notice that God didn't prevent the blowing up of the Maine, brings to recollection a similar query from the 'Social Contract' of Jean Jacques Rosseau: 'All power comes from God, I acknowledge it; but all sickness comes from Him, too: does that mean that it is forbidden to call a physician?'" Jack then devotes a paragraph to Schopenhauer's "terrific arraignment of women, or rather his philippic against them," and precedes some extracts: "Don't believe that I endorse them in toto." "Dear friend:-"June 7, 1899.

" . . . I have been busy. Have been going out more than at any other time in the past eight months; have been studying harder than ever in my life before; and have been turning out more copy than hitherto. Finding that I must go out more and that I was becoming stale and dead, I have really ventured to be gay in divers interesting ways.

"Yes; the time for Utopias and dreamers is past. Coöperative colonies, etc., are at best impossible (I don't mean religious ones), and never was there less chance for their survival than to-day."

"June 12, 1899.

"My dear friend:—

"Yes, I agree with you, 'In a Far Country' should have been the best of the series, but was not. As to the clumsiness of structure, you have certainly hit it. I doubt if I shall ever be able to polish. I permit too short a period—one to fifteen minutes—to elapse between the longhand and the final MS. You see, I am groping, groping for my own particular style, for the style which should be mine but which I have not yet found.

"As to plagiarism: you seem very hypersensitive on the subject. Know thou, that 'In a Far Country' was written long after I had read your 'Norton-Drake Co.' Yet I had no thought of the coincidence till you mentioned it. Great God! Neither you nor I have been the first to make use of a broken back, nor, because of this fact, should we be debarred from using it. How many broken legs, broken backs, broken hearts, etc., have been worked up, over and over again? . . . Take 'White Silence,' how many have made use of a falling tree. For instance, Captain Kettle in June Pearson's. . . . I see no reason in the world why you should cut the broken back out of 'Charge it to the Company.' . . .

"Pardon brevity. I have been writing this and entertaining half a dozen friends at the same time. Really don't know what I have been saying."

A second letter of June 12:

" . . . How I envy you the thrill of life, such as must surely have been gained through your mix-up with the Greasers. In this prosy city existence I have even failed to tangle up with a lone footpad. And one cannot really come to appreciate one's life, save by playing with it and hazarding it a little.

" . . . Have also tried my hand at storiettes for Munsey, but without success, then I ship same off to Tillitson & Son, 203 Broadway, N. Y. C. Figuring it up, it seems to me they pay somewhere around four dollars per thousand. . . . They are a syndicate . . . but their demand for such stuff seems unlimited. I don't like that kind of work, myself, as I can readily see you do not. . . .

"Yes; going out more isn't a bad idea; but as to the less study, can't agree with you. My mind has at least reached partial maturity and I believe I know how far I may go without injury to it. And when I do go out, I assure you I go out with a vengeance, and throw utterly to the winds all thought and worry of my everyday life. And it has been my luck never to be without the one companion to share with me temporary oblivion. No; I don't mean dope, but a proper unadulterated good time with one who knows a good time when it is seen.

"How rabid you are! I feel called upon, for that matter, to tell you that you are really narrow in some things. Remember, the infidel that positively asserts that there is no God, no first cause, is just as imbecile a creature as the deist that asserts positively that there is a God, a first cause. Have you ever read Herbert Spencer's First Principles of synthetic philosophy, and noted the line, the adamantine line of demarkation he draws between the knowable and the unknowable. Pardon me, I should not have allowed myself this discursion, for I have never heard you make that rash negative assertion. But, as regards your Anglo-Saxon views. In one breath you say you are of pure Anglo-Saxon descent on both sides and that your descent (evidently on one side at least) can be traced to the Welsh kings. Know thou, that the Welsh blood is really no nearer (save geographically) and no farther away from the Anglo-Saxon, than is the Hindoo blood of India or the Iranic of Persia. The Welsh, of which breed were the Welsh kings you mention, belongs to the Celtic branch of the Aryan Family, as the pure Russian does to the Slavonic, the Hindoo and Persian to the Indo-Iranic. All the same family, but distinctly different branches. What is the Anglo-Saxon, as we understand it to-day? Let me make you miserable with a little history and ethnology." And he goes on at some length polishing up his memory of what he has read, continuing:

"But enough, this is not my hobby, as you may think, but only one portion of my philosophy or whatever you wish to call the entire edifice of my views. Some day we shall meet and I may be able to explain myself better."

His next letter, of June 23, proceeds with the racial discussion. This paragraph is of especial note as regards his biological attitude toward women:

"Remember, there is even a higher logic than moral or formal logic. Moral and formal logic demonstrate thoroughly that woman shall vote; but the higher logic says she shall not. Why? Because she is woman; because she carries that within her that will prevent, that which will no more permit her economic and suffragal independence, that it will permit her to refrain from sacrificing herself to the uttermost to man. I speak of woman in general. So, with the race problem. The different families of man must yield to law—to LAW, inexorable, blind, unreasoning law, which has no knowledge of good or ill, right or wrong; which has no preference, grants no favors, whether to the atoms in a molecule of water or to any of the units in our whole sidereal system; which is unconscious, abstract, just as is Time, Space, Matter, Motion; of which it is impossible to postulate a beginning nor an end. This is the law, the higher logic, which the petty worms of men must bow to, whether they will or no.

"Socialism is not an ideal system, devised by man for the happiness of all life; nor for the happiness of all men; but it is devised for the happiness of certain kindred races. It is devised so as to give more strength to these certain kindred favored races so that they may survive and inherit the earth to the extinction of the lesser, weaker races. The very men who advocate socialism, may tell you of the brotherhood of all men, and I know they are sincere; but that does not alter the law—they are simply instruments, working blindly for the betterment of these certain kindred races, and working detriment to the inferior races they would call brothers. It is the law; they do not know it, perhaps; but that does not change the logic of events."

"War," Jack declared upon a later occasion, "is a divine beneficence compared with mixed breeding!" During the several years before his death, his experimentation with livestock only cemented his convictions. As witness this letter, written in his last year, to a young Athenian who had dared pit his unripened opinions against the elder's philosophy:

"In reply to yours of Dec. 24, 1915. . . . God abhors a mongrel. In nature there is no place for a mixed-breed. The purest breeds, when they are interbred, produce mongrels. Breed a Shire stallion to a Thoroughbred mare, and you get a mongrel. Breed a pure specimen of greyhound to a pure specimen of bulldog, and you get mongrels. The purity of the original strains of blood seems only to increase the mongrelization that takes place when these strains are interbred or cross-bred.

"Consult the entire history of the human world in all past ages, and you will find that the world has ever belonged to the pure breed and has never belonged to the mongrel. I give you this as a challenge: Read up your history of the human race. Remember, Nature permits no mongrel to live—or, rather, Nature permits no mongrel to endure.

"There's no use in your talking to me about the Greeks. There are not any Greeks. You are not a Greek. The Greeks died two thousand years ago, when they became mongrelized. Just because a lot of people talk the Greek language, does not make those people pure Greeks. Because a lot of people talk Italian, does not make them Roman. The Greeks were strong as long as they remained pure. They were possessed with power, achievement, culture, creativeness, individuality. When they mongrelized themselves by breeding with the slush of conquered races, they faded away, and have played nothing but a despicable part ever since in the world's history. This is true of the Roman; this is true of the Lombards; this is true of the Phoenicians; this is true of the Chaldeans; this is true of the Egyptians; this is not true of the Gipsies, who have kept themselves pure. This is not true of the Chinese, it is not true of the Japanese, this is not true of the Germans, this is not true of the Anglo-Saxons. This is not true of the Yaquis of Mexico. It is true of the fifteen million mongrels of Mexico; it is true of the mongrels that inhabit the greater portion of the West Indies, and who inhabit South America and Central America from Cape Horn to the Rio Grande. This is true of the mongrelized Hindoos.

"Read up your history. It is all there on the shelves. And find me one case where you can breed a greyhound with a bulldog and get anything but a mongrel. Read up your history. You will find it all there on the shelves. And find me one race that has retained its power of civilization, culture, and creativeness, after it mongrelized itself. Read up your history, and try to find any remnant of a pure Roman race, of a pure Hindoo race. . . .

"You know how I am. I talk straight out. When I am asked to hit straight from the shoulder, I hit straight from the shoulder. It is now up to you to come back at me on the very question at issue. . . .

"And, in conclusion, let me repeat—you know the straight talker I am—that no matter how straight-out and savagely I talk, my hand rests no less warmly upon your shoulder, and that only you can be offended by me, and that you cannot offend me.

"Affectionately yours."

To Cloudesley he goes on:

" . . . 'The artist is known by what he omits.' That is my chiefest obstacle, one that I am fully aware of, and one that I struggle ceaselessly to overcome. That is why I am trying my hand at storiettes. I do not like them, but I realize what excellent training they give. Also, the shekels they bring in are not exactly distasteful to me. To me, all my work is practice, experimentative, and I consider myself lucky to be able to sell the sheets of my copybook.

"Forty-six stories—I have not written that many in all my life—why it's a book! Neither have I ever written a book. Nor shall I till I consider myself prepared, and time and place, and man are met."

On July 5, 1899, reference, I believe, is made to the young woman he subsequently married:

"Just got home this morning, and have been hard at it ever since. Have written fifteen hundred words of a new story, transacted all my business, started a few more of my returned children on the turf (as you put it), and am now winding up the last letter of my correspondence. Go away again on Friday, for a jaunt on wheels down country with a young lady whom I have been promising for some time. She made me a call to-day and foreclosed. We stop with mutual friends along the way."

Then he comments upon some editorial errors in his story "The Priestly Prerogative," published in the July *Overland*, ending his letter: "Damn editors!"

The letter of July 22, illustrates Jack London's law-abiding proclivity, as well as his determination to be an artist:

"As for myself, I believe in these present marriage customs and laws, but that is no reason why I should sway my tale one way or the other for aught save the tale's sake. As for my judgment of the tale, I like it least of the series. Just about as much as I do the next which is now in press and which is the last of the *Overland* series. ["The Wife of a King."]

"As to the hog-train—when a passenger goes by in the daylight, shunning six-wheelers it has been my custom to swing under between the trucks and ride the rods—by this I do not mean the gunnels, brake-beams, or springs, or brake-rods. I have often gone along that way in the daytime, with feet cocked up, reading a novel, peering out at the scenery, and enjoying a comfortable if sometimes dusty smoke.

" . . . As soon as I get well ahead of the game—very problematical—I shall escape all my friends, and creditors alas! by engaging cabin passage on a big English ship for a voyage round the Horn to Europe. Shall go aboard with a box of books, a typewriter, and several boxes of paper, and say! I won't do a thing to things in general and particular. I'll write some sea yarns soaked in the atmosphere, besides other and what I would consider more important work, and do no end of reading up all that which the present and continuous flood of current literature will not permit me to enjoy. Ah plans, plans! How many have I builded! and how few have I realized."

"July 29, 1899.

"My dear friend:—

"Trip knocked out in the middle. Whole lot of company came to house—very small house. . . . Well, we had some of our fun anyway.

"Guests are at last gone, and am too flabbergasted to get to work. Have all kinds of work awaiting me, too. Did you ever write a yarn of, say, twelve thousand words, every word essential to atmosphere, and then get an order to cut out three thousand of these words, somewhere, somehow? That's what the *Atlantic* has just done to me. Hardly know whether I shall do it or not. It's like the pound of flesh. [This was "An Odyssey of the North," published in *Atlantic* the following January.] Say, am hammering away at that *Cosmopolitan* essay, at spare intervals. . . . Am thoroughly satisfied, as far as I have gone, which is saying a good deal for me—am usually sick at this stage, and it's such dry, dissertative stuff after all.

" . . . Drop in on us when you do come. Small house, but usually plenty of fair steak, chops, etc., in the larder. I am a heavy eater, but a plain one, fruit, vegetables and meat, and plenty of them, but with small regard for pastries, etc. If you've a sweet tooth you will not receive accommodation here except in the fruit line and the candy stores.

" . . . O, by the way, just to show how this business of placing MSS. is a despairing one. Long years ago—three, anyway, I wrote a synopsis of 'The Road,' under that title, describing tramps and their ways of living, etc. It has been everywhere—every syndicate and big Sunday edition refused it as a feature article; but I kept it going. And lo, to-day, came a note of acceptance of same from the *Arena*. Think I'll resurrect some of my old returned third rate work and send it to *Harper's, Century*, etc. That is, if there is any chance of their accepting what tenth class publications have refused. . . .

"And say, when a third rate magazine publishes something of yours, and you wait thirty days after publication for pay, and then dun them, and then they do not even answer your note, what do you do? Is there any way of proceeding against them? Or must one suffer dumbly? Tell me, tell me—I'd like to make it hot for some of those Eastern sharks.

"And in these pay-on-acceptance fellows, did you ever get your check at the same time you were notified of acceptance? They always make me an offer, first, and then I needs must sit idly and grow weary and sick at heart waiting during the period between my closing with offer and the arrival of the all-needful. . . .

" . . . As you say, I am firm. I may sometimes appear impatient at nothing at all, and all that; but this everybody who has had a chance to know me well have noticed: things come my way even though they take years; no one sways me, save in little things of the moment; I am not stubborn but I swing to my purpose as steadily as the needle to the pole; delay, evade, oppose secretly or openly, it's all immaterial, the thing comes my way. To-day I have met my first serious wall. For three long years the fight has been on; to-day it balances; is a deadlock; I may have met my master; I may not; the future will tell, and one or the other of us will break—and on top of it all I may say it concerns neither my interest or theirs, nothing except the personal vanity and the clash of our wills. 'I won't' and 'I will' sums the whole thing up.

"Firm? But I am firm in foolishness, as well as other things. Take things more seriously than you? Bosh! You don't know me. Ask my very intimate friends. Ask my creditors. Pshaw—let this illustrate: a very dear friend, a woman charming enough to be my wife, and old enough to be my mother, discovered that my most precious possession, my wheel, was hocked. You know I only live for the day. She at once put up the all-needful so that I might regain it. She could well afford it, so that was all right; but mark you, she virtually had a lien upon it. Well, to top it—had been extravagant on the strength of receiving money which did not materialize. Creditors waxed clamorous; a few dollars judiciously scattered among them would have eased things; but credit exhausted; along comes a particularly nice person for a good time. A very nice person who wished to see things; wheel hypothecated and things seen for some forty odd hours. This is me all the time and all over—seriously take things of life—does it look like it? Pshaw. Ask those who know me.

"And I am firm in my foolishness.

"I am glad you took Jordan in the right way. He is, to a certain extent, a hero of mine. He is so clean, and broad, and wholesome. Would to God he were duplicated a few thousand times in the U. S. Working for a sheepskin! That's what most fools do who go in for education, and most of the rest are geniuses and cranks, who get the kernel and then don't or won't use it.

" . . . As for my writing histories and works on economics—I may, some day—but I have little ambition to do so. The same may be said of any kind of writing under the sun. My only wish that way is the all-needful—it seems the easiest way. Had I an assured income, my ambition would be for music, music, music. As it is, impossible—I bend."

Aug. 10, 1899.

"Dear Friend:

"Same old tale. Wound off one visitor the first of last week, to receive at once two more—they have just now gone home. I'll get even with them yet, so that even their letters, much less themselves shall not reach me. I see you have been suffering a similar affliction.

"Say, remember telling me if I got a check from *Town Topics* to frame it? After acceptance I let them slip for several months, then wrote them a nice little note of enquiry—five lines—and behold! They dug up a dollar for that triolet—'He Chortled with Glee', and two twenty-five for the poem 'If I Were God One Hour. ' You mentioned the *Owl* as a snare and a delusion. Well, they haven't got the best of me yet, at least that's all I can say. You know I wrote long ago a lot of stuff upon which I wasted many stamps. Nor would I retire it if hope of getting my postage back still lived. And I must say I have succeeded in disposing of quite a lot of rubbish that way by sending it to the way down publications. The *Owl* published a skit of mine a couple of months ago. When they made the offer for it, I almost fainted—One Dollar and Fifty cents for two thousand words. But it more than paid for the stamps I had wasted on the thing, and gave promise of release from at least one of my early nightmares, so I closed with the offer. But they have not yet paid me. Then the question arises: why should they have made such a miserable offer if they intended to take the whole works? And one answer suggests itself: that from very shame at the smallness of the selling price, the author would refrain from making any trouble in the event of non-payment. However, I am devoid of that kind of shame.

"Yes, I cut the story for the *Atlantic*. There were 12,250 words; but while they wanted it reduced three thousand, I only succeeded in getting it down to an even ten thousand. So I don't know what they will do about it. They seem very nice people from their letters, but that, however, remains to be substantiated by something solid. Have also sent Houghton, Mifflin & Co., collection of tales. [This was "The Son of the Wolf" collection.]

"I closed with a cash offer of ten dollars, and five yearly subscriptions with the *Arena*, so probably it is alright with them. Say, it's great, learning the inner nature of some of these concerns!

"O but I do take myself seriously. My self-estimation has been made in very sober moments. I early learned that there were two natures in me. This caused me a great deal of trouble, till I worked out a philosophy of life and struck a compromise between the flesh and the spirit. Too great an ascendancy of either was to be abnormal, and since normality is almost a fetish of mine, I finally succeeded in balancing both natures. Ordinarily they are at equilibrium; yet as frequently as one is permitted to run rampant, so is the other. I have small regard for an utter brute or for an utter saint.

"A choice of ultimate happiness in preference to proximate happiness, when the element of chance is given due consideration, is, I believe, the wisest course for a man to follow under the sun. He that chooses proximate happiness is a brute; he that chooses immortal happiness is an ass; but he that chooses ultimate happiness knows his business.

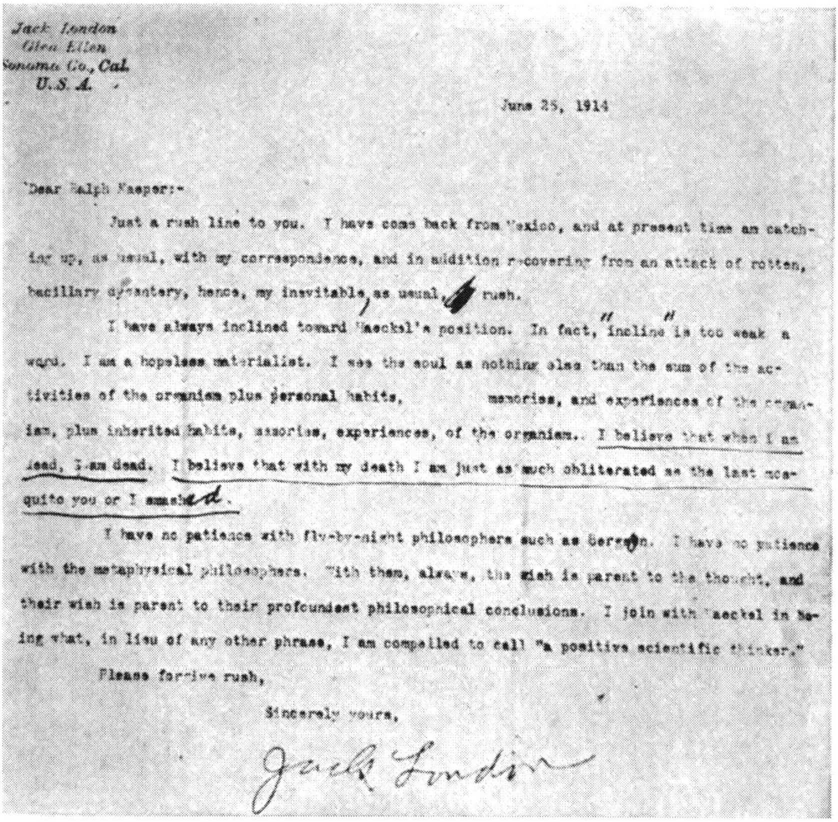

Jack London
Glen Ellen
Sonoma Co., Cal.
U.S.A.

June 25, 1914

Dear Ralph Kasper:-

Just a rush line to you. I have come back from Mexico, and at present time am catching up, as usual, with my correspondence, and in addition recovering from an attack of rotten, bacillary dysentery, hence, my inevitable, as usual, rush.

I have always inclined toward Haeckel's position. In fact, "incline" is too weak a word. I am a hopeless materialist. I see the soul as nothing else than the sum of the activities of the organism plus personal habits, memories, and experiences of the organism, plus inherited habits, memories, experiences, of the organism. I believe that when I am dead, I am dead. I believe that with my death I am just as much obliterated as the last mosquito you or I smashed.

I have no patience with fly-by-night philosophers such as Bergson. I have no patience with the metaphysical philosophers. With them, always, the wish is parent to the thought, and their wish is parent to their profoundest philosophical conclusions. I join with Haeckel in being what, in lieu of any other phrase, I am compelled to call "a positive scientific thinker."

Please forgive rush,

Sincerely yours,

Jack London

1914. LETTER FROM JACK LONDON STATING HIS MATERIALISTIC BELIEF

" . . . I doubt if even you would consider the novel avowedly with a purpose to be real literature. If you do, then let us abandon fiction altogether and give the newspaper its due, for the fixing or changing of public opinion especially on lesser things. But Spencer's 'First Principles' alone, leaving out all the rest of his work, has done more for mankind, and through the ages will have done far more for mankind than a thousand books like 'Nicholas Nickleby','Hard Cash,' 'Book of Snobs,' and 'Uncle Tom's Cabin.' Why, take the enormous power for human good contained in Darwin's 'Origin of Species' and 'Descent of Man.' Or in the work of Ruskin, Mill, Huxley, Carlyle, Ingersoll. . . .

"As to 'that retired stuff'—many thanks for your kind offer; but really, I shall never resurrect it again. Whenever I get to thinking too much of myself I simply look some of it up, and am at once reduced to a more becoming modesty. No, it's put away for good. I have very little out, just now. And it's growing less all the time. It will soon catch me up, I'm afraid, if I don't get down and dig.

"Well, say, hold on a minute. Let me explain. But first let me say how glad I was that you liked 'The Wife of a King.' But I was candid, though I cannot for the life of me remember what 'shameful comparison' I made in letter to you concerning it. This is the way it happened. I had the most terrific dose of blues I ever was afflicted with in my life. I couldn't think of anything original, so I made a composite of three retired MSS., slapped them together, as I at the time considered, haphazard, with the crudest of dove-tailing, Shipped the result off in disgust, and forgot all about it, save a most uncomfortable sense of general dissatisfaction. And for the first time, when I looked upon it printed, I was not wholly-disgusted with myself—not because it was the best I had done, but because I had rated it so low that disappointment or disgust seemed impossible.

"Are there any phases of humanity, under any combinations which have not already been exploited? Yet I think I have for some time had an entirely original field in view, so why should I ask? But who knows. . . . I should think the only way to write a novel would be to do it at a fair rate per day, and then ship off at once. If I can only get ahead of the game, I'm going to jump back to Jerusalem in the time of Christ, and write one giving an entirely new interpretation of many things which occurred at that time. I think I can do it, so that while it may rattle the slats of the Christians they will still be anxious to read it."

The next is a handwritten note dated:

"College Park, May 13/99.

"Dear Friend:—

"A friend has taken it into his head to die; so, in resultant tangle, am at present wasting time at present quarters. Must acknowledge receipt of

'Splendid Spur,' also of two letters, which same I shall answer on my return home. Yes, 'Q' did good work when he completed 'St. Ives.' . . . How do you like my scrawl?"

"962 East 16th St.,
"Aug. 24, 1899.

"My dear friend:—

"'Frisco and Oakland have been roaring since last evening, when the Sherman was sighted. Nor will things quiet down till the week is past. So no work for me—besides, have had another friend to stop with me.

" . . . Am going down country the first of next month to pose as best man for a foolish friend of mine who has abandoned the torturing of catgut for the harmony of matrimony. And I have to dig up a wedding present besides! Wow! . . .

"Have you read anything of Weismann's? He has struck a heavy blow to the accepted idea of acquired characters being inherited, and as yet his opponents have not proved conclusively one case in which such a character has been inherited. Another idea he advances well, is that death is not the indispensable correlative of life, as hitherto it has been supposed to be. In fact, his researches in the germ-plasm have proven quite the contrary. Read him up, you will find him interesting. But it's heavy. If you have not studied evolution well, I would not advise you to tackle him. He takes a thorough grounding in the subject for granted.

"Are you going in for that *Black Cat* Prize Competition? It has just been announced, and the time is not up till the 31st of March, 1900. The style, etc., is worth imitating for the money—if one thinks he is able to do it. I intend having a go at it. I . . . to-day received confirmation of acceptance of my MS. from the *Atlantic*. But say, can you explain this to me? I understand that they pay on acceptance. Well, to-day acceptance comes with assurance of publication in an early number, and that is all. No check, no nothing concerning rate of payment, when, or how.

" . . . Was there ever a luckier fellow than I when it comes to friends? I doubt it. And between you and myself, I likewise greatly fear for the bit of femininity who takes me for little better and much worse. . . .

" . . . But really, I shall have to ask you to accept this stuff as a letter. I have striven and striven and striven. It is warm; doors and windows are open. Three youngsters are playing on the porch before my window. Their elders are in the parler. My guest and a temporary visitor are in the same room with me, waxing hotter and hotter over some mooted point in that much mooted question of telepathy, so I must call quits. . . . "

"Sept. 6, 1899.

"My dear friend:—

"Back again, but not yet settled down. Have blown myself for a new wheel ('99 Cleveland), and hence, between appearing at weddings in knickerbockers and rampaging over the country with bloomer-clad lassies, and celebrating the return of the Californians, I have been unable to chase ink. The way I happened to get said wheel is an illustration of how little rhyme or reason there is in placing MSS. Some time ago I wrote an avowedly hack article for an agricultural paper, expecting to receive five dollars for the same, and to receive it anywhere from sixty to ninety days after acceptance. But it was rejected, and, being short at the time, I was correspondingly dejected. But straight away I shipped off the MS. to the *Youth's Companion,* and lo and behold, without any warnings, they forwarded me a check for thirty-five dollars—eleven dollars per thousand. How's that for luck?

" . . . Don't weep over what the *National* did—they pay poorly. Some time ago they accepted one of my ancient efforts, for which they gave me five yearly subscriptions, and five dollars cash, pay on publication. I expect it to come out in the September number. God bless the publishers.

" . . . Go it for the *Black Cat!* I cannot even think of a suitable plot—my damnable lack of origination you see. I think I had better become an interpreter of the things which are, rather than a creator of the things which might be.

" . . . Well, time is flying; I've got a visitor as usual, spending a few days with me, and as I hear the tinkle of his bicycle bell approaching, I must cut off. But just you watch my smoke some of these days—I intend shaking every mortal who knows me and going off all by myself."

"Sept. 12, 1899.

"My dear friend:—

"Between engagements, visitors, and friends, I have not yet succeeded in doing a tap. And to-morrow I start out on that postponed trip of mine to Stanford University and Mt. Hamilton, to say nothing of way points. And when I return from that I am going to lock myself up." [In an unimportant handwritten postscript he signs himself "J. G. L."—the only instance I know where he used his middle initial.]

"Sept. 20, 1899.

"Dear Cloudesley:—

"Back again. Had a glorious time. Stopped over at Stanford, where I met several students I know, sat under the various profs., etc. And looked through the thirty-six inch reflector on top of Mt. Hamilton. There we saw the moon, Saturn and his rings, and quite a number of bourgeois pigs. Yes, they were pigs, dressed like tourists. My companion and I, after seeing them, were exceeding proud of the fact that we were mere proletarians. . . .

" . . . Ah, therein you differ from me—it's money I want, or rather, the things money will buy; and I could never possibly have too much. As to living on practically nothing—I propose to do as little of that as I possibly can. Remember, it's the feed not the breed which makes the man. . . .

" . . . As an artisan cannot work without tools, so a man cannot think without a vocabulary, and the greater his vocabulary the better fitted he is to think. Of course, an ass may acquire the tools of an artisan and be unable to work with them, so with words. But that does not interfere with the broad statement I have laid down." . . .

"Sept. 26, 1899.

"Dear Cloudesley:

" . . . Did I ever mention a MS. I received in response to a trailer, which same MS. had been O.K'd and blue-penciled? Well, such happened to me some time ago. Without removing marks or anything I shipped it off to *Youth's Companion*. There were fifteen hundred words to it. Last week a check comes for twenty-five. Say I'm having lots of luck with the *Companion*, sending them my old, almost-ready-to-be-retired stuff. . . . They pay good and promptly. Though such work won't live, it at least brings the ready cash.

" . . . How I envy you when you say that you do not write for publication. There is certainly far greater chance for you to gain the goal you have picked out than for me who am in pursuit of dollars, dollars, dollars. Yet I cannot see how I can do otherwise, for a fellow must live, and then there are also others depending upon me. However, I shall once and a while make it a point to sit down and deliberately not write for publication. . . .

" . . . Have begun to isolate myself from my friends—a few at a time. But those I have managed to dispense with are the easy ones. I can't see my way clear to the others except by running away. But instead of the desert I'll take to sea. Many who know me, ask why I, with my knowledge of the sea, do not write some sea fiction. But you see I have been away from it so long that I have lost touch. I must first get back and saturate myself with its atmosphere. Then perhaps I may do something good. . . .

" . . . Viewing this world through the eyes of science I can see no reason at all why a person should be the slightest bit pessimistic. Why, it's all good, considering man's relation to it. . . .

P.S.—Did I inform you that I am once more an uncle. It was born nearly a month ago. [This was Eliza Shepard's only child, Irving, before mentioned.]

"Oct. 3, 1899.

"Dear Cloudesley:—

" . . . Last Sunday I went off with a very nice young lady on a bicycle trip up to Mill Valley, among the redwoods at the base of Mt. Tamalpais. To do this we had to go to 'Frisco and take the ferry to Sausalito, and from thence to destination via pedals. Any number of lively young 'Frisco people take the same outing on Sundays, except that they do not ordinarily or extraordinarily go on bikes. They patronize the railroad. Well, on the back trip to 'Frisco, a bunch of them took the deck and raised hell generally, to the shocking of many of the more sedate passengers. Am happy to state, however, that the girl I was with, while the kingdoms of the earth could not have lured her into getting up and doing likewise, at least highly enjoyed the performance. All of which is neither here nor there. But for myself, I was attacked by all kinds of feelings. Therein you and I differ—dissipation is alluring to me. Why, my longing was intense to jump in and join them after the fashion of my wild young days, and go on after we arrived in 'Frisco and make the night of it which I knew they were going to make. Alluring? I guess yes.

"And then again, I could feel how I had grown away from so much of that—lost touch. I knew if I should happen to join them, how strangely out of place it would seem to me—duck-out-of-water sort of feeling. This made me sad; for, while I cultivate new classes, I hate to be out of grip with the old. But say, it wouldn't take me long to get my hand in again. Just a case of lost practice.

" . . . Have been going on chess drunks of late. Did you ever yield to the toils of the game?—toils in more ways than one. It's a most fascinating game, and one which has devoured well nigh as many of my hours as cards. However, I've done very little chess in the last year or so, and this is merely a temporary relapse.

"Have also been feasting my soul with some of the new books: Kipling galore, Bullen's 'Sea Idyls,' Grant Allen's 'Adventure of Miss Gayly,' and among others, Beatrice Harraden's 'Fowler'. . . . "

At this period Jack London put into practice his thousand-words-a-day stint, which he maintained for the rest of his life:

"Am now doing a thousand words per day, six days per week. Last week I finished 1100 words ahead of the required amount. To-day (Tuesday), I am 172 ahead of my stint. I have made it a rule to make up next day what I fall behind; but when I run ahead, to not permit it to count on the following day. I am sure a man can turn out more, and much better in the long run, working this way, than if he works by fits and starts. . . .

"How time flies! Here is Christmas at hand, and Paris approaching—ah! I wonder if the gods will smile so that I may go."

"October 24, 1899.

"Dear Cloudesley:—

"Everything in confusion, visitors still here. So you're a chess player. And it's the one form of dissipation which has any attraction for you. As I can hardly look upon it in that light concerning myself, I can but conclude that you are by far the better player. Why, I have never met a good player—spent all my time teaching beginners, and you know nothing is worse for chess than that. And besides, I have never had the time to devote to it. For a year at a stretch I never see a board, and then, for a few short weeks I happen to mildly indulge. As I have not taken the time to learn properly, so I cannot play an intensive game; instead, I play viciously, not more than four moves ahead at the best, and endeavor to break up combinations as fast as my opponent forms them—that is, first, if they are threatening; and second, if the slightest and most insignificant gain will accrue to myself, such as the getting of another piece of mine in position by a trade, or by double-banking my opponent's pawns, or preventing his castling by forcing him to move his king in a trade. For the sake of this latter, when the gambit goes my way, I always trade queens. But a heavy player, once growing accustomed to my play, doesn't do a thing to me. So be it. I shall never learn chess.

"Last article published by me, had, among other typographical errors, 'Something fresh for the jaded care of the world,' instead of 'something fresh for the jaded ear of the world.' On second thought it might have been worse.

"Think you could train yourself into becoming a hermit? For me that would be far harder than to train myself to become a suicide. I like to rub against my kind, with a gregarious instinct far stronger than in most men. A hermitage—synonym for hell.

" . . . Lucrative mediocrity? I know, if I escape drink, that I shall be surely driven to it. By God! if I have to dedicate my life to it, I shall sell work to Frank A. Munsey. I'll buck up against them just as long as I can push a pen or they can retain a MS. reader about the premises. Just on general principles, you know.

" . . . Am reading Stevenson's 'Virginibus Puerisque' just now. Find in this mail his 'Inland Voyage.' Return it when you have finished, as I wish to pass it along. Have read it myself. Get such books for 'Bull Durham' tobacco tags. Have sent for his 'Silverado Squatters'—don't think much of it from previous reading, but it was a long time ago, and I did it too hurriedly, I'm afraid. . . .

"So you try experiments in letter writing. I never do nor never have. Haven't the slightest idea what I'm going to say when I sit down—just hammer it out as fast as I can. And right well am I pleased when I have finished the hateful task. I wouldn't do it at all, no more than I would work, were it not for the compensation. As for you, I get more originality in your letters than from all my rest put together—rather jerky and jagged but refreshing and interesting. Believe me, I'm not fishing for a loan.

" . . . Have been reading Jacobs' 'More Cargoes'. . . . Also have been going through Kendricks Bangs' 'The Dreamers' and 'The Bicyclers and Other Farces.' He's clever and humorous, in a mild sort of way.

"Have been digging at 'Norman's Eastern Question,' preparatory to a certain economic dissertative article I intend writing—Asia touches one of the phases I wish to deal with. Besides, I have gone through Curzon's similar work, and wish to take up soon Beresford's 'Breakup of China.' Am going through Drummond on evolution, Hudson on psychology, and reviewing Macaulay and De Quincey in the course of English in Minto which I am giving to a friend—the photographer. She's well up in the higher Math., etc., but not in general culture—coaches in the exact sciences for would-be university students, etc. Say, that reviewing does a fellow good. I had no idea how lazy I had gotten.

"Society will never injure me—the world calls too loudly for that."

"Oct. 31, 1899.

"Dear Cloudesley:—

" . . . So you deem the world as fair a synonym for hell as I do hermitage. Can't see it. There are some redeeming features. As long as there is one good woman in it, it will not hold. Why, I remember, once, when for several weeks I meditated profoundly on the policy of shuffling off. Seemed the clouds would never break. But at last they did, and I doubt if you could imagine the cause of my sweetened mood. A memory of a day, of an hour—nay, a few paltry minutes—came back to me, of a time almost lost in the dim past. I remembered—what? A woman's foot. We were by the sea. In a dare, we went wading: had to stick our feet in the hot sand till they dried; and it was those few moments which came back to me, dripping with 'sweetness and light.' Hell? Nay, not so long as one woman's foot remains above ground.

"Please don't thing I'm in love. Simply sentiment. Don't get that way often.

"Well, some time since, I started in to write a twenty-five hundred word article on 'Housekeeping in the Klondike.' [This was published in *Harper's Bazaar*, on September 15, 1900.] In choice of theme I had been forced to narrow, being aware of my miserable predilection. And lo, before I had got into full swing, I found that the whole article could be comfortably taken up in a discussion of bread-making. And, still narrowing, it was soon apparent that this should be divided, one single subhead to be discussed, viz.: sourdough bread-making. And so it goes. Never did a person need the gift of selection more than I.

" . . . Have just completed Horace Vachell's 'The Procession of Life' . . . quite interesting, but not of the first water. . . . And any way, did you ever read that boyhood classic, 'Phaeton Rogers'? Rossiter Johnson, who edits the Whispering Gallery of the *Overland*, is the author. . . .

"My *Atlantic* story will come out, I believe, in the January number. Received a check for one hundred and twenty dollars yesterday for it, with a year's subscription thrown in. They are very slow, but very painstaking. They even questioned the propriety of using my given name—unconventional. But they came around all right.

"Have heard nothing more concerning my collection. They do take their time about it. Nothing from the *Cosmopolitan* prize essay either.

"How do you like my new machine? Haven't got used to it yet. Came to-day. When I get married, guess I'll have to marry a typewriter girl. I do most heartily hate the job.

"So the poor little Boers have risen in their might. God bless them! I can admire their pluck, while at the same time laughing at their absurdity. There be higher things than formal logic or formal ethics. When a detached, antiquated fragment of a race attempts to buck that race, a spectacle is presented at once pitiful and impotent. Fools, to think that man is the object of his own volition, inasmuch that a few of him may oppose the many in a movement which does not spring from the individual but from the race, and which received its inception before even they had differentiated from the parent branch!"

"November 11, 1899.

"Dear Cloudesley:—

"You say: 'This is the beginning of the end—you'll see—and within ten years the British Empire will have followed its predecessors, the Greek, the Roman, and the French.' Well, well, well. I'd like to talk with you for a few moments. It's simply impossible to take it up on paper. The day England goes under, that day sees sealed the doom of the United States. It's the Anglo-Saxon people against the world, and economics at the foundation of the whole business; but said economics only a manifestation of the blood differentiations which have come down from the hoary past.

"This movement, dimly felt and working in strange ways, is not to be stopped in a day, or by a lesser people, or by a bunch of the same which have become anachronisms. The Boers are anachronisms. There is no place for them in the whirl of the world unless they whirl with it.

"You say, if subjugated they will still be Boers. Do you remember the Norman invasion of England? How long the Saxons held strictly apart? And how in the end, the Saxon, as a Saxon, vanished from the face of the earth? Took several centuries, but it was accomplished.

" . . . I believe Bret Harte wrote a story of a natural fool who got along nicely till he struck it rich. I'm hard at it. Am just finishing an ambitious Klondike yarn which is a failure, and before the twenty-fifth of this month have to write and read up for two essays and prepare for a speech before the Oakland Section. Haven't addressed an audience for three years; it'll seem strange.

" . . . As to your suggestion regarding the finish of 'To the Man on Trail': I had never been satisfied with that ending, though too lazy to even think for an instant of attempting to better it. Your ending could not be bettered, and I shall hasten to take advantage of it. Many thanks for same. It will then leave one with a pleasant taste in the mouth. The alliterative effect you mention strikes my gaudy ear; I shall certainly use it. I want you to read my 'Odessey of the North ' when it comes out. . . . "

"Nov. 21, 1899.

"Dear Cloudesley:—

"Hard at it—mostly history and economics. And yet I don't work a tithe of what you work. Why should you work seventeen hours a day? As regards your writing you positively should not do more than six—four were better. But any excess of six cannot be good stuff. . . .

" . . . I never pity anybody but myself. Life is too short.

"The *Overland* declined my offer on specious grounds. Twenty-five dollars was stiff under the circumstances. However, I have placed a yarn with them to come out in the Christmas number. ["The Wisdom of the Trail."] they're great people, of great heart: but heart and finance do not usually go together. . . .

" . . . Very few American educated people have little else but rancor for England—a rancor which is bred by the school histories and the school traditions. All of which is utterly wrong. I have to laugh when you call Kipling a narrow, hidebound, childishly pettish, mean little man. . . . Any masculine who delights in taking down a woman's back hair will find a warm welcome in my heart.

" . . . Find, with 'Editor,' when it comes along, some more proofs of yours truly, taken down by the sounding sea. Also one of the young woman who sometimes accompanies me in my far from conventional rambles. Last Sunday, threatening rain, we wandered off into the hills, cooked our dinner (broiled steak, baked sweet potatoes, coffee, etc., crab, French bread, and a patty of dairy butter), and were a couple of gipsies. To-morrow we may jump on our wheels and ride off forty or fifty miles. And yesterday we may have taken in the opera and dined fashionably. Never the same, except the camera, which same I am slowly mastering.

"Yes; I read 'A New Magdalen' when I was about twelve, and then shocked a very nice young lady by starting to discuss it with her."

Continuing the discussion that runs throughout the correspondence, and which I must cut, he argues:

"When England is so decadent as to lose her colonies, then England falls. When England falls the United States will be shaken to its foundations, and the chances are one hundred to one that it ever recovers again. Why, England is our greatest purchaser, and our greatest maker of markets, and the only nation which is not deep down hostile to us. Germany, France, Austria and Russia can supply the world with all that the world needs, if they could only get a chance by having England and the United States eliminated from the proposition. And once one were eliminated the ruin of the other were easy. But England is not going to fall. It is not possible. To court such a possibility is to court destruction for the English speaking people. We are the salt of the earth, and it is because we have it in us to frankly say so that we really are so. No hemming or hawing; we state the bald fact. It is for the world to take or leave. Take it may, but it shall always leave us. . . .

" . . . So? Why, the United States never had but one fight in its history; that was when it fought with itself. England never bothered her. Read up history and you will find that England's hands were full of other things, and preferring other matters, she let the colonies slip away. Do you really think we whipped the whole of England in the Revolution? Or in 1812, when her hands were full with Napoleon, and she was fighting in every quarter of the globe? Mexico was play. But the civil war was a war, a death grapple. And all hail to the South for the fight it put up against stiff odds.

"You little know Canada. Why don't those other European countries, standing by themselves, fall? Because, they are but ostensibly alone. In reality they stand together—whenever it comes to bucking the Anglo-Saxon.

Dropping to the personal, he announces:

"If cash comes with fame, come fame; if cash comes without fame, come cash."

Dec. 5, 1899.

"Dear Cloudesley:—

"First letter-writing I have done for quite a while. . . . Have not had an evening at home for nigh on to two weeks, what with suppers, speaking, functions, and last but not least, FOOTBALL. Did you see what we did to Stanford? In case that benighted region in which you reside has not yet received the score, let me have the privilege of blazoning it forth. Thirty to nothing, Berkeley.

"It was magnificent, to sit under the blue and gold and see the Berkeley giants wade through the Cardinals, and especially so when one looks back to the times he sat and watched the Stanfordites pile up the score and hammer our line into jelly. Do you care for football? In case you do not, I shall not permit my enthusiasm to bore you further.

". . . Heaven save us from our friends! Last Sunday evening I spoke before the San Francisco Section. Unknown to me, and on the strength of divers newspaper puffs which recently have appeared, they posted San Francisco, and also perpetrated the enclosed hand bill. I knew nothing about it till just the moment before I was to go on the platform. Can I sue them for libel? [I find the hand bill in Jack's scrapbook for 1899-1900, advertising his name in blatant type, "The Distinguished Magazine Writer," a lecture in Union Square Hall, 421 Post Street, Sunday Ev'g, Dec. 3rd, 1899.]

". . . Your criticism of my 'Editor' article is exactly my own criticism. We could not disagree on that if we tried. By the way, there were 1750 words in it. The 'Editor' was billed to pay liberally, and they told me on acceptance, promptly. It was published last October, I received for it five dollars which came to hand day before yesterday.

"O Lord! Good-by."

Dec. 12, 1899.

"Dear Cloudesley—

" . . . You mistake, I do not believe in the universal brotherhood of man. I think I have said so before. I believe my race is the salt of the earth. I am a scientific socialist, not a Utopian, an economic man as opposed to an imaginative man. The latter is becoming an anachronism.

"Nay, nay, bankruptcy is not an ideal state, at least for me. It's too horrible for words. Give me the millions and I'll take the responsibilities.

"Later on I shall forward you an article of mine on the 'Question of the Maximum,' which contains within it, though not the main theme, the economic basis for imperialism or expansion. This, I know, is directly opposed to the current ethics. But it is the one which will dominate the current ethics."

CHAPTER XIX

INTRODUCING ANNA STRUNSKY, AND JACK'S LETTERS TO HER; ALSO FURTHER CLOUDESLEY JOHNS LETTERS

JUST about this time Jack London's orbit crossed that of Anna Strunsky. Anna was a Stanford University student—a round, brown slip of a girl, a Russian Jewess, no older than the little women of his precocious boyhood, for she was barely seventeen. A glowing, flaming creature she was, intellectual, brilliant and friendly, with a deep and lasting loyalty that we were all to learn. She was so different from anything he had ever known of woman—neither lily-pallid nor boldly passionate; but wide-hearted like all her family, and deliciously, naively frank. She met one so wondrous-comradely. Every one loved Anna, women as well as men; no one could resist the drawing power of her, she the Much-Desired. Who was Jack, to hold aloof from the warmth of her presence? Who, indeed! As naturally as breathing, their friendship waxed, and they could not but regard their need of each other in the big world that is lovely to souls like theirs, stainless of deceit toward each other. But it was their mental and spiritual companionship that most counted, and that endured.

Rose, Anna's younger sister, was likewise uncommonly brilliant for her years—no less remarkable than Anna: "There's Rose," Jack once said to me,—"She's as wonderful, in her way, as Anna. Watch Rose." Rose has indeed been worth watching, from her early work to her extraordinary book on Abraham Lincoln, her translation of Tolstoi's "Journals," and Gorky's "My Confession."

The whole Strunsky family, with its arms-around hospitality, its long table always laid for a problematical number of interesting guests (for no dull one ever drew chair to its abundance)—the whole Strunsky brood stamped its intelligence and its lovableness and its charm upon Jack London until he came in after years to call it his Love Family. Once in a letter to me, he said: "They are fine splendid people to know. They are individuals, not a mess. And they stand for high things, and are good to know."

Anna Strunsky, co-author with Jack of "The Kempton-Wace Letters," (and since, of "Violette of Pere La Chaise,") loved mate of a distinguished husband, William English Walling, and mother of four glorious children, wrote me from her home in Greenwich, Connecticut, under date of January 17, 1919:

"Dearest Charmian:

"This is perhaps a pretty complete statement of the psychical aspect of our friendship. I have nothing but love and gratitude for him, and that he has lived at all and I have known him is a miracle of happiness, a miracle of miracles. . . . If there is anything more that suggests itself, please ask. . . . Your loving sister, always,

"Anna."

What she sends me I give in advance of the letters written her by Jack, which she has as freely contributed to my picture of her friend:

"Jack and I met for the first time at a lecture by Austin Lewis, I believe, in the fall of 1899 at the old Turk Street Temple. It was either Cameron King or Strawn-Hamilton who introduced us. *Herman* Whitaker had 'discovered' Hamilton and had made him acquainted with Jack, and Hamilton and Cameron were intimate friends.

"It is owing to a kind of spiritual secret diplomacy that the details of our meeting are vague in inverse ratio to the importance of the moment. The essentials, however, are stamped on my mind. He and I gravitated towards the platform to congratulate the speaker. A whispered 'Do you want to meet him?' from either Strawn-Hamilton or Cameron—'he is Jack London, a Comrade who has been speaking in the street in Oakland. He has been to Klondike and writes short stories for a living.' We shook hands, and remained talking to each other. I had a feeling of wonderful happiness. To me it was as if I were meeting in their youth, Lasalle, Karl Marx or Byron, so instantly did I feel that I was in the presence of a historical character. Why? I cannot say, except perhaps because it was the truth and he did belong to the undying few. This certainty with which he inspired me was the vital subjective fact about our meeting.

"Objectively, I confronted a young man of about twenty-two, and saw a pale face illumined by large, blue eyes fringed with dark lashes, and a beautiful mouth which, opening in its ready laugh, revealed an absence of front teeth, adding to the boyishness of his appearance. The brow, the nose, the contour of the cheeks, the massive throat, were Greek. His form gave an impression of grace and athletic strength, though he was a little

1904. JACK LONDON, IN KOREA ON HIS AUSTRALIAN BARB-MARE, "BELLE"

1905. JACK LONDON ON "WASHOE BAN"—"BROWN WOLF" BESIDE

under the American, or rather Californian, average in height. He was dressed in gray, and was wearing the soft white shirt and collar which he had already adopted.

"Then began our friendship. If at the time, to the inexperienced heart of our youth, it seemed tempestuous, almost terrible, storm-bound as it was by our intellectual and psychical differences, now I see in it only the dearness and beauty of a force that outlasts life, a world, indeed, without end, something more precious and more significant to both of us than we could then understand. Those differences—what were they but the healthy expression of our immaturity, of our aspirations toward the absolute of truth and right and justice, the normal expression, perhaps, of the man and woman equation in the abstract questions concerning life! The differences tortured us as they did precisely because in the great essentials we were at one—but this, youth could not know! Did he not years later write 'The People of the Abyss,' 'The Dream of Debs,' 'The Iron Heel'? How then, could I have challenged his Socialism? Was he not an ardent feminist and suffragist? Why then, did I suspect him of thinking women the inferiors of men? Did he not finally marry with love and for love, and exemplify in his own life the need of love that men and women have in common, the greatest miracle of all, the miracle of interdependence? Why, then, did we spend twenty-two months writing 'The Kempton-Wace Letters,' trying to convert each other to positions which, at bottom, we must both have held?

"Individualized as his personality was he was yet symbolic. In him was expressed what a human being escaping from the Abyss might become. Charles Ferguson, the other day, spoke of Jack London as having been the most aristocratic of men. If to be gifted beyond others, stronger than others, more beautiful in person, warmer of heart than others is to be a natural aristocrat, then this super-democrat, this man identified with the People and with the Class War was one. To me his qualities were interesting more because they showed what was in all of us than because they were exceptional. He was a genius and yet that was only to be—the ordinary human being extended. To know him was immediately to receive an accelerated enthusiasm about everybody.

"Our friendship can be described as a struggle—constantly I strained to reach that in him which I felt he was 'born to be.' I looked for the Social Democrat, the Revolutionist, the moral and romantic idealist; I sought the Poet. Exploring his personality was like exploring mountains, and the valleys which stretched between troubled my heart. They did not seem to belong to the grandiose character he was, or could, by an effort of the will, become. He was a Socialist, but he wanted to beat the Capitalist at his own game. To succeed in doing this, he thought was in itself a service to the Cause; to 'show them' that Socialists were not derelicts and failures had a certain propaganda value. So he succeeded—became a kind of Napoleon of the pen. This dream of his, even when projected and before it became a reality, was repellant to me. The greatest natures, I thought, the surest Social Democrats, would be incapable of harboring it. To pile up wealth, or personal success—surely anybody who was a beneficiary of the Old Order must belong to it to some extent in spirit and in fact.

"So it was that our ancient quarrel, and many, many others took their rise in the same source—a doubt, not as to himself—I never doubted the beauty and the warmth and the purity of his own nature—but as to the ideas and the principles which he invited to guide his life. They were not worthy of him, I thought; they belittled him and eventually they might eat away his strength and grandeur. . . .

" . . . I have felt so much for Jack London because I saw in him potential martyrs and heroes. . . . He was symbolic of the Movement and its struggle and its sorrow; he was the dawn of the future, and in his beauty was the pristine beauty and greatness of the race. So I said when I first beheld him; so I say now, after his death. . . . "

Herewith are her friend's first impression of Anna Strunsky:

"Jack London,
"962 East 16th St.,
"Oakland, Calif.,
"Dec. 19, 1899.

"My dear Miss Strunsky:—

"Seems as if I have known you for an age—you and your Mr. Browning. I shall certainly have to reread him, in the hope after all these years of obtaining a fuller understanding.

"What did I start to write you about, anyway? Oh! First, that toasting the old year out affair—does it take place on the last Friday or Thursday of the month; and secondly—well, it doesn't matter. I have forgotten.

"Please don't carry a wrong impression of my feelings regarding Hamilton. Because I happen to condemn his deficiencies is no reason that I do not appreciate his good qualities, nor that I should not love him. Indeed I do. Do you remember how I said I ran down the street after him on a circus day, our engagements, etc.? My feelings and personal liking swayed me there; but in summing up the man I set such things to one side and perform the operation with the cold-bloodedness of the economic man. I hope you will understand. My regard for him is such that were I to accumulate a treasure I think I would advertise for him in the agony columns throughout the United States and bring him to me, give him a home, a monthly allowance, and let him live out his life whatsoever way he willed.

"You said at parting that you also were a literary aspirant. I may be able to help you, perhaps—not in the higher criticism but in the more prosaic but none the less essential work of submitting MS. Through much travail I have learned the customs of the 'silent sullen peoples who run the magazines.' Their rates, availability, acceptability, etc. Should you stand in need of anything in this line (economic man), believe me sincerely at your service.

"Of course, I do not know what lines you deem yourself best fitted for: however, as I sat there listening to you, I seemed to sum you up somewhat in this way: A woman to whom it is given to feel the deeps and the heights of emotion in an extraordinary degree; who can grasp the intensity of transcendantal feeling, the dramatic force of situation, as few women, or men either, can. But, this question at once arose: Has she expression? By this, I mean simply the literary technique. And again, supposing that she has not, has she the 'dig', the quality of application, so that she might attain it.

"In a nut-shell—you have the material, which is your own soul, for a career: have you the requisite action to hew your way to it?"

"Dec. 21, 1899.

"Dear Miss Strunsky:—

"Surely am I a barbarian, lacking in cunning of speech and deftness of touch. Perhaps I am only a Philistine. Mayhap the economic man incarnate. At least blundering and rough-shod, lacking even that expression which should properly voice my thoughts. I call for a trial by jury. I throw myself on the mercy of the Court. Nay, after all is said and done, I plead not guilty.

"Somehow it is a new note to me, that of being seen as 'aimless, helpless, hopeless,' and I am uneasy under it all.'

"I rarely remember what I say in letters, sometimes retaining only vague recollections of what I do not say; but in the present case I am sure I said nothing like the above. I speculated on you as impartially as had you been a hod-carrier, a Hottentot, or a Christ. It was a first speculation; it dealt with but one portion of your being. And as I could not divorce Christ or the Hottentot from the rest of humanity as having nothing in common with it, so I could not divest you of the weaknesses which I know your fellows to suffer from. But such weaknesses are not to be classed under your three-fold caption, 'aimless, helpless, hopeless,' I granted aim. I then asked myself whether you had the qualities by which to realize it. I did not answer that question, for verily I did not nor do I know. I was even more generous, I granted the basic qualities, all-necessary for attainment, and only questioned the existence of the medium by which they could be made to meet with their proper end. And that question I did not answer (to myself), for I did not know, nor do I know.

"This is my case. I call for your verdict.

"Somehow I am like a fish out of water. I take to conventionality uneasily, rebelliously. I am used to saying what I think, neither more nor less. Soft equivocation is no part of me. As had I spoken to a man who came out of nowhere, shared my bed and board for a night, and passed on, so did I speak to you. Life is very short. The melancholy of materialism can never be better expressed than by Fitzgerald's 'O make haste.' One should have no time to dally. And further, should you know me, understand this: I, too, was a dreamer, on a farm, nay, a California ranch. But early, at only nine, the hard hand of the world was laid upon me. It was never relaxed. It has left me sentiment, but destroyed sentimentalism. It has made me practical, so that I am known as harsh, stern, uncompromising. It has taught me that reason is mightier than imagination; that the scientific man is superior to the emotional man. It has also given me a truer and a deeper romance of things, an idealism which is an inner sanctuary and which must be resolutely throttled in dealing with my kind, but which yet remains within the Holy of Holies, like an oracle, to be cherished always but to be made manifest or be consulted not on every occasion I go to market. To do this latter would bring upon me the ridicule of my fellows and make me a failure; to sum up, simply the eternal fitness of things:

"All of which goes to show that people are prone to misunderstand me. May I have the privilege of not so classing you?

"Nay, I did not walk down the street after Hamilton—I ran. And I had a heavy overcoat, and I was very warm and breathless. The emotional man in me had his will, and I was ridiculous.

"I shall be over Saturday night. If you draw back upon yourself, what have I left? Take me this way: a stray guest, a bird of passage, splashing with salt-rimed wings through a brief moment of your life—a rude and blundering bird, used to large airs and great spaces, unaccustomed to the amenities of confined existence. An unwelcome visitor, to be tolerated only because of the sacred law of food and blanket.

"Very sincerely,"

"Dec. 29, 1899.

"My dear Miss Strunsky:—

" . . . Expression? I think you have it, if this last letter may be any criterion. How have I felt since I received it? How shall I say? At any rate, know this: I do agree, unqualifiedly, with your diagnosis of where I missed and how. If I recollect aright, it was my first and last attempt at a psychological study. I say that I had much before me yet to gain before I should put my hand to such work. I glanced over several pages just before sending, noted the frightful diction and did not dare go on to the meat of it. I knew, I felt that there was so much which was wrong with it, that the ending was inadequate, etc., and that was all. But you have given me clearer vision, far clearer vision. For my vague feelings of what was wrong, you have given me the why. It is you who are the missionary. . . . My extenuation is my youth and inexperience. . . . It really was false-winged, you see, that flight of mine. Not only have you shown me my main flaw, but you have exposed a second—the lack of artistic selection.

"And above all, you have conveyed to me my lack of spirituality, idealized spirituality—I know not if I use the terms correctly. Don't you understand? I came to you like a parched soul out of the wilderness, thirsting for I knew not what. The highest and the best had been stamped out of me. You knew my life, typified, maybe, by the hastily drawn picture of the forecastle. I was troubled. Groping after shadows, mocking, disbelieving, giving my own heart the lie oftentimes, doubting that which very doubt made me believe. And for all, I was a-thirst. Stiff-necked, I flaunted my physical basis, hoping that the clear water might gush forth. But not then, for there I played the barbarian. Still, from the little I have seen of you my lips have been moistened, my head lifted. Do you remember? 'It was my duty to have loved the highest; it was my pleasure had I known?' Pray do not think me hysterical. In the bright light of day I might flush at my weakness, but in the darkness I let it pass.

"Only, I do hope we shall be friends.

" . . . I see this 'just a line' has grown. Please do not answer until after your examinations. Know that I pray for the best possible best. And please let me know the outcome, for I shall be as anxious almost as yourself . . . .

"Very sincerely,"

Either Jack was economizing on ink, or on energy, or improving his chirography, or using a finer pen-point; for his signatures early in 1900 present a reduced appearance. Evidently, from these letters, he is in a low state of cheer and funds and is putting pressure on himself, since on January 22, 1900, still dating from 962 East 16th Street, he writes to Cloudesley Johns:

"Have pawned my wheel, bought stamps, and got things in running order again. . . . Have to get in and dig now—have jumped my stint to 1500 words per diem till I get out of the hole." And on the 30th: "Am hard at it. Have not missed a day in which I have turned out at least 1500 words, and sometimes as high as 2000. How's that? And at the same time I have broken no engagements, gone on with my studying, and corrected daily from 16 to 48 pages of proofsheets. Sometimes forty-eight hours pass without my even stepping foot on the ground or seeing more of outdoors than the front porch when I go to get the evening paper. Hurrah for hell. . . . So you fell! Sensible lad! The damn dollars do carry some weight after all. I am frankly and brutally consistent about money; you are neither, nor are you consistent. . . . "

Nine days earlier he had written to Anna Strunsky, at Stanford:

"Dear Miss Strunsky:—

"O Pshaw!

"Dear Anna:—

"There! Let's get our friendship down to a comfortable basis. The superscription, 'Miss Strunsky,' is as disagreeable as the putting on of a white collar, and both are equally detestable. . . . Now I feel comfortable. Nobody ever 'Mr. Londons' me, so every time I opened a letter of yours I felt a starched collar draw round my neck. Pray permit me softer neckgear for the remainder of our correspondence. . . . I did not read your last till Friday morning, and the day and evening were taken up. But at last I am free. My visitors are gone, the one back to his desert hermitage, and the other to his own country. And I have much work to make up. Do you know, I have the fatal faculty of making friends, and lack the blessed trait of being able to quarrel with them. And they are constantly turning up. My home is the Mecca of every returned Klondiker, sailor, or soldier of fortune I ever met. Some day I shall build an establishment, invite them all, and turn them loose upon each other. Such a mingling of castes and creeds and characters could not be duplicated. The destruction would be great. . . .

"Find inclosed, review of Mary Austin's book. Had I not known you I could not have understood the little which I do. Somehow we must ever build upon the concrete. To illustrate: do you notice the same in excerpt from her, beginning, 'I thought of tempests and shipwrecks.' How I would like to know the girl, to see her, to talk with her, to do a little toward cherishing her imagination. I sometimes weep at the grave of mine. It was sown on arid soil, gave vague promises of budding, but was crushed out by the harshness of things—a mixed metaphor, I believe. . . .

"Ho! ho! I have just returned from the window. Turmoil and strife called me from the machine, and behold! My nephew, into whom it is my wish to inoculate some of the saltiness of the earth, had closed in combat with an ancient enemy in the form of a truculent Irish boy. There they were, hard at it, boxing gloves of course, and it certainly did me good to see the way in which he stood up to it. Only, alas, I see I shall have to soon give him instructions, especially in defense—all powder and flash and snappy in attach, but forgetful of guarding himself. 'For life is strife,' and a physical coward the most unutterable of abominations.

"Tell me what you think of MS. It was the work of my golden youth. When I look upon it I feel very old. It has knocked from pillar to post and reposed in all manner of places. When my soul waxes riotous, I bring it forth, and lo! I am again a lamb. It cures all ills of the age and is a sovereign remedy for self-conceit. 'Mistake' is writ broad in fiery letters. The influences at work in me, from Zangwill to Marx, are obvious. I would have portrayed types and ideals of which I know nothing, and so, trusted myself to false wings. You showed me your earliest printed production last night; reciprocating. I show you one written at the time I first knew Hamilton. I felt I had something there, but I certainly missed it. . . . Tell me the weak points, not of course in diction, etc. Tell me what rings false to you. And be unsparing, else shall I have to class you with the rest of my friends, and it is not complimentary to them if they only knew it. . . . "

Here, in form of query, one comes upon his first enunciation of a civil policy which he often repeated as the years went by:

"Feb. 10, 1900.

"Dear Cloudesley:

" . . . What do *you* think about marriage being made more difficult, and divorce correspondingly easy?

"I have had quite good success with *McClure's*. You remember my mailing that story of a minister who apostasizes? And the vile sinner who did not? *McClure's* accepted it if I would agree to the cutting of the opening and the elimination of certain swear-words. Of course I agreed, as it was an affair of 6000 words. Two days after that came an acceptance, from *McClure's*, of 'The Question of the Maximum'—that socialistic essay I read to you. What do you think of that for a conservative house? I mean conservative politically. . . . They also wanted to see more of my fiction, wanted to have me submit a long story if I had one, and if I had a collection of short stories they wanted to examine them for publication.

"Have finished 'The Son of the Wolf' proof sheets—251 pages of print in it.

" . . . 'I have told you that I consider absolute pauperism almost as objectionable as wealth.' Now, say, I wonder if you mean it? Of course you are inconsistent. Of course you sacrificed (serially) your name and workmanship by changing the story. And further, you did it for money. You can't defend yourself, you know you can't. Why not come out and be brutally frank about it like I am? You are doing the very same thing when you write hack-work. *Press* or *Journal* and *Black Cat* prize stories—money, that's all. Simmer yourself down and sum yourself up in a square way for just once. Be consistent, even though you be vile as I in the matter of dollars and cents.

" . . . Have lost steerage way in the matter of writing. Have done twenty-two hundred words in five days, and gone out every night, and feel as though I can never write again. Isn't it frightful! Lord! Who wouldn't sell a farm and go to writing! Say, I think I have stuck *Munsey's* with a thirty-two hundred word essay. I wonder if it can be possible. 'Wave' has not ponied up yet."

And he tenders a bit of futile prophesy:

"Have evolved new ideas about warfare, or rather, assimilated them. If my article is published soon, upon that subject, I shall send it to you. Anyway, to make it short, war as a direct attainment of an end, is no longer possible. The world has seen its last decisive battle. Economics, not force, will decide future wars. Of course all this is postulated between first-class powers, or first-class soldiers; not frontier squabbles. Nor would I classify the fighting in the Transvaal as a squabble. Unless there is a grave blunder, and unless the British do not too heavily reinforce, it will be found that neither British nor Boers can advance. Which ever side advances, advances to its own destruction."

Miss Strunsky had "enticed" him into abrogating a "pet aversion"—the reading of a magazine serial—being Mr. J. M. Barrie's "Tommy and Grizel." "I found I could not lay it down," he confesses to Cloudesley, "so I am stuck to the job for a year."

Then come a few remarks upon lost manuscripts:

"Your 'Call' and 'Wave' rackets remind me of what happened to me recently. Last fall I lost a forty-six hundred word story with *Collier's Weekly*, I wrote them, after due time, and they sent me a full-page letter explaining that it had never reached them, and that they had no record of it. To show them I still had confidence, I later on sent them another. It too became overdue and I trailed it. And lo and behold, the other day arrived both MSS. The first one I had long since retyped.

"My dear fellow, had I not been 'an animal with a logical nature' I should not be here today. It is only because I was so that I did not perish or stagnate by the wayside. I have been called stern, cold, cruel, unyielding, etc., and why? Because I did not wish to stop off at their particular station and remain for the rest of my days. Money? Money will give me all things, or at least more of all things than I could otherwise possess. It may even take me over to the other side of the world to meet my affinity; while without it I might mismate at home and live miserable till the game was played out.

"Got an acceptance from *Youth's Companion* the other day—qualified—if I would make the opening a little longer. . . . You remember the 'Wave'? I sent them yesterday a brief note, enclosing with it half a dozen pawn checks and a two-cent stamp. I am wondering what they will do."

"Feb. 17, 1900.

"Dear Cloudesley:—

"Thanks for Julian Ralph's 'Picture of New War Problems.' Find it herewith returned. If it has interested you, I am sure my article will, for I treat the machinery of war at length, and then go into the economic and political aspects. . . . I am intending to write an essay entitled 'They That Rise by the Sword' shortly. And just you wait till I come out with my 'Salt of the Earth.'

"So, when you are doing your best work you only do about four or five hundred a day. Good. Most good. I hope you will live up to it. I insist that good work cannot be done at the rate of three or four thousand a day. Good work is not strung out from the inkwell. It is built like a wall, every brick carefully selected, etc., etc.

" . . . Ruskin, at the height of his fame, and turning out his best work in the Cornhill, had the series of essays stopped in the middle by Thackeray because they were daring. And daring, mark you, not for their attacks on religion, but for their attacks on the prevailing school of political economy. The same Thackeray refused one of Elizabeth Barrett Browning's best poems because it was risque. . . . I'm afraid Thackeray was a snob, a cad, and a whole lot of other things which he in turn has so successfully impaled for the regard of the British reading public."

In a letter dated March 1 after a dissertation upon an article by William H. Maple, "Does Matter Think?" Jack concludes with:

"Why, the man positively reeks of Herbert Spencer interpreted by Prof. Haeckel. Not that I am impugning his article; far from it. But he has simply put into his own words what he has learned from them, and he has done it well. Spencer was not openly, that is, didactically favorable to a material basis for thought, mind, soul, etc., but John Fiske has done many queer gymnastics in order to reconcile Spencer, whose work he worships, to his own beliefs in immortality and God. But he doesn't succeed very well. He jumps on Haeckel, with both feet, but in my modest opinion, Haeckel's position is as yet unassailable.

"Am working busily away; have to finish a *McClure's* story, an *Atlantic* story, and my speech before the Oakland Section for the eleventh of this month. Then I positively must write a *Black Cat* story. As yet haven't even worked out a plot, or idea. Was going to send them my 'Man with the Gash,' but *McClure's* accepted it. It was the MS. which I recently told you of—lost at *Collier's Weekly*, etc., and returned after I had taken a duplicate from the original longhand. Been refused by all sorts of publications and now *McClure's* are to publish it in the magazine. They paid me well. The two stories and essay which they accepted aggregated fifteen thousand words, for which they sent me three hundred dollars—twenty dollars per thousand. Best pay I have yet received. Why certes, if they wish to buy me, body and soul, they are welcome—if they pay the price. I am writing for money; if I can procure fame, that means more money. More money means more life to me. I shall always hate the task of getting money; every time I sit down to write it is with great disgust. I'd sooner be out in the open wandering around most any old place. So the habit of money-getting will never become one of my vices. But the habit of money spending, ah God! I shall always be its victim. I received the three hundred last Monday. I have now about four dollars in pocket, have not moved, don't see how I can financially; owe a few debts yet, etc. How's that for about three days?

" . . . If a man, in controversy, becomes undignified, he certainly is beneath your notice, and you likewise lose your dignity if you do notice him. And surely, if he remains dignified, you are the last in the world to become undignified. Life is strife, but it also happens to stand for certain amenities."

" . . . Sold *Youth's Companion* a four thousand word story which they say is the best I have yet sent them; that makes two since you were up."

About this juncture, shortly after the first of March, I made the acquaintance of this vivid character, so paradoxical to the chance observer, but whom I have failed to find paradoxical. In the next letter, dated March 10, 1900, Jack mentions our meeting, which I have treated in detail in the Prologue of this book.

"Dear Cloudesley:—

" . . . Honestly, though, rubbing with the world will not harm you if you take the rubs aright. Not only wild and woolly rubbing, but intellectual rubbing. The most healthful experience in the world for you who are rather versatile and universal, would be bumping into specialists who would handle you without gloves. Such has been for me the best education in the world, and I look for it more and more. Man must have better men to measure himself against, else his advance will be nil, or if at all, one-sided and whimsical. The paced rider makes better speed than the unpaced.

"I can sympathize with you in your disgust for Harold. [A town.] A year of it would drive me mad, judging from the pictures. Outside of your own work what intellectual life can you have? You are thrown back upon yourself. Too apt to become self-centered; to measure other things by yourself than to measure yourself by other things. . . . Man is gregarious, and never more so when intellectual companions are harder to find than mere species companions.

" . . . I am only averaging about 350 words per day, now, and can't increase the speed to save me; but, it's either very good work, or else it is trash; in either case I am losing nothing, for I am measuring myself and learning things which will bring returns some future day." [Here follows the reference to his call at my home.]

"March 15, 1910.

"Dear Cloudesley:—

"Your Wave episode reminds me of my *Journal* one. I have sold 2000 words for one dollar and a half; but the work was bad and I would do the same again. But I can't exactly see it when I am offered three fifty for 2200 words of very good work. I wonder what such people think a fellow lives on.

" . . . To be well fitted for the tragedy of existence (intellectual existence) one must have a working philosophy, a synthesis of things. Do you write, and talk, and build upon a foundation which you know is securely laid? Or do you not rather build with a hazy idea of 'to hell with the foundation?' In token of this: What significance do the following generalities have for you: Matter is indestructible; motion is continuous; Force is persistent; the relations among forces are persistent; the transformation of forces is the equivalence of forces; etc., etc.? And if you do find in these generalities some significance relating to the foundation (way down) of your philosophy of life, what general single idea of the Cosmos do they (which are relative manifestations of the absolute), convey to you? How may you, therefore, without having mastered this idea or law (they are all laws), put down the very basic stone of your foundation? Have you ever thought that all life, all the universe of which you may in any way have knowledge of, bows to a law of continuous redistribution of matter? Have you read or thought that there is a dynamic principle, true of the metamorphosis of the universe, of the metamorphoses of the details of the universe, which will express these ever-changing relations? Nobody can tell you what this dynamic principle is, or why; but you may learn *how* it works. Do you know what this principle is? If you do, have you studied it, ay, carefully and painstakingly? And if you have not done these things, which have naught to do with creeds, or dogmas, with politics or economics, with race prejudices or passions; but which are the principles upon which they all work, to which they all answer because of law; if you have not, then can you say that you have a firm foundation for your philosophy of life? . . .

" . . . 'Screaming nonsense'—my article on war. You amuse me. Permit me to demolish you. What do you know of the Mauser rifles which are not as yet even in use in South Africa? They have only recently been tested in Holland. Let me demolish you out of your own mouth. Can you conceive of a man pointing, without removing from shoulder, a gun in any given direction for one second, or moving it, during that second at an approximately same elevation for a second? (this isn't sharpshooting, but repelling a rush attack of a body of men). Also, can you conceive that man is capable of pressing a finger steadily (no clicking, no removing or ejecting of shells on his part) upon a trigger for one second? And can you conceive a man capable of inventing a device, which, under steady pressure, will deliver six blows sufficiently heavy to explode by impact six caps set in the ends of six cartridges? If you cannot conceive these things, then I do sincerely pity you; it would be then the fault of your ancestors.

"Did you think that it was necessary for a sharpshooter to shoot so rapidly as all that? Did you think I was fool enough to think so? Cloudesley! Cloudesley! You say that you firmly believe that any position which can be approached at doublequick can be carried at the point of the bayonet by a body twice the strength of the defenders. Cold steel, mind you. Do you happen to know that Hiram Maxim writes his name with a Maxim gun upon a target at two thousand yards? Cold steel!

"You misunderstand the whole trend of my article, which meant first the struggle between first-class soldiers of the first-class European powers, and said powers are on about an equal war-footing. Secondly, my aim was to show, that war being so impossible, that men would not go up against each other to be exterminated, but that a deadlock would happen instead. Thus bringing in the economic factor. Because I stated that warfare was so deadly, I did not state that it would be applied. Rather would the deadlock occur. Read my article again. You missed the whole drift of it.

"Here comes Whitaker, I have to speak over in Alameda in an hour, so must quit.

" . . . I expect to have a try at the *Black Cat* in a couple of days, if only the damned plot will come. Am too busy now to think upon it."

It is noteworthy that in the article referred to above, "The Impossibility of War," Jack London actually foretold the method of warfare that obtained in the Great War fourteen years thereafter:

"Soldiers will be compelled to creep forward, burying themselves in the earth like moles. Future wars must be long. No more open fields; no more decisive victories; but a succession of sieges, fought over and through successive lines of widely-extending fortifications. The defeated army—supposing it can be defeated—will retire slowly, entrenching itself step by step, and most likely with steam entrenching machines. "And he went on to emphasize the greater deadliness of artillery owing to "the use of range-finders, chemical instead of mechanical mixtures of powder, high explosives, increase of range, and rapid fire."

To Anna Strunsky, March 15, 1900, whom he had sent a box of his early MSS:

"Dear Anna:—

"Regarding box . . . please remember that I have disclosed myself in my nakedness—all those vain efforts and passionate strivings are so many weaknesses of mine which I put into your possession. Why, the grammar is often frightful, and always bad, while artistically, the whole boxful is atrocious. Now don't say I am piling it on. If I did not realize and condemn those faults I would be unable to try to do better. But—why, I think in sending that box to you I did the bravest thing I ever did in my life.

"Say, do you know I am getting nervous and soft as a woman. I've got to get out again and stretch my wings or I shall become a worthless wreck. I am getting timid, do you hear? Timid! It must stop. Enclosed letter I received to-day, and it brought a contrast to me of my then 'unfailing nerve' and my present nervousness and timidity. Return it, as I suppose I shall have to answer it some day.

" . . . I have to speak in Alameda tonight—'Question of the Maximum.' Might as well work it for all there is in it, before it is published. [In "War of the Classes."]

"Am thinking about moving—getting cramped in my present quarters; but the turmoil and confusion and time lost during such an operation!

"Freda and Mrs. Eppingwell [Characters in short story 'Scorn of Women'] have fought it out, and I have just reached the climax of the scene with Floyd Vanderlip in Freda's cabin. I did not treat it in the way I suggested. Instead of her wasting a sacredly shameful experience upon a man of his stamp, I had her appeal to him sensuously (I think I handled it all right). So the conclusion of the story is only about a day away from now. Then hurrah for the East—if McClure accepts it, it will mean about one hundred and eighty dollars. He (McClure) sent me a photograph, large and framed, yesterday, and when I could find no free place upon my walls to hang it, I decided to perambulate. Almost wish a fire would come along and burn me out. It would be quicker, you know.

" . . . I am cursed with friends. I have grown accustomed to their clamoring for my company, and unconsciously feel that my presence (to them) is desirable. This mood is dangerously apt to become chronic. Need I say it so manifested itself Saturday night? And need I say that your company has ever been a great delight to me? That I would not have sought it had I not desired it? That (like you have said of yourself), when you no longer interest me I shall no longer be with you? Need I say these things to prove my candor?

"As to the box. Please take good care of the contents. And don't mix them up, please. I haven't written any poetry for months. Those you see

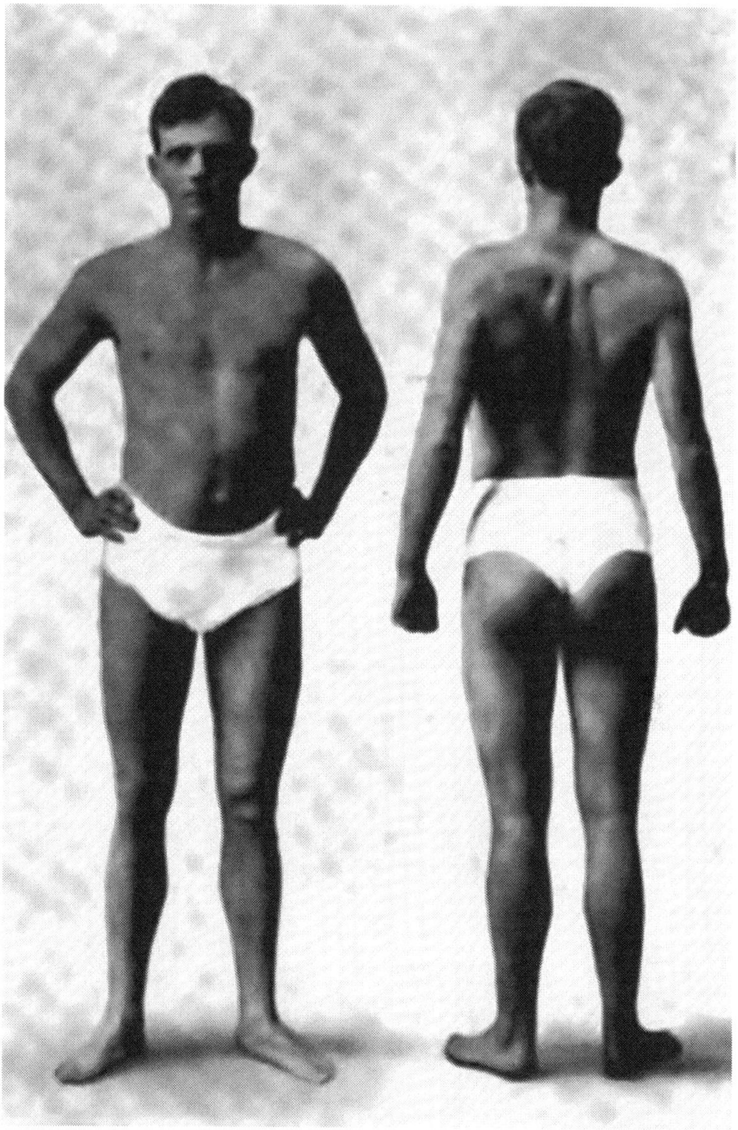

1904. JACK LONDON

are my experiments . . . and though they be failures I have not surrendered. When I am financially secure, some day, I shall continue with them—unless I have prostituted myself beyond redemption.

"To-day I am just learning to write all over again. When you can display as many failures, and have yet achieved nothing, then it is time for you to say that you cannot write. You have no right to say that now. And if you do say so, then you are a coward. Better not begin unless you are not afraid to work, work, work, to work early and late, unremittingly and always.

" . . . Do you show them to no one. Like the leper, I have exposed my sores; be gentle with me, and merciful in your judgment. And remember, they are for your encouragement. Anna, you have a good brain, also magnificent emotional qualities, and insofar you are favored above women in possession. But carry Strawn-Hamilton before you. No system, no application. But carry also Mr. Bamford's quoted warning from Watson's 'Hymn to the Sea.' Don't apply what you have, wrongly. Don't beat yourself away vainly, etc. This was not the lecture I intended giving you; that was on other lines.

"But Anna, don't let the World lose you; for insomuch that it does lose you, insomuch you have sinned."

"962 East 16th St., March 24, 1910.

"Dear Cloudesley:—

"Am pulling out on my wheel for San José; so pardon rush.

"I, at the eleventh hour, from a chance newspaper clipping, caught the motif for a *Black Cat* yarn. Behold, it is finished and off. How's this for a title? 'The Minions of Midas'? . . . 5000 words in length. ['Moon-Face' collection.] I did not write it for a first, second or third prize, but for one of the minor ones. I knew what motif was necessary for a first prize *Black Cat* story, but I could not invent such a motif.

" . . . Shall be back next Tuesday 27th. "

CHAPTER XX

MARRIAGE TO ELIZABETH MADDERN; MORE LETTERS

"1130 East 15th St.,
"Oakland, Calif.,
"April 3, 1900.

"Dear Cloudesley:—

"Thanks for the stamps. And by the way, before I get on to more serious things, let me speak of 'The Son of the Wolf.' For fear you invest in a copy if I don't I want to tell you that I shall send you one as soon as they come to hand. There is only one advance copy on the Coast, and I haven't seen that one yet. They say it is all right.

"You must be amused, lest you die. Here goes. You will observe that I have moved. Good! Next Saturday I shall be married. Better? Eh? Will send announcement of the funeral later.

Jack London."

Mr. Johns's acknowledgment of the foregoing was laconic in the extreme, consisting of a sacred name of two words with an initial between, followed by an exclamation point. The same mail had brought to my Aunt, Mrs. Eames, the letter quoted in the Prologue. In her hands was the one advance copy of "The Son of the Wolf," to which Jack refers above.

Briefly, it seems to have come about in this way: Pressed for space in the small cottage, especially in the 10 by 10 den which served as work-room, bedroom for himself and any chance guest, and for living-room as well, Jack at last found means to make a change and move his mother and nephew and himself to a nice two-story house at 1130 East Fifteenth Street, flanked by a neat garden. In it were seven rooms, including a large bay-windowed parlor, and an upstairs study 13 by 15 feet. And joy upon joy, an attic where Jack could store his accumulating "gear."

Jack and Elizabeth Maddern had been exchanging instruction in English and "math" in the Fifteenth Street dwelling and the young woman had joined with Eliza in fixing up Jack's new den. His idea of adding a member to the household was born of the moment. He lay on his back in the middle of the floor, lost in a book, while sister and friend put his small but swelling library on some shelves he had had thrown together by a carpenter. Eliza, happening to glance aside, saw him turn over on his elbows, and, supporting his head on his hands, regard Miss Maddern fixedly as she moved about. His eyes filled with visions, and he dropped his face and lay still for a long time. Eliza, with a pang, sensed what had come to him, but held her peace. Looking back upon it, he wrote: "I was convinced absolutely that I knew the last word about love and life."

That evening, by force of argument, Jack convinced the girl of the wisdom of a union such as he proposed, or at least gained her consent, and next morning dropped into his sister's house:

"I am going to be married," he said without preamble. Eliza, as mask-like of face and feelings as ever he could be, replied, "Good! I'm glad of it!" and undertook, at her brother's request, to break the news to his mother. Flora London, who had been basking in the dream of this large, new, clean house where she would be mistress, was not enthusiastic at the idea of being superseded. Jack's cozy little plan did not work out so automatically as he had hoped; three months after the return of the bride from honeymoon to home all decorated with flowers by Eliza, that same sister-in-law, again at Jack's plea, superintended another removal, namely of Flora London and Johnnie Miller, into a cottage on Sixteenth Street, almost behind Jack's home. Eliza appears to have avoided all interference and only consented to step in from time to time when Jack's feminine affairs tangled to the imminence of his great disgust. Little was said upon these occasions between brother and sister. One look at his gray face, a word or two from the tightened bow of his lips concerning the nature of his need, and Eliza, without undue antagonizing of the others, set about regulating matters as fairly as possible.

While one delves for further enlightenment upon Jack London's sanction for this abrupt and loveless union, it may well be surmised that his feeling for Anna Strunsky played its part. Up to now, and beyond, his head determined the way of his life, for the day had not come when the big, ripe, man-heart of him overturned the fanes he had so carefully erected, and caused him to volunteer that "Love is the greatest thing in the world." As for Anna, the very dart and smart of their intellectual comradery rendered her an unrest. His plans for the future were so nicely ordered toward a systematic schedule of writing—to the aim of successful living, to be sure—that he could not consider the feverish temperamental life that was likely to be if he joined his with Anna's. How much the very fear of being drawn into such a situation entered into his sudden resolve to take no chances on that side, and to marry, as he did marry, we shall never know.

Cloudesley Johns, upon receipt of the printed announcement, wrote Jack:

"Harold, Cal, April 12, 1900.

"Dear Jack:—

"May I defer my congratulations of you and Mrs. Jack for ten years? Then I shall hope to tender them—Thursday, April 7th, 1910. Don't forget: try to expect them.

"Your mind will be much occupied for a time with your change of residence and condition, and mine is hibernating at present, so I would suggest that you take up my last letter, and reply to it,—say June 1st.

"I heartily wish you both permanent satisfaction.

"Cloudesley Johns."

"1130 East 15th St., April 16, 1900.

"Dear Cloudesley:—

"Why certainly you may defer congratulations till April 7, 1910. Permit me to felicitate you upon your last letter bar this one I am answering. We all had a good laugh over it and enjoyed it immensely. I was away on the little wedding trip when it arrived, and my sister (you met her), looked at it and said she'd give ten dollars to see what you had to say. And it was worth it.

"No, I'll not answer it. Am not laconic enough.

" . . . Got settled down to work to-day, and did the first thousand words in three weeks, and hereafter the old rate must continue. Say, a year ago I wrote a two thousand word skit or storiette called 'Their Alcove.' First, second, and third raters refused out of hand. Sent it to the *Women's Home Companion,* and without a word of warning, and in quick time, came back an acceptance accompanied by a twenty dollar check. Most took my breath away. "

"May 2, 1900.

"Dear Cloudesley:—

" . . . No; at the moment I get a good phrase I am not thinking of how much it will fetch in the market, but when I sit down to write I am; and all the time I am writing, deep down, underneath the whole business, is that same commercial spirit. I don't think I would write very much if I didn't have to."

Also on May 2, Jack wrote to Anna:

"How sorry I am. Friday I am chairman at the Ruskin Club dinner and cannot possibly escape. Thursday I speak in 'Frisco, and Saturday am bound out to dinner. . . . However, may I put you down for afternoon and dinner on Wednesday, May 9th?

"How enthusiastic your letters always make me feel. Makes it seem as though some new energy had been projected into the world and that I cannot fail gathering part of it to myself. No; God does not punish confidence; but he grinds between the upper and the nether millstone all those of little faith and little heart, and he grinds them very fine. Of course you will succeed—if you will work—and certainly you seem to suffer from a superabundance of energy. Apply this energy, rightly and steadily, and the world will open its arms to you. You are all right; the world is all right; the question is: will you have the patience to gain the ear of the world. You will have to shout loud, for the world is rather deaf, and you may have to shout long. But the world sometimes opens its ears at the first call. May it be thus with you.

"Jack."

In a letter of June 3, he mentioned having received a letter from Charles Warren Stoddard. The correspondence between these two prospered for years, during which the older man addressed Jack "Dear Son," and Jack responded with "Dear Dad." They never met. In this same letter of June 3 to Mr. Johns, Jack goes on:

"Have sold a couple of hundred more dollars worth of good stuff to *McClure's*—at least I think it is good—'The Grit of Women' [published August, 1900] and 'The Law of Life' [published March, 1901, both stories in *McClure's*, and later collected in volumes 'The God of His Fathers' and 'Children of the Frost,' respectively.]

"Got the proofsheets of a 'S. F. Examiner' story in and am correcting them . . . 'Which Makes Men Remember.' [Published June 24, 1900, under title 'Uri Bram's God.']

" . . . So! I am married, and I cannot start to Paris in July, dough or no dough—that's why I got married.

"But none the less I heartily envy you your trip. I think maybe I'll take a vacation on the road this summer just for ducks and to gather material, or rather, to freshen up what I have long since accreted—how would you judge of my use of that last word?

"*Smart Set?* I may go in for one of the lesser prizes. Can't tell yet. *Outing* has asked a bunch of Northland stories of me and I am busy hammering away at them just now."

In the next letter, June 16, he winds up advice to writers:

" . . . Pour all yourself into your work until your work becomes you, but nowhere let yourself be apparent. When, in the 'Ebb Tide,' the schooner is at the pearl island, and the missionary pearler meets those three desperate men and puts his will against theirs for life or death, does the reader think Stevenson? . . . Nay, nay. Afterwards, when all is over, he recollects, and wonders and loves Stevenson—but at the time? Not he . . . study your Beloved's 'Ebb Tide.' . . . Study your detestable Kipling. Study them and see how they eliminate themselves and create things that live, and breathe, and grip men, and cause reading lamps to burn overtime. Atmosphere stands always for the elimination of the artist, that is to say, the atmosphere is the artist. . . .

" . . . Think it over and see if you catch what I am driving at. Of course, if you intend fiction, then write fiction from the highest standpoint of fiction. . . . Put in life, and movement—and for God's sake no creaking. Damn you! Forget you! And then the world will remember you. . . . Pour all yourself into your work until your work becomes you, but nowhere let yourself be apparent. "

Upon a long-coveted day when, debts cleared and cash left in pocket, for once square with the world, Jack strolled along Oakland's Broadway, it occurred to him that he could actually step into any of the familiar shops and purchase things that had burned in his desire since he could remember. Smiling to himself, he stopped before one window after another until he came to halt beside some small boys gloating and whispering before a candy store display. And suddenly an emptiness gnawed in him—something had gone out of his life. It was too late—desire had fled upon tired wings, and there was nothing that he, with silver at last heavy in his pocket of excellent cloth, cared to buy. It came with a shock. From the pocket he withdrew a hand bulging with loose change and bestowed it upon the little boys, with a catch in his throat almost marveling at the eagerness in their faces—which turned into something akin to suspicion, for a man must be crazy to shell out so much money at one time. And Jack passed on sadly enough, doubtlessly a trifle sorry for himself. "There wasn't a thing I wanted any more," he told his sister. "It had come too late."

Jack and his wife take a holiday at the seashore, at Santa Cruz, upon return from which he writes:

"July 23, 1900.

"Dear Cloudesley:—

"Back from vacation at last! And hard at it. This is thirty-fifth letter. Ye Gods!

"Did I tell you McClure has bought me (as you would call it), but as I would say, has agreed to advance me one hundred and twenty-five per month for five months in order that I may try my hand at a novel? Well, it is so, and I start in shortly, though filled with dismay in anticipation.

"Did you read that storiette of mine 'Semper Idem; Semper Fidelis'? About fifteen hundred words, dealing with a man who cut his throat, bungled it, was cautioned by the doctor at the hospital as to how he might bungle it, and who went out, profited by the advice, and did it successfully? Well, I have sent it everywhere. At last I sent it to *Black Cat.* I would have sold it for a dollar. But the *Black Cat* gave me a sort of poor mouth, said it had hospital stuff to last it two years, etc., and that under the circumstances it could only offer me fifty dollars for it! Say! Most took my breath away. A fifteen hundred word sketch, 'The Husky,' I refused to sell some time ago for $3.50, and *Harper's Weekly* bought it for twenty dollars. Say, those hang fire MSS. seem the best after all."

The next letter, dated July 31, 1900, is to Anna Strunsky:

"Comrades! and surely it seems so. For all the petty surface turmoil which marked our coming to know each other, really, deep down, there was no confusion at all. Did you not notice it? To me, while I said, 'You do not understand,' I none the less felt the happiness of satisfaction—how shall I say? felt, rather, that there was no inner conflict; that we were attuned, somehow; that a real unity underlaid everything. The ship, new-launched, rushes to the sea; the sliding-ways rebel in weakling creaks and groans; but sea and ship hear them not: So with us when we rushed into each other's lives—we, the real we, were undisturbed. Comrades! Ay, world without end!

"And now, comrade mine, how long are those Shakespeare papers to keep you from 'Consciousness of Kind?' You know how anxiously I wait the outcome, and how much you have improved. And Anna, read your classics, but don't forget to read that which is of to-day, the new-born literary art. You must get the modern touch; form must be considered; and while art is eternal, form is born of the generations. And O, Anna, if you will only put your flashing soul with its protean moods on paper! What you need is the form, or, in other words, the expression. Get this and the world is at your feet.

"And when are we to read 'The Flight of the Duchess'? And when are you coming over?"

"Sept. 9/00.

"Dear Cloudesley:—

"So am I up against it—and just got started against it. Am winding up the first chapter of novel ['A Daughter of the Snows']. Since it is my first attempt, I have chosen a simple subject and shall simply endeavor to make it true, artistic, and interesting. But afterward, when I have learned better how to handle a sustained effort, I shall choose a greater subject. I wish I were done.

" . . . There are a number of Le Gallienne's quatrains which I like better than corresponding quatrains of Fitzgerald's. Perhaps the literary mentors will not bear me out in this, but none the less, so far as I am concerned, it is so. . . .

"Am beginning to take exercise once again. Indian clubs, jumping, etc., every day, wheelrides every day, and baths three or four times per week—swimming I mean. Am just back from practising in diving, and am stiff and sore with practising front and back somersaults. . . . Expect to take up fencing later on, and the gloves, and shooting. It is Voltaire, I believe, who said: 'The body of an athlete and the soul of a sage; that is happiness.' I am trying to assimilate Spencer's philosophy just now, so there is a chance that I may yet attain to happiness."

Meanwhile, Jack and Anna had formulated the project of writing in collaboration, to thresh out their opposing ideas by means of a correspondence as between two men, upon the subject of Love.

To Mr. Johns, Oct. 17, 1900, Jack mentions this work:

"Didn't I explain my volume of letters? Well, it's this way: A young Russian Jewess of 'Frisco and myself have often quarreled over our conceptions of love. She happens to be a genius. She is also a materialist by philosophy, and an idealist by innate preference, and is constantly being forced to twist all the facts of the universe in order to reconcile herself with herself. So, finally, we decided that the only way to argue the question out would be by letter. Then we wondered if a collection of such letters should happen to be worth publishing. Then we assumed characters, threw in a real objective love element, and started to work. Of course, don't know yet how it will turn out. We're both doing some very good work—in spots; but we are agreed, in case they merit it, to go over when we are done."

"Nov. 27th.

"Dear Anna:—

"I have been sitting here crying, like a big baby. I have just finished reading 'Jude the Obscure.' Perhaps it is not as great as 'Tess,' but in a way it is greater. When are you coming over that I may lend it to you? With two such books to his name Hardy should die content. Well may he look upon his work and call it good.

"Jack."

To Mr. Johns, Dec. 10, 1900:

"You can't get away from the materialistic conception of history. . . . Ideas do not rule, never have ruled; where they have appeared to rule, it was merely because economic or material conditions were such as to have first generated the ideas, and secondly, to have been in harmony with the working of them."

And Dec. 22:

"Yes, after much delay, I captured *Cosmopolitan* prize. I flatter myself that I am one of the rare socialists who have ever succeeded in making money out of their socialism. Apropos of this, I send you copy of a letter received day before yesterday from Brisbane Walker. Of course I shall not accept it. I do not wish to be bound. Which same you do think I am. Not so. *McClure's* have not bound me, nor will they. [This refers to the offer of an editorship.] I want to be free, to write of what delights me, whensoever and wheresoever it delights me. No office work for me; no routine; no doing this set task and that set task. No man over me. I think *McClure's* have recognized this, and will treat me accordingly. Aside from pecuniary considerations, I think they are the best publishers, or magazine editors, in their personal dealings, that I have run across.

"Speaking of illustrations, did you see how beautifully *Ainslie's* did by my story in December number? Incidentally, without asking my permission, here and there they succeeded in cutting out fully five hundred words, which I shall reinsert when published in book form. I suppose the one hundred and twenty-five they paid for it was considered sufficient justification for mangling."

On the day after Christmas, he wrote to Anna:

"Comrade Mine:—

"Thus it was I intended addressing you a Christmas greeting, saying, as it seemed to me, for you, the finest thing in the world. But it was impossible. For a week I have been suffering from the blues, during which time I have not done a stroke of work. Am writing this with cold fingers, at six in the morning—going for a day on the water, fishing, shooting, etc., to see if there are any curative forces left in the universe.

"Ah, we refuse not to speak, and yet we speak brokenly and stumblingly! True, too true. The paradox of social existence, to be truthful, we lie; to live true, we live untruthfully. The social wisdom is a thing of great worth—to the mass. For the few it is a torment, upon it they are crucified—not for their salvation, but for the salvation of the mass. I grow, sometimes, almost to hate the mass, to sneer at dreams of reform. To be superior to the mass is to be the slave of the mass. The mass knows no slavery. It is the task master.

"But how does this concern you and me? Ah, does it not concern us? We may refuse not to speak, yet we speak brokenly and stumblingly—because of the mass. The tyranny of the crowd, as I suppose Gerald Stanley Lee would put it. As for me, just when freedom seems opening up to me, I feel the bands tightening and the riveting of the gyves. I remember, now, when I was free. When there was no restraint, and I did what the heart willed. Yes, one restraint, the Law; but when one willed, one could fight the law, and break or be broken. But now, one's hands are tied, one may not fight, but only yield and bow the neck. After all, the sailor on the sea and the worker in the shop are not so burdened. To break or be broken, there they stand. But to be broken while not daring to break, there's the rub.

"I could almost advocate a return to nature this dark morning. A happiness to me?—added unto me?—why, you have been a delight to me, dear, and a glory. Need I add, a trouble? For the things we love are the things which hurt us as well as the things we hurt. Ah, believe me, believe me. 'I have not winced or cried aloud.' The things unsaid are the greatest. Surely, sitting here, gathering data, classifying, arranging; writing stories for boys with moral purposes insidiously inserted; hammering away at a thousand words a day; growing genuinely excited over biological objections; thrusting a bit of fun at you and raising a laugh, when it should have been a sob—surely all this is not all. What you have been to me? I am not great enough or brave enough to say. This false thing, which the world would call my conscience, will not permit me. But it is not mine: it is the social conscience, the world's which goes with the world's leg-bar chain. A white beautiful friendship?—between a man and a woman?—the world cannot imagine such a thing, would deem it inconceivable as infinity or non-infinity."

CHAPTER XXI

LETTERS: CLOUDESLEY JOHNS AND ANNA STRUNSKY

LETTERS opening the year 1901, hint at Jack's general state of inner consciousness, his worldly condition, and sentiments on the consummation of fatherhood, so dearly desired from merest boyhood.

"1130 East 15th St., Jan. 5/01.

"Dear Cloudesley:—

"... I have written probably one hundred and ten thousand this [past] year, against your ninety-odd; but I think that I loafed or did other things less, and that each thousand took me longer than each of your thousands did you.

"To tell you the truth, Cloudesley, I haven't had any decent work published recently—work which I would care to have you read—socialistic essay excepted, and that I was unable to get a whack at in the proof sheets.

"... Christmas is just past. Further a friend has taken up writing with seven children and an undeveloped ability, which said friend I have been helping to finance. Another, both ankles broken badly some time since. Then my mother, to whose pension I add thirty dollars each month, got back in her debts and I have just finished straightening her out. And my Mammie Jennie (negro foster mother) came down upon me for December quarterly payment of interest on mortgage, and delinquent taxes. Furthermore, within a week I expect my wife to be confined. . . . January check non est, and I have been going along on borrowed money since before Christmas."

"Sunday Morning, Jan. 6/01.

"Dear Anna:—

"I had intended writing you yesterday, asking you to come over Monday evening and go with me to that equal suffragist club before which Whitaker was to read. Then Tuesday I could have taken your picture. But I had forgotten Mrs. Gowell's lectures. . . . Also found out that Monday was not the night and that we would have our regular boxing bout.

"So Saturday, but come early . . . so that I may take advantage of the sun. This, then, be the qualification: if I do not telephone you otherwise. Possibly ere that time, the boy—I do pray for a boy—shall have arrived. In which case, you must come. So, Saturday, early. . . . My birthday. A quarter of a century of breath. I feel very old.

"Of the New Comer, I thank you for what you say. It will be in itself a dear consummation. Then must come the patient determining. And, Anna, it must be make or break. No whining puny breed. It must be great and strong. Or—the penalty must be paid. By it, by me; one or the other. So be.

"I shall be glad to go in for the Ibsen circle. I need more of that in my life."

Feb. 4/01.

"Dear Cloudesley:—

"Not dead, but rushed as usual. Have got down to my regular five hours and a half sleep again and running by the clock. Am just answering a whole stack of letters.

"Well, there's no accounting for things. I did so ardently long to be a father, that it seemed impossible that such a happiness should be mine. But it is. And a damn fine, healthy youngster. Weighed nine and a half pounds at birth, which they say is good for a girl. Up to date has shown a good stomach and lack of ailments, for it does nothing but eat and sleep, or lie awake for a straight hour without a whimper. Intend to call her 'Joan.' Tell me how you like it, what associations it calls up.

" . . . As regards 'bumming by force from peoples inhabiting lands we cannot thrive in?' Does not our modern slavery serve to deteriorate us, affecting our own government? While counting the profit you must not ignore the loss. . . . Do you not realize that whatever is 'is right and wise.' Certainly it may be made wiser and more right in the natural course of evolution (and then again it mayn't), but the point is that it is the best possible under the circumstances. Given so much matter, and so much force, and beginning at the beginning of things as regards this our world, do you not know that it could not have worked out in any other way, nay, not in the least jot or tittle could it have been other than it was. We may make it better; and then again we may not.

"As Dr. Ross somewhere says: 'Evolution is no kindly mother to us. We do not know what moment it may turn against us and destroy us.' Don't you see; I speak not of the things that should be; nor of the things I should like to be; but I do speak of the things that are and will be. I should like to have socialism; yet I know that socialism is not the very next step; I know that capitalism must live its life first. That the world must be exploited to the utmost first; that first must intervene a struggle for life among the nations, severer, intenser, more widespread, than ever before. I should much more prefer to wake to-morrow in a smoothly-running socialistic state; but I know I shall not; I know it cannot come that way. I know that a child must go through its child's sicknesses ere it becomes a man. So, always, remember that I speak of the things that are; not of the things that should be.

"Find enclosed *Cosmopolitan* letters. I stood off first one and wrote to *McClure's*. They have agreed to go on with me, giving me utter freedom. So you see, at least they have not bought me body and soul. Honestly, they are the most human editors I ever dealt with. When I think about them, it is more as very dear friends, than people I am doing business with. However, in refusing *Cosmopolitan* offer, which meant giving up freedom, I think I have acted for the best. What think you?"

"Feb. 13/01.

"Dear Cloudesley:—

"Well, I am on the home stretch of the novel, and it is a failure. This is not said in a fit of the blues, but from calm conviction. However, on the other hand, I have learned a great deal concerning the writing of novels. On this one which I have attempted, I could write three books of equal size showing wherein I failed, and why, and laying down principles violated, etc. O, it's been a great study. I shall be at work finishing it for the rest of the month—you know I always finish whatever I begin. I never leave a thing in such a state that in the time to come haunting thoughts may creep in—'If I only had gone on,' etc.

"*McClure's* are getting ready to bring out a second collection of Klondike stories—not so good as the first, however.

"March I shall take a vacation, and April I intend writing my long-deferred 'Salt of the Earth.' . . .

"I see you laugh at me and my optimistic philosophy. So be. I only wish you would study up the materialistic conception of history, then you would understand my position."

Again Jack moves his family, this time to an ornate Italian villa, "La Capriccioso," on the shores of Oakland's pleasure-pond, Lake Merritt, designed and built by his good friend the sculptor, Felix Peano:

"1062 First Avenue,
"Oakland, Calif.,
"March 15/01.

"Dear Cloudesley:—

"Note by address that I have moved. Last seen of old house there was a foot and a half of water under it, and the back yard a lake. Am much more finely situated now, nearer to Oakland, with finer view, surroundings, air, etc., etc. Do you remember Lake Merritt?—a body of water which you might have seen from the electric cars on the way to my place from down town. I am located right near it, and believe, with a sling shot from the roof of the house, that I could throw a stone into it.

"Shall have the novel done in ten days, now N.G. ["No Good"]. But I know I shall be able to do a good one yet.

" . . . Mr. Whitaker is selling some of his work, now—*Ainslie's*, The S. S. *McClure*, *Munsey's*, etc., etc. He's picking up.

"Jack."

"April 1/01.

"Dear Cloudesley:—

"The novel is off at last, and right glad am I that it is. . . .

"I send herewith a letter from Town Topics. They are paying two dollars for jokes now, and if you have any it wouldn't be a bad idea to send them along. I do not know much about joke writing, but I wouldn't send jokes in a bunch. I sent four triolets (the only four I ever wrote), to Town Topics. They took one, and sent three back. Later I resent one of the triolets: they took it. Later I resent another: they took it. But they balked on the fourth. " . . . By all means . . . come somewhere and live in the center of things. In this day one cannot isolate one's self and do anything. Get you a big city anywhere, and plunge into it and live and meet people and things. If you believe that man is the creature of his environment, then you cannot afford to remain 'way off there on the edge of things."

"April 3/01.

"Dear Anna:—

"Did I say that the human might be filed in categories? Well, and if I did, let me qualify—not all humans. You elude me. I cannot place you, cannot grasp you. I may boast that of nine out of ten, under given circumstances, I can forecast their action; that of nine out of ten, by their word, or action, I may feel the pulse of their hearts. But the tenth I despair. It is beyond me. You are that tenth.

"Were ever two souls, with dumb lips, more incongruously matched! We may feel in common—surely, we ofttimes do—and when we do not feel in common, yet do we understand; and yet we have no common tongue. Spoken words do not come to us. We are unintelligible. God must laugh at the mummery.

"The one gleam of sanity through it all is that we are both large temperamentally, large enough to often misunderstand. True, we often understand but in vague glimmering ways, by dim perceptions, like ghosts, which, while we doubt, haunt us with their truth. And still, I, for one, dare not believe; for you are that tenth which I may not forecast.

"Am I unintelligible now? I do not know. I imagine so. I cannot find the common tongue.

"Largely temperamentally—that is it. It is the one thing that brings us at all in touch. We have, flashed through us, you and I, each a bit of the universal, and so we draw together. And yet we are so different.

"I smile at you when you grow enthusiastic? It is a forgivable smile—nay, almost an envious smile. I have lived twenty-five years of repression. I learned not to be enthusiastic. It is a hard lesson to forget. I begin to forget, but it is so little. At the best, before I die, I cannot hope to forget all or most. I can exult, now that I am learning, in little things, in other things; but of my things, and secret things double mine, I cannot, I cannot. Do I make myself intelligible? Do you hear my voice? I fear not. There are poseurs. I am the most successful of them all.

"Jack."

"April 8/01.

"Dear Cloudesley:—

"I am sending you herewith pictures of the youngster at three weeks and two months.

"Every man, at the beginning of his career (whether laying bricks or writing books or anything else), has two choices. He may choose immediate happiness, or ultimate happiness. . . . He who chooses ultimate happiness, and has the ability, and works hard, will find that the reward for effort is cumulative, that the interest on his energy invested is compounded. The artisan who is industrious, steady, reliant, is suddenly, one day, advanced to a foremanship with increased wages. Now is that advance due to what he did that day, or the day before? Ah, no, it is due to the long years of industry and steadiness. The same with the reputation of a business man or artist. The thing grows, compounds. He is not only 'paid for having done something once upon a time,' as you put it, but he has been paid for continuing to do something through quite a period of time. . . .

"O no. My 'incentive' is not the 'assurance of being able some day to sell any sort of work on the strength of a name.' Every year we have writers, old writers, crowded out—men, who once had names, but who had gained them wrongfully, or had not done the work necessary to maintain them. In its way, the struggle for a man with a name, to maintain the standard by which he gained that name, is as severe as the struggle for the unknown to make a name.

"Jack London."

"Harold, April 13, 1901

"Dear Jack:—

" . . . Thanks for photos: my mother asked a while ago if you had sent any of 'the small one' yet. They are woefully helpless and stupid things—human infants—yet it is wonderful what expression they sometimes have. That of Miss London at two months impresses me as distinctly weird, as if she were perplexed by some weighty problem. I believe the mystery of existence agitates the mind at even so early a stage of its development as that.

"N.B. I think your machine needs boiling—try brushing the types for a starter though.

"Cloudesley Johns."

"April 19/01.

"Dear Cloudesley:—

"I agree with you in some of your criticism of 'The Law of Life,' but not in all. For instance, 'What was that?' Remember, the words occur, not in the writer's narrative—in such a place your criticism would hold good. But the words do occur in the mind of the Indian. He *thinks* them. And that it is the most natural thing in the world for a person to so think when something unknown or unusual occurs, you cannot deny.

" . . . Did I tell you?—novel is accepted to be brought out this fall. In the meantime immediate serial publication is being sought.

"Have to go read a poem over a coffin to satisfy the whim of a man who was quick and is now dead; so so long."

Saturday evening, April 26, 1901, he lectured in Forrester's Hall, Alameda, at corner of Santa Clara Avenue and Park Street, upon tramp experiences.

Home July 12, from a vacation which he wrote Cloudesley was a longer absence than he had intended, Jack sends Anna the letter quoted below. And right here it is well to insert Jack London's own words on his outlook toward newspaper work: "I could have made a good deal at newspaper work; but I had sufficient sense to refuse to be a slave to that man-killing machine, for such I hold a newspaper to be to a young man in his forming period. Not until I was well on my feet as a magazine writer did I do much work for newspapers."

"July 24/01.

My Little Collaborator:—

"Yes, and the Yellow is dead—at least for some little time to come. For all I know, I may be doing prize fights next.

"Explanations are hardly necessary between you and me, but this case merits one I think. Didn't get home till the middle of the day, Monday. Went to see my mother, sister, etc. Tuesday went to Santa Cruz to speak. Came back Wednesday and pitched into work on back correspondence. All the time intending to take up reply to Dane Kempton's last and surprise you with it. But the *Sunday Examiner* rushed me Thursday to have a freak story in by Friday noon. And Thursday also the *Daily Examiner* clamored to see me instanter. Put daily off, finished Sunday work on time, and on Friday also went to see *Daily Examiner*. They proposed the Schutzenfest to me. Saturday I started reply to Dane Kempton and paid bills. And on Sunday took up the Schutzenfest and have been at it steadily for ten days, publishing in to-day's *Examiner* the last of that work. My whole life has stood still for ten days. During that time I have done nothing else. Why, so exhausting was it that my five and one-half hours would not suffice and I had to sleep over seven.

"And just now, to-day, as I sat down to send you greeting, along comes yours to me. I kind of looked for you to be over to-day, though little right had I to, and I have now given up that idea.

"And further, I find I must do something for *McClure's* at once, or they will be shutting off on me. So I am springing at once into a short story, which will be finished by end of week, and then the Letters. You know I have striven to be on time, so forgive me this once. Tell you what I'll do, if you don't expect to be out—see you on Friday afternoon. Won't be able to stop to dinner, though, for have to go to 6:30 supper. [This was the delightful 'Six-Thirty Club,' of San Francisco.] If I do miss the supper, will be dropped from the rolls, for it will have been my third consecutive absence.

"Haven't finished 'Aurora Leigh' yet, but it is fine, greater, I think, than Wordsworth's ('Excursion' is it?) from the little you read me of it."

Early October finds Jack broken with S. S. McClure, and again moved, this time a little higher toward the western hills, with a long-envied view of the Golden Gate across the Bay. With each change of residence, he had a new rubber-stamp made for letter-heading:

"Jack London,
"56 Bayo Vista Avenue,
"Oakland, Calif.,
"October 9/01.

"Dear Cloudesley:

"Note change of address. Am now living out on the hills. . . . And how's New York? Are you going to settle down to writing for the winter? I nearly shipped across on a cattle boat when I was on the road, but somehow didn't.

"Am free lance again. Have just finished a 3700-word defense of Kipling against the rising tide of adverse criticism. Did you see the attack in current *Cosmopolitan*?

" . . . Well, haven't much news. Am hard at it. That series of letters with Miss Strunsky is three-fifths through. That is to say, we have three-fifths of a book done. Though the Lord only knows what publisher will dare tackle it. Also, am hammering away at a series of Klondike tales, which I shall assemble under the title 'The Children of the Frost.' They are all to be done from the Indian approach, you know."

Two letters unfold the first intimation that Jack London wanted to widen his field by getting away from Alaska:

"Nov. 8/01.

"Dear Cloudesley:—

"Of course the painter has to quit painting bears, but he has first to gather together his itinerary and select his route. (Say, is that what they call a mixed metaphor?)

"Anyway, it's the same old story. A man does one thing in a passable manner and the dear public insists on his continuing to do it to the end of his days. the humorists who try to be serious!

" . . . that letter series Miss Strunsky and I are writing? Well, we've got past the forty-thousand mark and the goal is in sight. Gee! I wonder how you'll jump upon it. My contention is the same as I heard you make once: That propinquity determines choice. Yet I am sure you will be after my scalp before you finish it—that is, if we can entice a publisher into getting it out.

"Whitaker has just sold a story to *Cosmopolitan*. Rah for Whitaker! O, he's going it scientifically.

"I wouldn't mind being with you next spring when you pull out for the old countries.

"Cosgrave mentioned having several interesting conversations with you, and that he expected to get some tramp work from you. How is it coming on?"

"Dec. 6/01.

"Dear Cloudesley:—

"Nothing doing. Am hammering away in seclusion, trying to get out of Alaska. Guess I'll succeed in accomplishing it in a couple of years.

" . . . Wyckoff is not a tramp authority. He doesn't understand the real tramp. Josiah Flynt is the tramp authority. Wyckoff only knows the workingman, the stake-man, and the bindle-stiff. The profesh are unknown to him. Wyckoff is a gay-cat. That was his rating when he wandered over the States.

"Well, good luck on the way to Cuba! Wish I were with you. I am rotting here in town. Really, I can feel the bourgeois fear crawling up and up and twining around me. If I don't get out soon I shall be emasculated. The city folk are a poor folk anyway. To hell with them."

Upon a not much later date, Jack London wrote: "Although primarily of the city, I like to be near it rather than in it. The country, though, is the best, the only natural life."

At the time he expressed the foregoing, I also find this: "I think the best work I have done is in the 'League of the Old Men,' ["Children of the Frost" collection] and parts of 'The Kempton-Wace Letters.' Other people don't like the former. They prefer brighter and more cheerful things. Perhaps I shall feel like that, too, when the days of my youth are behind me." But he never changed, always considering "The League of the Old Men" his finest story. Concerning the "Kempton-Wace Letters," note the following two communications, undated, to Anna Strunsky:

"Dear Anna:—

"Your letter is a splendid, a delicately splendid addition to the book. I am anxious to see it in type. I want to see it shape up.

"Your letter impelled me to work, and find here my attempt at rewriting my first letter. I have been two whole days on it, and working hard. From the trouble I have had with it, and from its original horribleness, I now know that I shall have to write it a third time (at the general revision), ere it is worth looking at. However, I send it for what it is worth. How bad my first letters were I never dreamed. I know now.

"You will notice that I have devoted little space to Hester, and more space to other and unimportant things. I have described her mental characteristics, her intellectual constitution, that which appeals to the non-loving Herbert Wace. For the reader I have already opened the breach between you (Dane Kempton) and me. When the book opens we are both aware of the slipping away, vaguely aware; one certain function of the book will be to differentiate us so that the breach becomes sharply defined. I change my landlord to my friend Gwynne. I shall develop a love experience for him, which shall culminate in one of the inserted letters—naturally the love experience will be evidence on my side of the contention."

"Dear Anna:

"Find here letter No. 2. And I must plead guilty to the same feeling which you were under when you wrote me. I don't know what to make of it. Seem all at sea. Feel that I am all wrong, that I am not building characters as I should, or even writing letters as they should be written. But I suppose the whole thing will grow, in time. Anyway, it's a good method for getting a fair conception of one's limitations.

"What do you think of my making a poet of Hester? Should it be poet or poetess? I detest poetess. Is there such a word as 'lyricist'? There is the word 'lyrist', meaning the same thing, but I do not like it. Do you catch my new school possibly to be founded by Hester?—Poetry of a Machine Age. I may exploit it in later letters. Do you, Dane Kempton, behold that I have not told you anything about Hester physically? I don't like the wind up, the treatment of the minor conflict. It seemed as though I begged the question, and yet I couldn't conceive a way of arguing it out. To me it seems almost unarguable. I do not know. Perhaps not. Can't tell.

" . . . And please criticize unsparingly, especially in errors of taste."

In an article written after Jack London's death, Mrs. Walling said, referring to the period when they were collaborating:

"He held that love is only a trap set by nature for the individual. One must not marry for love but for certain qualities discerned by the mind. This he argued in 'The Kempton-Wace Letters' brilliantly and passionately; so passionately as to again make one suspect that he was not as certain of his position as he claimed to be".

CHAPTER XXII

1902—PIEDMONT—27th YEAR

RETURNING at Christmas, 1901, from a fifteen-months visit in the eastern states, broken by several weeks of Europe, at my Aunt's suggestion I went to call at the Bayo Vista Avenue home of the Londons, but found no one at home. When I did renew acquaintance, that spring of 1902, it was in the old Worcester bungalow at Piedmont, set on a breezy high-hill slope amid pine and swaying eucalyptus, with a rich spread of golden poppy-field slanting toward the westering sun, across the blue bay to the bluer sea. George Sterling, the poet, had called Jack's attention to this neglected, picturesque spot beyond his own home, and it came nearer to Jack London's ideal than any house he ever dwelt in.

The squat, weathered thatch of shingle sheltered a large-beamed living hall, a small dining room, and three or four bedchambers, in one of which Jack eventually combined his sleeping-with working-quarters. Kitchen, laundry, and servants' rooms rambled like aimless if charming afterthoughts, with scant mercy to impatient feet, up-step and down, to the dismay of mistress and nursemaids and cook, of which assistants, whenever obtainable, there were, at one time or another, from one to three.

The long-deserted premises lacked certain modern touches, and Eliza was called in to oversee the rehabilition. A pretty box of a cottage in the grounds was furnished for Jack's mother, the which, after voluble objection, she had at length consented to occupy. By now Flora London had grown as averse to pulling up stakes as ever she had welcomed such diversion in a bygone day.

While on Bayo Vista Avenue, Jack had pursued the custom of receiving all and sundry callers upon one afternoon and evening a week, with welcome to dinner. Other days he must be uninterrupted. This was the untheatrical practicality of his dream—"keeping my house in order." All things, work and play, should be subject to an efficient discipline. "I am a disciple of regular work," he had to say, "and never wait for an inspiration. Temperamentally I am not only careless and irregular, but melancholy; still I have fought both down. The discipline I had as a sailor had full effect on me. Perhaps my old sea days are also responsible for the regularity and limitations of my sleep. Five and a half hours is the precise average I allow myself, and no circumstance has yet arisen in my life that could keep me awake when the time comes to 'turn in.'"

As for the domestic wear and tear involved to insure his one half-day of relaxation out of six or seven (he did not always rest on Sundays, and one day a week he devoted to helping a brother writer, since successful, and now deceased), he would cry:

"If there are not enough servants, get more; your credit is good. Our slim days are passing. Go ahead—get all that are needful to put a good hospitable meal on my table on my Wednesdays!"

Those Wednesday afternoons and evenings will never fade to the lucky souls privileged to share in them, filled as they were with merriest and noisest of jollity and sport; card-games—whist, poker, pedro, "black-jack;" rapid-fire of wits. And there was no lack of music—piano and singing, ringing voices—and poetry. Arthur Symons, Le Gallienne, Swinburne, the Rosettis, Fitzgerald, Bierce, Henley—these and many others were read aloud around the long oaken table, or lolling about the roomy veranda where swung the hammock. Now it would be George Sterling's hushed recitation, or Jack's vibrant tone, or Anna's mellow, golden throat—all the others hanging tremulous on the music of speech from these receptive ones who could not wait to make known their beloved of the poets. Blessing it was to sit under the involuntary young teachers of good and gracious ways of the spirit.

Frolicking outdoors and in, the company assisted their sparkling-eyed gay host, his formidably wise head "sunning over with curls," in the flying of huge box kites from stationary reels set about the acre or so of garden both tended and wild-poppied. Or sparred lustily with the gloves, or fenced with him or with the rising story-writer *Herman* Whitaker, who was Jack's English-pupil and incidentally his fencing instructor. Or with one another. Or rolled clamoring downhill in the tall grasses bloomed thickly amongst by the great, flaunting-orange poppies.

On working-days, for his conditioning Jack would inveigle anyone he could into a boxing-bout—even the little nurse-maids in their early teens had a rare chance to learn scientific self-defense with the well-padded gymnasium gloves. For in sport, as in everything else, Jack London adhered to the scientific approach. It was always an irk to him when hasty young male opponents lost their heads at his insistent, repetitive light-tapping on some persistently unguarded spot, and took to "slugging" in hot blood. In such case Jack necessarily defended himself with an occasional judicious "slug" of his own, until the other should learn the error of his ways. But more often he simply stalled and let the heated fighter absorb the disconcerting lesson of being hurt only by his own headstrongness.

Indoors, in the large room that was the apple of his eye, games were played of intellectual as well as hilarious "rough-house" varieties, in which all joined, boys and girls, men and women and children; and no one could surpass the joyous roar of Jack's fresh boyish lungs, nor out-invent him in bedevilment and sporting feats. Then suddenly he might shout, "Oh, wait—I've got to read you something! *Have* you seen W. W. Jacobs' 'Many Cargoes' and 'More Cargoes?' You've simply *got* to listen to 'In Borrowed Plumes.'" Thereupon, light-stepping with his blithe walk from fetching the book, he would settle deep into the yarn, perhaps propped on the floor with cushions, and repeatedly break down until he rolled and wept in a near-hysteria of uncontrollable mirth over the psychology of Jacobs's outraged skipper.

Romping, they were all one to Jack in this hearty crowd, the president of a great eastern publishing house, or say Sterling's several young and beautiful sisters, and the brilliant Partington sisters and brothers from San Francisco. They had to "take their medicine," Jack vowed, and they knew he despised a coward. The only difference he made with the girls was that he avoided being truly rough, except in such desperate encounters when they might overbear him by conspiracy or numbers or both. As, for instance, during a camping week in the farther hills, when these resourceful maidens, returning from a rattlesnake hunt one warm afternoon, sewed him napping in a hammock and built beneath him a crackling bonfire; or when, after a succession of clever indignities heaped upon him by their teeming trickery, he let them have a large panful of well-dressed salad of ripe red tomatoes, slung precisely chest-high in a sanguinary line the length of a picnic-table. After which perforce he took swift heels to the loftiest reaches of the landscape, pursued by a mad avenging mob of petticoats. Well I remember a day when Joaquin Miller strayed in upon us from his own home, "The Hights," not far away, and found Jack breathing hard and at wary distance from the exhausted feminine element of the camp. Some of the girls, as outcome of a blackberry "scrap," in which the August dust had also been used as ammunition, looked much like the day-after upon a battlefield. "I wish you would go and tidy your hair, young woman," Mr. Miller said to myself, who, though not one of the opposing factions, had accidentally intercepted a pailful of flying water. But presently, everything had quieted down, and the Poet of the Sierras, high-booted, hoary-bearded, serene, was reciting his own verses at our unanimous request. Still can I see Jack's drooped eyes, violet behind the long lashes, and hear the musical voice of the poet:

> "Many to-morrows, my love, my dove,
> Only one to-day, to-day."

Again, all frolic ceased, Jack could be so still, so low-toned with sudden access of beauty, or the sharing of beauty; as when, it may be, he would lead a friend into the rosy gloom of his redwood living-hall, that the glory of a single poppy, or two, or three poppies in a stem-slender vase, might be viewed against a window where a late sunray touched to burnished, palpitant gold the sumptuous petals. Many an one, thus favored, took to heart the unforgetable lesson in simplicity of detail, just as Jack had profited in Japan even with so youthful observation.

But in the many times I rode my chestnut mare to Piedmont that year, dropping in at one home or another where "The Crowd" forgathered in the best times they were ever to know, or at the picnic revels sometimes held Sunday afternoons, or sailed of a Sunday aboard some hired yacht like the *Jessie E.*, or Jack's own little sloop *Spray*, never once did I see or hear aught that was not all good, and clean, and wholesome. The healthful romping, be it ever so boisterous, of these "children of a larger growth," will never be misunderstood by the true hearts that still beat high at thought of those bright California days and nights—when care and spirit-ache were haply laid aside, days and nights "gone, alas, like our youth, too soon." In the very month of his passing, talking with one who had been of the Crowd, Jack wound up with: "Well, we were a pretty clean bunch all 'round."

Nor did I notice much drinking, though Jack, with that hospitableness which was one of his strongest passions, had stored a moderate supply of wines, beer, and whiskey behind the redwood-paneled doors of a built-in wall cabinet to one side the yawning fireplace; to say nothing of ginger ale and sodas and mineral waters. I think he would have loved great banquets in that roomy apartment, or at least a table resembling the Strunskys', always ready laid with abundance for the chance wayfarer. Perhaps Jack most strikingly embodied his magnificent ideal of entertainment in that succession of word-pictures painted in The Wit of Porportuk," the last story in the collection "Lost Face." Limitless, uncalculated hospitality, as attained in later years—but this belongs to another page.

I can see Jack London now, glass in hand, elbow lip-high, the freedom of the blue ocean in his deep sailor-eyes, joining departing guests each with stirrup-cup of whatsoever beverage raised for the pledging, his bright face and hair, played over by the firelight, standing out clearly from the dull-red paneling. Who, that knew him even slightly in those days, but can conjure a vision of him in one or another of his endless phases? Anna Strunsky Walling has given an authentic impression of him:

"I see him in pictures, steering his bicycle with one hand and with the other clasping a great bunch of yellow roses which he had just gathered out of his own garden, a cap moved back on his thick brown hair, the large blue eyes with their long lashes looking out star-like upon the world—an indescribably virile and beautiful boy, the wisdom of his expression somehow belying his mouth.

"I see him lying face-down among the poppies, or following with his eyes his kites soaring against the high blue of the California skies, past the tops of the giant eucalyptus which he so dearly loved.

"I see him becalmed, on the *Spray*, the moon rising behind us, and hear him rehearse his generalizations made from his studies in the watches of the night before of Spencer and Darwin. His personality invested his every movement and every detail of his life with an alluring charm. One took his genius for granted, even in those early years when he was struggling with all his unequaled energies to impress himself upon the world."

And yet, and yet, with his dream in effect, at least in its ordered intention, tied to the mate he had chosen, fatherhood in his hungry grasp at last, at last, and the deepest love in him for the tiny daughter with face so wistfully like his own—the Boy-Man was not happy. Some few of the merrymaking friends and neighbors may have suspected that his scheme of life had failed of triumphant joyousness; but he spoke no word to them, nor looked the sorrow that was his. Only to Anna and to Cloudesley did he let go ever so little the leash he put upon his tongue, and hint the barrenness of his soul for even the year last past. As Anna said of him at that time:

"His standard of life was high. He for one would have the happiness of power, of genius, of love, and the vast comforts and ease of wealth. Napoleon and Nietzsche had a part in him, but Nietzschean philosophy became transmuted into Socialism—the movement of his time—and it was by the force of his Napoleonic temperament that he conceived the idea of incredible success, and had the will to achieve it. Sensitive and emotional as his nature was, he forbade himself any deviation from the course that would lead him to his goal. He systematized his life. Such colossal energy, and yet he could not trust himself! He lived by rule. Law, Order and Restraint was the creed of this vital, passionate youth."

The first of Jack's 1902 letters is to Anna Strunsky, written on January 5:

"Your greeting came good to me. And then there was the dear little token for Joan. And it all impresses me with how much I am and always shall be in your debt. . . .

"You look back on a tumultuous and bankrupt year; and so I. And for me the New Year begins full of worries, harassments, and disappointments. So you? I wonder.

"I look back and remember, at one in the morning, the faces I saw go wan and wistful—do you remember? or didn't you notice?—and I wonder what all the ferment is about.

"I dined yesterday, on canvasback and terrapin, with champagne sparkling and all manner of wonderful drinks I had never before tasted warming me heart and brain, and I remembered the sordid orgies and carouses of my youth. We were ill-clad, ill-mannered beasts, and the drink was cheap and poor and nauseating. And then I dreamed dreams, and pulled myself up out of the slime to canvasback and terrapin and champagne, and learned that it was solely a difference of degree which art introduced into the fermenting. . . .

"Sordid necessities: For me Yorick has not lived in vain. I am grateful to him for the phrase. Am I incoherent? It seems very clear to me.

"And now to facts. Bessie wants me to ask you, if, on January 12th, we can stop all night, and if we can put Joan to bed also. You see, in Piedmont here, we have to leave San Francisco an hour earlier than we used to on account of the street cars. And Bessie cannot bring herself to be away from Joan a whole night."

This occasion was a birthday party given for Jack by the Strunsky family, on January 12. "The Crowd" were all there, and among them a young Norwegian writer, Johannes Reimers, whose novel, "The Heights of Simplicity," just out, he presented to Jack. This man became one of Jack's close friends, and in time one of his favorite painters. I asked Mr. Reimers the other day concerning the meeting with Jack that birthday night at the Strunskys' on Sutter Street:

"Jack looked like a young, ardent, hopeful fellow brimful of conviction. He instantly inspired me with his open comradeship. In appearance?—oh, I should say he struck me as resembling a powerful, healthy young Scandinavian, of a sea-roving type. I tried to get him into conversation about contemporary literature, and was impressed with an apparent bashfulness in him, for he seemed quite reticent of his opinions. And when we said good night, he asked me to come and see him in Piedmont—to come over and have lunch when there was to be nobody else there. And that's the way our friendship began. I read aloud one of my *Overland Monthly* stories to him, and when I had finished, Jack sat quietly for a minute or two, thinking; then he pointed: 'Look at that stack of manuscripts there? Those are just your kind of stories, and nobody wants to buy them.'—Whenever I saw him, he was always the center of a group; people flocked to his vital magnetism; everyone who came within its radius, loved him."

The day after his letter to Anna, whom he had nicknamed "Protean," and who honored him with "Sahib," in unrelieved despair Jack wrote to Cloudesley—January 6:

"Dear Cloudesley:

"But after all, what squirming, anywhere, damned or otherwise, means anything? That's the question I am always prone to put: What's this chemical ferment called life all about? Small wonder that small men down the ages have conjured gods in answer. A little god is a snug little possession and explains it all. But how about you and me, who have no god?

"I have at last discovered what I am. I am a materialistic monist, and there's damn little satisfaction in it.

"I am at work on a short story that no self-respecting bourgeois magazine will ever have anything to do with. In conception it is really one of your stories. It's a cracker jack. If it's ever published I'll let you know. If not, we'll wait until you come west again.

"As regards 'effete respectability,' I haven't any, and I don't have anything to do with any who have . . . except magazines. Nevertheless I shall be impelled to strong drink if something exciting doesn't happen along pretty soon.

"My dear boy, nobody can help himself in anything, and heaven helps no one. Man is not a free agent, and free will is a fallacy exploded by science long ago. Here is what we are:—or, better still, I'll give you Fisk's definition: 'Philosophical materialism holds that matter and the motion of matter make up the sum total of existence, and that what we know as psychical phenomena in man and other animals are to be interpreted in an ultimate analysis as simply the peculiar aspect which is assumed by certain enormously complicated motions of matter.' This is what we are, and we move along the line of least resistance. Whatever we do, we do because it is easier to than not to. No man ever lived who didn't do the easiest thing (for him).

"Or, as Pascal puts it: 'In the just and the unjust we find hardly anything which does not change its character in changing its climate. Three degrees of an elevation of the pole reverses the whole jurisprudence. A meridian is decisive of truth; and a few years, of possession. Fundamental laws change. Right has its epochs. A pleasant justice which a river or a mountain limits. Truth this side the Pyrenees; error on the other.'

"Nay, nay. We are what we are, and we cannot help ourselves. No man is to be blamed, and no man praised.

"Yes, Cosgrave wrote me instanter about the Letters. I'm afraid they're not for him. They would be utter Greek. Say, Cloudesley, did you ever reflect on the yellow magazinism of the magazines? —says I ought not to write for the *Examiner*. And in the same breath he says he will take what I write if I write what he wants. ye gods! Neither the *Examiner* nor Everybody's wants masterpieces, art, and where's the difference in the sacrifice on my part? . . .

" . . . Well, in six days I shall be twenty-six years old, and in nine days Joan will be one year old. . . . "

Here are excerpts from letters to Anna, showing his effort to bend her great talent to disciplined work on the Kempton-Wace correspondence:

"I have been in despair over this letter. Four days I have devoted to it. . . . Well, well, there will have to be no end of revising when we have finished. . . . The great thing after all is to get the letters shaped.

"The movement of this is too rapid and sketchy. It is too much in the form of a narrative, and narrative, in a short story, is only good when it is in the first person. The subject merits greater length. Make longer scenes, dialogues, between them.

"My criticism is, in short, that you have taken a splendid subject and not extracted its full splendor. You have mastery of it (the subject), full mastery—you *understand*; yet you have not so expressed your understanding as to make the reader understand. . . .

"Remember this—confine a short story within the shortest possible time-limit—a day, an hour, if possible—or, if, as sometimes with the best of short stories, a long period must be covered—months—merely limit or sketch (incidentally) the passage of time, and tell the story only in its crucial moments.

" . . . Now, don't think me egotistical because I refer you to my stories—I have them at the ends of my fingers, so I save time by mentioning them. Take down and open "Son of the Wolf."

On January 18, he wrote:

"You are getting a big grip on the written word. And I am whistling over my work at the way the Letters are coming on. We must finish them on this lap. I begin a reply to-day to your last in the series. But, Oh! won't we need to lick those first letters into shape!

"As for my not having read Stevenson's letters—my dear child! When the day comes that I have achieved a fairly fit scientific foundation and a bank account of a thousand dollars, then come and be with me when I lie on my back all day long and read, and read, and read, and read.

"The temptation of the books—if you could know! And I hammer away at Spencer and hack-work—try to forget the joys of the things unread."

He writes to Cloudesley on "Jan. 27/02":

"Dear Cloudesley:

"So you've been oystering? And at a beautiful time of the year—November, on the Atlantic seaboard! How did you like it? I note that you are non-committal on your postal.

"A line from Stoddard [Charles Warren], telling me that you had dropped in on him, led me into looking for your arrival in California at any time. When are you coming West? If you are not, then go on East, but don't stop in that man-killer New York. Mate with the 'wind that tramps the world,' do anything except stay in that 'fierce' burg. It will kill anybody with guts, even you.

"If you hit California you must drop in on me and stop for a spell. I am always hard up, but I '11 never again be as hard up as during your previous visit. You see, I do not have to worry about grub from day to day. I'm doing credit on a larger and Napoleonic scale. And gee! if at any moment I should die, won't I be ahead of the game!"

"Jack London,
"Piedmont,
"Alameda County, Calif.
"Feb. 23/02.

"Dear Cloudesley:—

"Behold, I have moved! Wherefore my long silence. I have been very busy. Also, I went to see a man hanged yesterday. It was one of the most scientific things I have ever seen. From the time he came through the door which leads from the death-chamber to the gallows-room, to the time he was dangling at the end of the rope, but 21 seconds elapsed.

"And in those twenty-one seconds all the following things occurred: He walked from the door to the gallows, ascended a flight of thirteen stairs to the top of the gallows, walked across the top of the gallows to the trap, took his position upon the trap, his legs were strapped, the noose slipped over his head, drawn tight and the knot adjusted, the black cap pulled down over his face, the trap sprung, his neck broken, and the spinal cord severed—all in twenty-one seconds, so simple a thing is life and so easy it is to kill a man.

"Why, he made never the slightest twitch. It took fourteen and one-half minutes for the heart to run down, but he was not aware of it. 1/5 of a second elapsed between the springing of the trap and the breaking of his neck and severing of his spinal cord. So far as he was concerned, he was dead at the end of that one-fifth of a second. He killed a man for twenty-five cents.

"You ask what else beside matter moves. How about force? Waves of light, for instance.

"We'll have to reserve the free will argument till God brings us together again. I've got the cinch on you.

"Did you go in on the *Black Cat*? I went in for a couple of stories, though I have little hope of pulling down even the least prize. I imagine I can sell the stuff somewhere else, however.

"Lord, what stacks of hack I'm turning out! Five mouths and ten feet, and sometimes more, so one hustles. I wonder if ever I'll get clear of debt.

"Am beautifully located in new house. We have a big living room, every inch of it, floor and ceiling, finished in redwood. We could put the floor space of almost four cottages (of the size of the one you can remember) into this one living room alone. The rest of the house is finished in redwood, too, and is very, very comfortable. We have also the cutest, snuggest little cottage right on the same ground with us, in which live my mother and my nephew. Chicken houses and yards for 500 chickens. Barn for a dozen horses, big pigeon houses, laundry, creamery, etc., etc. A most famous porch, broad and long and cool, a big clump of magnificent pines, flowers and flowers and flowers galore, five acres of ground sold the last time at $2000 per acre, half of ground in bearing orchard and half sprinkled with California poppies; we are twenty-four minutes from the door to the heart of Oakland and an hour and five minutes to San Francisco; our nearest neighbor is a block away (and there isn't a vacant lot within a mile), our view commands all of San Francisco Bay for a sweep of thirty or forty miles, and all the opposing shores such as San Francisco, Marin County and Mount Tamalpais (to say nothing of the Golden Gate and the Pacific Ocean)—and all for $35.00 per month. I couldn't buy the place for $15,000. And some day I'll have to be fired out."

But on March 14, 1902, he writes to Anna from the Piedmont eyrie, showing his sincere attitude toward debt:

"I find myself forced to get up at four o'clock now, in order to turn out my day's work. And of course, so long as tradesmen bicker and landlords clatter, that long must the day's work be turned out.

"Also, Joan has been under the weather, my sister's boy on the edge of dying for a number of days, my other sister very close to death herself, and the many and varied demands have consumed every minute of my time.

"Do run over and see us when you're in town. We are nearly settled now, and things will be more comfortable. . . . It will be delightful here this summer."

A week later:

"Many happy returns of the year, since I am too late for the day. And after all, it is the year that must count, and not the day. May it be a full year.

"And may it be an empty one, too—empty of heartache, and soul-silences, and the many trials which have been yours in the past twelve months.

" . . . I look out across the bay to a nook in the Marin shore where I know San Rafael clusters, and I wonder how it fares with you and how you are doing.

"I would suggest . . . that you gather together your belongings, gipsy fashion, and seek a change. New scenes, new inspiration. . . . Also, do not worry. Things are not worth worrying over, except bills and rent. Other things do not count.

" . . . And say, next Sunday, to-morrow, what's the matter with running over to see us? Charmian Kittredge, charmingly different from the average kind, is liable to be here. Perhaps you will like her. Also, Jensen, an old Klondike friend (the sailor whose letters I once showed you), is to be here. Also, possibly several others who will pitch quoits, and fence, and what not. Also, I am scheduled, in the company of Jim and George, to take hasheesh as a matter of scientific investigation. . . . Do come."

The "scientific investigation" proved a very unpleasant passage. Jack deliberately buttered a piece of bread with an excessive amount of the drug, and the overdosage counteracted all the promised joys of his dreaming. A horrible nightmare was the result, and much nausea to follow.

A fragment of a letter to Anna:

"In the last twelve days I have done over eleven thousand words, and that's the rate I have, and am keeping up. 'Writer's cramp' you know. Do run over and see us some day—any day. . . . The rest is bound to do you good. And stop all night—we've a little more room in our new quarters.

"And O, before I close, Whitaker has sold a story to *Harper's Monthly* for one hundred dollars, a story which had been refused divers times by lesser publications.

"I am to proceed right now to a review of "Foma Gordyeeff" for *Impressions*. Have you read it yet? I am saving it for you to read first of all if you haven't. It is a wonderful book. I wish I could allow myself the freshness of a whole day to it instead of going at it, as I now shall, jaded and tired."

To Cloudesley, from Piedmont, March 26, 1902:

"Have got another collection of stories done, 'Children of the Frost,' though they are waiting publication at various magazines."

To Anna, three days later:

"I had intended to write you a good long letter . . . but people have come, must shave now or never, and have some toning to do in dark room . . . do you know, leaving out the letters to be inserted, we have now 50,000 done on the book?

"I must get a Letter from you (Dane Kempton) saying that you are coming to California, and also, somewhere in your Stanford Letters a limit must be given to the effect of our meeting, which meeting I should imagine must precede your meeting with Hester.

"What ho! now, for the revision! You must come and live with us during the momentous period. It's glorious here, more like a poppy dream than real living. . . . Let me know if Letter fits, or if another is needed."

And a little later:

"I have just finished reading your last Letter, Dane Kempton, preparatory to replying to it, and before replying, I must tell you that I feel the Letters will *go! Go! Go!*

"Your last is good, is great! You do get your position stated better than I had thought it possible it could be stated. Come to-morrow. The reply will await you. How goes the novel? I must see and hear of it, all of it."

"Jack.

In the month of May, Jack suffered some newspaper notoriety of an unexpected and to him unusual sort. It was his custom to run accounts at the tradesmen's, pending the receipt of checks from the publishers, which were often delayed, sometimes for impatient weeks. A grocery bill, among others, was still unpaid when he moved to Piedmont, and he was waiting funds with which to liquidate all outstanding obligations when the grocer, sole one of the debtors to voice anxiety, to Jack's indignation dunned him over the telephone. His indignation was eloquently expounded, it may be taken for granted, the while he explained his position with regard to the delayed check. When the man persisted in refusal to deliver bread that day, Jack, now thoroughly aroused, assured him that the bill would be paid when and only when he, Jack London, thought fit and proper. And furthermore, if the grocery-man made any undue fuss, or complained, as threatened, to carry the matter up to the Grocers' Association—it never would be paid. The dealer promptly, in council convened, did precisely what he was warned not to do; and Jack did precisely what he had warned he would do: the bill never was paid. Evidently the Groceryman's Association appreciated his contention, or did not wish to encourage the onus of discourtesy in their ranks, for they failed to back up the complainant. As soon as Jack's check finally arrived, he settled all bills except this one, seeing to it that word of the same reached the groceryman.

"It's the only bill of mine that I ever defaulted on in my life," Jack said when relating the affair, "except $1.67, I think it was, I owed a man in Oakland at the time I jumped out tramping. And I've never been happy that I couldn't find that man after I came back, try as I would."

At the beginning of this incident of the grocery bill, I said that Jack "suffered" notoriety. It was only a way of speaking. I do not know that he suffered. In fact, whether or not his elation extended to the notoriety, no matter how jocosely stated in the press, in this affair or any other that made him conspicuous, is one of the few things about him which I have never fathomed with satisfaction to myself. He appeared to enjoy any kind of contest, as well as its attendant fruits; but I have oftentimes suspected—though never divulging this to him—a bold front to carry on a bluff that protested an underlying shrinking.

"Piedmont, June 7/02.

"Dear Anna:—

" . . . Bills are beginning to press, and I am behind in all my work. Just now I am hammering out juvenile stuff—the Fish Patrol stories for the *Youth's Companion.* [Book of this collection published 1905.] The proofsheets of the novel are giving me endless trouble. It is terrible to doctor sick things. Last night was business meeting of Ruskin. In morning did day's juvenile work. Expected to get off 7 pages of proofs in afternoon and go down town on business. At one o'clock I started in on proofs (7 sheets), at quarter past five I finished them! Every batch seems the worst till the next batch comes along.

"Second Tuesday in June, June 10th, is night you are billed for the lecture at 528 27th St."

On July 3, he writes her:

"I am wondering and wonder what you are doing, and as usual am too rushed to write. For three months I have been steadily dropping behind in all my work, and I have sworn a great vow to catch up. Yesterday I worked eighteen hours, and did clean up quite a lot—the same, the day before, and day before that, etc.

"Sahib."

In a letter to Cloudesley, who was still in New York, of date July 12, 1902, I come upon Jack's first voicing of his fear and regret concerning the gathering of too much knowledge—"opening the books" was his lifelong phrase:

"You must have been having one hell of a time. Aren't you disgusted with metropolitan life? If you aren't you ought to be. I am, and I've never seen it.

"This world is made up chiefly of fools. Besides the fools there are the others, and they're fools, too. It doesn't matter much which class you and I belong to, while the best we can do is not to increase our foolishness. One of the ways to increase our foolishness is to live in cities with the other fools. They, in turn, would be bigger fools if they should try to live the way you and I ought to live. "Wherefore, you may remark that I am pessimistic.

"Speaking of suicide, have you ever noticed that a man is more prone to commit suicide on a full stomach than on an empty one? It's one of nature's tricks to make the creature live, I suppose, for the old Dame knows she can get more effort out of an empty-bellied individual than a full-bellied one.

"Concerning myself, I am moving along slowly, about $3000 in debt, working out a philosophy of life, or rather, the details of a philosophy of life, and slowly getting a focus on things. Some day I shall begin to do things, until then I merely scratch a living.

"Between you and me, I wish I had never opened the books. That's where I was the fool."

It was in this summer, "pitifully, tragically hard at work," as Anna once phrased it, that about the middle of July an offer from the American Press Association found Jack London. This came by wire, and the following day he left for New York, the proposition being that he sail for South Africa to write a series of articles on the Boer War and the political and commercial status of the British Colonies. Sorely in need of diversion, and money with which to meet the lengthening scale of living, this commission, promising both, was welcomed and accepted with celerity, and Jack was the very picture of enthusiasm and relief when a God-speeding crowd of us saw him off on the *Overland* Limited at Oakland Pier. The only regret he showed was in his face, when he pressed Baby Joan in his arms at parting.

By the time he reached New York, it had been learned that the Boer generals had set sail for England. His plans were altered, but he continued on, in the hope of intercepting and interviewing these men. Meanwhile he had made tentative arrangements with the Macmillan Company to publish a contemplated book upon the slums of London. For through lack of foresight and faith, the McClures had let the bright young star slip through their fingers. But Mr. George P. Brett, President of the Macmillan Company, made no such blunder.

On the 29th of July, Jack wrote to Cloudesley Johns, who had temporarily left New York:

"It's a damned shame we missed each other. I sail to-morrow evening for Liverpool. I received your letter last night at 8 o'clock at the Harvard Club—too late to write you. . . . Write me, care of Am. Press Association, 45 Park Place, N. Y. C."

And to Anna, on the 31st, from "B. M. S. *Majestic*":

"I sailed yesterday from New York at noon. A week from to-day I shall be in London. I shall then have two days in which to make my arrangements and sink down out of sight in order to view the Coronation from the standpoint of the East Enders, with their stray flashes of divinity.

"I meet the men of the world in Pullman coaches, New York clubs, and Atlantic liner smoking rooms, and, truth to say, I am made more hopeful for the Cause by their total ignorance and non-understanding of the forces at work. They are blissfully ignorant of the coming upheaval, while they have grown bitterer and bitterer towards the workers. You see, the growing power of the workers is hurting them and making them bitter while it does not open their eyes."

Richard Lloyd Jones met Jack in New York at this time, and was impressed by the many facets he observed of the boy. "To me," Jack said in his hearing, "the world looks like a play that needs perfecting. The lines we speak are not well thought out. The stage business we perform is not well conceived. And the plots we put together are too often poor and mean. We need to work on higher and finer lines."

And the next day the young fellow was roystering through the recreational city of Coney Island, nothing too absurd or too wild for him to attempt. He insisted upon looping the loop. Mr. Jones accompanied him—once, which was the measure of *his* fun. "But London went down again and then again, and still again. He went down eleven times. After he was about half way of these trials, I asked him why he wanted to keep on, and he replied: 'I'm going down that thing until I can go clear around the loop without grabbing hold of it.' And he did, an evidence of his perseverance."

By the end of the first week in August Jack was installed in the East End of London, working under forced draft, and on the 17th scribbled a card to Cloudesley:

"Your letter, forwarded from California, just received. I enjoyed it immensely. I am located in the East End and am hard at work. Have finished 6000 words. Latter part of this week I go down into Kent to do the hop-picking.

"Been in England 11 days, and it has rained every day. Small wonder the Anglo-Saxon is such a colonizer."

On the 25th, to Anna:

"Saturday night I was out all night with the homeless ones, walking the streets in the bitter rain, and, drenched to the skin, wondering when dawn would come. Sunday I spent with the homeless ones, in the fierce struggle for something to eat. I returned to my rooms Sunday evening, after thirty-six hours' continuous work and short one night's sleep. To-day I have composed, typed and revised 4000 words and over. I have just finished. It is one in the morning. I am worn out and exhausted and my nerves are blunted with what I have seen and the suffering it has cost me. . . . I am made sick by this human hell-hole called the East End."

By the close of September, roughly in seven weeks he had lived his book, written his book, taken the photographs to illustrate his book, tried out some English publishers on his work, and was ready for a fleeting jaunt on the Continent. He had written Cloudesley on September 22:

"Yours of Sept. 9th received. I quite agree with you that not to be a free agent is hell. But I don't quite follow you when you say the particular hell lies in not being able to blame anybody, anything, and not even yourself. I don't see how that will help matters in the least. If you throw me down and break my back, of course I can blame you; but that doesn't mend my back.

"I am glad you liked 'Nam-Bok the Unveracious.' The idea of it always appealed to me (including the satire), but I was not satisfied when I wrote it. I feel that I missed somewhere. . . .

"In another week I shall have finished my book of 60,000 words. It's rather hysterical, I think. Look up a brief article of mine in the *Critic* somewhere in the last numbers. Also tell me how you like the 'Story of Jees Uck' in current *Smart Set*."

Near the end of his life, "Of all my books on the long shelf," Jack said to me, "I love most 'The People of the Abyss.' No other book of mine took so much of my young heart and tears as that study of the economic degradation of the poor."Always he was made wroth from a technical standpoint, when this work was ignorantly and maliciously termed a "socialistic treatise." "I merely state the disease, as I saw it," he would explain. "I have not, within the the pages of *that* book, stated the cure as I see it." Jack's earliest method seems to have been to entrench himself behind facts that others had overlooked or neglected, and deliver his challenge. To the wavering and hesitant tongue and eye of the unprepared or unwilling, he showed no mercy whatever. All the satisfaction he won from trying to stir the dead mass was his knowledge that he knew what he knew. Facts were facts, and the only foundation upon which to build righteous certitudes. Of work like "The People of the Abyss," he would say: "I treat of the thing that is, not of the thing that ought to be." To critics who rail at his propaganda, I like to point out how deliberately little he cluttered his art, his fiction, with propaganda.

As if in negation of his consistent attitude on the mighty dollar, Jack put his heart and precious time into this exposition of London's East End with full belief that it would not prove a money maker, either as a bound book or serially. No bourgeois magazine, able to pay its worth as a human document, would risk reputation on one so forthright of unsavory truths. So "The People of the Abyss" appeared in Gaylord Wilshire's socialist monthly, *Wilshire's*, and of course the price could not have been large. Only one of many instances was this, where Jack London acted what seemed paradoxically when sternest values were at stake. It was only a manifestation of his necessity, while perchance building temples in the sky, of keeping his feet on the ground—as he had written Anna, "Somehow, one must always build in the concrete." One critic has said, "With sincerity one may cleave to greatness and sit among the giants." And Jack was eminently sincere in all he did—whether pursuing a hard-headed course in order to discharge his patriarchial duties, or flaming his unremunerative soul-stuff upon the incombustible wall of public opinion. He must weave his best into a dog-story or other fiction medium; straight, unvarnished Truth about the human, no matter how gloriously portrayed, did not command an approval that paid for the beds and bread and coats he must supply his charges.

In Paris, Jack fell in with a spirit kindred to his own vein of French, who assured him: "Ah-h-h, we will not only *see* Paris: we will *live* Paris!"

It grimly amused him, in the early days of the Great War, to read or hear denial on the part of Germany and the Germans of their hatred for England and the English. His sharpest impression of Germany was of a day's journey that ended in Berlin. The compartment contained a half-dozen men besides himself, all Germans of the educated classes; but though they spoke English perfectly, any bid for companionship or request from Jack for information was met with boorish discourtesy of briefest reply, or no reply except lowering looks and cold shoulders. Upon alighting at Berlin, these men suddenly learned from some remark he dropped that he was American:

"Why didn't you tell us?" was the burden of their lament. "We thought you were an Englishman—your face, your figure, your clothes".

And thereafter nothing was too good to be done to make amends.

Italy he loved, and took many photographs with his big "panoram," which he enjoyed developing later in the little dark-room in Piedmont, and framing for his walls. And he climbed Vesuvius.

In all the great centers of civilization, as in New York City, his personal touches with and too-keen observation of the rich, set against his intimate knowledge of the Sub-merged, contributed toward a vast melancholy. Again he wished that he had never "opened the books." But having opened them, it was not in his nature to turn back; he must continue to the end to keep his eyes open their uttermost, for weal or woe.

While still on the Continent, a cable apprised him of the birth of his second child, Bess, who came along eighteen months after Joan, and Jack lost no time in terminating the vacation. On the evening of November 4, 1902, from New York he wrote to Cloudesley:

"Just arrived, and if I can raise $150 by to-morrow morning, shall put out for California to-morrow afternoon.

"Sorry I didn't have your room address, for I could have looked you up and talked the evening with you. As it is, shall have to be on the jump to get away to-morrow.

That autumn of 1902, as Jack London sped west once more, saw his bewildered reviewers facing three new volumes just on the bookstalls, from as many different publishers—namely, "Children of the

1903. JACK LONDON AT 27

1904. SAILOR JACK OF SLOOP "SPRAY"

1906. JACK LONDON IN BOSTON
The first President of The Intercollegiate Socialist Society

1909. JACK LONDON IN MELBOURNE, AUSTRALIA

Frost," (Macmillan); "The Cruise of the Dazzler," (*Century*); and "A Daughter of the Snows," (Lippincott.) In all, he had five books to his credit, with enough manuscript on hand for an equal number. There ensued lengthy reviews in America, where he was hailed alliteratively as "The Kipling of the Klondike," while England sat up and dared venture the assertion that he was America's most promising writer of fiction. "A Daughter of the Snows" called out much diversity of opinion, and no reviewer thought as poorly of it as the author himself. But in future years, looking over this his first long romance, Jack concluded: "It's not so bad, after all. I really believe I think it's rather good for a starter. Lord, Lord, how I squandered into it enough stuff for a dozen novels!"

CHAPTER XXIII

HOME FROM EUROPE; SEPARATION

1903

BACK from Europe, Jack's solemn purpose was to achieve harmony within himself when he should again be at home in the Piedmont bungalow. He devoted himself to this idea, with earnest intention toward the development of his children, and strove to convince himself that all was well with him. As note this paragraph to Cloudesley, dated January 27, 1903:

"By the way, I think your long-deferred congratulations upon my marriage are about due. So fire away. Or, come and take a look at us, and at the kids, and then congratulate."

The Wednesday evenings and Sunday outings were resumed, new acquaintances came and went. Among other writers who shared in the Piedmont gaieties were W. C. Morrow, Dr. C. W. Doyle, and Philip Verrill Mighels, whose novel, "The Inevitable," made simultaneous appearance on Lippincott's fall list with "A Daughter of the Snows." Frank Norris, with whom Jack London had previously gotten tangled in press controversy, had died the year before, or undoubtedly he would have been one in the Crowd.

To me Jack was always friendly, if a trifle impersonal; and once in a while he referred with genial quizzicalness to my failure to review his first book. He presented me with a copy of "The Cruise of the Dazzler," inscribing it:

"Dear Charmian:

"In memory of the *Jessie E.* and the run home before the wind.

"Jack London.

"The Bungalow, February 25, 1903."

Journalists came thousands of miles to interview him, and of them all I think he most cared for that brilliant and lovable soul Fannie K. Hamilton, whose surpassing appreciation of him was a sustained joy for all his years. As to his mode of life he said to her:

"I have adaptability, and can endure cities; but this suits me best. I like room."

Odd little experiences came his way, hurts delivered by pinch-natured debtors to his kindness. Two of them were totally unexpected—one, when a friend he had assisted in various ways spent an entire night showing him conclusively why he, Jack London, was doomed to failure in literature; the second, when another, far more indebted, cut him dead in a Piedmont home, before "The Crowd." He seemed a veritable mark for slights from persons whose touchiness and jealousies restrained them from truly knowing his unsuspecting good-nature and fellowship:

"Did you see———cut you when he came into the room

Sunday, when you and George were playing pedro?" asked his indignant hostess.

"No!" with incredulous, bright interest. "You don't say so! I was so intent on my rotten hand that I never noticed . . . why, I said Hello, didn't I? I'm sure I did. . . . Now I do remember—just for an instant it seemed the air was chilly, and then it went right out of my head.—Why, the son of a gun!" he added amiably, "what did he do that for? What have I done to him?"

And the short-lived wonder gave place to other and more profitable curiosities about the world in which he lived. For the largest part of his life, he stedfastly refrained to take to himself slights or petty humors of men and women. Near the end, sadly enough, they began to gather in a formidable cloud upon his horizon of values. To Anna, in a letter, he commented upon the incident:

"Oh, by the way. I have lost a friend. W. has canceled my name from his list and even cut me in public. For what reason I cannot imagine, for he has said nothing to me at all, though I have heard he was incensed because I told Leonard D. Abbot when I was in New York that he (W.) was a backslider from the Cause."

But it would appear that the young husband and father waged a losing fight for the livable contentment of his resolutions. As early as the middle of February, when again he wrote Cloudesley, his final words bespeak a desire for solitude:

"Feb. 21/03.

"Dear Cloudesley:—

"Well, I must say, from your letter, that my predictions concerning you and New York came pretty close to being verified. And I'm glad to hear you're shaking its dust from your shoes by May. Do it, by all means. The city life is too unnatural and monstrous for us folk of the West. To hell with it. There's more in life than what the social shambles offers.

"Do, by all means, stop over and see us. I hope, by May, to have a sloop on the Bay and be writing a sea novel. You and I can have some fine voyaging together."

A letter to Anna Strunsky, written a month later during an illness, illustrates the heavy pressure he was putting upon himself to gain financial footing to do justice to his little family, as well as an almost superhuman struggle to shake free from "hack-work" and get down to worthy achievement. (I remember dropping in one day to see the babies, and noticing Jack, much tousled, very pale, and with a don't-disturb-me look appealing through the welcoming smile. Jack, who a few short years earlier had been striving to master common grammar, to develop "grammatical nerves," was now typing the manuscript of a story that was destined to ring around the world and be treasured in the universities of his country as a jewel of English literature—"The Call of the Wild." At the same time he was shaping up material for the sea novel referred to in the above letter to Cloudesley, which was "The Sea Wolf," hardly less noted; while arrangements had been perfected with Macmillans to bring out "The Kempton-Wace Letters.") Below is the letter to Anna:

"March 13/03.

"Dear Anna:—

"I quite wondered if you were ever going to write to me again. And I should have wondered more, only I have been head over heels in work, getting things cleaned up, books partly finished, etc., so that I might start in on the sea novel for Mr. Brett.

"You found him reading the manuscript of what was probably my dog story. ["The Call of the Wild."] I started it as a companion to my other dog-story 'Batard,' which you may remember; but it got away from me, and instead of 4000 words it ran 32000 before I could call a halt. I hope you will like it when it appears.

"I wrote Hyman [her brother] a letter which he must have received just about the time he arrived in San Francisco. I have been unable to get over and see him. I go nowhere any more. Since my return, I have been to San Francisco but twice and do not dream of when I shall again go there.

"I have just finished writing two lectures, each 6000 words long and something like the 'Tramp.' They are 'The Scab' and 'The Class Struggle.' [Collected under title of "War of the Classes."]

"I can hardly contain myself, looking forward to seeing the Letters in print. Be sure to question anything and everything in mine that strikes you as wrong.

" . . . I am quite a hermit these days, going nowhere and seeing nobody. Between my crippled condition and the excessive delayed work it heaped upon me, I have been unable to see your people. . . .

" . . . I hear all kinds of flattering bits of news concerning you from Don and Wilshire, and know that you are glowing and rampant, living always at the pitch of life as is your way, pleasuring in your sorrows as ardently as in your joys, carelessly austere, critically wanton, getting more living out of hours and minutes than we colder mortals, God pity us, get out of months and years. Child, how one envies you. For child you are, as essentially a child as saliently you are a woman.

"I have reread what I have written. Believe me, there is nothing in it—only envy, honest envy, for one who will always titillate with desire, and with a thousand desires, who is content to pursue without attaining, and who enjoys more in anticipation than do others who grasp and satisfy and feel the pangs of hunger that is sated and yet can never be sated. Am I wrong? I hope not."

Desperate for funds, with bills pressing, Jack London hesitated not to accept two thousand dollars flat from The Macmillan Company for "The Call of the Wild," which was to be brought out in July, following serial publication begun immediately in the *Saturday Evening Post*, for which he received seven hundred dollars. And "The Call of the Wild," for which he pocketed only this total of twenty-seven hundred dollars, scored an instantaneous hit, leaped into the front ranks of the "best-sellers" and made money for everyone but the author. However, lest there be misunderstanding on this ground, let me go on record with the fact that Jack London came to maintain that he gained rather than sacrificed in the transaction, in view of the world-wide advertising upon which the Macmillans spent enormous sums.

"Mr. Brett took a gamble, and a big chance to lose. It was the game, and I have no kick," he stoutly asserted. "Also," Jack would add, "Mr. Brett stood almost certainly to lose on 'The Kempton-Wace Letters,' and I'm willing to lay a bet that the Company never much more than cleaned up expenses on that splendid but misunderstood and unpopular book."

"The Kempton-Wace Letters" subsequently went out of print in both the United States and England. In 1921 the book was resurrected, and reprinted in London by Mills & Boon, Ltd.

Jack's aptness for titles was never more happily evidenced than in "The Call of the Wild." And yet, both serial and book publishers entreated a different one. Jack concurred with their dissatisfaction, and told them he was quite willing they should invent a better. That they could not, or at least did not, gives one pause.

Jack was systematically criticized by a certain type of reviewers of all times, for his "brutality." I am inclined to think the following, from a letter to Mr. Johns of March 16/03, must have been the most surprising commission he ever received:

"If you have any 'horror' stories, submit them to *Bookman*. I have the following from *Bookman*:

"Don't you happen to have up your sleeve a dramatic tale with plenty of battle, murder, and sudden death—a story with real horror in it? Remember, the more gore the better."

One New York critic of "The God of His Fathers" had pleased Jack.

"Mr. Jack London's strength never degenerates into brutality. He deals with brutal things, with naked things, with the primitive life in a world barren of all save hardship, ice and snow, rich only in gold; but he remains an artist to the last. Whatever he tells us we accept because we feel its truth and the skill of its telling."

And an English reviewer characterized this collection as "Epic Stories of the North."

In another note to Anna, Jack is seen emerging from his hermit mood in a reference to the pleasure of a fortnight's visit each from the Lily Maid and Cloudesley Johns. And below are brief communications to his two friends upon one matter or another:

"Dear Anna:—

"Telegram received. I have no copy of the quotations lost by the printers. So book ["Kempton-Wace Letters"] will have to go without them. Too bad!

"... Am in tremendous rush. Hope you'll make this out. Wilshire was out to see me, with Rose, the Wallings, etc. All went to Ruskin Annual Dinner together.

"Shall send fotos of Joan and Bess as soon as I can get around to the making of them....

"By the way, the contract you signed with Macmillan Company is for the U. S. only. I feel quite certain that you and I will receive the same royalties from England from Messrs. Isbister & Co. . . . (This Isbister proposition is due to certain publishing arrangements I have on that side of the water.)"

"April 24/03.

"Dear Anna:—

"This is the first writing I have done for some time. Easter Sunday I elected to cut off the end of my thumb, and not finding the piece, have had a painful wound to heal. . . . Have a heart beating in the end of my thumb. . . . Am glad you liked the dog story. . . . "

Of same date to Cloudesley:

"Sedgwick has accepted 'Marriage of Lit-Lit' [In collection entitled "The Faith of Men"] if I put a 'snapper' on the end of it As it's already sold in England I guess I'll obey."

Referring to "People of the Abyss":

"May 5/03.

"Dear Cloudesley:

"Thank you very much for your criticism. The proofs are in, but I shall save your points (almost all of which I bow to) until I get another whack at the proofs, which I will get when I place the illustrations in it.

"My thumb is growing nicely—quite a chunk of new and very tender meat on the end of it. We went out sailing yesterday, and about everybody aboard, and there were fifteen, ran into it."

"May 29, 1903.

"Dear Cloudesley:

"When are you coming up? Am just in from a cracking good trip, in which I blew the *Spray*'s sails to ribbons. Am waiting ashore now while new ones are being bent. I find that I can work splendidly upon her.

"Nothing doing, no news, nothing. Thumb is getting along and have finished 30,000 words of sea story. ["The Sea Wolf."] When it is done am going to send you a MS. copy for criticism (if you don't mind), before I submit it."

"The Kempton-Wace Letters" was published in May, and Jack received his first copy of the book through the Glen Ellen post office, in Sonoma County, whither he had removed his family to camp on my Aunt's place on Sonoma Mountain, "Wake Robin Lodge." Here a congenial company of acquaintances met in the summers, making merry in the incomparable woods bordering Graham and Sonoma Creeks, swimming in the pools, tramping, boxing, fencing, kiting, and gathering about the campfire at dusk for discussion and reading. On one such night Jack, in firelight supplemented by a lantern, read aloud the "Letters." While several members of my family participated in all this rural delight, I was able to be present upon only an occasional weekend. I was fortunate enough to make one of the thralled circle that formed about the flickering logs on the June evening Jack London read aloud in his musical voice, at one sitting, "The Call of the Wild," which had just come to his hand.

Jack's state, and his method of speculation upon that of another, is shadowed in the following, written to George Sterling in June of 1903:

" . . . this I know, that in these later days you have frequently given me cause for honest envy. And you have made me speculate a great deal. You know that I do not know you—no more than you know me. We have really never touched the intimately personal note in all the time of our friendship. I suppose we never shall.

"And so I speculate and speculate, trying to make you out, trying to lay hands on the inner side of you—what you are to yourself, in short. Sometimes I conclude that you have a cunning and deep philosophy of life, for yourself alone, worked out on a basis of disappointment and disillusion. Sometimes, I say, I am firmly convinced of this, and then it all goes glimmering, and I think that you don't want to think, or that you have thought no more than partly, if at all, and are living your life out blindly and naturally.

"So I do not know you, George, and for that matter I do not know how I came to write this."

During this period, some of his friends sensed the breaking strain the young man was undergoing, and that all was not well in the Londons' ruddy-brown tent cottage and environs amidst the spicy-perfumed laurels edging the Graham's bank; but they would have been shocked had they known the strain was so taut that for some time back Jack had avoided sleeping with his old familiar pistol in the same room, lest he do himself an injury in his trouble-ridden slumber.

Which would point to the surmise that unhappy as he thought himself, he valued existence sufficiently to take steps to preserve his own.

Much suffering he concealed in the solitude of a leafy study on a mossy shelf down the bank, where at a rustic table he worked steadily on his novel, "The Sea Wolf"; or under an hilarious exterior as he played water-tag with a bevy of camp children, or blind-man's bluff among the trees and blossomy undergrowth on the Sonoma's marge. Mornings he rose betimes and went out ostensibly for small game, with a conspicuous absence of bags upon his returnings. This gave rise to an endless string of verses, goodnaturedly taunting and wholly affectionate, composed by little Dorothy Reynolds and Henry Breck and their playmates, and chanted shrilly by the juvenile company by campfire, to the tune of "Mr. Dooley." Here are some of the verses:

"O Mr. London,
O Mr. London,
The finest man the rabbits ever knew;
He always sought them
But never shot them,
For that was Mr. London's way to do.

"He started early
One Sunday morning:
He said, 'I will be sure to get one now!'
And gazing upward
Upon the hillside,
He saw a rabbit there as big as a cow.

"He raised his rifle,
He shook a trifle;
The rabbit looked at him reproachfully.
He said, 'I cannot,'
He said, 'I will not,'
And so he let the rabbit turn and flee.

CHORUS

"O it's strange when upon returning,
How his hunter's skill he'd praise,
About those monstrous rabbits
In his early morning chase.
O it's then that our hearts are gladdest,
And it seems it can't be true,
When he has to eat that bacon
Instead of rabbit stew."

It was during these dawn and sunrise hauntings of this sloping wall of Sonoma's valley that Jack London fell hopelessly in love with the "Sweet Land" he evermore was to adore and make his heart-home.

Evidently his plans were to spend as little time thence-forth as he could possibly avoid at the once desirable bungalow in Piedmont, as cited by his next contemplated absence, in a letter of July 2:

"Dear Cloudesley:

"Here I am, camping and knocking out 1500 words per day seven days in the week. If you're coming to see me, come just the same. Am only 2½ hours ride from San Francisco. So bring your traps right on up to camp here. Have a girl to do the cooking, plenty of grub, and plenty of blankets. So come along. Expect to stay here for a month yet. Then for the sloop!

"... You remember the rig we rode in the day I cut my thumb. Five of us were coming in on it, same road, down hill, horse hitting it up—when king-bolt broke and we spilled. I had five different places on arms and legs in bandages, also a stiff knee. Am almost recovered now.

"No, the Kempton Letters were written entirely by Anna Strunsky, though the ear-marks of each are to be found in the other's work—unconscious absorptions of style, I suppose."

In answer to some question from George Sterling, he again outlines his philosophy of work: "No, I don't approve of Pegasus plowing if he can fly. But I believe in his plugging like hell in order to fly."

Of course this tension of spirit could not last, in one so dynamic and intense as he. In spite of every effort, struggle as he would to carry out his scientific-mating experiment, he became beaten at his own game; and it was by a curious irony of events that his ultimate failure should have been coincident with the appearance of "The Kempton-Wace Letters," dealing the lie direct to his once boasted rule-of-thumb program.

Indeed, not long afterward we learned that in a copy of this book presented to a young cousin of mine, he had written refuting a brave argument once held with her in camp:

"One hour of love is worth a century of science."

This he repeated in my own copy three months after our marriage.

For now, abruptly, "out flew the web and floated wide," the fabric he had so carefully designed, so faithfully woven to its last least pattern of fidelity. It had got beyond him and he tore it and cast it to the winds. He did not care whither he went, nor how, nor with whom. He caught at a wild unthought-out suggestion for a northern trip without an ending—and not without a companion. Largely owing to restlessness, he renounced the steamer voyage as lightly as he had conceived it. But he remained unshaken in determination to start living by himself, at the first moment he could break up at the bungalow and see his family housed comfortably where he would have convenient access to his little ones.

Let no one, quick to condemn his action, dream that all this chaos of the established was easy for a man of Jack London's stamp. Deeply he loved his children, bone of his bone, flesh of his flesh. But he had committed a boundless mistake in his arrogant youth, and the penalty that was inevitable had overwhelmed him commensurately. "I must work hard to bring things out as right as I can," with sad eyes he said to one of us, "though it be work that shall wring my heart"—thinking of his babies, and not a little of the radical disturbance of their mother's round of existence. Sometimes, it seemed, he almost doubted his own strength to go through with what he had been driven to undertake.

But desire for freedom had wrung him vitally from all other considerations—he who could never be really free, in his whole life of responsibility for others. From Piedmont, in the midst of the rack of tearing up—everyone concerned oppressed with the impermanence of what had seemed so secure—Jack wrote:

"Dear Cloudesley:

"Just a line to let you know I am suddenly back from camping, that my affairs are all in confusion, that I do not know yet what I shall do, that I need and can use no help other than my own strength may give me, and that you do not come North till you hear from me again."

And on the 29th:

"Thank you, old man. Am moving house and splitting up, just now. Poor, sad little Bungalow!

"Should I need you, I will call upon you unhesitatingly."

He found a cozy five-room flat in Oakland, at what was then 1216 Telegraph Avenue, to which he moved his mother and Johnnie, setting aside space for his own belongings while he should be away in the sloop. The two babies and their mother were quartered in another flat a few blocks distant. From his new habitation he wrote Cloudesley:

"Aug. 21, 1903.

"Well, good luck to you, old man. If you love, that is all there is to it. I thought you downed my Herbert Wace philosophy rather squeamishly.

"And so we go zigzagging through life. When we first knew each other we were on the same tack. Then I filled away on the other tack and married. Now I have come about once more, and I find that you have put your helm down and are away on the opposite tack. May your reach be a longer one than mine—much longer."

That there was no lack of anguish on Jack's part for pain inflicted throughout this separation, may be judged, reticent though he was in general, from the closing remark of the next letter. Also he gives a line on his expectation of benefit to his work in the new order of life. To his mind, there could be no two ways about the latter, for the double homes demanded his very best effort to earn big prizes, although meanwhile he must deliver a certain amount of "hack:"

"1216 Telegraph Avenue,
"Oakland, Cal., Aug. 26, 1903.

"Dear Cloudesley:

"Yes, I shouldn't mind living for a while in Los Angeles; but, you see, I'm settled, am three months behind in all my work, letting my contracted work go and hammering away at hack in order to catch up with a few of my debts, and do not see my way to getting even with my work for all of a year hence.

"Hard-a-lee with me will not affect my work—in fact, I am confident it will be far otherwise.

"I laugh when I think of what a hypocrite I was, when, at the Bungalow, I demanded from you your long-deferred congratulations for my marriage—but, believe me, I was a hypocrite grinning on a grid.

"Concerning your affair, let me say this: It's all right for a man sometimes to marry philosophically, but remember, it's damned hard on the woman."

To Cloudesley, September 5, 1903:

"Tell you what I'll do. I'll take a flying trip down to Los Angeles, say somewhere in January—if not December, as soon as 'The Sea Wolf' is done and providing the *Century* takes it serially for 1904. The dicker is now on, and the only thing Gilder hesitates about is the last half (unwritten) wherein a man and woman are all by themselves on an island. I have just tried to assure him that I won't shock the American Prude, and, anyway, that he can blue-pencil all he wants.

"If *Century* doesn't take the novel, why, when I get done with it I'll have to plunge into hack-work up to my ears to escape bankruptcy. If *Century* does take it, why then I can take a vacation.

"As for living in Los Angeles—nay, nay. I am wedded to 'Frisco Bay.

"I should like to take the ride you mention. I love motion and can never go too fast. . . .

"I wouldn't care much for a woman capable of saying: 'A woman can lose everything, even her loved ones and her life, and still be rich in her purity.' I may respect her, but I could not admire her. She is a little cloudy and small in her ethical concepts even though it be not her fault."

The next letter shows his desire again to roam the world:

"Sept. 5, 1903.

"Dear Anna:—

"As usual, hard at work. It's been so long since I had a real vacation that I hardly know what such a thing would be like. Even when I was in Europe last year, instead of resting I wrote a book. Well, in about a year I am starting off around the world, and I expect to take years in going around.

" . . . Our Book——I haven't the least idea how it has sold; but, when all is said and done, it has been received far more favorably than might have been expected. It is a good book, a big book, and, as we anticipated, too good and too big to be popular. . . . "

On the 21st he wrote Cloudesley:

"I'm sending you, this mail, a copy of 'Call of the Wild.' You don't seem to care for the 'Daughter of the Snows.' I don't blame you. I wonder how you'll like the 'Sea Wolf.' I'11 bet you'll wonder how the *Century* dares to publish it."

"Sept. 26, 1903.

"Dear Cloudesley:

" . . . By the way, I learn Macmillan Company has made 'People of Abyss' into a $2.00 net book."

The reviewers, again with three new books thrown suddenly at their heads, making eight within three meteoric years since this astonishing young writer had shot into vision, were stunned not only by numbers but by the total dissimilarity of the three—"The Call of the

Wild," "The Kempton-Wace Letters," and now "The People of the Abyss." British critics, theretofore gathering in enthusiasm, were of two minds about "The People of the Abyss." Mainly it was resented and condemned as an inexcusable infringement on his part to come to their shores and turn out the London slums for the world to view. They thought he would be better occupied in those of his own land. A minority, however, accorded the book its due. And two years later, the Archbishop of Canterbury, inspecting New York's East Side, exclaimed: "Amazing! I am astonished at it all. The slums of New York are not nearly so bad as the slums of London. And the mean streets are not so mean as the East End of our great English city."

"Oct. 9, 1903.

"Say, Cloudesley:

"Thursday, Oct. 22nd, I set sail on the *Spray* for a couple of months cruising about the Bay, and up the Sacramento, San Joaquin and Napa rivers. Do you want to come along, just you and I?

"We can both get our writing in each day and have a jolly time. Also, I'll have a shotgun and rifle along and we can get in plenty of duck-shooting. It won't cost you anything. . . . Also, I have that Smith-Premier typewriter, and if you can use such a machine you won't have to bring your own along.

"What d'ye say? Let's hear soon."

"Oct. 13, 1903.

"All right, old man. I shall look for you, then, on Oct. 21st. You may desert or receive dishonorable discharge, whichever you will, whenever you wish. . . . We ought both of us get in plenty of work, and have a good time, and get health and strength".

1904. WAR CORRESPONDENTS EN ROUTE TO JAPAN

From Left to Right: 1. James H. Hare, Collier's; 2. Robert L. Dunn, Collier's; 3. J. Sheldon Williams; 4. Captain Lionel James, London Times; 5. Jack London, San Francisco Examiner; 6. Frederick Palmer, Collier's; 7. Percival Phillips; 8. O. K. Davis, N. Y. Herald

CHAPTER XXIV

JAPANESE-RUSSIAN WAR

Spring 1904

WITH war threatening to flare up any moment between Japan and Russia, the *San Francisco Examiner* asked Jack London if he would be ready to go out at call. Jack, near the close of his sea novel, sorely needing funds, held himself awaiting the summons. He arranged his finances so that regular payments would be made to his mother as well as to his children, with instructions to his eastern publishers to stand prepared to advance any necessary further sums should his wife call for the same. Meanwhile the Managing Editor haled him to San Francisco, to sit for photographs against the day of featuring a sensational departure. The pictures were posed on the roof of the *Examiner* Building, and portray a very lovable, very boyish, unmodish person, with tousled curls.

Although hostilities had not yet been actually declared, Jack was dispatched on the S. S. *Siberia*. To Cloudesley on January 7 he dashed off: "Sail to-day for Yokohama. Am going for Hearst. Could have gone for *Harper's*, *Collier's*, and *N. Y. Herald*—but Hearst made the best offer." Other newspapermen aboard were Captain Lionel James, *London Times*; Percival Phillips, *London Daily Express*; Sheldon Inglis Williams, artist for *London Sphere;* O. K. Davis, *New York Herald*; Frederick Palmer and R. L. Dunn, for *Collier's Weekly*, and *Collier's* veteran war photographer, James H. Hare.

En masse "The Crowd" saw Jack off at the dock; and of the Crowd, George Sterling and I were entrusted jointly with the *Century Magazine* and the Macmillan proofreading of "The Sea Wolf," the manuscript of which had been completed and signed the previous evening, and shipped off to the *Century Magazine* for immediate serialization. The original script of this novel lay in a steel safe throughout San

Francisco's Great Earthquake and Fire of 1906, and to this day the incinerated sheets preserve their form, the only visible markings being lead-penciled corrections, which withstood the heat.

Five days later, at the Sterlings' in Piedmont, a few of us gathered to celebrate Jack's twenty-eighth birthday.

Early in the voyage, he had an attack of grippe; and the day the *Siberia* cleared from Honolulu, during deck sports Jack's left foot was badly injured.

There is not space in this biography to incorporate Jack London's articles on the Japanese-Russian War. But I quote excerpts from letters written to me, and these will serve to illustrate the almost intolerable irk endured under the rigors of Japanese discipline toward the newspaperman. "They settled the war correspondent forever," he often exclaimed, "and they proved that he was a dispensable feature of warfare."

Near the time of Jack's death, among other collections of unpublished book material, he had arranged his Japanese-Russian and also his 1914 Mexican War-Notes, which shall presently be issued as he intended. His utter disgust with the lack of opportunity given the journalist, to deliver what would be really worthwhile articles, accounts for his long delay in bringing out his notes. His 3-A Kodak, however, had the distinction of being the first to supply pictures for the American public, although so poor was the mail service in and out of Korea, he never knew until his return six months afterward whether or not his films and cables had been received.

One can give no better idea of his experience and frame of mind than by quoting from his letters to myself:

"S.S. *Siberia*,
"Jan. 13/04.

"Somewhat weak and wobbly, but still in the ring. Came down with a beautiful attack of La Grippe. Of course, didn't go to bed with it, but spent the time in a steamer chair, for one day half out of my head. And oh, how all my bones ache, even now! And what wild dreams I had! . . .

"Honolulu is in sight, and in an hour I shall be ashore mailing this, and learning whether or not there is war.

" . . . Am, Grippe excepted, having a nice trip. The weather is perfect. So is the steamer. Sit at the Captain's table, and all the rest—you know. . . . "

"Jan. 15/04.

" . . . Well, we sailed yesterday from Honolulu. . . . Am still miserable with my Grippe, but getting better. Had a swim in the surf at Waikiki. Took in the concert at the Hawaiian Hotel, and had a general nice time.

"Had some fun. I bucked a game run by the Chinese firemen of the *Siberia*, and in twenty-five minutes broke three banks and won $14.85! So, you see, I have discovered a new career for myself.

"The war correspondents, the 'Vultures,' are a jolly crowd. We are bunched up at the Captain's table, now that the passenger list has been reduced by the lot who left at Honolulu. In fact, the trip to Honolulu had three bridal couples which sat at the upper end of the table. This is a funny letter—the correspondents are cutting up all around me; and just now I am being joshed good and plenty."

"S.S. *Siberia*, Jan. 20/04.

" . . . Quite a time since I last wrote. You'll wonder why. Well, know that I am the most fortunate of unfortunate men. The evening of the day we left Honolulu I smashed my left ankle. For sixty-five sweaty hours I lay on my back. Yesterday I was carried on deck, on the back of one of the English correspondents. And to-day I have been carried on deck again.

"The smashed ankle is the misfortune; the fortune . . . is the crowd of friends I seem to have collected. From six o'clock in the morning till eleven at night, there was never a moment that my stateroom did not have at least one visitor. As a rule there were three or four, and very often twice as many. I had thought, when the accident happened, that I should have plenty of time for reading; but I was not left alone long enough to read a line.

"I am looking forward with interest to the sixth day, when, if the surgeon does not change his mind, I may put my foot to the deck and try to walk with the aid of crutches.

"Of course, what you want to know is what the smash consists in. I was jumping and coming down from a height of three feet and a half. I landed on my left foot—having 'taken off' with my right. But my left foot did not land on the deck. It landed on a round stick, and lengthwise with the stick. Stick about diameter of broom-handle. Of course, my foot went up alongside my leg. My ankle was strained on one side, sprained on the other. That is, the tendons on the inside were stretched and ruptured, the bones on the outside ground against each other, bruising themselves and pinching the nerves—result, an irresistible combination.

"Now I have two weak ankles. I fear me I am getting old. Both my knees have been smashed, and now both my ankles. It might be worse, however. What bothers me just now is that I don't know just how bad this last ankle is. Absolute rest, in a rigid bandage, has been the treatment, so not even the surgeon will know till I try to walk on it.

" . . . Don't worry because I have let my worry out in this letter. Anyway, I'll be able to write you later, before we make Yokohama, and let you know more. I hope the report will be promising."

"S.S. *Siberia*, Jan. 21/04.

"You should see me to-day. Quite the cripple, hobbling around on a pair of crutches. I can't stand on the ankle yet, but hope to be able to walk by the time we make Yokohama. To-day is Thursday, and we expect to arrive next Monday morning. I hope war isn't declared for at least a month after I arrive in Japan—will give my ankle a chance to strengthen.

"All hands are very good to me, and I might say I am almost worn out by being made comfortable. . . . I am in for a game of cards now, so more anon."

"S.S. *Siberia*, Jan. 24/04.

"Yesterday I dragged about on crutches to the boat deck and to tiffin, and to bed. To-day I have ventured without crutches. But I walk very little—just from stateroom to boat deck.

"A young gale is on, but the *Siberia* is behaving splendidly.

"P.S. The young gale is still growing."

"S.S. *Siberia*, Jan. 24/04.

"Just packing up. Shall be in Yokohama at six to-morrow morning. Ankle is improving. Am walking (very slowly, and limpingly, and carefully) without crutches. I just missed breaking the leg—so you can see what a twist it was. Hope the war holds off for a month yet. . . . "

"Thursday, Jan. 28/04.

" . . . If you can read this. The train is joggling, and the temperature inside the car is 40. I am on the express bound for Kobe—where, on Jan. 31, if not sooner, I expect to get a steamer for Korea. I am bound for Seoul, the capital. Was pretty busy in Yokohama and Tokio. Arrived Monday, and have been on the jump until now, though this writing looks as though I were still jumping.

"Ankle is getting better very slowly."

"Jan. 29/04.

"You should have seen me plunging out of Kobe this morning, myself and luggage in three 'rickshaws, with push-boys and pull-boys and all the rest, and racing to catch the express for Nagasaki. No steamer out of Kobe till Feb. 3rd, so am going to try my luck at Nagasaki, twenty-two hours' ride on the train and no sleeping car.

"Weather is warmer down here. It was bitter cold up Yokohama-way.

"If I do not refer to war doings, know that there is a censorship, and cables, etc., are held up. . . . "

"Shimonoseki, Feb. 3/04.

"Still trying to sail to Chemulpo. Made an all-day ride back from Nagasaki to Moji to catch a steamer, Feb. 1 (Monday). Bought ticket, stepped outside and snapped three street scenes. Now Moji is a fortified place. Japanese police 'Very sorry,' but they arrested me. Spent the day examining me. Of course, I missed steamer. 'Very sorry' Carted me down country Monday night to town of Kokura. Examined me again. Committed. Tried Tuesday. Found guilty. Fined five yen, and camera confiscated. Have telegraphed American Minister at Tokio, who is now trying to recover camera.

"Received last night a deputation from all the Japanese Newspaper correspondents in this vicinity. Present their good offices, and 'Very sorry.' They are my brothers in the craft. They are to-day to petition the judges (three judges sat on me in black caps) to get up mock auction of camera, when they will bid it in and present it to me with their compliments. 'Very uncertain,' however, they say.

"Expect to leave for Chemulpo on the 6th or 7th inst."

"On board Junk, off Korean Coast,
"Tuesday, Feb. 9, 1904.

"The wildest and most gorgeous thing ever! If you could see me just now, captain of a junk with a crew of three Koreans who speak neither English nor Japanese and with five Japanese guests (strayed travelers) who speak neither English nor Korean—that is, all but one, which last knows a couple of dozen English words. And with this polyglot following I am bound on a voyage of several hundred miles along the Korean coast to Chemulpo.

"And how did it happen? I was to sail Monday, Feb. 8th, on the *Keigo Maru* for Chemulpo. Saturday, Feb. 6th, returning in the afternoon from Kokura (where my camera had been returned to me)—returning to Shimonoseki, I learned the *Keigo Maru* had been taken off its run by the Jap Government. Learned also that many Jap warships had passed the straits bound out, and that soldiers had been called from their homes to join their regiments in the middle of the night.

"And I made a dash right away. Caught, just as it was getting under way, a small steamer for Fusan. Had to take a third class passage—and it was a *native* steamer—no white man's chow (food) even first class, and I had to sleep on deck. Dashing aboard in steam launch, got one trunk overboard but saved it. Got wet myself, and my rugs and baggage, crossing the Japan Sea. At Fusan, caught a little 120-ton steamer loaded with Koreans and Japs, and deck load piled to the sky, for Chemulpo. Made Mokpo with a list to starboard of fully thirty degrees. It would take a couple of hundred of such steamers to make a *Siberia*. But this morning all passengers and freight were fired ashore, willy nilly, for Jap. Government had taken the steamer to use. We had traveled the preceding night convoyed by two torpedo boats.

"Well, fired ashore this morning, I chartered this junk, took five of the Japanese passengers along, and here I am, still bound for Chemulpo. Hardest job I ever undertook. Have had no news for several days, do not know if war has been declared and shall not know until I make Chemulpo—or maybe Kun San, at which place I drop my passengers. God, but I'd like to have a mouthful of white man's speech. It's not quite satisfying to do business with a 24-word vocabulary and gesticulations."

"Thursday, Feb. 11, 1904.

"On board another junk. Grows more gorgeous. Night and day traveled for Kun San. Caught on lee-shore yesterday, and wind howling over Yellow Sea. You should have seen us clawing off—one man at the tiller and a man at each sheet (Koreans), four scared Japanese, and the fifth too seasick to be scared. Of course, we cleared off, or you wouldn't be reading this.

"Made Kun San at nightfall, after having carried away a mast and smashed the rudder. And we arrived in driving rain, wind cutting like a knife. And then, you should have seen me being made comfortable last night—five Japanese maidens helping me undress, take a bath, and get into bed, the while visitors, male and female, were being entertained (my visitors). And the maidens passing remarks upon my beautiful white skin, etc. And this morning, same thing repeated—the Mayor of Kun San, the captain of police, leading citizens, all in my bedroom, visiting while I was being shaved, dressed, washed, and fed.

"And all the leading citizens of the town came to see me off, and cheered me, and cried 'Sayonara' countless times.

"New junk, manned by Japanese—five—and not one knows one word of English; and here I am, adrift with them, off the Korean Coast.

"No white man's news for a long time. Hear native rumors of sea-fights, and of landing of troops, but nothing I may believe without doubting. But when I get to Chemulpo, I'll know 'where I'm at.'

"And maybe you think it isn't cold, traveling as I am, by junk. . . . The snow is on the land, and in some places, on north slopes, comes down to the water's edge.

"And there are no stoves by which to keep warm—charcoal boxes, with half a dozen small embers, are not to be sneered at—I am beside one now, which I just bought for 12½ cents from a Korean at a village, where we have landed for water."

"Saturday, Feb. 11, 1904.

"Still wilder, but can hardly say so 'gorgeous,' unless landscapes and seascapes seen between driving snow squalls, be gorgeous. You know the tides on this Coast range from 40 to 60 feet (we're at anchor now, in the midst of ten thousand islands, reefs, and shoals, waiting four hours until the tide shall turn toward Chemulpo—30 *li*—which means 75 miles away).

"Well, concerning tides. Yesterday morning found us on a lee shore, all rocks, with a gale pounding the whole Yellow Sea down upon us. Our only chance for refuge, dead to leeward, a small bay, and high and dry. Had to wait on the 40-ft. tide. And we waited, anchored under a small reef across which the breakers broke, until, tide rising, they submerged it. Never thought a sampan (an open crazy boat) could live through what ours did. A gale of wind, with driving snow—you can imagine how cold it was. But I'm glad I have Japanese sailors. They're braver and cooler and more daring than the Koreans. Well, we waited till eleven A.M. It was 'twixt the devil and the deep sea—stay and be swamped, run for the little bay and run the chance of striking in the surf. We couldn't possibly stay longer, so we showed a piece of sail and ran for it. Well, I was nearly blind with a headache which I had brought away with me from Kun San, and which had been increasing ever since; and I did not much care what happened; yet I remember, when we drove in across, that I took off my overcoat, and loosened my shoes—and I didn't bother a bit about trying to save the camera.

"But we made it—half full of water—but we made it. And maybe it didn't howl all night, so cold that it froze the salt water.

"All of which I wouldn't mind, if it weren't for my ankles. I used to favor the right with the left, but with the left now smashed worse than the right, you can imagine how careful I have to be (where it is impossible to be careful) in a crazy junk going through such rough weather. And yet I have escaped any bad twists so far.

"Junks, crazy—I should say so. Rags, tatters, rotten—something always carrying away—how they navigate is a miracle. I wonder if Hearst thinks I'm lost."

"Monday, Feb. 15, 1904.

"Oh, yes, we waited four hours! When four hours had passed, wind came down out of the north, dead in our teeth. Lay all night in confounded tide-rip, junk standing on both ends, and driving me crazy what of my headache.

"At four in the morning turned out in the midst of driving snow to change anchorage on account of sea.

"It was a cruel daybreak we witnessed; at 8 A.M. we showed a bit of sail and ran for shelter.

"My sailors live roughly, and we put up at a fishing village (Korean) where they live still more roughly, and we spent Sunday and Sunday night there—my five sailors, myself—and about 20 men, women and children jammed into a room in a hut, the floor space of which room was about equivalent to that of a good double-bed.

"And my foreign food is giving out, and I was compelled to begin on native chow. I hope my stomach will forgive me some of the things I have thrust upon it: Filth, dirt, indescribable, and the worst of it is that I can't help thinking of the filth and dirt as I take each mouthful.

"In some of these villages, I am the first white man, and a curiosity.

"I showed one old fellow my false teeth at midnight. He proceeded to rouse the house. Must have given him bad dreams, for he crept in to me at three in the morning and woke me in order to have another look.

"We are under way this morning—for Chemulpo. I hope I don't drop dead when I finally arrive there.

"The land is covered with snow. The wind has just hauled ahead again. Our sail has come in, and the men are at the oars. If it blows up it'll be another run for shelter. O, this is a wild and bitter coast."

"Tuesday night, Feb. 16, Chemulpo.

"Just arrived. Am preparing outfit—horses, interpreter, coolies, etc., for campaign into the North toward the Yalu and most probably into Manchuria."

"Buy everything in sight and get ready to start for Ping-Yang!" Jack was greeted when he landed at Chemulpo. It was the first whiteman's speech he had heard in eight days. The welcome tongues were those of Jones and MacLeod, who had preceded him. One of these men, who had known Jack, did not recognize him, so disfigured and cadaverous was he from sunburn and illness, and so crippled. And now, for the first time, he learned that war was on—had been on for five days.

"Chemulpo, Feb. 17/04.

" . . . Am preparing to advance north—campaign to the Yalu and perhaps into Manchuria. I shall accompany. Am busy getting interpreters, coolies, horses, saddles, provisions, etc. Only four outside newspapermen here. The rest, a host, cannot get here."

"Grand Hotel, Seoul, Feb. 24/04.

" . . . Am starting in five minutes for the North. Have been about crazy trying to outfit and start:

"3 pack ponies
"2 riding horses

"1 interpreter (Jap.)
"1 cook (Korean)
"2 mapus (Korean grooms)."

Of all the correspondents in the field, Jack was the last to reach Seoul, but the first to the Front. At Seoul, no one seemed to have any orders about him, so he lost not a moment hitting the road for the North. But from Sunan, the farthest point yet reached by any correspondent, and near the firing line, he was ruthlessly ordered back to Seoul.

"Ping-Yang, March 4/04.

"Have made 180 miles on horseback to this place. I shall be able to ride a little with you when I return, for it appears there are months of riding before me. I have one of the best horses in Korea—was the Russian Minister's at Seoul before he went away.

"Very little chance to write these days—am not writing enough for the *Examiner* as it is. Worked to death with the trouble of traveling.

"Have received no more letters from you nor anybody.

"Am pulling North soon for Anju and maybe the Yalu. Am now in the midst of accounts with correspondents, interpreters, mapus and what not, so cannot think. . . . I do not know when I shall ever be able to write you a real letter—lack of time.

"But I'm learning about horses—last two days traveled 50 miles a day, and I was saddle-sore and raw.

"I am living in a Japanese hotel crammed with soldiers. (Only three of us—1 English correspondent—1 American photographer.) Am ordering whiskey just now for them."

"Poral-Colli, March 8/04.

"How the letters have roused me up! . . . Furthermore, they have proved to me, or, rather, reassured me, that I am a white man.

"As a sample of many days, let me give to-day. Was forbidden departure by Gen. Sasaki at Ping-Yang—argued it out through interpreters—vexations, delays, drive me mad. Should have started at 7 A.M. Scarcely started to load pack horses, when summoned by Japanese Consul—more interpreter—distraction—successful bluff—pull out late in afternoon.

"Arrive at this forlorn village; people scared to death. Already have had Russian and Japanese soldiers—we put the finishing touch to their fright. They swear they have no room for us, no fuel, no charcoal, no food for our horses, no room for our horses, nothing—no grub for our mapus and interpreters. We storm the village—force our way into the stables—capture 25 lbs. barley hidden in man's trousers—and so forth and so forth, for two mortal hours—chatter and chin-chin to drive one mad.

"And this is but one of all the days. One can scarcely think white man's thoughts. . . . As I write this, the horses are breaking loose in the stable—native horses are fiends, and I have desisted writing long enough to stir up the mapus.

"The horse I was astride of to-day is named Belle. I named her after your Belle. She is as sweet and gentle as yours, and she is the only sweet and gentle horse in Korea. She is an Australian barb, and have I told you she was the Russian Minister's at Seoul? She is gigantic compared with all other horses in Korea—Chinese, Japanese, and Korean horses—and excites universal wonder and admiration.

"As I write this a cold wind is blowing from the North, and snow is driving. Also, before my door are groaning and creaking a hundred bullock-carts loaded with army supplies and pushing North.

"My interpreter comes in with his daily report. Manyoungi, my Korean cook and interpreter, comes in with tea and toast. Dunn sends down half a can of hot pork and beans—and there are a thousand interruptions.

"

"Wednesday, Mar. 9/04.

"Here we are—captured and detained, while the wires are working hot between here and Ping-Yang and Seoul. I mean captured by Japanese soldiers who will not let us proceed North to Anjou. And five more vexatious hours have just elapsed—chin-chin and delay galore.

"As I write this, a thousand soldiers are passing through the village past my door. My men are busy drawing rations for themselves and horses from the Army.

"Red cross ponies, pioneers, pack horses loaded with munitions and supplies, for foot soldiers, are streaming by. Captains are dropping in to shake hands and leave their cards, and then going on.

"IMPORTANT. ANOTHER VEXATION!

"Just caught five body lice on my undershirt. That is, I discovered them, Manyoungi picked them off, the while he interpreted for me an invitation from a Korean nobleman to come to his place and occupy better quarters! The nobleman looked on, while the lice were caught and I changed my clothes. Lice drive me clean crazy. I am itching all over. I am sure, every second, that a score of them are on me. And how under the sun am I to write for the *Examiner* or write to you!

"Intermission—the horses, stabled within ten feet of me, have been kicking up a rumpus—kicking, biting, stampeding my Belle and my three other horses—and broken legs would not be welcome just now. I am advised to get my life insured.

"And the troops stream by, the horses fight—and mapus, cook and interpreter, are squabbling 4 feet away from me. And the frost is in the air. I must close my doors and light my candles.

"A Korean family of refugees—their household goods on their backs, just went by."

"Japanese Consulate,
"The 9th March, 1904.

"To Mr. Jack London:
Sir:

"I have the honor to inform you by the order that you would stay here until our Land Forces under Major General Sasaki proceed for the North.

"Yours truly,
(Signed) "C. Chinjo,
Jap. Acting Consul."

Jack, referring to the foregoing, notes as follows:

"This is one of many commands not heeded. This was issued yesterday at Ping-Yang. I am now North of that city and in advance of General Sasaki.

"The first command, had I obeyed it, would have held me in Tokio to this day, where are 50 other correspondents who did heed. I am prepared, however, to be held up by Japanese scouts at any moment and be brought back to Ping-Yang. But it's all in the game. I am the only correspondent thus far in advance. With me is Dunn, a photographer for *Collier's Weekly*. . . . In Ping-Yang are two other correspondents—and that is all the regular correspondents in Korea at present moment."

"Sunan, Mar. 11/04.

"Have just returned from a ride on Belle—doesn't that strike you familiarly? North I may ride for a hundred yards, and when I come thundering up at a lope the Japanese guard turns out on the run, presenting bayonets to me in token that I may proceed no farther. East, "West, and South I may ride as far as I wish, but North, where fighting is soon to begin, I may not go. Nor may I go until I receive permission from Lieut.-General Inouye, commander of the 12th Division of 12,000 men, and just now at Seoul, a couple of hundred miles to the South.

" . . . Your two letters I received several days ago were brought up, horseback, from Seoul. As I write I look out my door and a dozen feet from where I am sitting, see Belle munching away at her barley ration which I have drawn for her from the Army. She is a joy! . . . I am my own riding teacher. I hope I don't learn to ride all wrong. But anyway, I'll manage to stick on a horse somehow, and we'11 have some glorious rides together."

"Sunan, March 12/04.

" . . . You needn't worry about my welfare. The Japanese are taking very good care of me. Here I am, 40 miles from the front, and here I stay. The only other newspaperman who reached this far, Dunn, has gone back. So I'm farthest north of all the correspondents. Furthermore, no others may now pass out of Ping-Yang."

He quotes several short poems from the Korean, and comments:

"These are sweet, are they not? They are the only sweet things I have seen among the Koreans!"

"Ping-Yang, March 14/04.

" . . . Ordered back to Ping-Yang yesterday by the authorities—so here I am, and a chance to mail this."

"Ping-Yang, March 16/04.

"Here beginneth the retrograde movement. Have been ordered back 50 li from Sunan to this place. Am now ordered back 540 li from this place to Seoul—the Japanese are disciplining us for our rush ahead and the scoop we made—and they are doing it for the sake of the correspondents who remained in Japan by advice of Japanese and who have made life miserable for the Japanese by pointing out that we have been ahead gathering all the plums.

"540 li to Seoul and 540 li back = 1080 useless li I have to ride, plus 100 (Sunan and return) = 1180 useless li. Well, I'll become used to the saddle at any rate."

"Seoul, March 18/04.

"Just arrived, fired hence from the North. Pull out on a little side jump to Wei-hai-wei to-morrow morning early. Learn that a bunch of letters is chasing around after me up at Ping-Yang. . . . Shall get them a week hence when return from Wei-hai-wei."

"March 19/04.

" . . . Didn't go to Wei-hai-wei after all."

"Seoul, Korea, March 29/04.

"Here I am, still in Seoul, assigned to the first column but not permitted to go to the Front. None of the correspondents at front. All held back by Japanese, and in this matter we are being treated abominably.

" . . . I have decided that I shall remain away no more than a year. Ten months from the time I left San Francisco, I shall cable Hearst to send out another man to take my place at the front—if I've got to the front by that time.

" . . . Since writing you from north of Ping-Yang at Sunan, I have not only received not one letter from any one else, but not one letter from you. . . . You, at least, have my miserable letters to the *Examiner* to read. Have never been so disgusted with anything I have done. Perfect rot I am turning out. It's not war correspondence at all, and the Japs are not allowing us to see any war. Photographs inclosed taken at table upon which I am writing this."

"Grand Hotel, Seoul, Korea, April 1/04.

"And still no mail. . . . I'll never go to a war between Orientals again. The vexation and delay are too great. Here I am, still penned up in Seoul, my 5 horses and interpreters at Chemulpo, my outfit at Ping-Yang, my post at Anjou—and eating my heart out with inactivity. Such inactivity, such irritating inactivity, that I cannot even write letters.

"Mark you, while inactive, I am busy all the time. What worries is that I am busy with worries and nothing is accomplished. Never mind, I may not ride beautifully or correctly, but I '11 wager that I stick on and keep up with you in the rides we may have together.

"Just now I'm riding all kinds of Chinese ponies, with all kinds of saddles, in all kinds of places (and some of the ponies are vicious brutes). I was out yesterday, without stirrups, and loped all over the shop with another fellow, down crowded streets, narrow streets, crooked streets, over sprawling babies, for the ponies are hard-mouthed and headstrong (a thousand shaves), and live to tell the tale."

Here is a letter received by Jack from Mr. James, Chemulpo, at this juncture:

"Dear London:

"Your mare and the ponies are well looked after. Only a little influenza in her and she wants a lot more exercise. She is quite fat.

"Chin-chin, old chap.

"Yours as a Sourdough,
"James."

And at foot, this note from Jack's interpreter, K. Yamada:

"For you don't returned within long time there happened trouble yesterday that I had been arrested to Japanese gendarme as reporting military secret to you and after 10 hours examined several questions, I could come back to my boarding house. Received telegram and I shall do your order.

"Y.ff'ly [affectionately?!],
"K. Yamada."

"If you don't come back I can't help plenty troubles."

Jack comments upon the two communications above:

"These two letters, on same sheet, as indicative of some of my troubles. Here I am, compelled to remain in Seoul, my horses at Chemulpo. My interpreter, K. Yamada, left in charge of horses, arrested. My mare with influenza, and suffering from 'hay-belly,' which James mistakes for being in foal. Hay I had sternly forbidden, for I had learned effect on mare. James (an Ex-Klondiker) and making a dash for Chemulpo, I asked to take a look at my horses."

In very bad humor over the holding up of his mail, he writes:

"Seoul, Korea, April 5/04.

" . . . I am going out to ride off steam now on a jockey saddle and a spanking big horse, and if we don't kill each other we'll kill a few native babies or blind men. Had the horse out yesterday—hardest mouth—took half a block to bring it to a walk and half a dozen to hold it when I got off to pay a call. How I stuck on I don't know—but I never took the reins in both hands, a la Japanaise, nor did I throw my arms around his neck. Oh, I'm learning, I'm learning. I never had time in my life to learn to play billiards, but I'm learning now. I never had time to learn to dance, but if this war keeps on I'll learn that, too—only the missionaries don't dance, and the *Kresang* (Korean dancing girls) can't dance because the Emperor's mother is dead and the court is in mourning.

"To-morrow night I give a reading from 'Call of Wild' before foreign residents for benefit of local Y. M. C. A.—and I give it in evening dress!!! Custom of the country and I had to come to it. In Japan, however, one has to have a frock coat and top hat—imagine me in a Prince Albert and a stovepipe. Anyway, if Japan wins this war the Japs will be so cocky that white people will be unable to live in Japan. . . .

" . . . Here's the horse, and I go. Say, I have learned a new swear-word (Korean), 'Jamie.' Whenever you want to swear just say 'Jamie' softly, and people won't know you are swearing."

"O-Pay, Korea, April 16/04.

"In the saddle again . . . and riding long hours. Roads are muddy. Was putting Belle in up to the shoulders as darkness fell last night. Have breakfast eaten and am under way at 6 a.m. It is now 9:30 p.m., and I have just finished supper and am going (in about one minute) rather tired to bed."

"Anjou House, April 17/04.

"Plugging along in the race for Japanese Headquarters. Four men ahead of me, but expect to overhaul them, though I am bringing my packs along and they are traveling light. The rest of the bunch is left in the rear.

"Beautiful long hours in the saddle, and beautiful mud. . . . Am prouder than a peacock, for I am able to keep Belle's shoes on her, to tighten them when they get loose, and to put on a shoe when she casts and loses one. Of course, it is coldshoeing, but they *work*! they *work*!"

"Wiju, April 24th.

"Well, I didn't overtake the four men ahead of me, though I caught up with them where they were stopped farther back along the road, and arrived here with them, where we shall stop for some time.

"Now, to business. As I understand it, Macmillans expect to bring out 'The Sea Wolf' late this Fall. I shall not be able to go over the proofsheets. And you must do this for me. I shall write Macmillans telling them this and asking them to get into communication with you. In the first place, before any of the book is set up in print, you must get from them the original MS. in their possession. Much in this MS. will have been cut out in the *Century* published part. What was cut out I want put back in the book. On the other hand, many GOOD alterations have been made by you and George [Sterling], and by the *Century* people—these alterations I want in the book. So here's the task—take the Macmillan MS., and, reading the *Century* published stuff, put into Macmillan MS. the good alterations.

"Furthermore, anything that offends you, strike out or change on your own responsibility. You know me well enough to know that I won't kick."

"Headquarters 1st Japanese Army,
"Manchuria, May 6/04.

" . . . I am well, in splendid health, though profoundly irritated by the futility of my position in this Army and sheer inability (caused by the position) to do decent work. Whatever I have done I am ashamed of. The only compensation for these months of irritation is a better comprehension of Asiatic geography and Asiatic character. Only in another war, with a whiteman's army, may I hope to redeem myself. It can never be done here by any possibility."

"Feng-Wang-Cheng,
"Headqrs. First Jap. Army, "Manchuria, May 17, 1904.

" . . . I have so far done no decent work. Have lost enthusiasm and hardly hope to do anything decent. Another war will be required for me to redeem myself, when I can accompany our army or an English army. Well, time rolls on. In six weeks the rainy season will be here. The chances are that I'll pull out for some point in China where I can get in touch with a cable. . . .

"Do you know—beyond my camera experience at Moji (mailed before the War) I do not know whether the *Examiner* has received one article of mine (I have sent 19) or one film (and I have sent hundreds of photographs)."

"Headquarters First Japanese Army,
"Feng-Wang-Cheng,
"Manchuria,
"May 22, 1904.

"My heart does not incline to writing these days. It could only wail, for I am disgusted at being here. War? Bosh! Let me give you my daily life.

"I am camped in a beautiful grove of pine trees on a beautiful hill-slope. Nearby is a temple. It is glorious summer weather. I am awakened in the early morning by the songs of birds. Cuckoo calls through the night. At 6:30 I shave. Manyoungi, my Korean boy, is cooking breakfast and waiting on me. Sakai, my interpreter, is shining my boots and receiving instructions for the morning. Yuen-hi-kee, a Chinese, is lending a hand at various things. My Seoul mapu is helping in the breakfast and cleaning up generally. My Ping-Yang mapu is feeding the horses.

"Breakfast at 7. Then try to grind something out of nothing for the *Examiner*. Perhaps go out and take some photographs, which I may not send any more for the Censor will not permit them to go out undeveloped and I have no developing outfit or chemicals with me.

"I am at liberty to ride in to headquarters at Feng-Wang-Cheng, less than a mile away. And I am at liberty to ride about in a circle around the city of a radius little more than a mile. Never were correspondents treated in any war as they have been in this. It's absurd, childish, ridiculous, rich, comedy.

"In the afternoon, the call goes forth, and we (the correspondents) go swimming in a glorious pool—clear water, over our heads, plenty of it. It all reminds me of Glen Ellen. A campfire at night, whereby we curse God, or Fate, and divers peoples and things which I shall not mention for the Censor's sake, and the day is ended.

"Disgusted, utterly disgusted.

"I have this day written the *Examiner* that in a month or six weeks (at outside) I shall pull out of the country and go to some place where I can get in direct communication with them; that my position here is futile; that there is no reason for my continuing here, and that, unless arrangements have been made for me to go on the Russian side, I shall return to the United States—unless they expressly bid me remain.

"Now I don't think it is possible for them to make arrangements for me to go on the Russian side, so . . . as you read this I may be starting on my way back to the States, to God's country, the Whiteman's country. . . . Who knows? Who knows? At any rate, believe me . . . it would take a many times bigger salary than I am receiving to persuade me to put in a year again in Japan much less pay for the year out of my own pocket. In the past I have preached the Economic Yellow Peril; henceforth I shall preach the Militant Yellow Peril.

"And just imagine the Censor reading all this. . . . Not a letter, not a line. I know not what is happening.

" . . . I have no heart, no head, no hand, for anything. In preposterous good health, but ungodly sick of soul. . . . "

Jack London always cherished a high regard for Richard Harding Davis. Mr. Davis, together with John Fox, Jr., and a large contingent of other writers, were held tightly, though courteously and hospitably, bottled up in Tokyo by the Nippon Government. Here they were eating out their hearts in enforced inaction, doubtlessly envious, and excusably, of the seven men who, Jack among them, had somehow got ahead with the First Army. And yet, when it was rumored in Tokyo that Jack London, a white man, a countryman, was in sore straits with the brown military authorities away up in Korea, and like to be summarily dealt with, it was Richard Harding Davis, white man to white man's rescue, although personally he knew him not, who first set the wires burning to Washington, where Theodore Roosevelt sat in the President's chair.

I have heard Jack's account of the fracas that "put him in wrong" with General Kuroki. Later on, someone circulated that he had been sent back to America for "violation of neutrality." Being very rusty on the facts, I took occasion, during a visit from James H. Hare in 1917, to refresh my memory. When Jack renewed acquaintance with both "Jimmie" Hare and "Dick" Davis in 1914 at Vera Cruz, I had the pleasure of meeting them.

The seven who were lucky enough to be members of the Japanese First Army were Jack London, Captain Thomas (French), William Maxwell (British), Mr. Fraser, and, for *Collier's Weekly,* Mr. Hare, Mr. Palmer, and Mr. O. K. Davis—all absolute subjects of the iron machine of which they were part. Each possessed his own outfit and servants, including a mapu (horseboy), and every week these mapus went to the Japanese quartermaster to obtain feed for their masters' beasts. On one such day, Jack's boy had some dispute with another mapu. Going to see what the row was about, Jack's boy explained that the other had prevented him from getting his proper share of the feed.

This same offender Jack recognized as one who had been stealing his "grub" for some time back; but knowing how risky it would be for an unwelcome white correspondent to strike a Japanese, no matter how low in station, had regretfully refrained from taking it out on the other's hide.

On the present occasion Jack interposed, by word of mouth, and the impudent thief, presuming too far upon a fancied security, made a threatening bluff in his direction. Jack watched carefully, and only when the fellow came actually at him, did he let out that small, scientific fist. "Lord, Lord," I can hear him muse, "I only hit him once—stopped him with my fist, rather—you know, he fell right into it; and then down with a thud. And he went around whimpering in bandages for two weeks".

But Jack nor his friends minimized the danger he was in, for the beaten mapu lost no time reporting to headquarters, and there were black looks everywhere. Jack was called on the carpet by General Kuroki's chief of staff, General Fuji, while the six other white men armed themselves, determined to stand with their comrade against the whole brown Army if need be, and go down together—a lovely thing, the most inspiring and romantic in the world.

Matters looked very serious for a while, although General Fuji did at length condescend to listen to Jack's side. Richard Harding Davis's effort undoubtedly halted any sudden execution by court martial that might have been in the minds of the staff. At any rate the storm blew over; but for days the seven men kept closely together, ready for emergency. Again, in 1914, Mr. Davis extended a second white-man's hand in an unforeseen difficulty; but that story belongs elsewhere.

And when Jack sailed from Yokohama, coming home, he left Mr. Davis still awaiting, with the other soul-sick correspondents, their permission to go to the Front.

APPENDIX

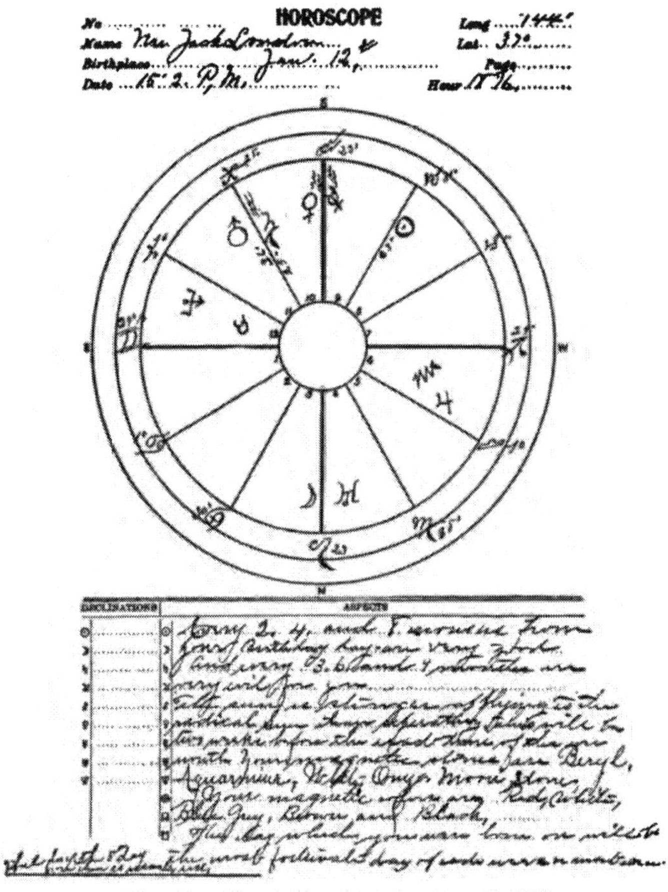

HOROSCOPE OF JACK LONDON, CAST IN 1905

HOROSCOPE OF JACK LONDON, CAST IN 1905

HOROSCOPE OF JACK LONDON, CAST AFTER HIS DEATH

Jack London State Historic Park

Located in Glen Ellen, California in the "Valley of the Moon", the park includes the large ranch and buildings owned by Jack London that he purchased over a number of years in the early 1900's. It includes the museum, several buildings, and a number of ruins of old structures including the burnt-out Wolf House.

Museum

The Museum was built by Charmian London after London's death in 1916. The House of Happy Walls was designed to be a museum as well as Charmian's home. She lived in the house from 1935 until 1945 (when she was not traveling abroad or staying with relatives). Today the museum includes displays in many rooms, with a complete set of first-edition books by Jack London, Charmian's 1901 Steinway piano, and many unique crafts and mementos Jack and Charmian collected in their travels.

This house is similar to the Wolf House in some ways—the Spanish-style roof tiles and walls of field stone, for example—but it is much smaller and more formal. Much of the furniture in the house was designed by the Londons and custom-built for use in Wolf House, though never used there due to the fire that destroyed Jack and Charmian's dream home. Several times a year small concerts are held upstairs in the historic building.

Grave Site

During the last few years of his life, Jack London's health declined rapidly from the effects of failing kidneys. On November 22, 1916, at only forty years old, Jack London died after a brief coma. His death certificate states that the cause was "Uraemia following renal colic".

On November 26, 1916, in a silent ceremony, Charmian London placed her husband's ashes on the chosen knoll under a large rock from the Wolf House. After she passed away in 1955, Charmian's ashes were laid under the same rock, next to Jack.

Wolf House

Started in 1911 and designed by architect Albert Farr, Jack's dream home was four levels comprising 15,000 square feet, 26 rooms and 9 fireplaces. It was constructed with beautiful locally-cut redwood logs, stone walls, and even contained a reflection pool.

Jack London wrote so many books about wolves and dogs that his friend George Sterling gave him the nickname 'The Wolf'. So when Jack started to build his dream house in 1911, it was only fitting that people would call it the 'Wolf House'.

Jack and Charmian never got to live in their home because one hot summer night in August 1913, spontaneous combustion

started a fire in the house. Nobody was living near the house so the fire was quite advanced before anyone became aware of it. The Londons were sleeping in the Cottage about a half mile away and were awakened by a farm worker who saw the red glow in the sky. They got on their horses and rode to their beloved dream house. By the time they got there, the house was completely engulfed in flames and beyond saving. Although Jack vowed to rebuild the house, he did not live long enough to rebuild. Today, we have a beautiful ruin.

Cottage

The Cottage was London's principal home on the Beauty Ranch. This wood-framed cottage was purchased by London in 1911 along with the Kohler and Frohling winery buildings. It was enlarged after 1911 until it included some 3,000 square feet of living space. Here he wrote many of his later stories and novels.

In 2006, restoration of the cottage was completed and the re-furnished cottage and Stone Dining Room were opened to visitors. These two buildings capture Jack and Charmian's bohemian lifestyle and close working relationship.

Beauty Ranch

The Beauty Ranch is the legacy of Jack's passion for the land. The Cottage, the Winery Ruin, the Silos, Barns and

Pig Palace are remnants of Jack and Charmian's life on the ranch. Combined with scenic beauty and miles of hiking and riding trails, the park attracts fans of the writer and nature lovers year round.

In 1905 London bought the first of several ranches on Sonoma Mountain in Glen Ellen, California. Using proceeds from his prolific writing career, London acquired adjoining parcels over several years and expanded his ranch, also known as the Ranch of Good Intentions.

By 1913 London owned 1400 acres on the slopes of the mountain and by 1916 employed nearly fifty workers building, farming, and tending prize livestock. Self-taught and inventive, London sought to improve farming methods using common sense, research, and concepts gleaned from travel. Visitors to the ranch today will see examples of his ingenuity and foreshadowing of organic and biodynamic methods popular today. He planted 65,000 eucalyptus trees hoping to use them for lumber but they eventually proved unsuitable.

The "Pig Palace"

Lake

Jack London designed a stone dam on the slope of Sonoma Mountain, creating a lake at the headwaters of Kohler Creek. His plan, to capture water for his farming needs and to remediate erosion from the logged out hillsides above, worked well. He also saw the resulting lake as a cool respite for swimming and boating with Charmian and friends during the hot summers. The four-acre lake was completed in 1914 and became the topic of the first water rights trial in California. When London won the dispute, he invited all the neighbors for a barbecue beside the lake. The floating walkway, along with piped in fresh

spring water for showering, was state of the art in 1915. Charmian and other riders used the lake to swim their horses. During the Depression, Beauty Ranch was converted to a Guest Ranch that offered fishing, swimming, boating and picnics at the lake.

In 2010, London's lake was designated "one of the ten most threatened cultural landscapes in America". An assessment is underway to repair the dam, refresh the lake, and revitalize the adjacent wetland. These improvements will substantially reduce sediment downstream and provide fresh open water and wetland habitat for amphibians, reptiles, birds, and mammals on the mountain. Park visitors can still view the graceful stone dam and log bathhouse.

I would rather be ashes than dust. I would rather that my spark should burn out in a brilliant blaze than it should be stifled by dry-rot. I would rather be a superb meteor, every atom of me in magnificent glow, than a sleepy and permanent planet. The proper function of man is to live, not to exist. I shall not waste my days in trying to prolong them. I shall use my time.

—Jack London, 1916

Map of the Park

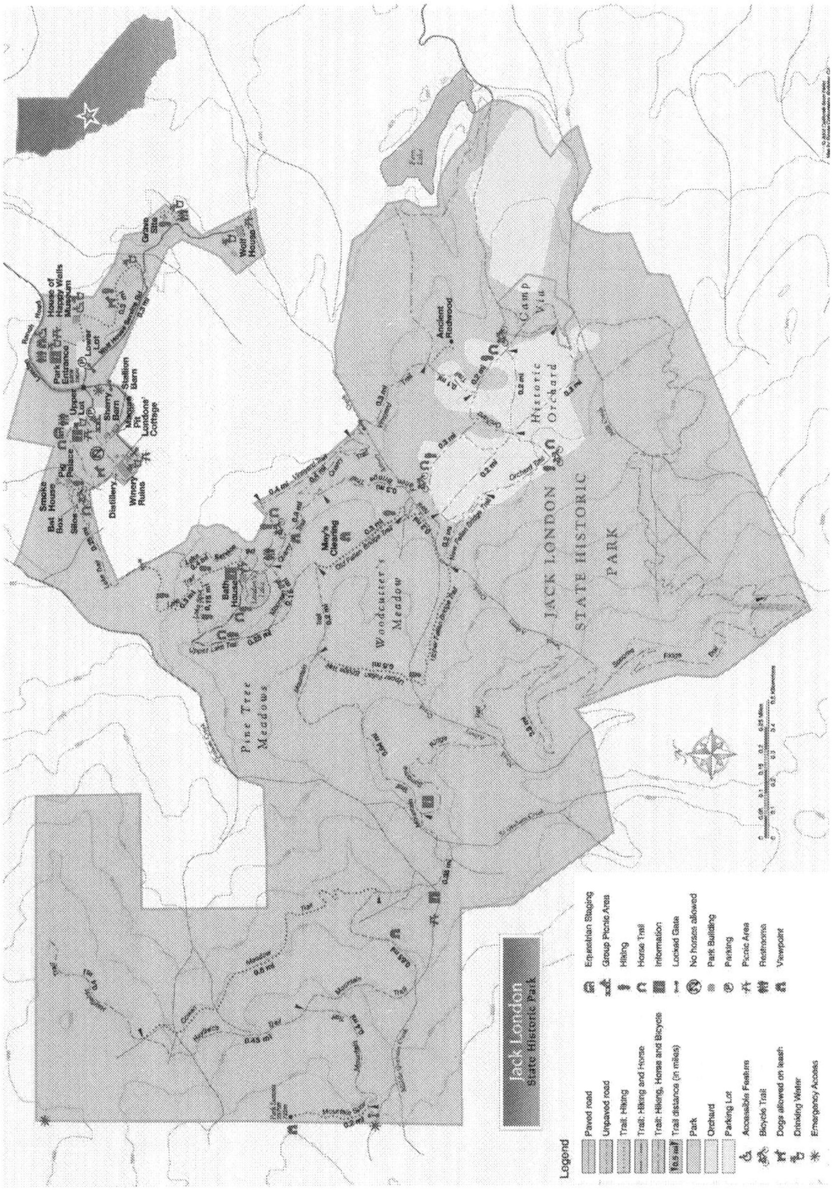